SACRED GROUND

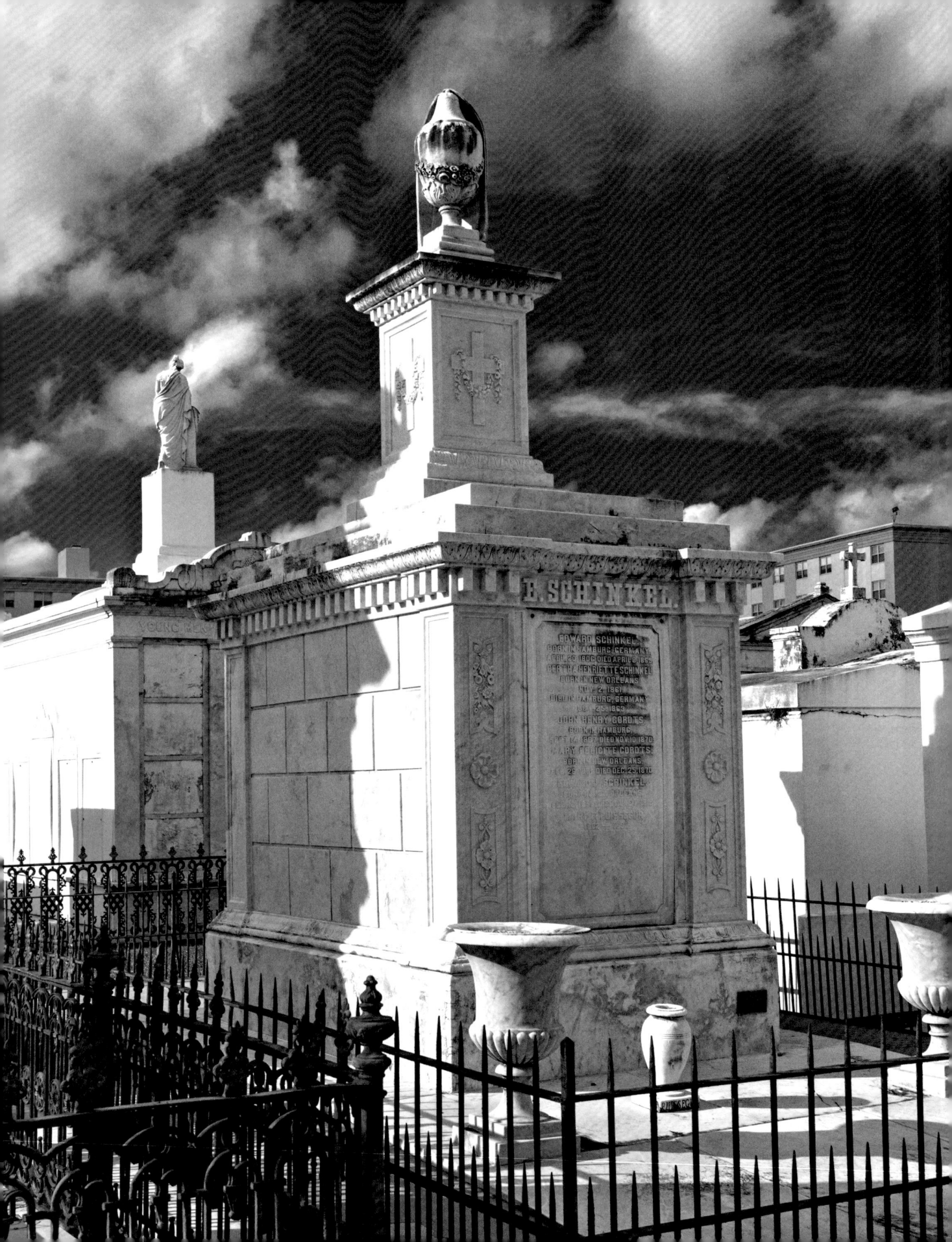

SACRED GROUND

The Cemeteries of New Orleans

Robert S. Brantley

Introduction by S. Frederick Starr

PRINCETON ARCHITECTURAL PRESS · NEW YORK

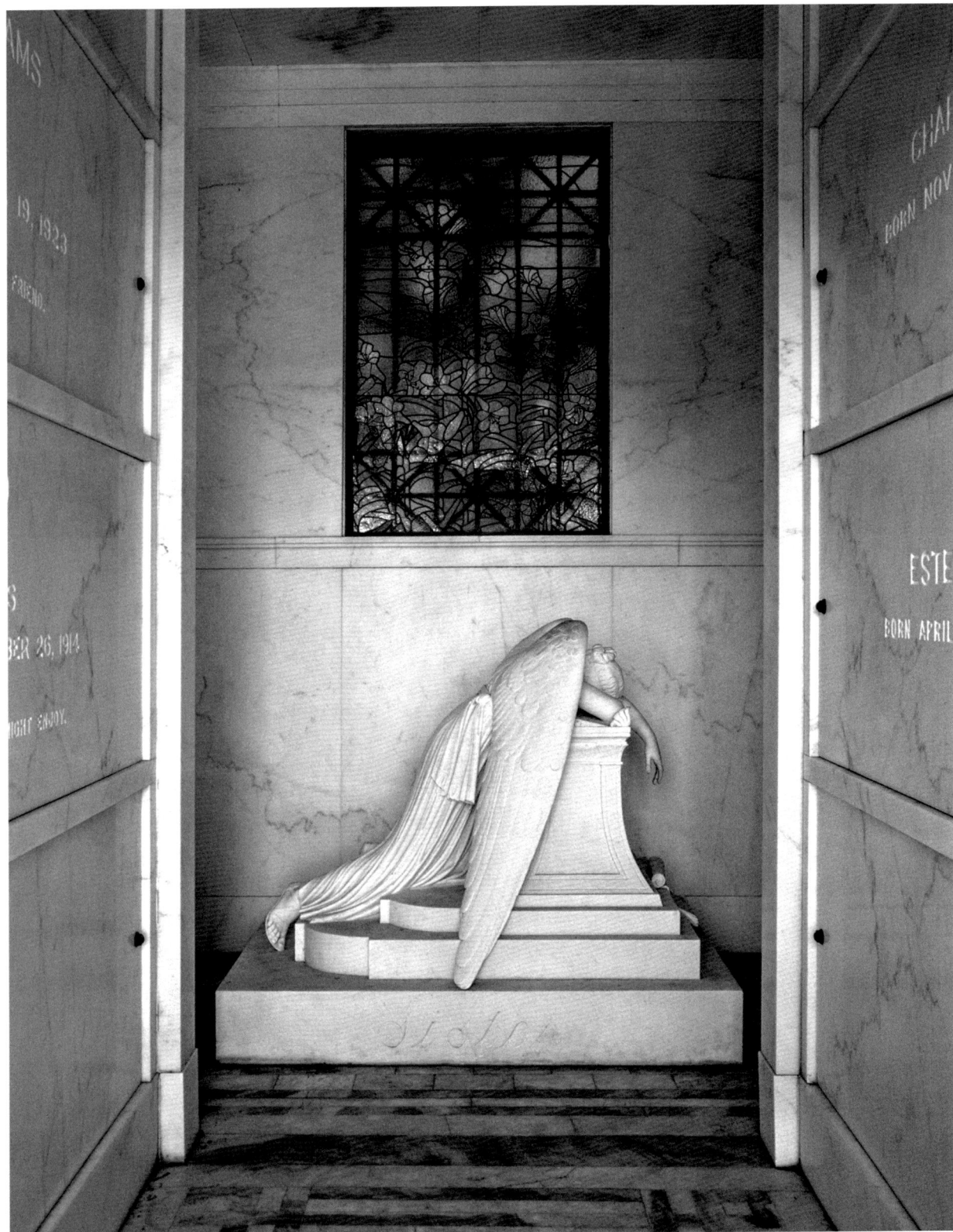

Photograph by Jan White Brantley

*To my grandparents Oliver & Annie Shipman and my parents,
Ben & Martha Shipman Brantley,*
thanks for teaching me that true strength, power, wisdom, and vision come from inside and culminate in love and gentleness.

To the love of my life, Jan White Brantley,
who knew my soul better than any other and who allowed me to share hers, and who taught me the simplicity and gentleness of true love and happiness.

The Truth in Art and Beauty is in the Love and Pain they Conceal.

Published by
Princeton Architectural Press
202 Warren Street, Hudson, NY 12534
Visit our website at www.papress.com

© 2019 Robert S. Brantley
All rights reserved
Printed in China
22 21 20 19 4 3 2 1 First edition

No part of this book may be used or reproduced in any manner without written permission from the publisher, except in the context of reviews.

Every reasonable attempt has been made to identify owners of copyright. Errors or omissions will be corrected in subsequent editions.

Editor: Sara Stemen
Designer: Paula Baver
Symbolic interpretation: Heather Veneziano, Cultural Heritage Advisor, Gambrel & Peak LLC

Special thanks to: Janet Behning, Abby Bussel, Jan Cigliano Hartman, Susan Hershberg, Kristen Hewitt, Stephanie Holstein, Lia Hunt, Valerie Kamen, Jennifer Lippert, Sara McKay, Parker Menzimer, Wes Seeley, Rob Shaeffer, Jessica Tackett, Marisa Tesoro, Paul Wagner, and Joseph Weston of Princeton Architectural Press
 —Kevin C. Lippert, publisher

Library of Congress Cataloging-in-Publication Data
Names: Brantley, Robert S., author. | Starr, S. Frederick, writer of
   foreword.
Title: Sacred ground : New Orleans cemeteries / Robert S. Brantley;
Introduction by S. Frederick Starr.
Other titles: New Orleans cemeteries
Description: First edition. | New York : Princeton Architectural
   Press, [2018] Identifiers: LCCN 2018055158 | ISBN 9781616898212
   (hardcover : alk. paper)
Subjects: LCSH: Cemeteries—Louisiana—New Orleans. | Cemeteries—Louisiana—Pictorial works. | New Orleans
   (La.)—Biography.
Classification: LCC F379.N562 A224 2018 | DDC
   363.7/50976335—dc23
LC record available at https://lccn.loc.gov/2018055158

TITLE PAGE:
Latin cross festooned with daffodils and roses. Side panels are decorated in sunflowers and primroses representing a devotion to God and eternal love. Tomb of Edward J. Schinkel

PREVIOUS PAGE:
White marble weeping angel; tomb of Chapman H. Hyams, designed by architect Charles L. Lawhon and made by the Albert Weiblen Marble and Granite Company in 1915, Metairie Cemetery. Photograph by Jan White Brantley

Contents

INTRODUCTION
10 *Sacred Ground: The Cemeteries of New Orleans*
S. Frederick Starr

Part I
—

Twenty-One Biographies: Identity, History, Rites of Passage

24 Silent Sentinels Against Time
30 Nicolas Mioton (1791–1834)
32 John Lawless (1810–1850)
33 Kasper Auch (1811–1886)
34 John Davidson (1816–1872)
 & Henrietta Sidle Davidson (1827–1891)
35 Richard Bartlet Sumner (1816–1868)
37 Edward Sweeney (1822–1874)
40 Reverend Emperor Williams (1826–1896)
44 Seymour Alexander Stewart (1835–1856)
46 John Oliver Locke (1839–1864)
47 Captain Eugene Pierre Gaspard (1839–1889)
48 Reverend Father René M. J. Vallée (1839–1892)
50 William H. Webb (1839–1884)
52 Constantine Otto Weber (1847–1901)
54 Martha Lena Little (1856–1920)
56 Heinrick "Henry" Benthin (1857–1928)
59 Reverend Albert Richard Edbrooke (1870–1925)
62 Virginia Gleaves Lazarus (1871–1897)
63 Charles Ferdinand Vorbusch (1891–1915)
65 Leslie Philip Backes (1897–1918)
67 Indigent Burial (unknown–2018)

Part II
—

Plates

70 Cypress Grove Cemetery
84 Dispersed of Judah Cemetery
90 Greenwood Cemetery
106 Lafayette Cemetery #1 & #2
122 Metairie Cemetery
144 St. Louis Cemetery #1, #2 & #3
164 St. Patrick's Cemetery #1 & #2
170 Additional Cemeteries
 St. Vincent de Paul Cemetery #1 & #2,
 Odd Fellows Rest Cemetery, Holt Cemetery,
 Hebrew Rest Cemetery, Anshe Sfard Cemetery,
 Chevra Thilim Cemetery, Masonic Cemetery #1,
 St. Joseph's Cemetery #1, and Carrollton
 Cemetery #1
—
184 A Photographer's Vision

186 INDEX OF PLATES
190 ACKNOWLEDGMENTS
191 MAP OF CEMETERY LOCATIONS

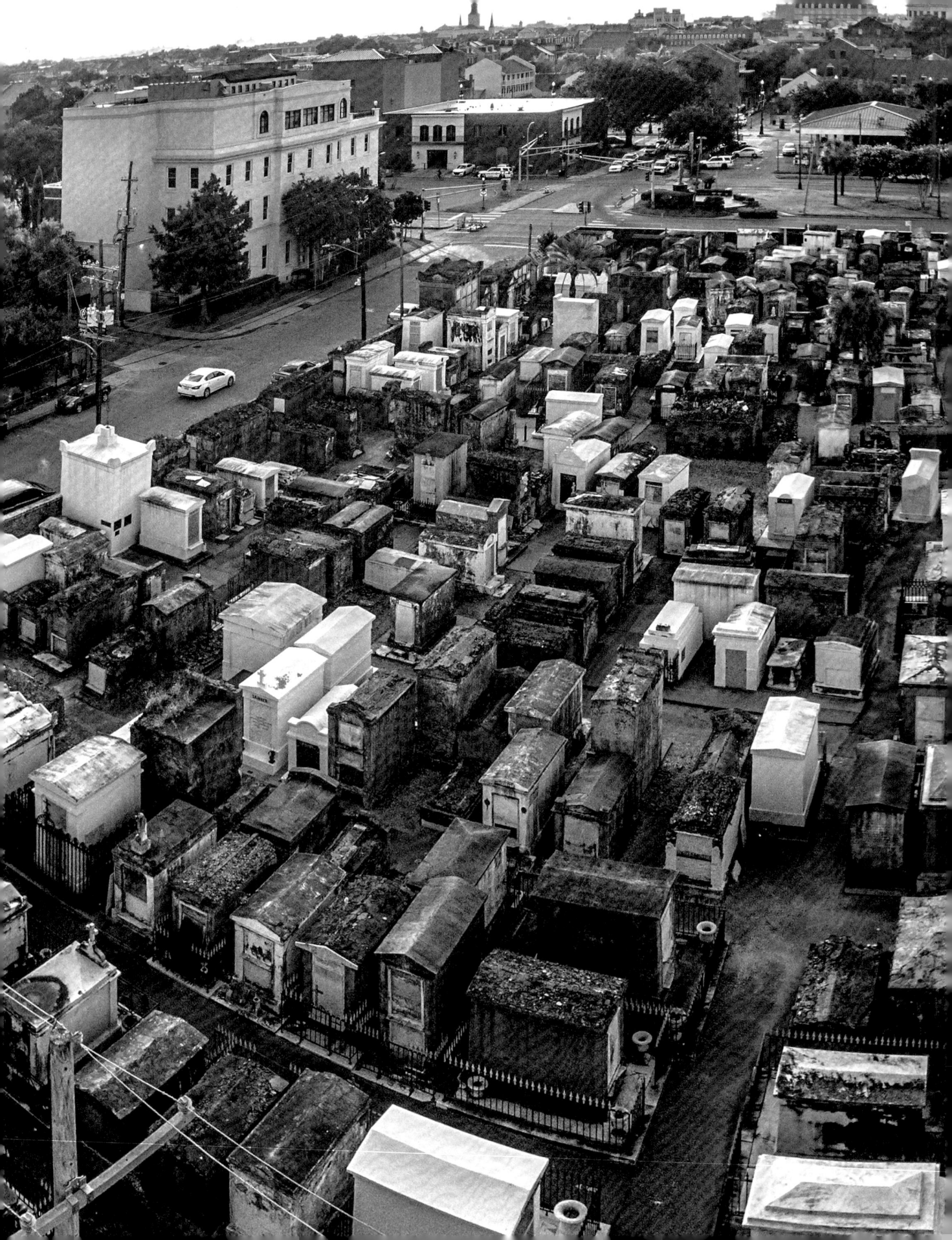

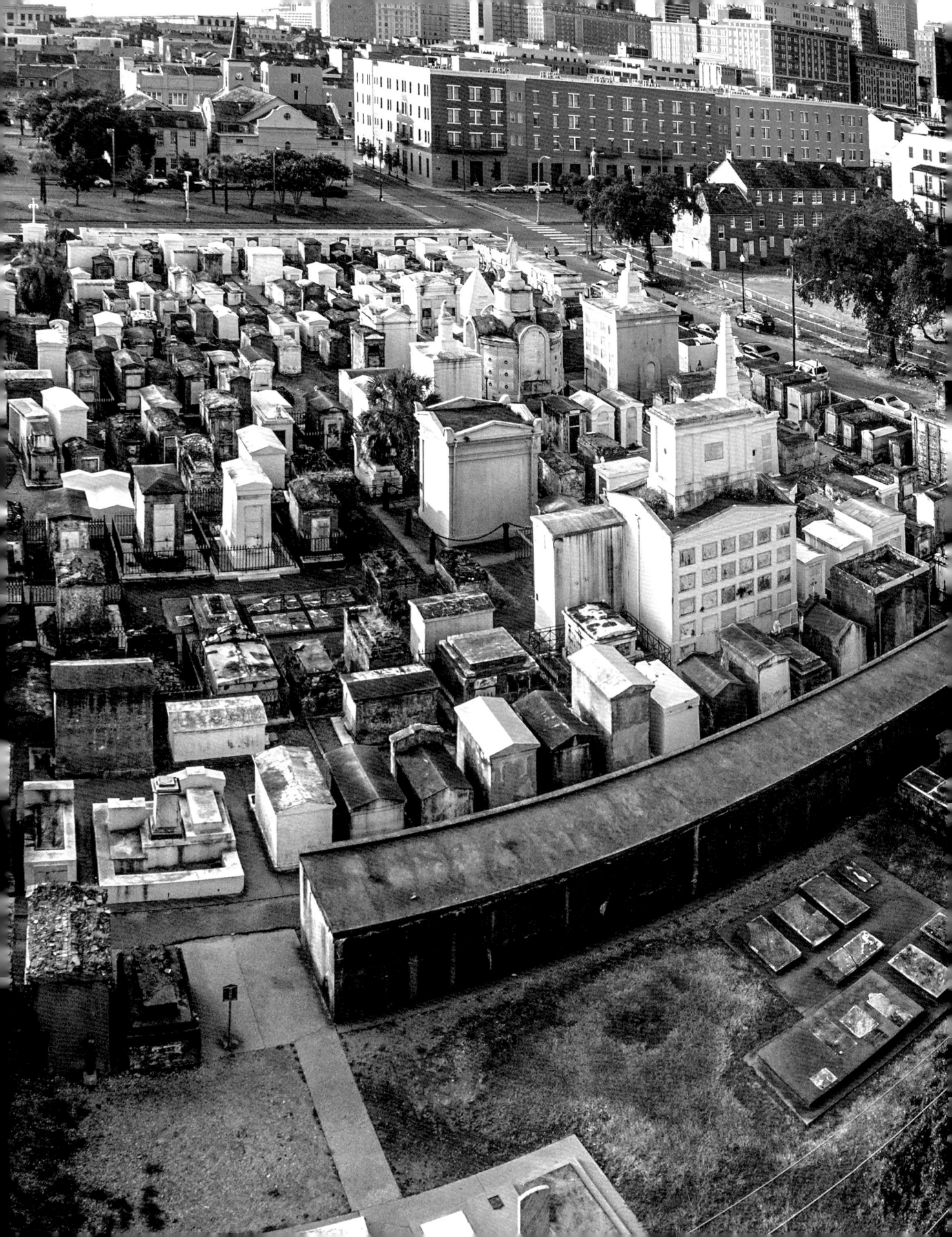

Sacred Ground: The Cemeteries of New Orleans

S. Frederick Starr

Benjamin Henry Latrobe had designed the US Capitol and was thoroughly conversant with European architecture and design. Yet when he found himself, in 1804, strolling through New Orleans's St. Louis Cemetery, he confessed that he was perplexed and astonished by the place, that its design and tombs were like nothing he had seen before. Little did he suspect that he himself would be buried there.

Writers have tried to summarize the essence of New Orleans's fifty-nine cemeteries in such clichés as "Cities of the Dead," which grow ever more trite over the years.[1] Maybe that essence cannot be captured in words. Hats off, then, to master photographer Robert S. Brantley, who has endeavored to capture the essence of New Orleans's cemeteries in subtle photographic images. These pictures enable the thoughtful reader to ponder the subject and to consider New Orleans's funereal monuments as reflections of our eternal quest for permanence in an impermanent world.

In some respects New Orleans's cemeteries are indistinguishable from their counterparts in Boston, Baltimore, or Cincinnati. Their distinctiveness is real, however, and can be traced to four factors, three natural and one human. The first of these is the best known, namely, the city's high water table. With water lurking just under the ground's surface, it is impossible to bury the dead. Yet the Gospel according to John (19:39–42) admonishes Christians to wrap the dead in linen and bury them, as was done with Christ himself. The only recourse was to lay down a brick foundation and place the corpse on a low floor, to which was then added simple sides and a roof. The corpse was still subject to the region's humidity and fierce summer heat, its quick decay reminding everyone of just how fragile is the flesh.

A second determining natural factor concerns the geology of the Lower Mississippi, which left the region with rich soil from the Midwest but no building stone or clays that could be transformed into hard bricks. Tombs had to be constructed of soft local bricks, which were then plastered and painted to imitate stone. Only a few of the rich could afford to clad their tombs with thin marble.

The third factor that defined New Orleans cemeteries was the prevalence until the early twentieth century of epidemics of cholera and yellow fever. Having chosen to live close by their neighbors, and with no understanding of the causes of the pestilences, the citizens of New Orleans died by the thousands in epidemics that recurred nearly every decade down to the last century. In one month alone, during the cholera epidemic of 1832, more than one thousand died, with their corpses piled up outside the city's main cemetery. Priests pronounced the last rites while standing by the mounds

---

1. For an early view, see "The City: Our Cemeteries and Their History," *Times-Picayune*, October 30, 1859. Recent studies include Peter B. Dedek's descriptive *The Cemeteries of New Orleans: A Cultural History* (Baton Rouge, LA: LSU Press, 2017); Robert Florence, *New Orleans Cemeteries: Life in the Cities of the Dead* (New Orleans: Batture Press, 2005); and Henri A. Gandolfo, *Metairie Cemetery: An Historical Memoir* (Metairie, LA: Stewart Enterprises, 1981). By far the best study of the cemeteries remains Leonard V. Huber, Peggy McDowell, and Mary Louise Christovich, *New Orleans Architecture*, vol. 3 of *The Cemeteries* (New Orleans: Pelican Publishing, 1996).

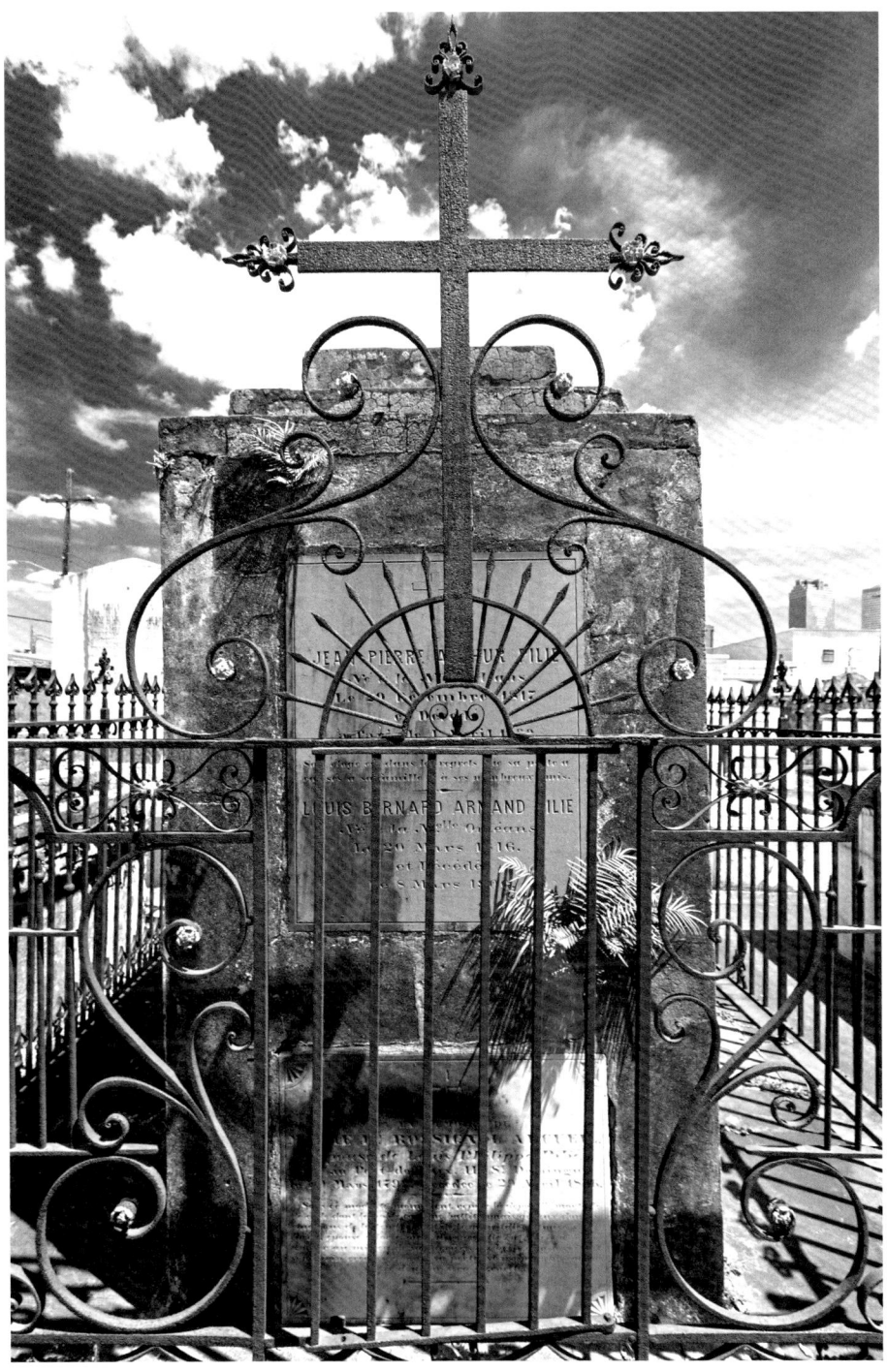

Wrought-iron gate, tomb of Jean Pilié family, St. Louis Cemetery #2, Square 1
Previous Page: Bird's-eye view of St. Louis Cemetery #1

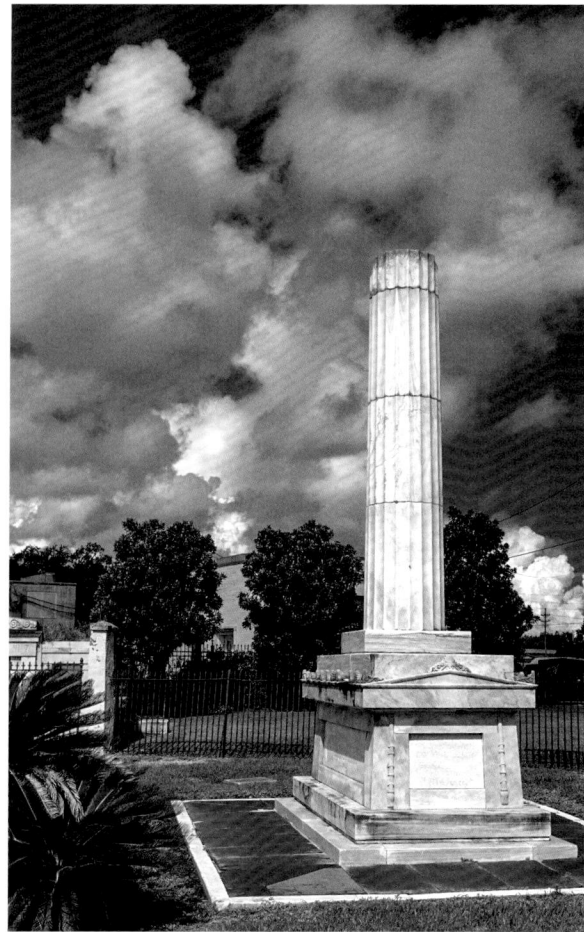

Monument of Irad Ferry, Cypress Grove Cemetery

of bodies. True, the Mortuary Chapel, now Our Lady of Guadalupe, had just been completed on Rampart Street, but even without pews, it could not accommodate the crowds of mourners.

To contain the periodic inundation of human remains, New Orleans borrowed from Spain the construction of wall vaults, each of which could accommodate tens or even hundreds of the dead. Resembling closed ovens, these came to be called "oven vaults." Each consisted of up to a dozen small vaults placed side by side and surmounted by rows of further vaults, piled up in as many as four ranks. Within each wall vault was a flat surface for the corpse, behind which was a closed shaft to the ground, which enabled the proprietor or family to push out the bones left from earlier interments and make way for fresh corpses. As a result, a simple oven tomb consisting of a dozen vaults could house the remains of ninety or more of the dead.

The one human factor that most defined New Orleans cemeteries was the absence of easy transport up and down the Mississippi River before the 1830s and the resulting slowness of bringing goods from eastern ports by sail before the 1840s. Both were overcome only by the rise of steam-driven vessels. Only then could New Orleans think of bringing granite from New England, limestone from Indiana, and other stones from as far afield as Italy. Once this was possible, however, the modest old brick-and-mortar vaults quickly gave way to extravagant monuments and to fierce but unacknowledged competitions among their sponsors and namesakes.

If steamboats and steamships opened the way for more elaborate grave monuments, the rise of local iron foundries in New Orleans provided material for sculptural ornaments for graves. The earliest of these were restrained and elegantly classical, but over time virtuoso ironmongers worked with stonemasons and architects to produce opulent effects for graves in metal.

With New Orleans unable to bury its dead, with poor local materials for constructing tombs, and with members of the community dying sometimes by the thousands at one time, who was responsible for organizing the disposition of the dead? This fell to the Catholic Church—not because it was expert at the design and construction of cemeteries but because, as the heir of St. Peter, it was responsible for the transition of human souls to the realm beyond death. Death, in other words, was above all a relationship between humans and God, and as such was mediated by the church. With a large part of the population being French or Spanish deep into the nineteenth century, and with a flood of new immigrants arriving from Catholic parts of Germany and from Ireland, this arrangement seemed natural and right to most of the population.

All people being equal before the Lord in death, the church did not encourage or welcome extravagance in the construction of tombs. Life and death being mere preparations for eternal life, it frowned upon overzealous effort to express distinctions of rank or wealth in the cemeteries. Nonetheless, even in the half century after the opening of St. Louis Cemeteries #1 (1789), #2 (1823), and #3 (1854), it welcomed a few grandiose monuments to honor distinguished citizens. The arrival in 1833 of the young architect Jacques Nicolas Bussière de Pouilly (1804–1875) brought to town the latest ideas on monument design from the great Père-Lachaise Cemetery in Paris.[2] Neoclassicism turned modest monuments into Roman or Greek temples, while broken columns, as in the Irad Ferry tomb in Cypress Grove, provided vivid reminders of human frailty.

Notable Catholics found prominent places in the early New Orleans cemeteries. Each of the many aisles in St. Louis Cemetery #3 bears the name of an early New Orleans bishop or priest. Yet from the outset, local cemeteries were open to non-Catholics. Many prominent Protestants are interred in St. Louis #1, while the later Cypress Grove, with its massive neo-Egyptian gate, and the Girod Street cemeteries were used almost exclusively by Protestants. Jews found burial in the earliest cemeteries, but in 1828 they formed their first congregation on Jackson Avenue and established there the Gates of Mercy (Shanarai Chasset), the first of what would become several Jewish cemeteries.

Just as blacks and whites always worshipped together in St. Louis Cathedral, New Orleans from the outset opened its cemeteries to blacks, both free and enslaved. While their graves were intermingled with those of other citizens, the entire square of St. Louis #2 between Iberville and Bienville Streets was set aside for black residents.

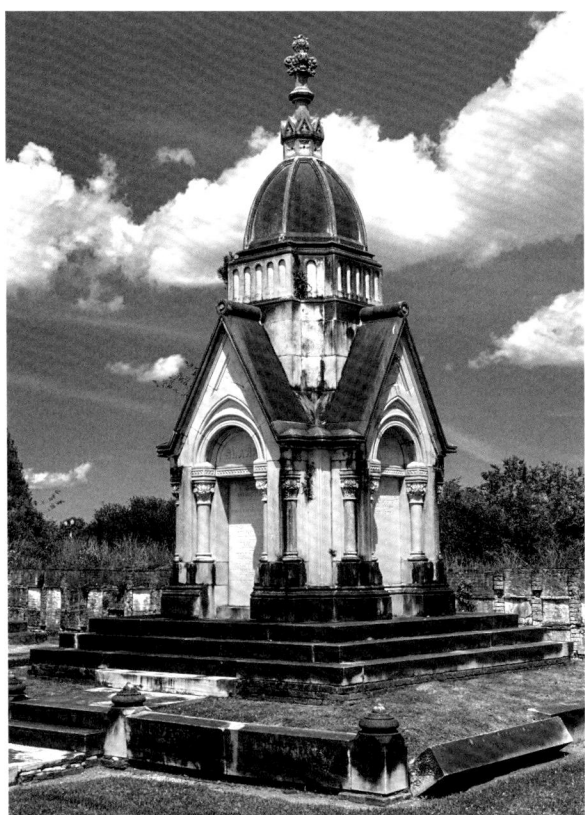

Diagonal elevation; tomb of Robert Slark family, Cypress Grove Cemetery

This intermingling of graves led naturally to an intermingling of funeral customs. During the nineteenth century, customs that had originated in the Catholic community spread to other faiths. Dominating all other civic funeral customs were, and are still today, those associated with All Saints' Day (November 1). This ancient Christian holiday celebrates the holiness of the saints and also the spiritual tie that is possible between saints and the pious among the living.

As in the Mediterranean and West Indian worlds, preparations for All Saints' Day in New Orleans began weeks beforehand. Chandeliers, candles, and even full-length portraits of the dead were brought to the tomb site. Local military units stood at attention at the entrances to the cemeteries. On the day itself, celebrants roamed the aisles pushing carts with flowers, sweets and other foods, and candles, while extended families gathered and renewed links with one another

---

2. On Pouilly, see Edith Elliott Long, "Jacques Nicolas Bussière de Pouilly," in Huber, McDowell, and Christovich, *New Orleans Architecture*, vol. 3, 135–37.

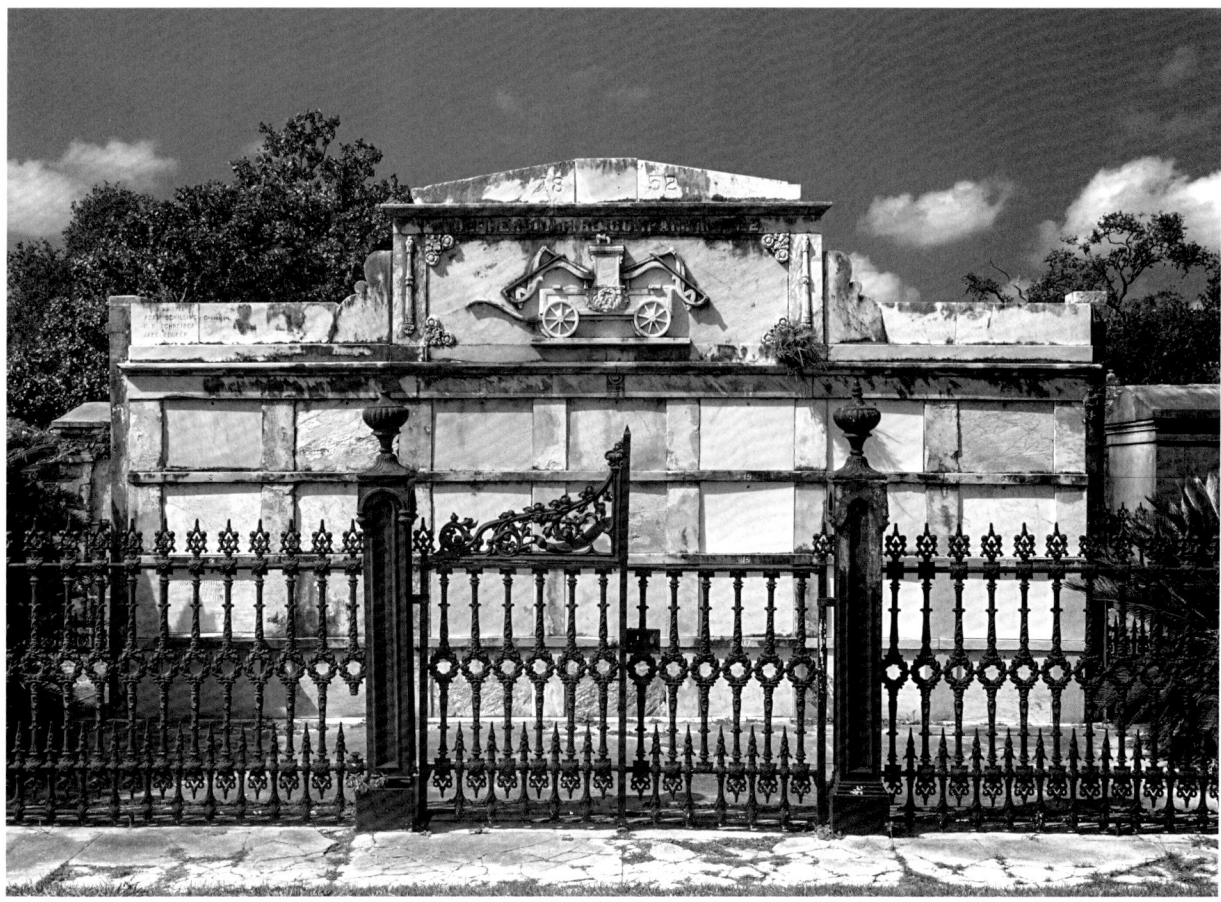

Society tomb of Jefferson Fire Company No. 22, Lafayette Cemetery

and the past. Departing the cemetery late in the evening, families might leave behind beads, wreaths, framed tufts of hair, and other "Immortelles" as permanent reminders of the departed. Such rituals peaked before the Civil War but continued to thrive well into the twentieth century. Curiously, over the years they became generalized, with Methodists and even Jews sharing funereal practices that originated with French and Spanish Catholics. Although many of the customs are no longer practiced, thousands of families today are working to maintain or revive the old traditions.

New Orleans in the 1840s and 1850s was a boom town, with many self-made men and their families wanting to memorialize themselves and their good fortune. Also, many heroes of the era of the 1815 Battle of New Orleans were dying off, and the community called for them to be appropriately commemorated by funeral monuments. This all coincided with an important transportation revolution. Proliferating steamboats on the Mississippi now enabled New Orleans to import stone from the Midwest, and oceangoing steamers could bring marble and granite from New England. This launched the golden age of New Orleans cemeteries, which extended until the 1920s.

During the mid-nineteenth century, relatively few grandees were able or inclined to erect grand monuments to themselves. One who did so was Robert Slark (1795–1868), a successful hardware merchant, whose tomb in Cypress Grove stands as a lasting reminder of his earthly success. Another, in St. Louis #1, memorialized Myra Clark Gaines (1805–1885), whose claim to fame was her involvement as plaintiff in an inheritance

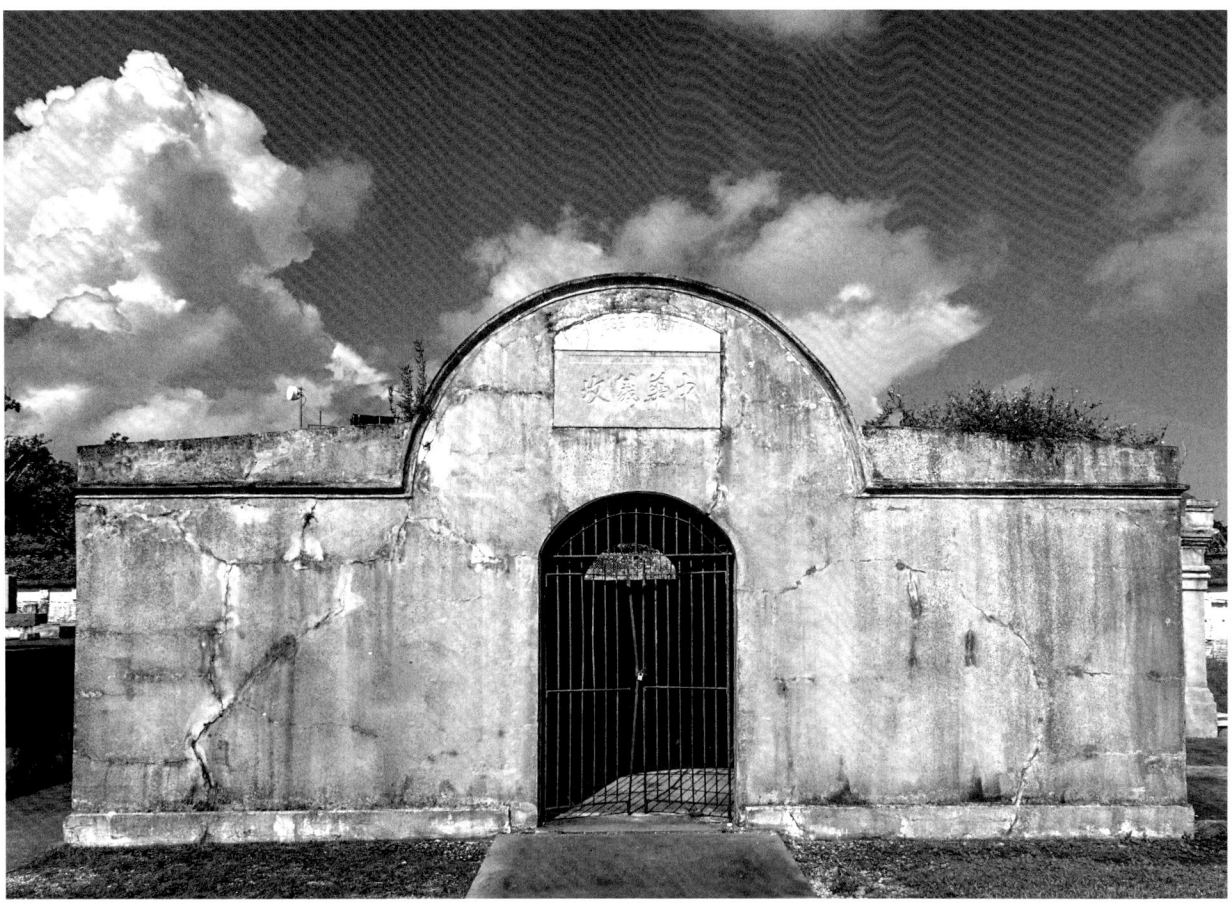

Society tomb of Soon On Tong Association, Cypress Grove Cemetery

dispute that became the United States' longest lawsuit of the nineteenth century.

Financial constraints, modesty, and a desire to avoid complicated dealings with the cemetery bureaucracies caused most people to look to mutual aid organizations to manage their funeral and interment. Beginning in the mid-nineteenth century, religious, fraternal, and trade organizations joined together and began building group tombs. These benevolent societies sprang up like mushrooms, with one of their main purposes being to build and maintain institutional tombs for their members. There were patriotic groups, like the Howard Association; branches of national benevolent societies, like the Odd Fellows and Elks; and a statewide Masonic group. Associations of professionals also erected impressive monuments, among which the Jefferson Fire Company No. 22 tomb in Lafayette Cemetery #1 is particularly grand. And later, as labor unions arose, they too erected tombs for their members and their families, the first of which was the tomb of the New Orleans Polygraphic Union in Greenwood Cemetery, which dates from 1911.

Far overshadowing these entities were the many organizations based on their members' national origins. Indeed, virtually every ethnic group represented in New Orleans's swelling population formed a mutual aid society and built one or more collective tombs for their members. The French and Italians were organized by 1848, the Portuguese had formed their Lusitania Society by 1850, the Dalmatians and other Slavs by 1876, and the Greeks shortly thereafter. The Chinese Soon On Tong Association erected its austere tomb in Cypress Grove

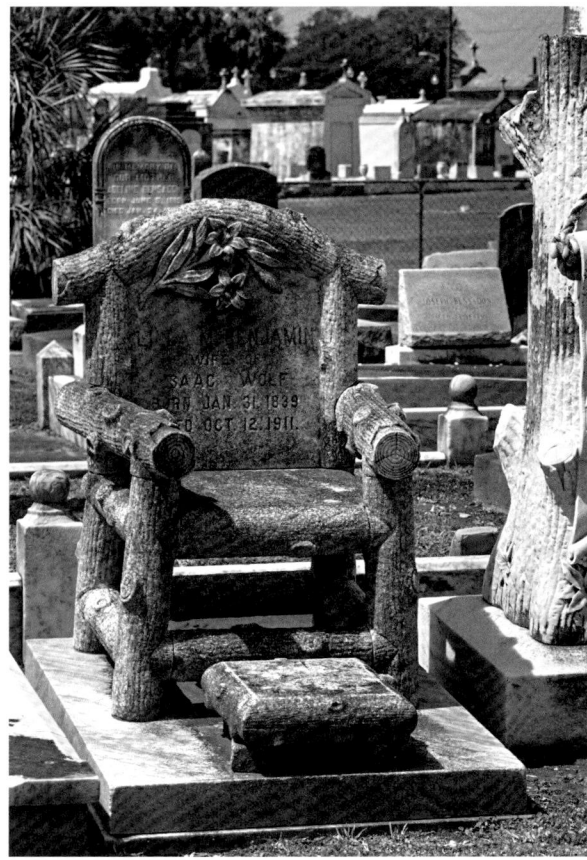

Granite chair; monument of Lilla Wolf, Dispersed of Judah Cemetery

only in 1904. Some groups, like the Spanish, with their Iberian Society and Cervantes Mutual Benevolent Society, formed two organizations corresponding to differences that traced back to their homeland. The proliferating Italian societies reflected conflicts in Sicily dating as far back as the thirteenth century!

Two national groups starkly underrepresented among the society tombs are the Germans and the Irish, who happened also to be the most numerous immigrants, along with the Italians. True, one can visit the Teutonia Lodge No. 10 Society's tomb in the Odd Fellows cemetery, but it is extraordinary that the city's large Irish population left the cemeteries bereft of Hibernian Society tombs. Yet the Italian, Irish, and German peoples assimilated so quickly that they felt no need for the mutual aid societies that so many other newcomers formed.

Much the same can be said for New Orleans's growing group of African Americans. More free people of color (*gens de couleur libres*) resided in New Orleans than in any other American city, and the enslaved population boasted levels of modern skills that surpassed those of their rural counterparts. From this arose such groups as the Wide Awake Benevolent Society, the Young and True Friends, the Ladies of Labor, and the Pure In Heart, each of which constructed its own large collective tomb.

Did women also form mutual aid organizations to ensure themselves an honorable burial? Visitors will quickly note that many women were memorialized, among them several who gained wide notoriety. Joining the persistent litigator Myra Clark Gaines were "voodoo queen" Marie Laveau (1801–1881) and the Storyville madam Josie Arlington (1864–1914). Daniel Moriarty's monument to his wife, Mary (1822–1887), is by any measure the largest in any New Orleans cemetery, while one of the city's most charming monuments is to Lilla Benjamin Wolf (1869–1911), who sat for years outside her family's shop on South Rampart Street and is remembered by the empty chair that adorns her tomb. But despite these monuments, and the fact that the overwhelming majority of symbolic funereal sculptures represented females (for instance, the Lucien Denopolis family tomb in Metairie and the Syme-Hardy tomb in Cypress Grove), women did not form benevolent associations to provide for their funerals. French law, which formed the basis of Louisiana law down to the mid-twentieth century, placed all women, including single women and widows, solidly in the context of their families. Because of this, women did not organize collectively to ensure decent burials, nor did they commonly build their own tombs until well into the twentieth century.

New Orleans's cemeteries developed organically. This steady process opened the possibility of stable careers for sculptors, architects, and ironmongers, not to mention suppliers of exotic stones, coffin makers, and providers of horse-drawn hearses. Some of these figures became highly regarded local personages. Newton Richards (1805–1874) not only erected some of the most impressive tombs but imported marble from New England to build them. Charles A. Orleans (1839–1923) followed in Richards's footsteps, expanding his sources for marble to the most renowned quarries in Italy. Scarcely had Ohio-born sculptor Alexander Doyle (1857–1922) arrived from New York than he gained a virtual monopoly in sculpting, as reflected in his grandiose Firemen's Charitable and Benevolent Association Monument (1887) in Greenwood Cemetery.

But what about the monuments themselves? Until the 1830s—and in many cases long thereafter—the field of architecture provided the main source of design ideas for New Orleans tombs. From neoclassicism and the Greek Revival movement came a wealth of simple but effective ornaments for what had heretofore been little more than brick boxes plastered with stucco. Soon, miniature temples were to be seen in all the cemeteries, at first mainly Greek in style but increasingly drawing on more lavish Roman prototypes. Scarcely had this international current been absorbed than a taste arose for more exotic architectural forms. By the late nineteenth century, New Orleans's cemeteries were festooned with marble structures in the Byzantine, Second Empire, Rococo, Renaissance Revival, and Gothic Revival styles, not to mention colorful and sometimes bizarre stylistic combinations.

Even the most modest graves proclaimed human mortality. Prior to the Civil War, New Orleans's funereal architects and designers shared a body of symbols of death, which they applied to the tombs they designed. All these symbols were well established in the architectural vocabulary of France, England, and North America and could be adopted without modification.

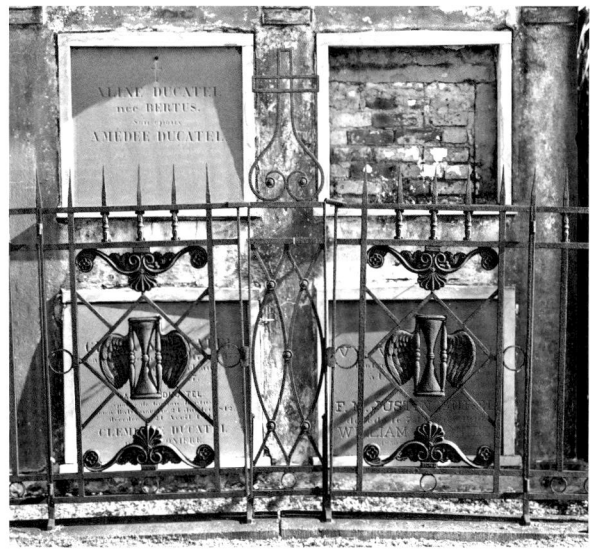

Tomb of Amédée Ducatel with winged hourglass, St. Louis Cemetery #2, Square 2

Memorial poem; tomb of John Oliver Locke, Greenwood Cemetery

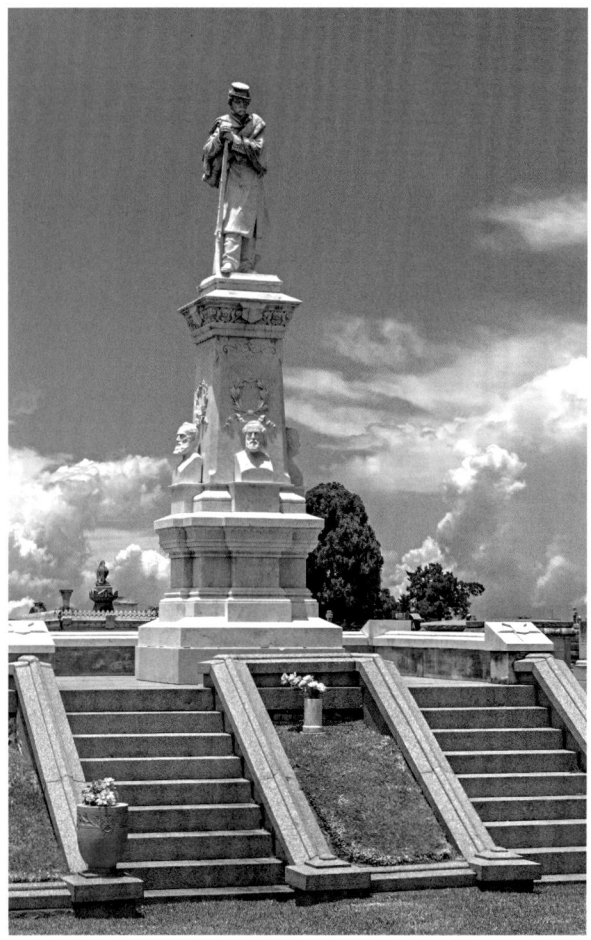

Monument to Confederate soldiers, Greenwood Cemetery

These symbolic statements included images of weeping mothers, lambs, lilies as symbols of purity, weeping willows, and winged hourglasses. All transcended specific languages or cultures.

No event did more to elicit large and impressive cemetery monuments than the Civil War. Of course, countless monuments to individual soldiers were erected, including one at Greenwood Cemetery dedicated to John Oliver Locke (see page 46), who perished in 1864. The heartfelt poetry on the simple tomb is as moving today as on the day it was engraved. But the primary demand was not for individual memorials but for large memorials to the major commands of the Confederate army and to those who gave their lives serving in them.

This popular wish was fostered by the many rank-and-file veterans in the city and spurred by the fact that several major Confederate generals (P. G. T. Beauregard, John Bell Hood, and others) made their postwar homes in New Orleans. The president of the Confederacy, Jefferson Davis, died there, and the city held some of the largest reunions of Southern soldiers. It was therefore natural that the new Metairie Cemetery and neighboring cemeteries would be chosen for major monuments to the Southern cause and as the place of interment for thousands of veterans.

One of the earliest such monuments was erected in 1874 near the entrance to Greenwood Cemetery to honor the memory of the six hundred Louisianans known to have perished while serving in the Confederate army. Prominently situated on an earthen mound, it was conceived and funded by the Ladies Benevolent Association of Louisiana. The imposing white marble structure was largely fashioned in Italy, while both Italian and local artists executed the many associated memorial sculptures of prominent Confederate generals.

This was followed in 1880 by a monument to the venerable Washington Artillery Battalion, which was present at the 1815 Battle of New Orleans. Three years later the Association of the Army of Northern Virginia dedicated the thirty-eight-foot-high monument to those several of its units from Louisiana. Surmounting the immense shaft is a statue of the indomitable Thomas Jonathan "Stonewall" Jackson by the Italian-born sculptor Achille Perelli. Close by is the related tomb structure featuring a larger-than-life statue of General Albert Sidney Johnston by Alexander Doyle. Four thousand Louisianans attended the dedication of this monument, and when President Davis died in 1889, he was interred there, as was local hero General Beauregard four years later.

Many assume that the Civil War led to a period of hardship and struggle in New Orleans. On the contrary, its conclusion ushered in an era of opulence that lasted until the Panic of 1873. During those years New Orleans architecture assumed a more lavish and grand face, which was reflected equally in the design of tombs in the city's proliferating cemeteries. Meanwhile, population growth generated a demand for more cemeteries, which was met less by the Catholic Church and mutual aid organizations than by private entrepreneurs who saw cemeteries and the funeral business as a whole as an opportunity for enrichment. A pioneer of this new current was Albert Weiblen (1857–1957), who in 1887 leased an entire quarry in Stone Mountain, Georgia, to secure his supply. Beginning in the late 1920s, the German-born sculptor Albert Rieker (1889–1959) discovered a demand for figures cast in bronze and, discovering that New Orleans had no bronze foundry, set up a regular relationship with a foundry in the Swabian town of Geislingen an der Steige. Meanwhile, a locally raised designer, George Stroud, became so well known for his mammoth and pretentious funeral monuments that when he died, he marked his own tomb in the main aisle of Metairie Cemetery simply as "Stroud's Tomb."

Such entrepreneurs appealed especially to the newly rich and to those who ranked higher in wealth or notoriety than in civic distinction. Thus, Weiblen did not hesitate to design an austere and handsome tomb for the renowned Storyville madam Josie Arlington, featuring the sculpture of a young girl at its door. This evocative bronze from the year 1911, a near duplicate of one in a Munich cemetery, was signed by F. Bagden and cast in Düsseldorf, in the early twentieth century one of the acknowledged art capitals of Europe.

Over time an unacknowledged competition existed with respect to size, adornment with sculptures, and the costliness of materials. The Irish-born grocer and real estate mogul Daniel Moriarty became the clear winner in 1905, when he erected the sixty-foot-high obelisk in Metairie Cemetery in honor of his late wife, Mary. With sculptures representing Faith, Hope, Charity, and Memory, the monument was composed of elements so

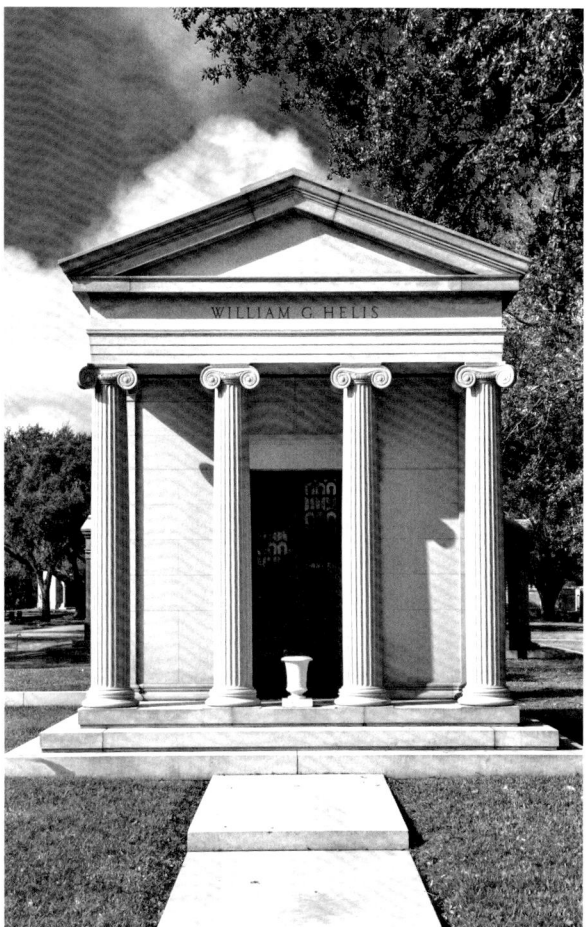

Tomb of William G. Helis family, Metairie Cemetery

heavy—four hundred tons—that at both the quarry in Barre, Vermont, and the one in Metairie, special railroad lines had to be laid to enable a fourteen-car train to pick up and deliver them.

The late nineteenth and early twentieth centuries marked the zenith of locally owned and locally based businesses in New Orleans. Immigrants, many of whom were fast assimilating and forming lucrative businesses of their own, wanted to join the ranks of the earlier establishment. Nothing symbolized worldly success more than an imposing marble or granite tomb in Metairie Cemetery or one of the several others nearby. And so, many New Orleans males wanted to cap their careers with the largest and most opulent tomb for themselves and their family. This was by no means unique to New

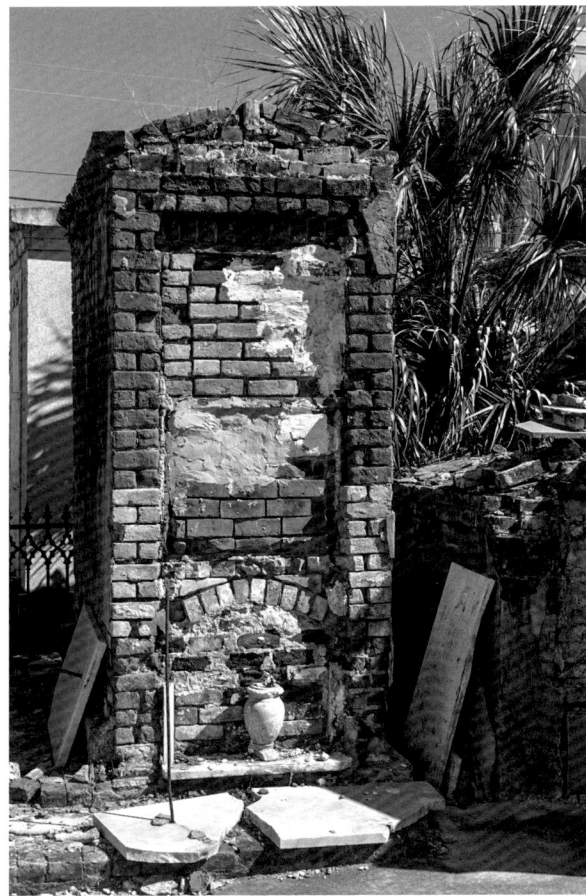

Three vaults of a decaying tomb, St. Louis Cemetery #1

Orleans: one need only look at Spring Grove Cemetery in Cincinnati, Lake View Cemetery in Cleveland, Allegheny Cemetery in Pittsburgh, or Bellefontaine Cemetery in St. Louis. But New Orleanians fully kept pace with this exuberant national effervescence of immodesty and even led it in ways that are evident to every visitor today.

The construction of grandiose tombs continues in Metairie Cemetery. To cite only two well-known examples, both Ruth Fertel, the hardworking and congenial founder of Ruth's Chris Steak House, and Alvin C. Copeland, the frenetic founder of the Popeyes fried chicken chain, were locally born and raised and wanted to be interred in the best New Orleans fashion. One senses an element of competition in their respective tombs, with the Copeland structure placed prominently near the Bell Avenue entrance of Metairie Cemetery and the Fertel monument close by on the same avenue. In planning their monuments, both reverted unapologetically to the marble, granite, and high-blown architectural styles that prevailed until the 1920s.

It was in the 1920s that profound changes began to unfold in the local economy and society that were to transform New Orleans's historic cemeteries. Many families began moving to the suburbs or elsewhere in the country, depleting the numbers of those who might maintain tombs and the old rites and rituals. As occurred elsewhere in America, distinguished locally owned firms sold out to national conglomerates, greatly reducing the number of New Orleans–based business leaders. Television and air conditioning weakened the neighborhood ties that had been so important to New Orleans's cemetery culture. And the successful assimilation of hundreds of thousands of Italians, Dalmatians, Greeks, Spaniards, and Germans meant that the old nationality-based mutual aid associations lost members and in many cases closed. Declining membership meant they could no longer maintain their collective graves, which were left to molder. Finally, a 1974 revision of Louisiana's constitution abolished the traditional annual family meeting, thus removing another support for New Orleans's cemetery culture.

The physical decay of New Orleans's cemeteries over the last few decades has been appalling. Besides the demolition of many monuments, including, sadly, the chapel of the Jesuit Fathers in St. Louis Cemetery #2, there has been ongoing deterioration, especially of those early tombs constructed of brick and plaster. Yet there is hope. A larger percentage of Louisianans are native born than in any other state, holding out the possibility of living customs being embraced anew and then once more passed down through the generations. Many families never interrupted the old traditions, and more than a few that had fallen away from them are now seeking

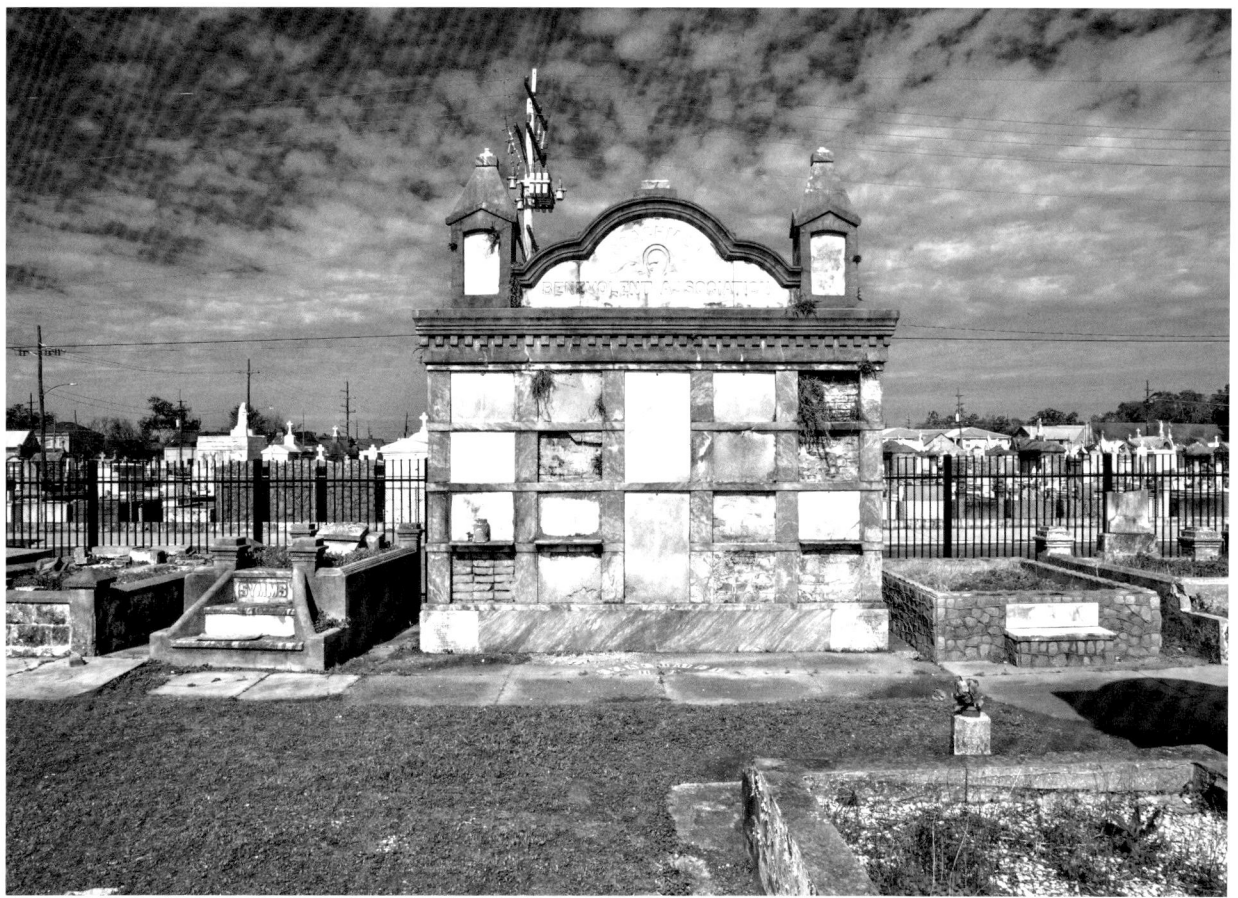

Society tomb of Coachmen Benevolent Association, Lafayette Cemetery #2

to revive what they knew or heard about as children. Meanwhile, concerned native residents and newcomers have combined forces to support such groups as Save Our Cemeteries, which are committed to documenting and preserving New Orleans's decaying cemeteries.

Today's visitors can choose from a dozen guidebooks or sign up for a professionally guided tour. Indeed, cemeteries have claimed a prominent place among the city's attractions. Related to this, the city's fifty-nine burial grounds are a source of income for hundreds of local citizens. It is nothing new for cemeteries to be deeply enmeshed within the New Orleans economy. One recalls, for example, Valentine Munck, who back in the 1850s made a lucrative business of building and renting out horse-drawn funeral cars. Unfortunately, the economics of New Orleans's cemeteries in both past and present remains largely unstudied. A careful examination may identify sources of income and help that are unknown or underused today. Even without such a study, we can be sure that the cemeteries bring huge value to the city. In 2013 Stewart Enterprises, which owned and managed Metairie Cemetery and several others, as well as several thousand cemeteries nationally, sold out to the Houston-based Service Corporation International for $1.13 billion. The owners of New Orleans's cemeteries include the Catholic Archdiocese, civil and religious groups, and private businesses. If they come to embrace the cemeteries as civic and economic assets, as well as monuments to the city's traditional culture, there may yet be hope for the future.

PART ONE

Twenty-One Biographies

Identity, History, Rites of Passage

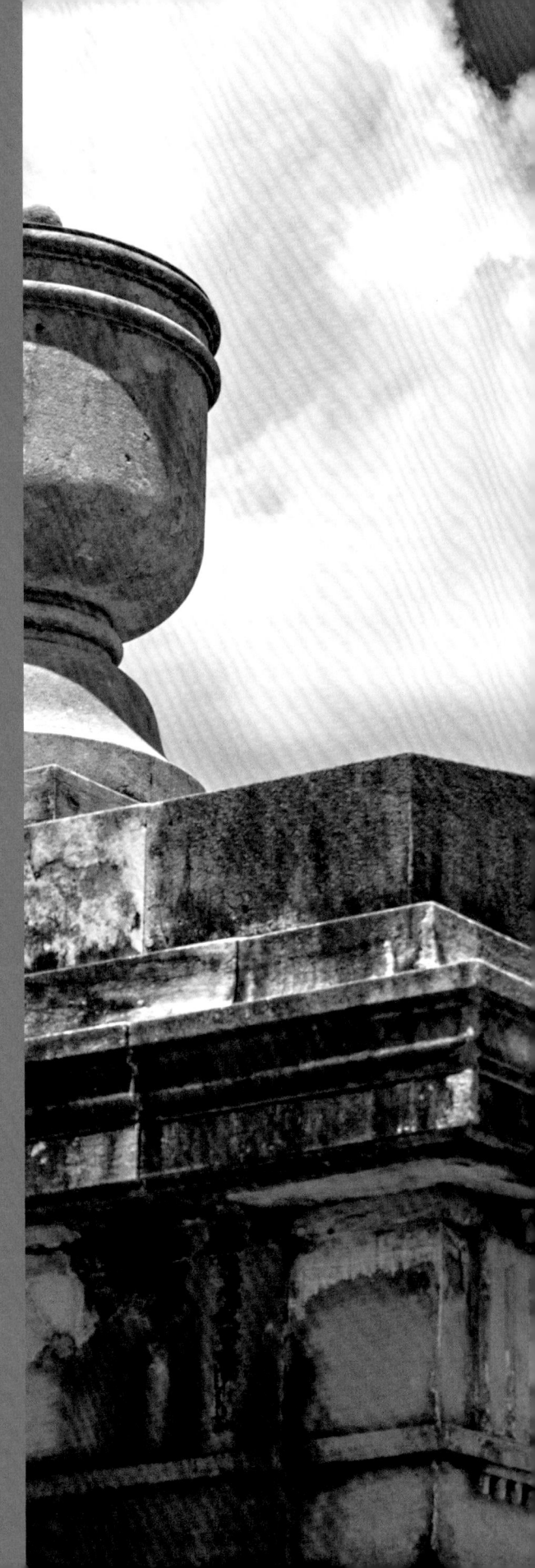

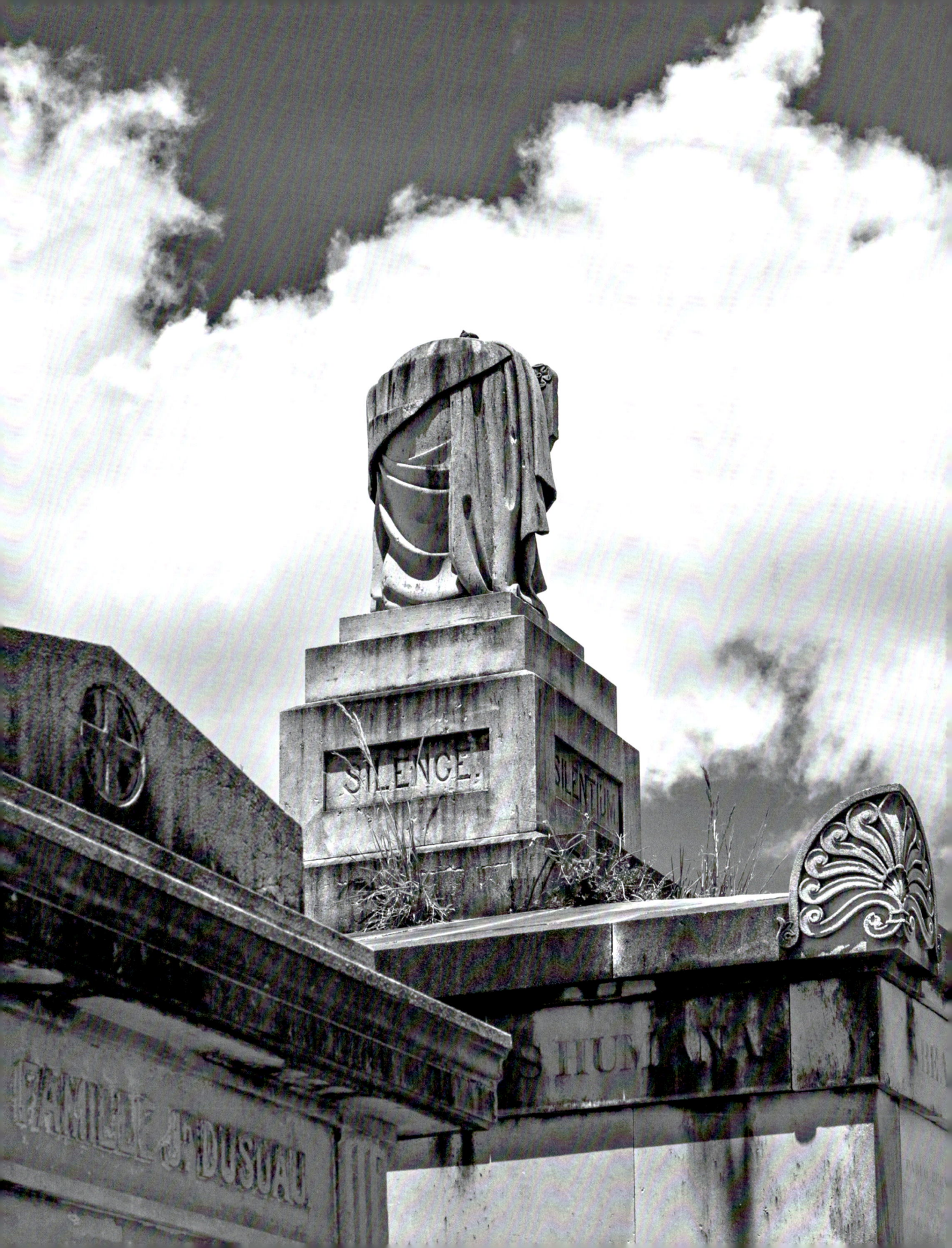

Silent Sentinels Against Time

SILENCE.

A simple word carved into the pedestal atop a large society tomb in St. Louis Cemetery #2, Square 2. Was the word meant for the living or the dead? In religions around the world, silence is revered as a meditative tool to come closer to God, the creator, and to all living things. Silence allows us to delve deep within ourselves and experience the thread that runs through all things and joins all creation as one. The Buddhist and Zen masters call it enlightenment; Christians, the love and peace of God. We call out by our silence to the One who hears all.

When St. Louis Cemetery #2 was first founded, it was a place of quiet and peace. There were no automobiles, ringing cell phones, airplanes, or interstate highways. By the time I saw that word *silence* carved deeply into white marble, I was struck by all the noise about me. Now the cemetery lies next to a raised freeway that delivers constant noise and distraction. But if you listen and concentrate, quiet again comes to the cemetery—your mind simply eliminates the background noise and slips into realms of silence and the dead. As you wander about, you begin to read the names and inscriptions on the tombs. Each name carved into the marble, slate, granite, or plaster represents a life lived; with the exception of the famous, we know little if anything about them. These people lived in another time; they are not like us nor we them. We each choose a path, each live our lives and hope to find love along the way. No one is guaranteed anything but a beginning and an end. It is how we live that matters.

✦ ✦ ✦

Whether old and simple or relatively new and grand, each monument is a visual feast. Attached to crumbling brick tombs, magnificent carved tablets with names mostly eroded by wind, rain, and time seem to be sentinels staring back at us. Next to them may stand a large mausoleum of granite and marble in near-perfect condition. Each is a resting place of people and their dreams, whether fulfilled or not. The wealthy and the poor, the powerful and powerless, owners and slaves—all have shared the same fate and all are finally equal.

As an architectural photographer and researcher, I was initially attracted by the architecture of these small cities, with their rows and aisles like streets in any neighborhood. This evolved into wondering, puzzling over what these people were like. What were their favorite foods, books, pleasures, games, songs—all those things and events that composed their daily lives? I could no longer look only at the structures, no matter how majestic or simple, without thinking of the people interred there. I knew that there was no possible way

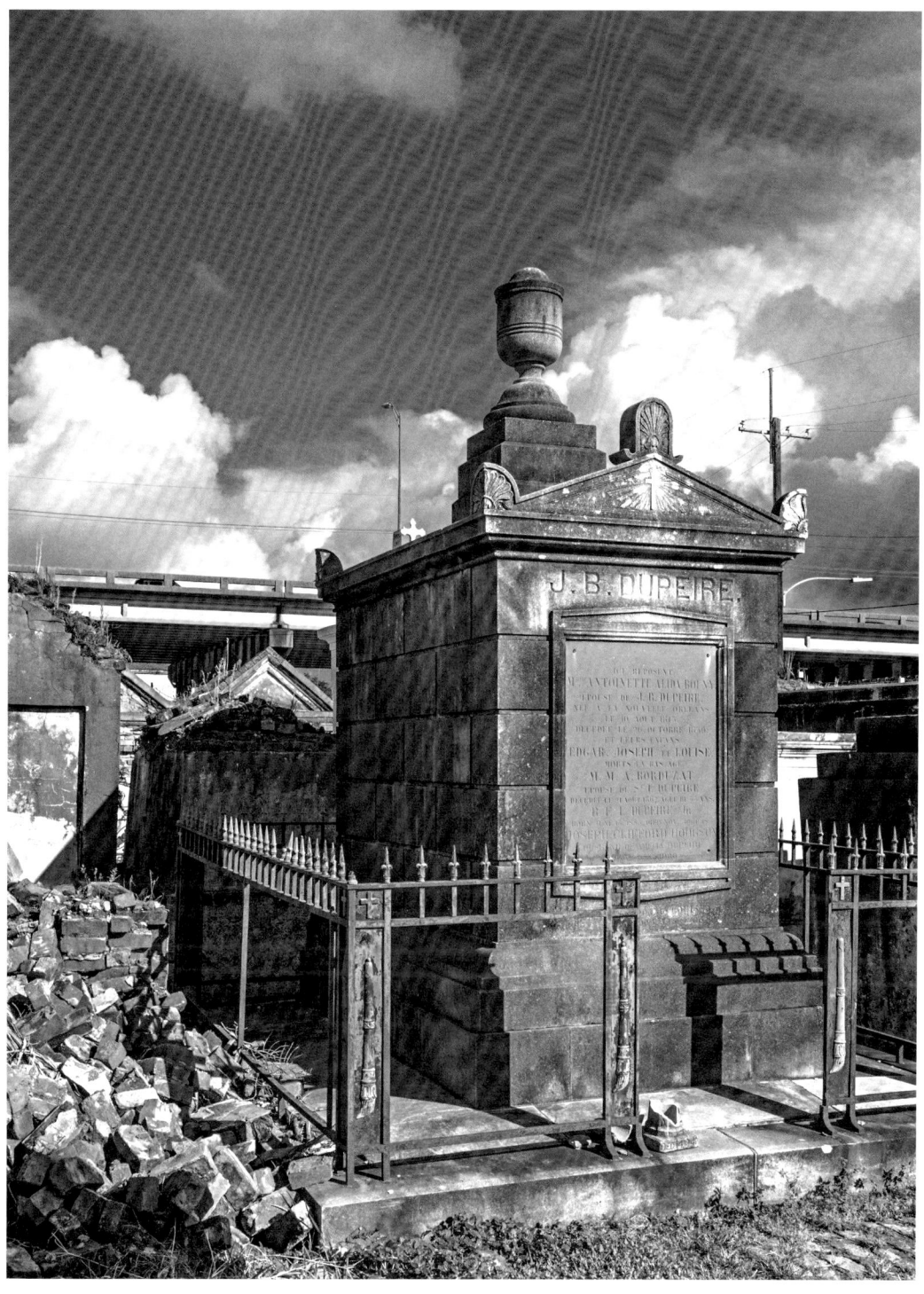

Tomb of Jean Baptiste Dupeire, St. Louis Cemetery #2, Square 2
Previous Page: "Silence" pediment; tomb of Iberian Society, St. Louis Cemetery #2, Square 2

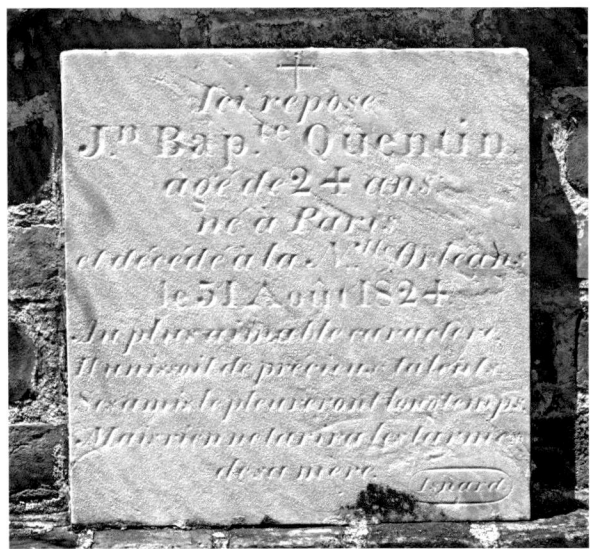

Jean Baptiste Quentin died at twenty-four in 1824. His tablet extols his virtues and tells of a life cut short. Wall vault tablet of Jean Baptiste Quentin, St. Louis Cemetery #2, Square 2

I could answer these questions or the other thousand that came to mind. The full stories would always remain a mystery. What I could do was simple: point a camera and release the shutter.

I began photographing cemeteries little by little. In early 1980 the pioneer preservationist and founder of Save Our Cemeteries, Mary Lou Christovich, asked me to join her on Saturday mornings to clean cemeteries. I began to see the deterioration firsthand as we cut trees out of the top of tombs, pulled weeds, and raked away debris. Along the way she became a close friend and mentor. I do not remember how many Saturday mornings we spent getting completely covered in dirt and grime, but I have never lost the sense of accomplishment in doing something for someone I have never known who has been long deceased. Mary Lou gave me a gift I cannot repay, but I hope that the work in this volume will speak for me.

In 1981 I was asked to head an inventory of historic cemeteries in New Orleans. The project began modestly, with St. Louis #1 and #2 chosen for study. It soon gained a momentum of its own and expanded into several other city and private cemeteries. Each tomb was described, and anything written on the closure tablets was transcribed exactly on a card, with care to match the upper- and lowercase lettering and punctuation. The tombs were then photographed. All this information is now housed at the Historic New Orleans Collection, the originator of the project. It covers thousands of tombs and wall vaults. Sadly, the photographs and written descriptions are now testimony to how much has since been broken and stolen, including wrought- and cast-iron fences and gates, marble vases, urns, crosses, and, in a few cases, entire tablets. Time has taken a serious toll on the cemeteries. They have suffered damage from hurricanes, hailstorms, freeze expansion within marble, neglect, theft, and vandalism. These monuments to the history of the people of this city are fragile and in need of utmost care and preservation.

As people wander about these cemeteries reading names and dates, they sometimes come across heart-rending inscriptions—emotional pleas from another age. They are messages in a bottle sent floating on time, awaiting the right person to read them. Perhaps to some passersby, the words on these tablets cause a swell of tears because they know all too well the emotions behind the epitaphs. One man tried to express the agonizing loss of his beloved wife with "All the Beauty that Could Die." A younger brother wrote a poignant statement after all his brothers had died; it is simplicity itself: "My Last Brother." One epitaph seems to convey the last words of a ten-year-old child heard by his mother shortly before he drowned, "Mother, I'm going out to play." A small, simple tombstone bears only two words: "Our Babies." There are thousands of examples such as these—we try to call back to them with

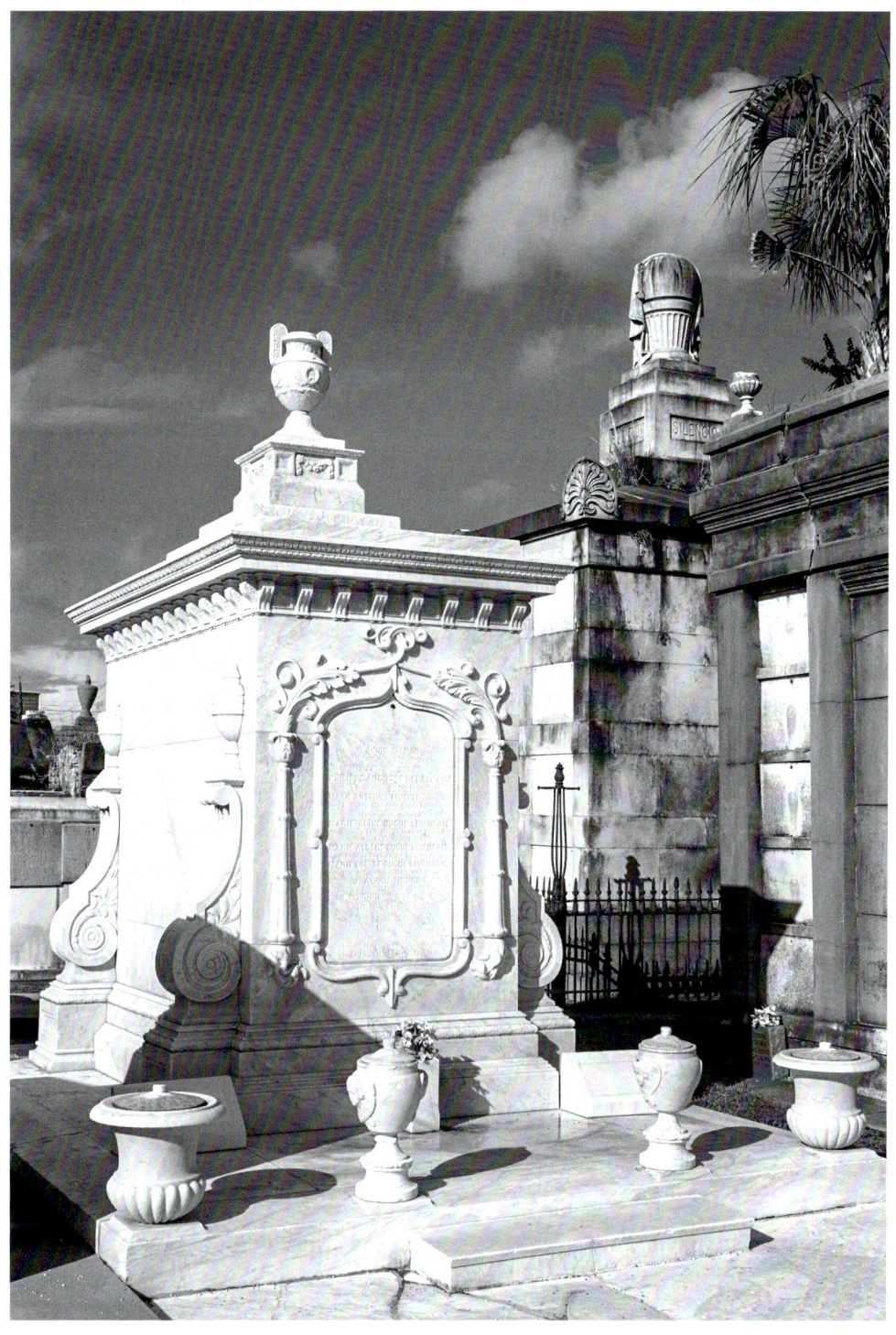

Tomb of Delachaise and Livaudais families, St. Louis Cemetery #2, Square 2

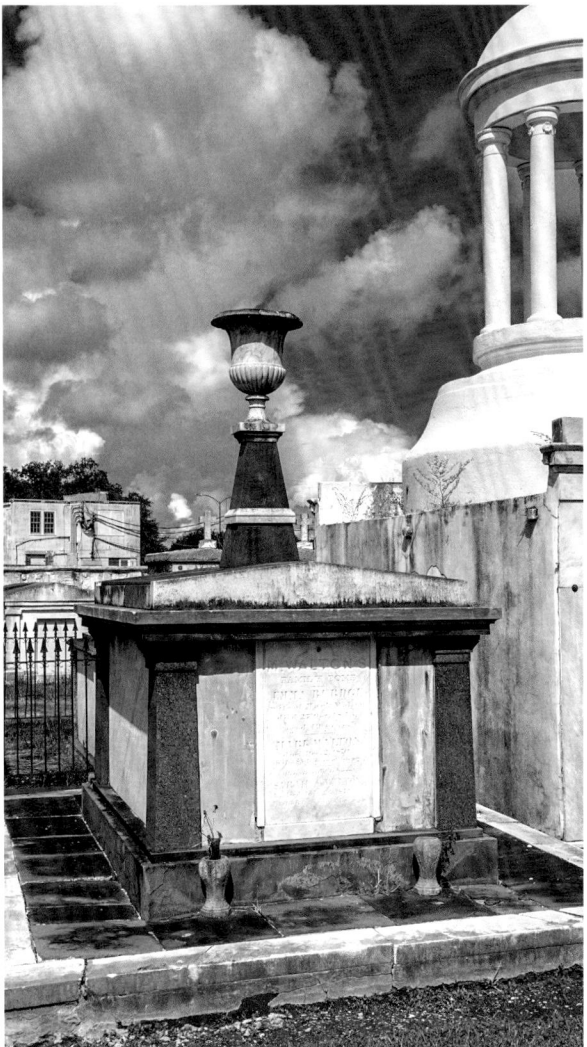

Tomb of Mark Walton family, Cypress Grove Cemetery

compassionate understanding, no matter how limited. The thread of humanity connects us to those who have gone before; these people interred are teachers of life, for they all knew great suffering and triumphed over it.

Walking through the aisles of the cemeteries, one notices features carved into the stone accenting the names and dates. Are they mere decorative ornamentations, or are they meant to convey meaning and events? They can be both. From the rather common variations of the weeping willow to the rare chalice with Host and the insignia of the Knights of Pythias, each communicates information or events about the deceased. We have only to stop and look at these symbols representing organizations, professions, talents, religious beliefs, or the pain of the surviving friends and family. Who cannot be stirred by the Weeping Willow cascading over an altar with a man bent over it in convulsive tears, longing for his lost love? These symbols are meant to tell stories about men and women who can no longer speak for themselves.

In my quest over the years to photograph and document tombs and their appurtenances, my fascination has grown about the people within. I would look at the names—some famous or notorious but mostly unknown to me. These individuals, nameless faces in old photographs, built the city I love so much. They were born and lived their lives quietly without conquering nations or writing great passages of literature; instead, they lived each day as best as they were able, caring for their loved ones and suffering their losses. These were people I wish I had known—it matters not to me their skin color, affiliations, accomplishments, religious denomination, or worldly possessions. I want to know the how and the why of their lives. The tombs kept drawing me closer to these people. I cannot laugh with them, console them, celebrate with them, or even simply take a walk with them. Instead, I have chosen twenty-one people from tablets and researched them. In all honesty, I do not know if the choices were random or if these individuals were calling out to be remembered. I have tried to write each story from the information I could find. These stories are not complete by anyone's imagination, but they are an attempt to make these New Orleans citizens live again, to be appreciated and, most important, remembered.

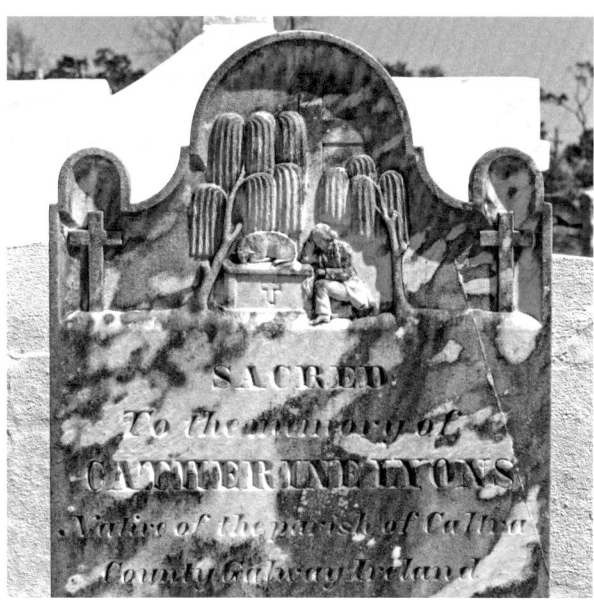

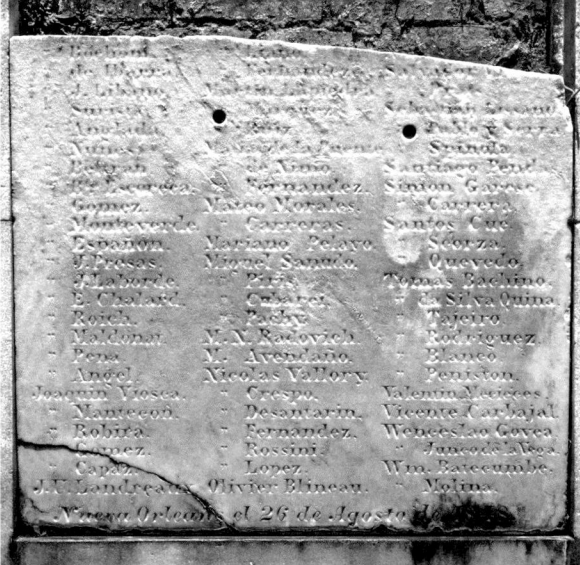

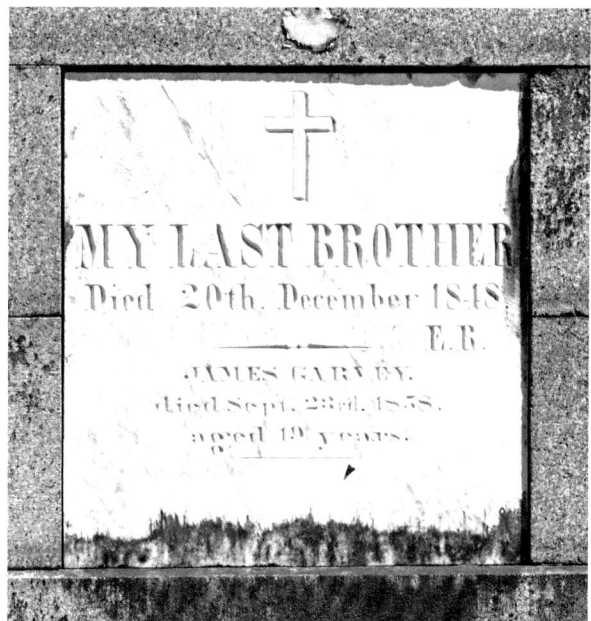

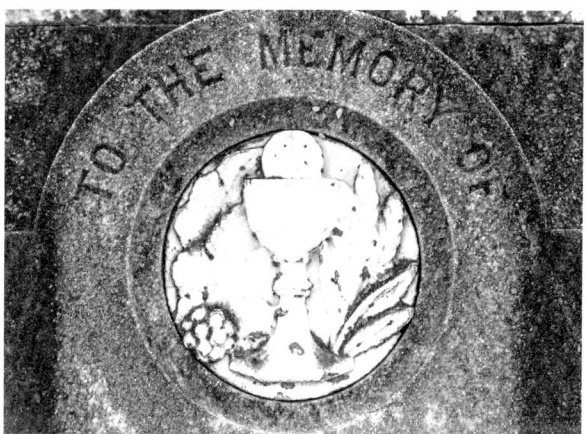

TOP LEFT
Weeping willow symbolizing mourning (especially for a spouse), and a sleeping lamb representing peace, innocence, and sacrifice; headstone of Catherine Lyons, St. Patrick's Cemetery #2

TOP RIGHT
Detail; tomb of James Garvey, St. Patrick's Cemetery #2

BOTTOM LEFT
Membership list; tomb of the Iberian Society, St. Louis Cemetery #2, Square 2

BOTTOM RIGHT
Chalice and Host detail; monument of Reverend Father René M. J. Vallée, Carrollton Cemetery #2

Silent Sentinels Against Time

Nicolas Mioton
1791–1834

Within the labyrinth of tombs that is St. Louis Cemetery #1 stands a three-tier stucco-covered tomb known as No. 440 in the South Quadrant. It bears a simple inscription:

NICOLAS MIOTON
19 FÉVRIER 1834

Nicholas Mioton married Anne Emilie Daram, who went by Emilie, in 1810. The onset in June 1812 of war between the United States and Great Britain slowed New Orleans's economy but did not cripple it until late 1814, when a large troop contingent from the British navy, fresh from the Napoleonic Wars, drove westward from Lake Borgne to capture New Orleans and the vast lands of the Louisiana Purchase. General Andrew Jackson arrived in the city on December 1 and began rallying the citizenry to face the inevitable. War was on their doorsteps.

Mioton, twenty-three, along with over a thousand others—including bankers, farmers, doctors, shopkeepers, slaves, and Native Americans—took up arms to protect their families and city. Land skirmishes began on the night of December 23 and continued sporadically over the next several weeks. Fortifications were dug below the city, lines formed, and the wait began. Mioton was a corporal under Major Jean Baptiste Plauché of the Orleans Battalion of Volunteers Foot Dragoons. By Saturday night, January 7, he was a veteran and found himself assigned to the far right end of the line. Heavily outnumbered, the Americans stood their ground. Before dawn the following morning, under cover of a heavy fog and a withering barrage of British rockets and artillery, Mioton would see the heaviest fighting, yet his ragtag army fought with distinction and dealt the British a humiliating defeat. The British never again threatened the United States.

Emilie and Nicolas Mioton's first child, Celina, had been born in 1812. After the war, Nicolas's early business life was not recorded until 1822, when he was a confectioner at 64 Chartres Street, near Bienville. That year, he bought a building nearby, at 136 Chartres, and moved his family and business there. His confectionery was on the first floor, and the family lived upstairs, where they settled into a quiet life with their five children. In 1831 Mioton bought a parcel of land about two-and-a-half miles below the city, facing the river, where the family moved before 1834. The confectionery business remained in town.

Seventeen-year-old Celina married Robert Stephen Hill, a tailor, in the spring of 1829; her sister Aline married Adolph Tremé, a planter, in 1832. The following year, Mioton gave each sister $2,000 (about $60,000 today). Celina gave the money to her husband to open a tailoring establishment, whereupon he traveled to Europe to procure cloth and other articles. During his absence Celina lived with her parents, close to the pregnant Aline Tremé's plantation. Frequent visits to her sister, brother-in-law Adolph, and his brother, Edouard, both veterans with Mioton in the late war, gave Celina great comfort. Edouard and Adolph were sons of Claude Tremé, who had developed the suburb (or "Faubourg") just behind the French Quarter that is known today as Faubourg Tremé.

Celina and Edouard indulged in an affair that left her pregnant. When her husband returned in November 1833, he discovered his wife's infidelity. Raging, he demanded to know the man's name. When she finally confessed, her father went to see Edouard, asking him to honor his actions and marry his daughter if a divorce could be arranged. (In Louisiana at the time, adultery was one of the few ways a divorce could be granted.) Edouard agreed, and the divorce was hastily arranged and finalized on January 15, 1834. Edouard Tremé's name was scratched off the divorce documents and did not appear in the newspapers, speaking to the influence of Nicolas Mioton. Yet, when the divorce document is examined closely, traces of Tremé's name remain visible.

The divorce final, Tremé surprised Celina's father by turning on his promise and saying there would be no wedding. Mioton left him with an ultimatum: he had fourteen days to decide. If his daughter could not be satisfied with marriage, Nicolas Mioton would give him what he deserved. The threat of a duel weighed heavily. The two weeks passed, and Tremé refused to relent. Mioton declared him a villain and challenged him to a duel.

Dueling was prevalent in New Orleans and elsewhere in the country (the most famous duel being the one between Aaron Burr and Alexander Hamilton, which left Hamilton dead). The weapon of choice was the pistol, for its flintlock-style smooth bore that ranged from a .45 to .52 caliber ball shot. A good percentage failed to strike the intended target, and many a duelist walked away unscathed or only slightly wounded. It was the facing one another that mattered. Yet because of the ball's large size, if it did hit near a vital body part it inflicted horrific damage.

Mioton and Tremé met on Bayou Road in the late afternoon of February 19, 1834, standing twenty feet apart. They both fired. Mioton's shot went wide, but Tremé's ball pierced the heart of his lover's father. Mioton's sister, Eleonore, ran to him and held him as he took his last breath. He was just forty-two years old.

Time does not allow us to witness the aftermath of the event except what was written in several obituaries and flowery testimonials given at the funeral. What went through Edouard's mind as he watched Nicolas die? The *L'Abeille* article of February 22, 1834, suggested regret: "And how much remorse must not the one who fired the mortal shot feel?... But the deed is done!" The

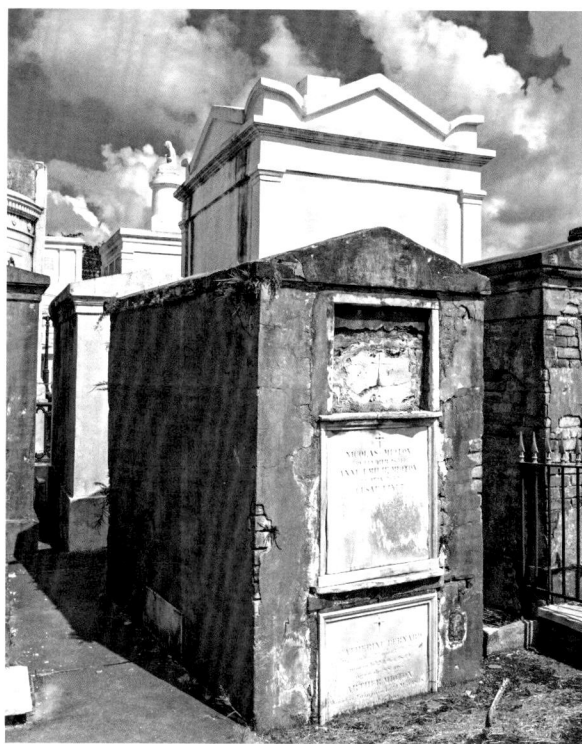

Tomb of dueler Nicolas Mioton, St. Louis Cemetery #1

article cautioned, "When will people cease to avenge an insult with a crime?" Shortly after his death, Mioton's many friends and relatives organized the Association Against Dueling and urged the police to enforce the 1812 law against dueling. Decades passed before the time-honored tradition became a thing of the past, by around 1890.

Emilie Mioton was left a widow and her children without their father; she never remarried, and she died in 1852, whereupon she was buried with her husband. Her daughter Celina gave birth to a son, Jean Baptist, on April 3, 1834, less than two months after her father's death. Within the year, she married Etienne Cesar Vinet, who raised her son as his own; together they had eleven children. Celina died in 1886 at the age of seventy-four and was buried in the Mioton tomb. Aline Tremé, the wife of Adolph, would not have wanted Edouard, her father's killer, near, and she turned him out of Tremé plantation to live in his father's home in Faubourg Tremé until his death in 1862, at the age of sixty-six.

The decayed Mioton tomb in St. Louis Cemetery No. 1 is all that remains of this tragic tale.

John Lawless
1810–1850

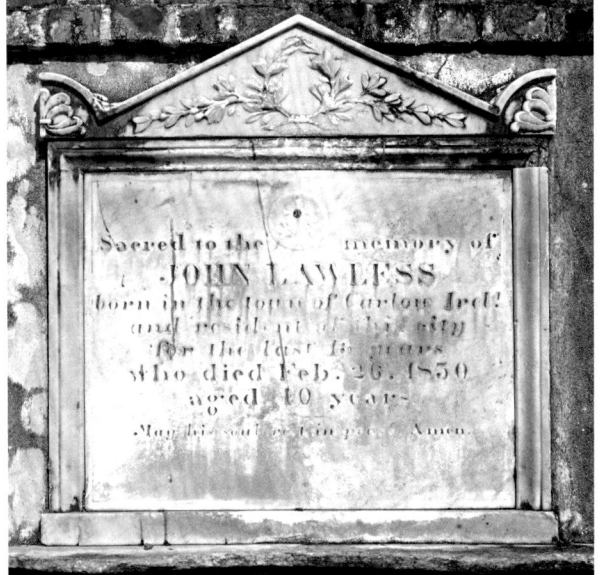

White marble olive wreath representing God's forgiveness, healing, and victory; wall vault of John Lawless, St. Louis Cemetery #2, Square 2

In Square 2 of St. Louis Cemetery #2, among the wall vaults along Conti Street, is a delicate white marble enclosure and tablet. It belongs to John Lawless, an Irishman born in County Carlow in 1810. At twenty-six he, with his sixty-year-old father and four siblings, crossed Ireland to Galway and booked passage for America aboard the *Brig Pratincole*. The family arrived at New York Harbor on June 1, 1836. John listed himself as a laborer. The exact date of his arrival in New Orleans is unknown, though probably sometime in 1837, for according to his obituary of 1850, he had been living in the city thirteen years.

The 1840 federal census, which named only the "head of household" while others were not identified, recorded John Lawless, age thirty, living with a woman between thirty and thirty-nine and a boy of less than five years. If these were his wife and son, they remain nameless. The city directory of 1842 has a John Lawless living at the corner of Hospital (today Governor Nicholls) Street and Burgundy Street in the French Quarter. The 1850 census is silent on a man, woman, or child named Lawless within the correct age range.

In October 1847 Lawless seems to have had a run of bad luck. Early that month a newspaper article states that a slave named Bill broke into a new building under construction on Rampart Street and stole a quantity of tools belonging to Lawless. Later that month a John Lyon was accused of breaking into Lawless's carpenter shop on Franklin Street and making off with the contents of two chests and a trunk containing clothes. Little else can be learned about Lawless other than that he worked in the building trades as a carpenter and later as a plasterer until his death on the afternoon of February 26, 1850, at his home on Jackson Avenue between Jersey (today Annunciation) and Laurel Streets. His epitaph is brief: "May his soul rest in peace, Amen." It is not known who had the tablet carved and placed on the wall or the cause of his death at age forty.

Kasper Auch

1811 – 1886

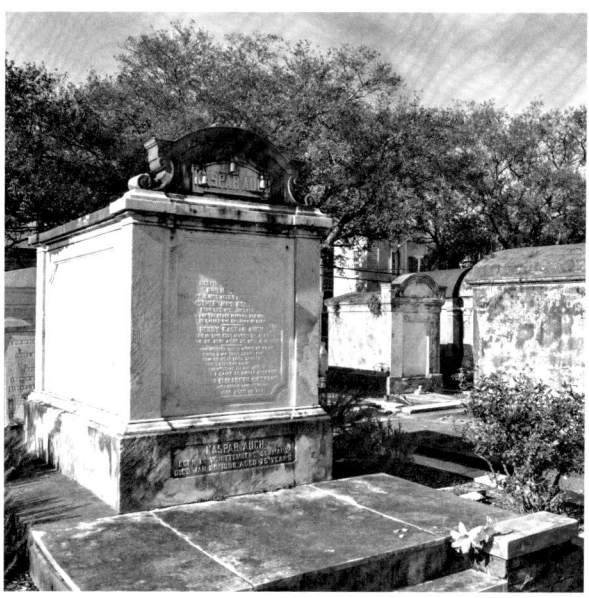

Tombs of Kasper Auch and John Richardson families, Lafayette Cemetery #1

Near the Sixth Street wall of Lafayette Cemetery #1 in the Garden District stands a white marble tomb. It is topped with a large scroll pediment decorated with marble tassels hanging about the raised letters "Kasper Auch." Now forgotten, at one time Auch was one of the most prominent men in the city of Lafayette, now part of New Orleans, serving on the city council and in the legislature.

Born in 1811 in Germany, Auch came to the United States with his parents when he was about seven years old. His exact time of arrival in New Orleans is unknown, but he began working in the lumber business around 1825, when he was fourteen or fifteen years old. It suited him well, and by 1840 he was prosperous enough to buy an omnibus line and extend its service to Canal Street. He found time to organize the Volunteer Fire Company No. 1, serving as a member for many years, and was one of the founders of the German Presbyterian Church and the Lafayette Presbyterian Church.

Auch married Mary Elizabeth Kieskamp in 1844. They had five children, all of whom died much too early: Joseph at eighteen months, David at twenty-one days, John at one day, and Philip St. John at three years. Their firstborn child, Henry, died at the age of twenty-six in 1871. At the time, Henry was working with his father, who had founded the Lafayette Fire Insurance Company in 1869. Kasper continued on as president of the company for several more years and then retired to care for his wife. She died on January 6, 1886, at the age of sixty-two, from what the doctors termed general debility. Her husband, distraught and inconsolable, died twenty-three days later from surgical complications. He left an estate of over $300,000, the majority of which he left to the Presbyterian Church for educational pursuits. Known in his lifetime for his generosity, he even remembered his children's nanny with a legacy of $500. The white marble tablet on his tomb is concise and cold:

**BORN IN WURTTEMBERG, GERMANY
DIED JAN. 28, 1886 AGED 75 YEARS.**

His faith had not been broken; he was triumphant in life.

John Davidson
1816–1872

Henrietta Sidle Davidson
1827–1891

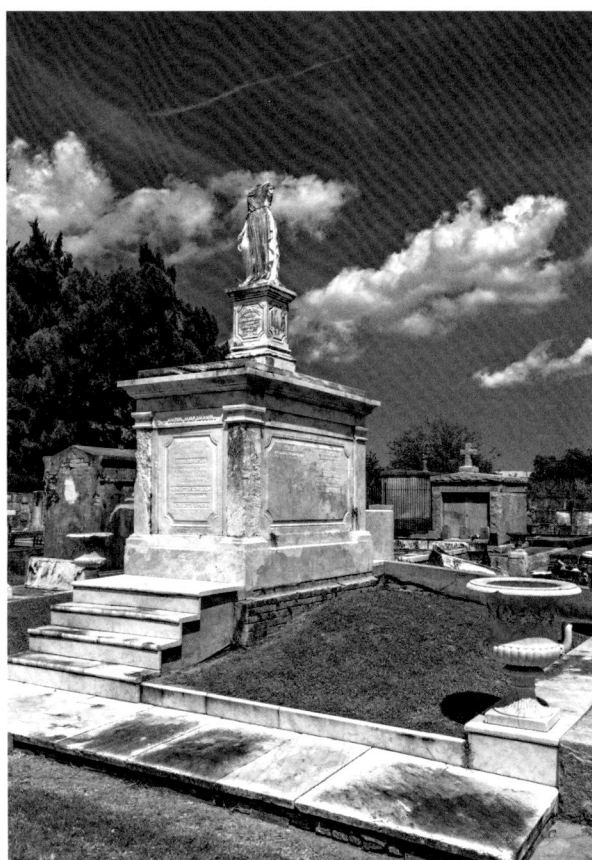

Tomb of John and Henrietta Davidson family, Cypress Grove Cemetery

On the main aisle of Cypress Grove Cemetery is the large, white marble tomb of the John and Henrietta Davidson family. The corner pilasters are worn and eroding. The tomb is topped by a marble pedestal inscribed "Henrietta Sidle wife of John Davidson," as well as a robed statue of a woman who is missing her left arm and has been decapitated by vandalism.

John Davidson grew up in Dundee, Scotland. In 1837 he boarded the ship *Governor Troup* in Liverpool and sailed for New York City, arriving on June 9. On the ship's passenger list, his occupation is given as carpenter. Thirty months later he made another journey, this time to New Orleans by way of Galveston, Texas, aboard the steamship *New York*. Within a year he had formed a partnership with fellow Scot John Lyall, a slater. The firm of Lyall & Davidson would become widely known among the architects and builders of the city as suppliers of Welsh slate for roofing and paving. In the late 1840s, John married Henrietta Sidle, the daughter of prominent builder David Sidle.

Both Davidson and Lyall began to speculate in real estate. Davidson began to accumulate substantial wealth and built a palatial home simply known as the Davidson Mansion on St. Charles Street. On the morning of January 3, 1872, when Davidson was driving his buggy across the Magnolia Street Bridge over the New Basin Canal, someone yelled out that the train was coming. With his view blocked by the buggy canopy, he thought he was about to be hit and hurriedly turned the buggy to get off the tracks. A wheel wedged against a post. As Davidson leaped from the buggy, his clothing became entangled and he fell directly in front of the oncoming coal train. Two men standing nearby ran to his aid and tried pulling him to the side. The train struck him in the back. Severely injured, he rolled to the side and the train wheels ripped his trousers. Bystanders took him home where doctors treated him, bleeding from multiple wounds and in shock. Surgeon Warren Stone, who in 1847 became the first Louisiana doctor to use ether in an operation, could do little, and Davidson died that evening at 11:30 p.m.

The following year his sixteen-year-old daughter, Henrietta Davidson Pike, died from complications in childbirth. Davidson's wife, Henrietta, would carry on the slating business until she began to suffer from paralysis in 1888. She died three years later.

Richard Bartlet Sumner
1816–1868

On Live Oak Avenue in Cypress Grove Cemetery is a small marble monument with a delicately carved bas-relief—a sheaf of wheat bound by an ivy vine. It is dedicated to the memory of Richard Bartlet Sumner, known as R. B. to his friends. The symbols tell of a life fulfilled and one of loyalty. Sumner was born in December 1816 in Newburyport, Massachusetts, into a merchant family with interests in the sea trade. His father, Michael, had a business associate and close friend named Richard Bartlet with connections in New York. Both Michael and Richard had advertised for sale a whaling ship named the *Newbury* in 1835. R. B.'s mother, née Mary Bartlet, may have been Bartlet's sister.

When Sumner reached the age of twenty-one in 1837, he moved to New Orleans and joined the shipping and commission firm of S. & J. P. Whitney & Co. Seven years later, in May 1844, Samuel Whitney, the senior partner, retired and left the newly renamed firm of J. P. Whitney & Co. to the partnership of R. B. Sumner and John P. Whitney. Sumner was soon one of the most influential businessmen in the city. The following year he married Harriet Johnson of Maine. They would have three children.

John P. Whitney's sudden death from scarlet fever on January 30, 1848, was a tragedy to his friend and partner. He had been ill for just three days, after watching his daughter die from the same infection. Age forty-two, Whitney was buried in his hometown of Waldoboro, Maine. The company and all its assets now fell to Sumner. In 1848 he reorganized one of their business partnerships, the Belleville Iron Works, which stood across the Mississippi River in Algiers, to sign on twenty prominent investors. Two years later, he was among the founders of the Crescent Mutual Insurance Company, devoted to fire, marine, and river insurance, investing $200,000 of capital. That same year, Sumner took on another partner, New York–born Edward Hyman, age thirty, who had been with the firm since the age of twenty.

The 1850s were a prosperous period for New Orleans, and Sumner took full advantage of the opulence. He helped organize the New Orleans, Opelousas & Great Western Railroad (known today as the Southern Pacific) and became one of its first directors in 1852. The following year he was elected vice president of the New Orleans Chamber of Commerce. But amid this success, he experienced yet another tragedy in Edward Hyman's sudden death on April 4, 1855, at the age of thirty-four, leaving a wife and children. Sumner would continue the business alone.

By this time, Sumner had as many as twenty to thirty ships in port loading and unloading cargo. The firm owned or had consignments on these ships, which represented a staggering amount of money. One of these ships was the 924-ton *R. B. Sumner*, which he commissioned in 1852 and began sending on routine trips to Europe. In November 1858 it would founder and capsize in the stormy and shallow seas off Chappaquiddick

Island, part of Martha's Vineyard. Sumner continued his entrepreneurial endeavors in 1856 by founding the Algiers Dry Dock Company No. 2, no doubt to service his own vessels.

The outbreak of the Civil War brought a virtual standstill to business in New Orleans. By the end of 1861, most construction of houses or businesses had come to a halt. The city fell to the Union Navy at the end of April 1862, yet this did little for the economic welfare of the city. Shipping trade with New York resumed by 1863 and steadily increased, yet the income was essentially worthless, as silver and gold currency had been replaced by paper. It is possible that Sumner saw his world crashing in on him when in May 1863 he sat down and wrote his holographic will. Soon thereafter he traveled to Europe, where he would remain until the fall of 1865. It is not known whether his family accompanied him; he returned alone to New York harbor.

There, he boarded the side-wheel steamship *North Star* on October 21, 1865, bound for New Orleans. The ship belonged to the New York–based Star Line, which ran eleven steamships between New York and New Orleans. Three nights after setting out, the ship sailed into a hurricane in the waters off Cape Hatteras, notoriously the fiercest seas along the Atlantic coast. The smokestack of the ship broke and swept away, and she began to take on water at an alarming rate. The passengers and crew spent the night and following day bailing seawater and doing anything they could to keep the water from reaching the boilers. After three days and nights, on October 27, the *North Star* was towed into Norfolk, Virginia. The same storm sank her sister ship, the *Evening Star*, also bound for New Orleans. It was carrying gold and silver coins worth an estimated $120 million today, coinage sent to help relieve the privation that was taking place in New Orleans. Over three hundred

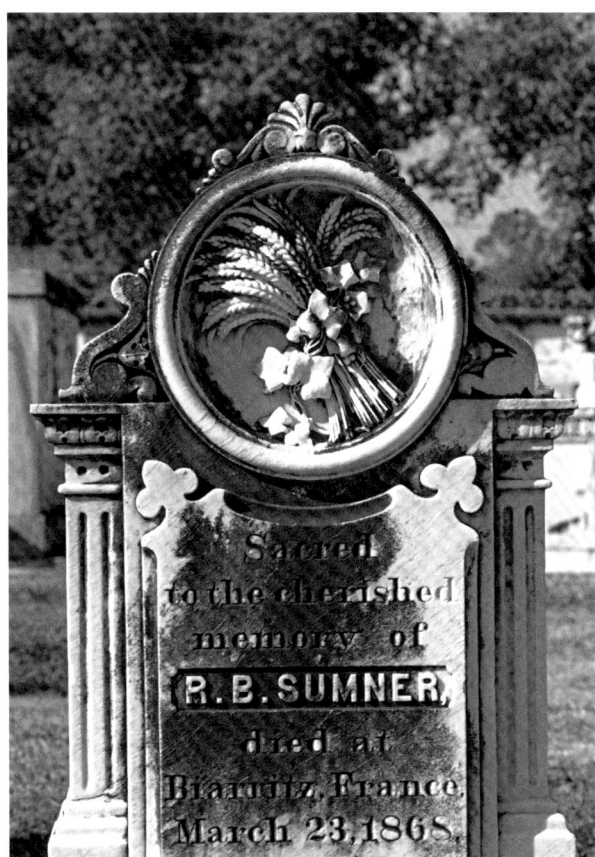

Monument of Richard Bartlet Sumner, Cypress Grove Cemetery

people lost their lives, including the great New Orleans architect James Gallier Sr. and his wife.

Sumner decided the railroad would be safer for his final passage from Norfolk; he arrived home on November 6. For reasons lost in time, he gathered his wife and children and sailed for Biarritz, France, where they had booked rooms at the Hotel Gardères.

There he died suddenly on March 23, 1868. He was fifty-one. His youngest daughter was just seven years old. The *Daily Picayune* published what can be described only as a bitter obituary. It stated that had Sumner not withdrawn from the bracing conditions in New Orleans and remained to provide his leadership, he might still be alive. It seemed to offer some sympathy only in the last line: "We record his death with profound sorrow."

His wife, Harriet, died almost four decades later, on March 20, 1904, in Chicago.

Edward Sweeney
1822–1874

On Locust Aisle in Greenwood Cemetery, a tall marble headstone stands at the rear of a large coping tomb, a concrete encasement filled with soil. The white marble, now gray from pollution and age, is dedicated to the Edward Sweeney family, and it tells a story of poverty, success, tragedy, love, kindness, generosity, and an unbreakable faith.

Edward as a young man knew hunger and want in Dublin. During the 1840s and early 1850s, the entire country was starving in the Potato Famine, which took the lives of one million people. One million more would flee, and in that number were Edward and his two sisters, Margaret (twenty-two) and Eliza (twenty). He was twenty-four when they boarded the bark *Fagan Bealac* (the ship's name was an old Gaelic battle cry meaning "Clear the Road"). They arrived in New York City on May 17, 1847, forty-five days after they had left Dublin harbor. Aboard ship were 198 passengers—like the Sweeneys, mostly in steerage.

Edward departed New York shortly after his arrival, heading south to New Orleans, although it is not known if he had relatives there. He took whatever job he could find; because he was Irish, the work would be hard. Gaels faced an uphill battle for survival. The Know-Nothing Party, which opposed immigration and especially the Catholic Church, fixated on nationalism and native-born supremacy and tried to restrict the newly arrived Irish to menial work. The party was quite successful until the outbreak of the Civil War. Prospects and living conditions for the Irish were dire, and they were viewed by many as disposable for their willingness to work for low wages in disgusting and dangerous positions.

The building of the New Basin Canal from 1832 to 1838, three miles from Rampart Street to West End at Lake Pontchartrain, epitomized the worst of this. It took the lives of an estimated eight thousand to twenty thousand Irishmen during its construction. Most fell to the cholera and yellow fever epidemic of 1832, as they struggled to dig through the marshes and swamps, while other diseases continued to take lives. Most were buried indiscriminately in several mounds behind the nearby Girod Street Cemetery.

After Edward arrived in New Orleans, he found work unloading ships and riverboats, a backbreaking and hazardous trade. Upon meeting a fellow worker, George Canby, from England, they turned the job of dockworker, or stevedore, into a lucrative business. They formed a partnership, Sweeney and Canby, that lasted the rest of Edward's life. (He named his second son after his partner.) Sweeney and Canby prospered by obtaining contracts for loading and unloading cotton bales on the riverboats—bales that arrived in New Orleans by the thousands every day. The *Sailor's Magazine* of September 1858 stated that New Orleans shipped an average of 1.5 million bales of cotton per year, with a value of $90 million. There was a lot of money to be made.

In January 1857 Edward Sweeney married Ellen Ralph; together they had five children. Their first child,

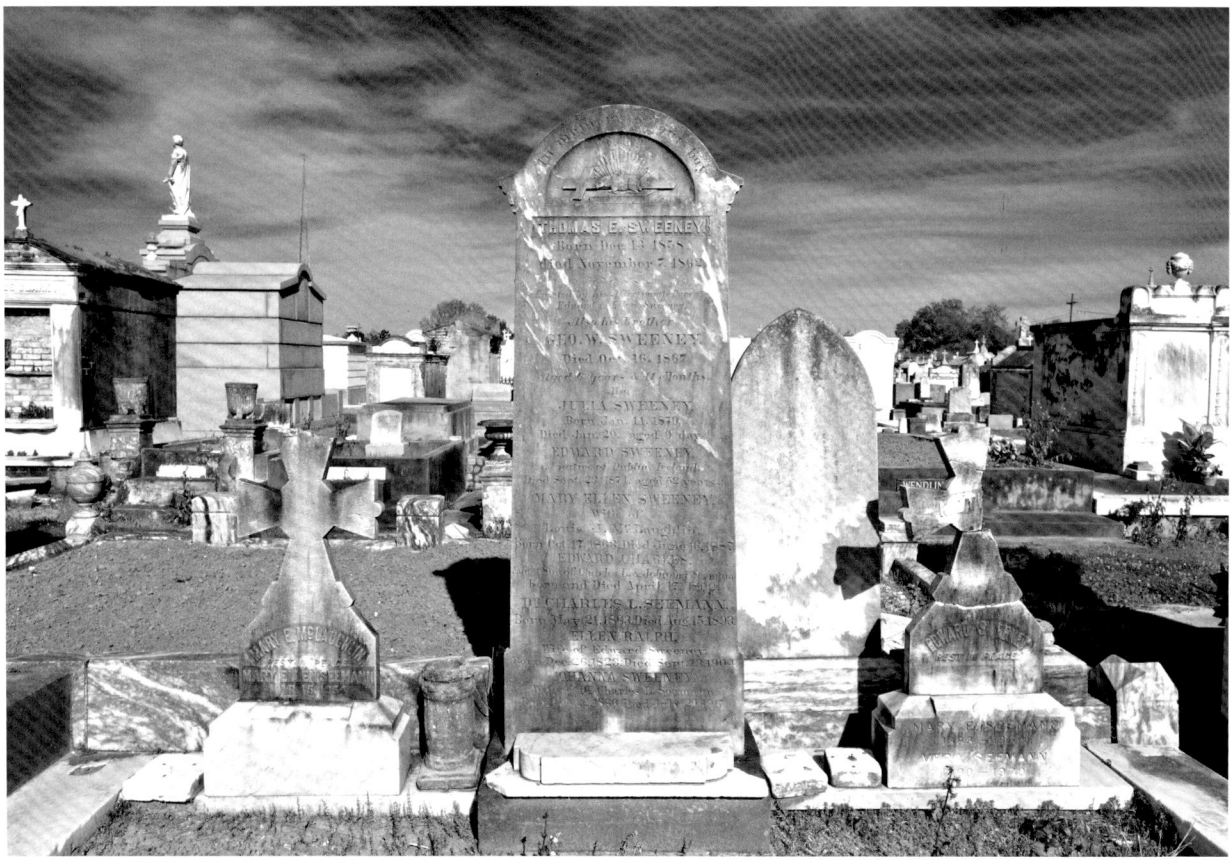

Monument of Edward Sweeney family, Greenwood Cemetery

Thomas Edward, was born in December 1858. He lived almost four years, dying in November 1862. Their second son, George W., was born in November 1860. The *Daily Picayune* of September 10, 1867, lists Edward Sweeney and son arriving in New Orleans from New York aboard the steamship *Gen. Meade*. We can only speculate about the trip's purpose. It may have been to seek medical treatment for George, who was probably suffering from headaches, sleeplessness, dizziness, and numbness in his legs or arms. If this was the reason for the trip, the prescribed treatments failed, and in just over a month he died. The death certificate states the cause of death was "congestion of the brain," a slow buildup of excess blood in the cerebral tissues that frequently causes a stroke. His grieving parents had two surviving children, Mary Ellen, age four, and Johanna, age one year. The family experienced the death of yet another child, Julia, who was born in January 1870 and lived only nine days. Loss was a part of life in 1800s New Orleans.

Throughout the nineteenth century, the city of New Orleans was constantly ravaged by yellow fever and cholera, creating orphans in the thousands. Edward saw the need and stepped up to help. Along with Father Cornelius Moynihan, pastor of Sts. Peter and Paul Catholic Church, he organized entertaining fund-raising events for St. Mary's Orphan Boys Asylum and St. Vincent de Paul Orphans' Home. He became an officer on their boards and served as president. In fall 1869 he bought a bay horse in Missouri, considered quite a distance at that time. He notified all the city fire departments that there would be a competition and that the winner would receive the horse, with all proceeds benefiting St. Vincent's.

Sweeney also became active in the volunteer fire companies by donating and raising money to buy modern equipment. At the time, the fire companies were entirely crewed by volunteers; it wasn't until 1891 that a professional fire department was founded. Edward was also instrumental in acquiring Amoskeag double-pump steam engines for the Crescent Steam Fire Engine Co. No. 24 and the Phoenix Fire Co. No. 8. During the dedication of one of these engines, he was described as a man "whose big heart is as large as the old Third District," where he lived and which was (and still is) the largest district in the city. He was a member of both fire companies as well as Creole Steam Fire Engine Co. No. 9.

Since the Civil War's end the city had been under the Reconstruction government; corruption was rampant, and the citizens were desperate to end the stranglehold that was slowly plunging the city into economic turmoil. Sweeney did more than his fair share. In the summer of 1870, he was one of the founders and directors of the new Hibernia Bank of New Orleans. The following summer, he was among the founding members and directors of the Hibernia Insurance Company of New Orleans. In 1872 he became the treasurer of the Hibernia Benevolent and Mutual Association of Louisiana. He was president of the New Orleans Homestead Association. Sweeney joined the Orleans Parish executive committee of the Reform Party when it organized in 1872, though the entire point of the party became moot with the onslaught of the Panic of 1873. New Orleans suffered more from that depression than most large American cities and did not fully recover until the 1880s. Despite these setbacks, Edward continued to raise money for the orphanages and maintain his position with the bank and insurance company.

He celebrated his fifty-second birthday in 1874. He was devoting most of his time to charitable institutions.

It is not known when he suddenly began experiencing painful abdominal cramps or how much medical help he sought. The pain grew worse, until at nine o'clock on the morning of September 23, he died at home from congestion of the bowels.

The Hibernia Bank closed its doors for one day in mourning. Numerous testimonials appeared in newspapers, glowing with praise for his selfless work to relieve the suffering of others. They noted his belief that "the deed had lost its merit if the world should know of it." Perhaps he was driven by a desire to prevent others from knowing the privation and hunger he had known in Ireland. His bereft widow, Ellen, lived three decades longer and died in September 1904; like her husband's, her funeral took place at Sts. Peter & Paul Church. She had lived long enough to see her husband and all but one child die. Their daughter Johanna lived until 1917.

Reverend Emperor Williams
1826–1896

Born into slavery in 1826, the aptly named Emperor Williams helped reshape the Methodist Episcopal Church and forge a path clearly marked for African Americans to follow.

Emperor was the son of Green and Louisiana Williams, and he stated that he was born into the General Gaines family in Nashville. General Gaines remains somewhat of a mystery. There was the Virginia-born general, none other than Edmund Pendleton Gaines, a hero in the War of 1812. He had been a citizen of Tennessee since childhood. Yet this writer has not found evidence that he owned slaves. (In 1838, during a military campaign, he defied the sheriff of New Orleans, who instructed the army to return escaped slaves from Florida to their owners. Instead, Gaines freed them and sent them west.)

There was also the planter Benjamin Gaines of Robertson County, only a few miles from Nashville, and it is possible that this is the Gaines family to which Emperor referred. Williams was taken to Louisiana in 1839 and sold to a free man of color in 1840 for $600. This unidentified African American, said Emperor, "treated him badly." A year later he was sold to James McIntosh of Jameson & McIntosh, New Orleans builders, and it is here that his life changed, pointing him in a direction he only could have dreamed about.

McIntosh taught Williams the skills to become a master mason. The relationship between the two men must have been one of respect because in 1846 Williams was named to the trusted position of foreman, a title he held until 1858. Something else highly unusual took place in those early years: McIntosh was instrumental in teaching Williams how to read and write, an act that could have landed both in prison because it was against the law to teach a slave to read or write. Williams began reading the Bible and speaking about what he read. He joined a church in 1845 and devoted more time to talking about the Bible. In 1849 Emperor claimed he married a slave woman, Dinah or Diana Harris, owned by another man. Their daughter, Frances, was born in 1852. It is questionable whether they were formally married at that time because their official wedding took place many years later, on August 1, 1869. In Diana's probate, both Emperor and Frances swore that Frances was the daughter of Emperor and Diana.

During Emperor's lifetime he told three different stories of his emancipation. Perhaps he meant the stories as an embellishment of his early years. We will never know the reason, but he fabricated not only the emancipation but also the death of his father, Green Williams.

The first story has Emperor writing a pass for himself to travel freely about New Orleans. He signed it "Mr. Williams." When his owner confronted him and asked if the name was a forgery—was his African American owner's name also Williams?—he replied, "No sir, that is not your name, but mine. I would not commit a forgery." The owner asked where he had learned to read and write. He said, "While I was collecting your rents."

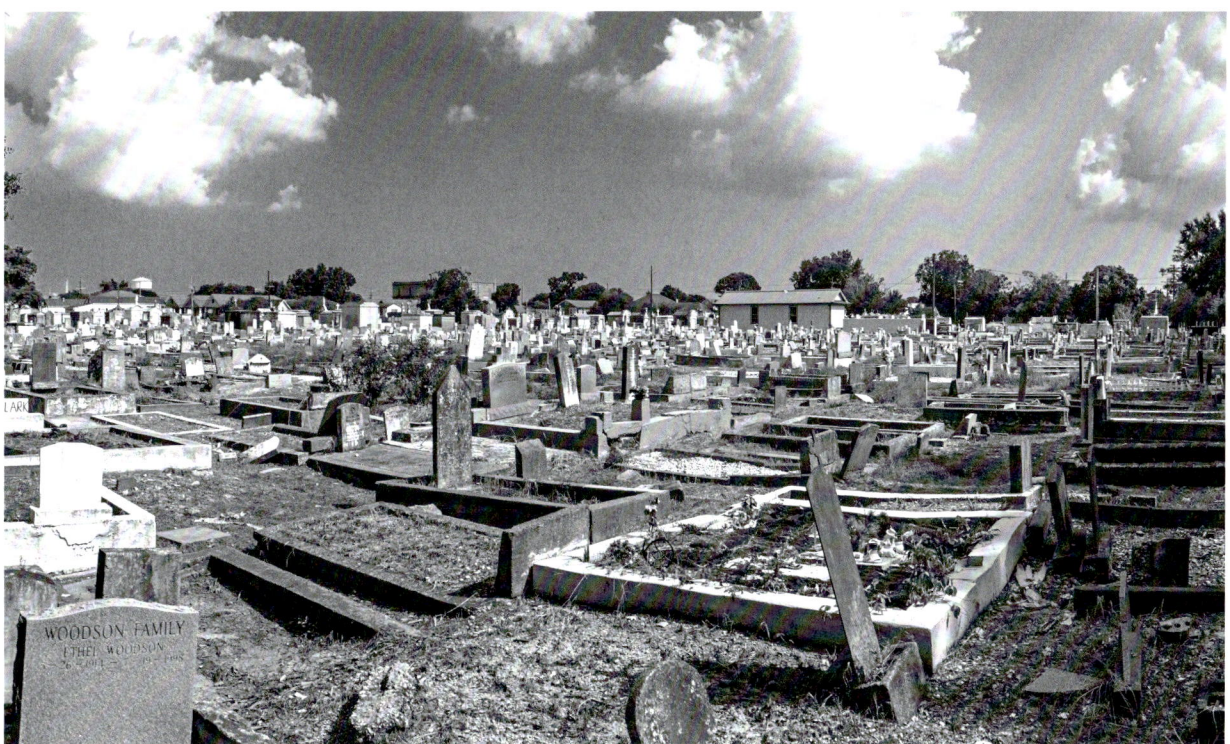

Somewhere within this panorama lie the remains of Reverend Emperor Williams in an unmarked grave, Carrollton Cemetery #1

At this point, Emperor stated that the man gave him seventy-five dollars, a suit of clothes, a cane, and said, "Go and preach until you die. I am tired of you and your God bothering me anymore." If this story is true, why would this owner sell him to McIntosh in 1842? And what about his earliest known affiliation with a church, which was not until 1845?

The second story was set in 1852, when his owner told him that he was nothing more than chattel. He said he took offense at this; the two had a severe fistfight, and three weeks later he was freed.

Both are excellent stories of defiance, but from extensive research, they appear to be just that—stories. What follows (the outlines of which were also told by Williams as a third variation) are the facts that this author has been able to gather, which give an account of two men who held each other in high regard.

McIntosh had promised Williams his freedom, and in a small way he already had given him a taste of it because Williams was allowed to walk about freely. He also had his own house. In 1858 Jameson & McIntosh were putting up a three-story brick building with a cast-iron front at the corner of Carondelet and Perdido Streets, now called Factor's Row. Attaching the cornice proved almost impossible. As foreman, Emperor took the plans home and studied them. The next morning he told McIntosh he knew how to fasten the molding. The builder replied that if he succeeded, he would make Williams a free man. Several days later, the cornice was on and McIntosh kept his word. Emperor was free.

He continued working for McIntosh and shortly afterward offered $2,000 in gold to buy Diana; her owner refused. (Williams probably had earned some of the money before his emancipation, since the Code Noir—a proclamation issued by the French king Louis XV in 1724, which governed slavery in Louisiana—allowed slaves to have extra jobs and be paid for them.) McIntosh died on December 1, 1860, at the age of fifty-five. Just over

Reverend Emperor Williams

a year after the outbreak of the Civil War, New Orleans fell to the Union forces during the last week of April 1862. Freedom for Diana Harris came shortly after, and the money her former owner refused bought the couple a house.

During the early 1860s, Emperor applied himself to becoming a minister, and on Christmas Day 1865, in Wesley Chapel, Bishop Thompson of the Methodist Episcopal Church ordained him and assigned him as a missionary. During the next thirty years, Reverend Williams accomplished remarkable things within both the church and the community. In 1866 he founded a missionary church in Carrollton, known today as the Williams-Ross United Methodist Church. In 1867 he helped found the Freedman's Savings and Trust Company in New Orleans. Emperor was keenly interested in education. In the late 1860s and early 1870s, he was an adviser and representative of the division of education for the Freedmen's Bureau, of which he was the "presiding Elder of the Red River District." He was elected to the school board in 1870 and served several years. He was instrumental in forming the Christian Republican Association and was a representative at national Methodist Episcopal conferences, an activity he continued throughout his life.

Tragedy struck on October 20, 1879, with the death of his beloved wife, Diana, from heart disease. Her succession, or probate, consists of only four pages, with Emperor and their daughter, Frances Williams, wife of Harrison Johnson, as sole heirs. Emperor's signature reflects a shaky hand. Frances's is smooth and fluid, while her husband signed with an "X." Diana was buried in the Carrollton Cemetery. The sexton neglected to note the location.

On July 21, 1880, the minister married a forty-seven-year-old widow named Caroline Reily Rankins, a laundress.

On April 5, 1880, as rector of the African American Wesley Chapel on South Liberty Street, Williams was the host for a speech given by former president General Ulysses S. Grant. The heroic Civil War Union general attracted a large crowd. The church was filled to overflowing, and the surrounding streets were packed with people. His address was short and focused on education and freedom of movement. He stated, "I hope the work which has been commenced to secure the Gospel and spelling-book to every class will be continued, so all denominations and individuals, white or black, may have these blessings."

A few days after that event, Williams was off to Cincinnati for a Methodist General Conference. At the conference, German delegates joined the African American delegation, which petitioned for naming a bishop from their own race. Emperor's name was placed in nomination but was not chosen, perhaps because one criterion would have been robust health; this may be a clue that his health was not the best.

During this time, the Democratic Party was passing oppressive Jim Crow laws, designed to take away as many rights from African Americans as possible. It was at the Methodist conference in Cincinnati that Emperor made yet another false claim concerning his father and again told the story of being freed in 1841. During a pause he asked the audience if they remembered John Brown and then said, "Green Williams, who was hanged with him, was my father." The facts refute the entire claim. The man hung with Brown was named Shields Green, who was sometimes called Emperor. He was born in 1836, ten years after Emperor Williams's birth. Emperor could have been using these stories almost as parables, perhaps showing how he and others had been defiant against the oppression of slavery and that they should be equally so against the Jim Crow laws. Sadly, it would be the twentieth century before people came together and tried to rectify previous wrongs. Reverend Williams would have been proud if he could have been a part of that reformation of beliefs and seen a day when all doors were open.

In 1873 he had been one of the founders and charter board members of New Orleans University, one of the first African American universities in the country. It began in a modest building on Camp Street at the corner of Race. By the mid-1880s the property was sold and a new location was selected on St. Charles Avenue at Valmont Street. Emperor was one of the speakers at the groundbreaking ceremony on January 23, 1886. Not known for his eloquence, on this occasion he spoke with acuity: "I wonder if this is the world I was born in. For twenty years I was a slave on these streets. It was a penitentiary offense to educate a Negro. I have seen my fellow servants whipped for trying to learn; but today, here I am on this great avenue in this great city with the bishops and elders and people of the Methodist Episcopal Church speaking at the breaking of ground for the education of my people. I wonder if this is the world I was born into." The university merged with Straight University in 1930 to become Dillard University, one of the finest traditionally black universities in the country.

Williams also was instrumental in the 1892 opening of the Medical College of New Orleans University on Canal Street for African Americans. In the same year, he became vice president of the Orphan's Home Society. In May 1894, after almost thirty years of endless devotion to his calling, he was exhausted and announced his retirement. Newspapers from New York to Seattle carried the retirement notice. Just two years later, on August 25, 1896, he died of a massive stroke caused by an embolism. His death notice consisted of one line: "Emperor Williams, 71 years, 2013 S. Rampart." Nothing else was written, and a great man passed into obscurity. His grave site has yet to be found. The sexton records for Carrollton Cemetery #1 are missing from that period, but I believe that he would have wanted to be buried with his first wife, Diana.

His widow, Caroline, went back to what she had done before her marriage. The 1900 federal census listed her as a washerwoman. She died at the age of eighty, on March 14, 1913. The newspapers of New Orleans did not carry her death notice.

Seymour Alexander Stewart
1835–1856

An inscription inside an elongated white marble Gothic tomb in Metairie Cemetery tells of one of the worst catastrophes in Louisiana history. In early August 1856 the young Seymour Alexander Stewart boarded a steamboat headed for Last Island, or Isle Dernière, southwest of New Orleans. Since the mid-1840s the island had become a resort destination, attracting some of the wealthiest families in Louisiana. The twenty-five-mile-long island boasted two two-story frame hotels and about one hundred privately owned houses spread throughout sand dunes, grasslands, and live oak groves. All of the structures were simply designed wooden buildings on raised piers. The highest point on the island was a mere five feet above sea level. Seymour had a good reason to celebrate by going to the resort: his twenty-first birthday was the twenty-first of August.

On August 21, 1835, Seymour was born into a family of mixed origins. His mother, Nisida Giguel, was from a creole family, and his father, Samuel Stewart, was an Irish immigrant from County Down who had arrived in the city in 1822. Samuel began his career in the building trades and erected two of the city's most iconic structures, the Pontalba Buildings, on either side of Jackson Square in the French Quarter. By 1850 he was one of the wealthiest men in the city. His firstborn son, Seymour, entered Spring Hill College at Mobile in the 1846–47 academic year. He finished his education there, graduating with an AB degree in October 1853. The following month he applied for a passport. He was described as eighteen years old, five foot nine, with hazel eyes, very dark brown hair, and Grecian features. It is unknown whether he took a trip or what the destination might have been.

Stewart could have reached Last Island by taking the New Orleans, Opelousas railroad that left Algiers, across the river from New Orleans, to Bayou Boeuf station in today's Morgan City. From there, he would have boarded the semiweekly packet steamship, the *Star*, which left each Saturday and Tuesday, returning on Mondays and Thursdays. He would have arrived on Sunday the third or Wednesday the sixth. After disembarking from the *Star*, he would have recognized many of the people already gathered to enjoy the cool Gulf waters and the social events that were so prominent in their lives. The Grand Dress Ball on Saturday nights was of special interest to the young men and women.

The weather began to deteriorate throughout the day on Saturday, August 9. Had Seymour stopped and looked out at the confused sea on Saturday afternoon, he would have seen an eastbound schooner silhouetted against a darkening sky suddenly drop its sails and reverse course, making a run for Galveston and safety. As evening fell, dinner was served and preparations for the dance were made. The partiers danced

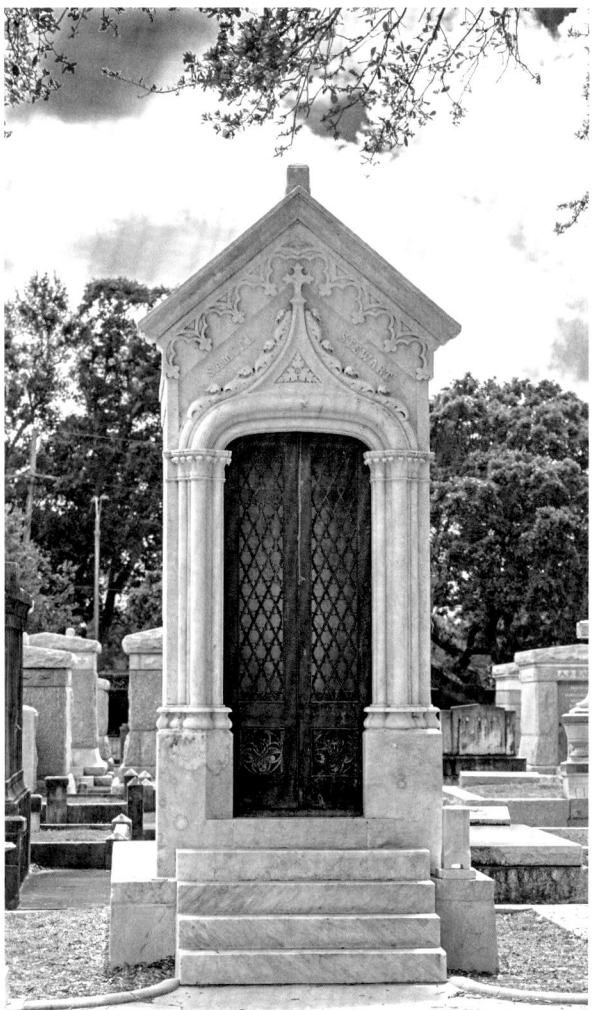

Tomb of Samuel Stewart family, Metairie Cemetery

until after midnight, when they made their way back to their rooms or house. Outside, the wind was whipping up, sand stinging the faces of those walking home. By morning, water was rising up the beach and the wind was beginning to tear the roofs from some houses. It would only get worse. A storm surge of twelve feet came quickly, destroying almost all of the buildings on the island. People were left scrambling for anything to hold on to. The storm at its fiercest had winds of 150 mph, strong enough to rip clothing from their bodies. There is no record of where Seymour was on the island or exactly what happened to him. When the storm passed, survivors looked on a scene beyond description. Every building on the island had been swept away, and lifeless bodies lay in every direction.

When the news of the disaster arrived in New Orleans, Seymour's parents became frantic for information about their son. Several days passed, and his name was not listed among the survivors or the dead. His father decided to go to Last Island. He arrived aboard the *Texas* on Tuesday, August 12, along with scores of armed men tasked with seeking out looters and pillagers of the dead. Samuel Stewart spent days searching the island in severe heat. Finally, on August 18, the body of a young man was found under debris in the marshes, miles from the island. It was disfigured and unrecognizable. Thankfully, looters had not robbed the body. A silver watch was retrieved, but Stewart said it could be anyone's silver watch. He did not recognize the other items, including a handkerchief. Discouraged, Stewart boarded the *Texas* for the return trip. Within several hours, a man approached him with the now-washed handkerchief. There, in the corner, he saw his son's initials. Seymour Stewart's *Daily Picayune* obituary of August 22 noted that he was just eleven days shy of his twenty-first birthday.

The storm split the island in half and took the lives of about two hundred people out of an estimated four hundred who had been on the island. Later storms have left the once-expansive barrier island in five fragmented islands, with only seabirds for residents.

John Oliver Locke

1839–1864

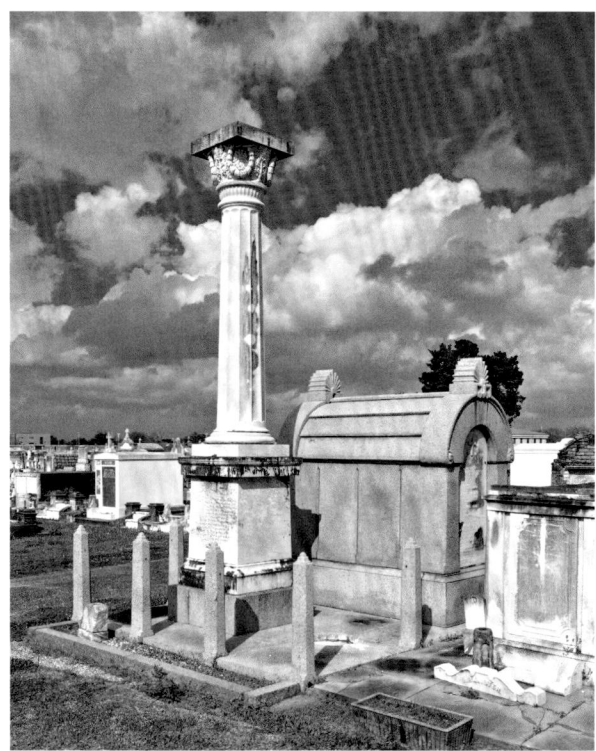

Column symbolizing a noble life, with its capital covered in oak and laurel leaves for victory, honor, virtue, and strength; memorial of John Oliver Locke, Greenwood Cemetery

In Greenwood Cemetery, a large fluted column on a marble pedestal stands next to a granite tomb surrounded by short granite piers. The monument is to the memory of John Oliver Locke, the son of New Hampshire–born Samuel Locke, a wealthy hardware merchant of New Orleans. His family and friends called him Oliver. In 1861, as the talk of war turned into action, young Locke was attending college. There is no record of whether his father was a Southern or Northern sympathizer or the types of discussions heard round the table in his Canal Street mansion.

John left college and joined the Confederate infantry as a first lieutenant on October 22, 1861, then resigned due to a knee injury the following February. Six months later, he traveled to Jackson, Mississippi, and enlisted as a private in Fenner's Battery, Louisiana Light Artillery. He saw action at Port Hudson, the Big Black campaign between Jackson and Vicksburg, and the Battle of Jackson in 1863. The unit was then transferred to Mobile, Alabama, where it remained until ordered to join the Army of Tennessee. The company arrived at Dalton, Georgia, on November 27, the day the Battle of Ringgold Gap, a few miles north of Dalton, took place. Roll calls for both November and December 1863 listed Private Locke as absent, "sick in hospital," at the Academy Hospital in Marietta, Georgia, south of Dalton on the same railroad line as Ringgold Gap. Was he injured in the battle at Ringgold Gap, or did he arrive already ill or wounded? In either event, he was twenty-five years old when he died in the Academy Hospital on January 12, 1864. The cause of death was not recorded, yet his family said he died from wounds.

During the Civil War, it was not uncommon for soldiers to die from wounds months or even years after they were inflicted. Locke's father, Samuel, died the next year during a trip to Massachusetts. Several years later, his mother hired a young man from their hardware business to go to Georgia and find her son's remains. Months later, he returned, and Locke was given a military funeral with honors and placed in the Greenwood tomb, along with his father, on May 12, 1870. In his verbose obituary, of February 7, 1864, in the *Daily Picayune*, the writer found a few simple words: "To know him was to love him."

Captain Eugene Pierre Gaspard

1839–1889

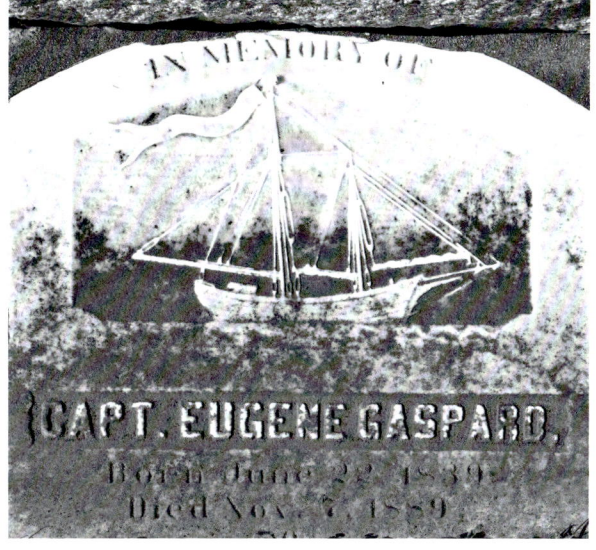

Tablet; tomb of Captain Eugene Pierre Gaspard, Greenwood Cemetery

Possibly from the Lorraine region in France, the twenty-one-year-old Eugene Pierre Gaspard traveled to Le Havre and boarded the brig *Amity* for New York City. He walked onto American soil on August 25, 1860, with two boxes and listed himself as a farmer. He arrived in New Orleans soon after, now identifying himself in the city directories of the period as a sailor. He married seventeen-year-old Barbara Martin on December 17, 1868. During their marriage they had five children: four daughters and a son who died at eight months in 1877.

Gaspard worked coastal schooners between New Orleans and the ports of Mississippi, Alabama, and Florida. He took command of his own vessel in 1880, rising through sheer hard labor and courage. In 1882 he commissioned a shipyard on the Jordan River in Mississippi, just north of Bay St. Louis, to build a new schooner. She was fifty-eight feet long and just over twenty feet wide, with a draft of almost five feet and a capacity for fifty-two thousand pounds of cargo. He named her *E.T.C. Gaspard*. She was an ideal vessel for the coastal trade: inland waterways were accessible because of her shallow draft. One of these was Bayou St. John, in the rear of New Orleans, connecting to the Carondelet Canal, which ran from the bayou to a large turning basin one block from the French Quarter. Gaspard made regular runs to Pascagoula, Mississippi, to take on cargoes of charcoal, a valuable commodity used in blast furnaces for iron smelting and manufacturing brass. He frequently arrived at the Old Basin stocked with almost three thousand barrels of charcoal.

The sea trade brought him success and wealth, but also bad health. In 1889 he went see Dr. Rudolph Matas, one of New Orleans's preeminent surgeons, who diagnosed Gaspard with diabetes. Infectious and painful boils developed across his body, most likely caused by conditions on the boat; charcoal was a filthy payload. Complicated by the diabetes, his condition worsened. Gaspard died on November 7, 1889, at the age of fifty, with the youngest of his four daughters only nine. He was buried in Greenwood Cemetery; his wife immortalized her husband by having a white marble tablet carved with a replica of his cherished schooner. The ship, described in the *Daily Picayune* as "The Fine, Well-Built Schooner *E.T.C. Gaspard*," was sold at auction two months later, on January 18, 1890, whereupon the new owner changed her name to *Lolita*.

Reverend Father René M. J. Vallée
1839–1892

A simple granite monument topped by a white marble angel and cross stands on St. Augustine Avenue in Carrollton Cemetery #2, the old St. Mary's Cemetery. Recessed into the granite is a delicately carved white marble bas-relief of a chalice with a raised Host. It is a testament to a beloved priest and is unique in the city's cemeteries.

Father René M. J. Vallée was born in the small French village of Poubalay, near the Brittany coast, on April 18, 1839. He grew up wanting to become a priest. After twelve years in seminaries, he was recruited by Archbishop Jean-Marie Odin of New Orleans to come to Louisiana. Vallée, along with fifty-one other seminarians, boarded an old converted warship, the *St. Genevieve*, chartered by the archbishop at Le Havre, France, and began the journey to a new life. Seminary studies were continued on the ship throughout its fifty-three-day passage to New Orleans. It arrived April 4, 1863, and one of the passengers is listed as Joseph Vallée. Also aboard the ship were three hundred baskets of Krug Champagne and hundreds of cases of wine, along with cartons of potatoes and other produce. Archbishop Odin wasted no time in preparing the young men for the priesthood. Vallée was ordained just seven months to the day after his arrival, on November 4, 1863. He would forever afterward be called René.

His first assignment took him to Opelousas, Louisiana, where he spent several months before becoming rector of Sacred Heart at Ville Platte, Louisiana.

In a letter to Archbishop Odin in 1864, Father Gilbert Raymond of Opelousas described Father Vallée as absolutely independent and liking a good life. In April 1866 Father Raymond wrote again to the archbishop that someone had said Vallée was "drinking a little too freely" but conceded that it may have been an exaggeration. During Vallée's three years at Sacred Heart, from 1864 to 1867, he expanded the parish and made attempts to build a church, acquiring a donation of six acres and building a presbyter.

Vallée left Ville Platte in April 1867 to return to France and visit his aging parents while himself recovering from latent weakness from typhoid, which he had contracted the previous December. Renewed, he returned to New Orleans at year's end to be assigned to the parish of St. Raphael at Bayou Goula. The church's building had first been used as a courthouse and then a dance hall. Then, in 1870, the archbishop assented to the construction of a new frame church, including pews, at a cost not less than $5,000. Upon completion of the new building in 1871, the old church was abandoned and the parish was named St. Paul's.

Vallée was recalled to New Orleans in 1873 to become the parish priest of a missionary church in Carrollton, St. Mary's Nativity. The parishioners fondly called it St. Mary's. He remained there for the rest of his life. Vallée began to acquire a reputation as an indefatigable worker; his devotion to his calling was absolute. He attended to the ill and dying, no matter the hour. He never wavered in his duties until, at the age of fifty-two, he began to grow weak and pale; any exertion brought on faintness and shortness of breath. He had gastrointestinal hemorrhaging. Urged by friends and doctors to take the cure at mountain springs, Vallée took leave from his St. Mary's responsibilities during the summer of 1892 and returned much improved. Yet soon the symptoms returned, and he became too weak to stand. His friend and assistant pastor, Father Ferguson, spent hours sitting by Vallée's bedside, holding his hand, and was there when he died in the early afternoon of Monday, September 19, 1892. He was fifty-three years old. His obituary carried high praise for this humble man, speaking for those who "esteemed him as a priest of this mental ability and loved him as a man. He was gentle and kind to all, attended to his duties as rector of the parish, neglecting none and with a smile and a pleasant word for all." At his funeral High Mass, Archbishop Francis Janssens delivered simple praise in a shaky voice: "Faults he had, but they were not faults of the heart." Father Rene M. J. Vallée was a true priest.

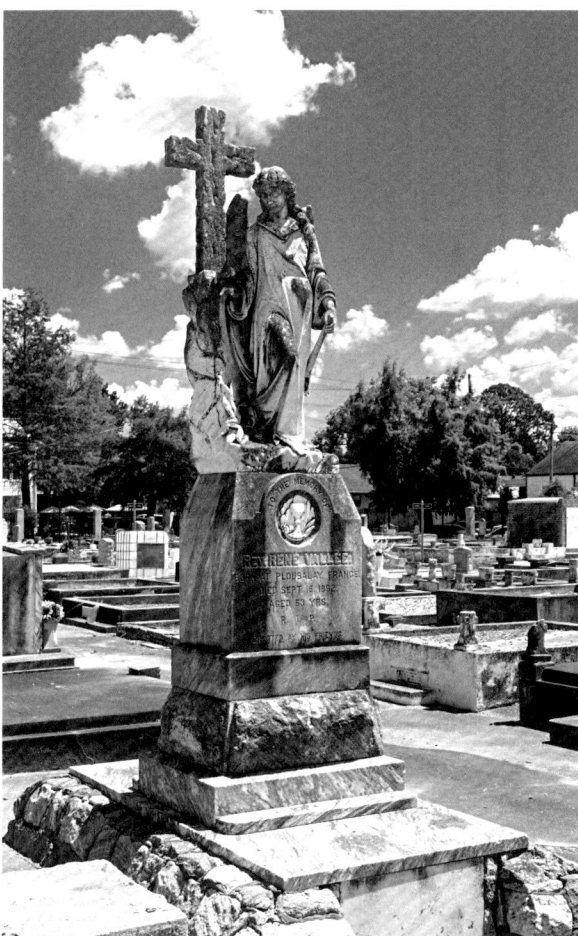

Monument of Reverend Father René M. J. Vallée, Carrollton Cemetery

William H. Webb
1839–1884

William H. Webb was born in London in 1839; at the age of four he sailed with his parents from Liverpool to New York harbor aboard the ship *United Kingdom*, arriving on May 28, 1845, after forty-one days at sea. The *New York Daily Herald* noted the ship's passengers as "481 in the steerage, one born on the passage." Shortly after, the family traveled to New Orleans to begin a new life. The 1870 and 1880 federal censuses recorded William Webb as a native of New York. This is also carved on his headstone. Why he disclaimed his birthplace is a mystery. This was not uncommon in nineteenth-century New Orleans. Many Irish professionals listed themselves as being English, and Germans changed their names to French ones—some to avoid prejudice and others to assimilate into the population. Perhaps the main reason was the strength of the Know-Nothing Party and its bigotry toward immigrants of all origins.

As young William grew into manhood, he became interested in the steamboats plying their trade on the Mississippi River. At some point in the late 1850s, approaching age twenty, he signed on to work aboard. He held this profession until the Civil War broke out in April 1861. In the patriotic fervor that swept across the South, he enlisted on June 23 in the Eighth Infantry Louisiana Volunteers and was assigned to Company B, the Bienville Rifles. He trained at Fort Moore, near Kentwood, Louisiana, but was there only for a matter of days before boarding a train for Manassas Junction, Virginia, just in time for the First Battle of Manassas on July 21. There he sustained a foot injury that took him out of the war. He was medically discharged on July 28, 1861, just a month after joining. This twist of fate was to prove a blessing: his regiment went on to fight in every major engagement fought by the Army of Northern Virginia. In April 1862 it had a complement of over 1,100 men; in 1865 there were only 75 remaining. In Webb's discharge record, he was described as twenty-three years old and five foot seven, with light-colored hair and blue eyes, born in London. He was paid $33.81 for his time in the army and the return trip from Manassas to New Orleans.

Soon after, he married. His bride's name was Susan Agnes Moses, and she was twenty years old and still a minor according to the law. She was the daughter of Abram Moses. Her mother, Jane Edwards, signed approval of the wedding that took place June 28, 1862. In 1865 Webb avoided an urgent military draft for the war, as did all fire company volunteers. Webb's historical record is then silent until fall 1866, when he was a police officer. In August 1868 he petitioned the Board of Assistant Alderman to pay him $77.35, the amount of his salary during an illness. The committee approved the request because it recognized his condition was the result of exposure while "in the performance of his duties." During this period he joined the Columbia

Steam Fire Engine Company No. 5, an affiliation he maintained for the remainder of his life.

In 1869, as a fireman on a locomotive, he fell and slipped boarding a train at Crystal Springs, Mississippi, and lost one leg. After he recovered, the New Orleans, Jackson & Great Northern Railroad reassigned him to a position as a receiving clerk, which he held through three mergers of railroad companies that culminated in the Illinois Central Railroad. The 1880 census taker recorded that Webb had a broken leg, no doubt a mistaken reference to his amputated leg. It also listed in the household a Minerva Webb, born in 1876, yet no relationship was given. Perhaps she was a niece, for Webb's obituary stated that he and his wife were childless.

Webb was in the minority in joining the Irish Republicans Workingmen's Club in 1876, located in the city's Ninth Ward. He apparently disliked the Jim Crow laws enforcing racial segregation in the South, for the club's goal was to elect Republican candidates to office in order to fight discrimination.

At some point during late 1883, Webb began coughing up blood. Known as consumption at the time, tuberculosis was the leading killer in nineteenth-century America, so prevalent that it became known as the White Plague. For William Webb, the end came on January 4, 1884. He was forty-five years old. The fire company published a lengthy memorial of sorrow and praise

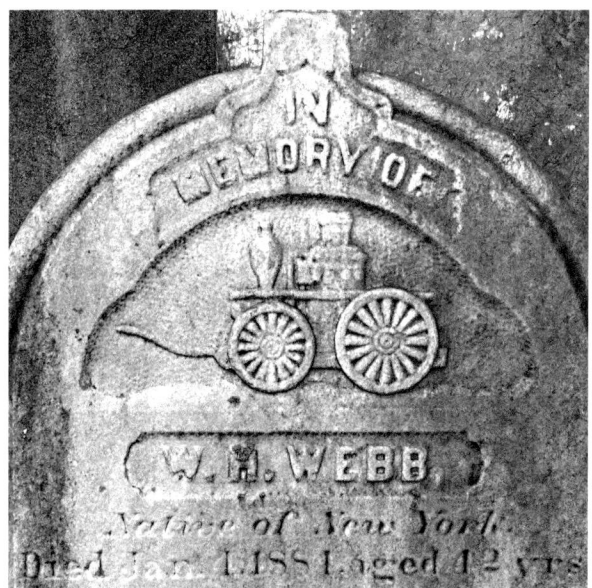

Fire engine detail; monument of William H. Webb, Cypress Grove Cemetery

on January 13, honoring "one who always proved himself a good, true and steadfast friend, and one who [displayed] conscientious devotion to his duties as a man and fireman." The testimonial concludes with a further description of his affable nature and devotion to his family. At the time of his death, he was still a receiving clerk for the Louisville and Nashville Railroad.

Webb's epitaph reveals great love: "Death came as gently, as the light wind wandering through groves of bloom." Susan published a "Card of Thanks" in the *Daily Picayune* on January 13, 1884, that expressed her gratitude to the members of the Columbia Fire Company No. 5 for their attention and aid during her husband's illness. Two years later, at the age of forty-three, on May 24, 1886, Susan died of peritonitis. Her mother, Jane Edwards, now the widow of Captain J. W. Clark, had a headstone erected for the couple, with a fire steam engine carved in bas-relief atop the headstone. Its final inscription is another profound show of love: "By her devoted mother." This loving mother herself died in 1891 of tuberculosis, which she may have contracted from her son-in-law. Today, the headstone has been moved and leans against the rear of a tomb in Cypress Grove Cemetery, where it seems sadly forgotten.

Constantine Otto Weber

1847–1901

A white marble coping tomb is located on Avenue F in Metairie Cemetery. In the center is a pedestal topped by a fluted column and finial. The pedestal is simply inscribed "C. Otto Weber 1847–1901" and elaborately decorated with beautifully carved symbols representing the life of a talented musician, teacher, and composer.

When Weber was a boy growing up in Karlsruhe, Germany, music was his first love and passion. It remained first for his entire life. He was admitted to the prestigious Conservatory of Music in Leipzig, founded in 1843 by Felix Mendelssohn, and graduated with honors. Believing that America afforded him greater prospects than Germany, in 1869 Weber traveled to New Orleans in relative style as a cabin passenger aboard the steamship *Teutonia*. Not long after arriving, he took a position as organist in the Unitarian Church on St. Charles Avenue. He also began teaching music, and by 1871 the city directory lists him as a professor of music living in a boardinghouse on Baronne Street. Within a few years, his reputation as an organist and choir director grew. During the 1870s he served as the director of music for Temple Sinai and the organist and choir director at Jesuit's Church on Baronne Street. During this period, he was able to send money to his mother and sister in Germany; in later years he paid for the education of his sister's children.

Weber, who went by Otto, was a quiet man who rarely spoke about his work. He preferred that his music speak for him. His first known public appearance was on the evening of April 22, 1872, when he was one of the featured artists at a performance of "parlor concerts" at Odd Fellows Hall. His next public appearance was in late May, at the Volksfest at the newly opened Fair Grounds. The exhibition hall was decorated with a myriad of international flags; before a packed house, Weber directed a glee club of about 150 members, his baton controlling every nuance. He began to compose songs, cantatas, compositions for string quartets, and sacred music for both Christian and Jewish services. Over the years he wrote music and directed performances at concerts benefiting the Unitarian Church, the Little Sisters of the Poor, the Hebrew Educational Society, and many others. During those early years, he discovered a young lady with a velvet voice and began to instruct her in vocals. Her name was Lena Little (see page 54), and she went on to become one of the most important singers of the period, both in Europe and in the United States.

While writing music and directing choirs at different churches and synagogues, Weber continued to teach piano, organ, singing, and cello, his favorite instrument. He was also professor of music at the Sylvester Larned Institute for Young Ladies between 1873 and 1875, and in the mid-1870s he joined with Rabbi J. K. Gutheim to compose music for both solo and choral performances, often at Temple Sinai; Weber wrote music set to Rabbi Gutheim's lyrics. From this humble beginning he began to have a profound influence on Jewish Reform repertoire in the city. Several of his songs were published and performed in 1875 at the Conservatory of Music in Leipzig, Germany. That same year his cantata based on Psalm 29 had its first performance with Rabbi Gutheim at Temple Sinai.

It was at a choir rehearsal at the Jesuit Church that he first heard a young woman whose voice stood out from all others. She was Nita Bohn, the daughter of an affluent commission merchant. They shared an intense love of music, and that attraction led them into a romantic relationship that lasted for the rest of Otto's life. They were married at St. Anna's Episcopal Church on December 13, 1886. Otto, who was known to sing his songs for friends, began to sing only to Nita. Years later, in his obituary, their relationship was described as one of total devotion to each other; their selflessness was plain for all to see and was "an admiration of their friends."

Not long after their marriage, the couple bought a house on Harmony Street and later a cottage on the outskirts of Asheville, North Carolina. They frequently spent the hot summer months in their Blue Ridge Mountains retreat. Throughout the 1890s this was a refuge from Otto's constant obligations as a teacher and choir director. It afforded him time to concentrate on his own music and a place of peace where he wrote numerous compositions, many in the genre of *musica sacra*, or sacred music. During this period five of his compositions were published in Regensburg, Germany.

At some point, probably in mid- to late 1900, Weber first noticed that he was having difficulty swallowing, followed by a slight pain in his ear. He and Nita went to their cottage near Asheville in the early summer of 1901, intending to return to New Orleans at their usual time in early October. This year would be different, however; as the New Orleans *Times-Democrat* stated on August 11, "Otter Weber's grave illness…necessitated his return with Mrs. Weber." By the time he was admitted to Touro Infirmary, the constant pain in his mouth and ears had become unbearable, and he was losing his voice. His speech was a whisper, and he was no longer able to sing to his beloved Nita. The diagnosis was cancer of the tonsils; it had spread incurably to the lymph nodes in his neck. Hoping the salt air might help provide relief, the couple traveled to the Gulf Coast, but Otto's condition worsened and they returned to New Orleans after only a few days. Somehow he maintained a cheerful demeanor, yet nothing could change the inevitable. Surrounded by friends and Nita, Otto Weber died on November 13, 1901, at his home at 1432 Harmony Street.

An obituary stated, "The tinsel and gauze of titles, the fleeting honors which follow on the heels of

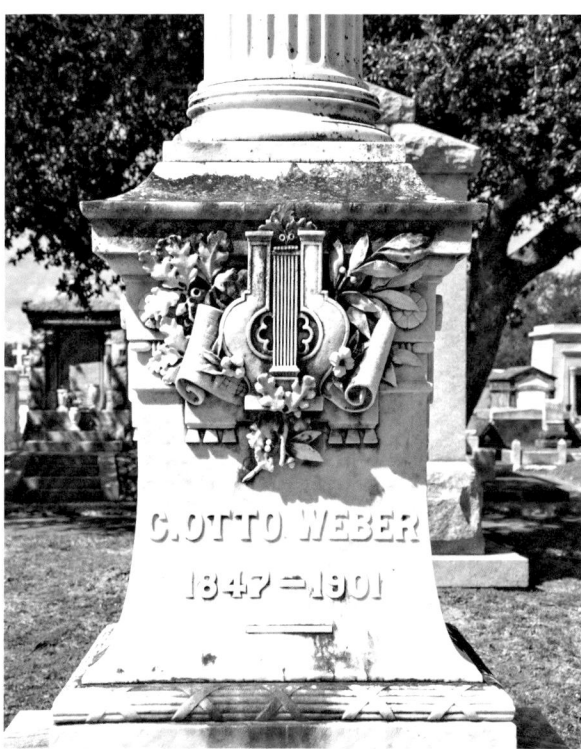

Base detail; monument of Constantine Otto Weber, Metairie Cemetery

applause, the cheap gee-gaws of high standing, had no charm for him." His friend of over thirty years, Rabbi Isaac L. Leucht of Touro Synagogue, said it best: "There was something essentially spiritual about him, and in all that he did or uttered." He was just fifty-four years old.

In 1905 Bloch Publishing Company of New York published his *Songs of Judah: Hymns, Psalms and Anthems*. His compositions continued to be played at Temple Sinai. The greatest tribute to Weber and his music came in 1925 and 1926 in a series of concerts highlighting his music, organized by his former students. In May 1926 the New York music-publishing firm G. Schirmer released Otto Weber's *Musica Sacra*, comprising seventeen never-before-published compositions. The cover featured a photograph of Weber's kindly face.

Nita Bohn Weber lived another twenty-one years. She died from breast cancer at her home in Biloxi, Mississippi, on February 23, 1928, having lived long enough to see her husband recognized for his exceptional talents as an artist and composer.

Martha Lena Little
1856–1920

If we knew the hour and manner of our deaths, would we ever commit an act of total desperation? A plain, brick tomb, whitewashed and well kept, on Locust Aisle in Greenwood Cemetery hides a story of a life filled with achievement and accolades in music, its coda being a desperate act.

Martha Lena Little was born September 19, 1856, to Robert and Rebecca Little. (The tablet fronting her tomb mistakenly gives her birth year as 1853.) Robert Little, along with his partner, Peter Middlemiss, was among the most successful builders in New Orleans. He and Rebecca called their daughter Lena, a name she used her entire life. As a child, she showed promise in music, and as she grew, so did the beauty of her voice. She and seven other girls were members of the first graduating class of Trinity Episcopal School for Girls on Christmas Eve, 1872. She entertained the packed church that night and would do so over the years in hundreds of venues. She could not have known that evening that she would become one of the premier singers in England and the United States. Thankfully, her parents, who had divorced in 1868, recognized her gift.

Lena's early musical training took place under the tutelage of C. Otto Weber, a professor of music who had graduated from the prestigious Leipzig Conservatory of Music (see page 52). He was among the few to recognize the potential of this sixteen-year-old contralto. Lena was tall and thin, with auburn hair and a graceful demeanor. During the remainder of the 1870s, she took part in numerous concerts at various churches and synagogues, the Exposition and Grunewald Halls, and the French Opera House. As recognition of her talent grew, the newspapers filled with admiring reviews of her performances, frequently calling her the "gem of the evening." In early 1880 one city newspaper lamented the exodus of musical talent because of the lack of "financial encouragement"; by this time, Lena had moved to New York City.

She quickly acquired work singing in church choirs. More important, she caught the attention of Dr. Leopold Damrosch, who had founded the New York Symphony Society in 1878. He began to feature the young singer. Timid at first, she performed songs of Richard Wagner, George Frideric Handel, Robert Schumann, Franz Liszt, and others. *A New York Times* review said she possessed a weak voice, but one that showed great promise with training. Damrosch suggested that she go to Germany and study under the great vocal teacher Julius Christian Stockhausen. On Wednesday, June 13, 1883, Lena boarded a ship to Frankfurt am Main, Germany, where she began her formal training. She remained a year with Stockhausen, who sent her to London, carrying a letter of introduction to the painter Lawrence Alma-Tadema, who welcomed her into the city's coveted artistic society. Lena Little soon found herself singing throughout Great Britain and touring with the conductor of the Vienna Opera, Hans Richter. Her reputation as a great singer had arrived. She was sought after by London society and lived there until 1889.

Returning to New York City aboard the steamship *Teutonic* on December 8, 1889, she gave a concert with the Symphony Society at the Metropolitan Opera House within just five days. Her hectic London schedule was maintained in New York and Boston. In February 1890, the Saengerfest in New Orleans (and later in Shreveport, Louisiana) invited her to perform. She then gave a farewell concert at the Grunewald Hall to rave reviews. That spring, she traveled to Chicago, possibly to visit her brother Robert, who was working as a reporter. Then she returned to Europe to spend the summer at Lake Geneva, returning to London in the fall and headlining concerts throughout the autumn and winter. In the spring of 1891, Little returned to New York to perform at Steinway Hall, as well as the Chickering Halls in New York and Boston. One of the great honors of her life was to stand as principal singer at the funeral of the great poet Oliver Wendell Holmes Sr., who had died on October 7, 1894, in Boston and whose elaborate memorial was celebrated at King's Chapel. It was there, in Boston, where she chose to live until 1908, while concertizing in New York and throughout New England and occasionally touring the South.

In a 1901 interview Little described loving Boston because it had higher music standards than other cities in the country. She offered that ragtime was ruining music (but ignored a question about her sensational gowns). Perhaps her style of singing was beginning to fall from vogue in favor of the more robust popular music of the day or she was beginning to tire of the frenetic pace of concerts and performances. The number of her appearances began to decline in the first decade of the twentieth century. She still gave concerts in both Boston and New York, but by 1907, possibly at the suggestion of her reporter brother, she began a series of musical reviews for the New Orleans *Times-Democrat* to earn extra money. She wrote of attending performances in Boston, New York, and Paris.

Little's mother, Rebecca, had died in July 1899; her father had previously passed away, and by 1900 she had only her brothers, Robert and William. In 1909 William died from stomach problems, possibly cancer or tuberculosis. It was then, possibly because of her brother's death, that she chose to return to New Orleans. At age fifty-four, she became a singing teacher. Her income must have declined dramatically, while her voice may have weakened and begun to lose its force and nuance.

Between 1910 and 1920, Little gave an occasional recital. She made summer trips to New York City to visit friends (and no doubt to avoid the oppressive New Orleans heat and humidity). In March 1913 her surviving brother, Robert, was diagnosed with stomach cancer and, following treatment and convalescence, slipped quietly

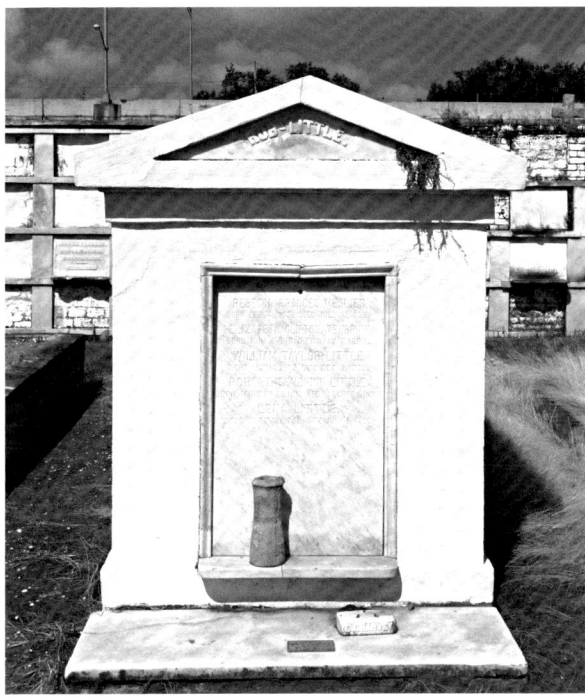

Tomb of Martha Lena Little, Greenwood Cemetery

into death on October 31. His sister was devastated. The decade was proving to be a difficult one as her students began to receive attention, leaving her for further training in New York, where newspapers reviews mentioned her as their early teacher. Lena Little had walked across her final stage. Accolades and performances had become a thing of the past.

A newspaper article from July 10, 1920, gives a hint at what happened in the home of her sister-in-law on Esplanade Avenue the night of July 5. Little was by then an invalid, confined to bed from a "protracted illness." She made a decision that apparently was born in despair. Shortly after midnight she pulled herself from her bed, taking with her a pillow, and entered the bathroom. She stuffed every crack, including the keyhole, then turned on the gas and lay down in the bathtub, her head resting on the pillow. Little was found early the next morning. The coroner's report stated simply that she was found in a tub and that the cause of death was asphyxiation. Her final note left only questions: "No one is to blame for any act of mine, Lena Little."

Heinrick "Henry" Benthin
1857–1928

Heinrick Benthin, known as "Henry Bentin," was born on February 16, 1857, in Nakel, West Prussia, Germany, now Nakło, Poland. The son of Sophie and Heinrick Benthin, he was the son and grandson of violinmakers. At an early age he possessed an aptitude for the family heritage in this fine craft. He did not have long to study under his father, for according to family tradition, in 1867 the elder Benthin emigrated to the United States, settling in Iowa. The December 3, 1867, census of Mecklenburg-Schwerin, Germany, lists two Benthin families, both headed by a woman named Sophie and both having a son Heinrick, born in 1856 and 1857, respectively. While impossible to verify which Heinrick was the future violinmaker, the most probable of the two is Sophie (age thirty-nine), whose children were Heinrick and Anna (both age ten) and Lisette (age seven). Sophie was a teacher at a poorhouse, and the children were attending school. (The other Sophie was a cook.) It is not known to which household our subject belonged. The absence of the father is striking and gives credence to the family story of the senior Heinrich departing for America. The reasons he left his family remain unknown, and a search of immigration records has not yielded a Benthin, Benton, or Bentin between 1865 and 1869.

When Henry's father left for America, his son had had only a few years of study, while a violinmaker's training requires many years. In a later interview in November 1922, Henry discussed the critical importance of varnish: "My Father taught me this secret, for he was a violin maker before me in Posen, Germany, where I was born, [and] he had plied his trade for a lifetime." Where and how he acquired the additional training is a mystery, yet a clue may exist in a 1904 *New Orleans Item* advertisement, which stated that he formerly practiced his trade in Berlin. It is quite possible that he completed his training there to become a violinmaker.

The events of Henry Bentin's early life in Germany are largely unknown until 1881, when he married Anna Victoria Froelich in Posen, Prussia, today Poznań, Poland. He and his wife settled in Berlin. Their first child, John Slavaski Bentin, was born there on July 18, 1882. The young family emigrated to America in 1885, according to the 1910 federal census. As is the case with his father before him, no record has been found of his immigration.

The Bentins probably went to Iowa to visit Henry's father, and there they stayed. Their second and third children were born in Dubuque—Leon "Leo" Joseph on October 23, 1887, and Hilda in 1888. How long the family remained in Iowa is unknown, yet Henry later admitted he found the Midwestern town unsatisfactory; no doubt a violinmaker's work was sparse.

The chronology of the Bentins' several residences is a bit difficult to piece together from various newspaper interviews, yet a rough timeline emerges: when he and his family left Iowa in around 1889, Henry set up shop in New York City. About a year later, they moved to St. Louis, arriving in 1890. There, the Bentins' son Edward was born on November 26. Bentin's shop was in his residence at 1136 Washington Avenue (according to an advertisement for "Violin Maker and Repairer" in the city's *Post-Dispatch*), where the family remained until 1896, when they moved to New Orleans. A July 1897 newspaper advertisement announced, "Hy. Bentin, violin maker and repairer of all kinds string instruments. 1132 Felicity between Camp and Magazine." (In 1899, he became a naturalized US citizen.) Bentin frequently

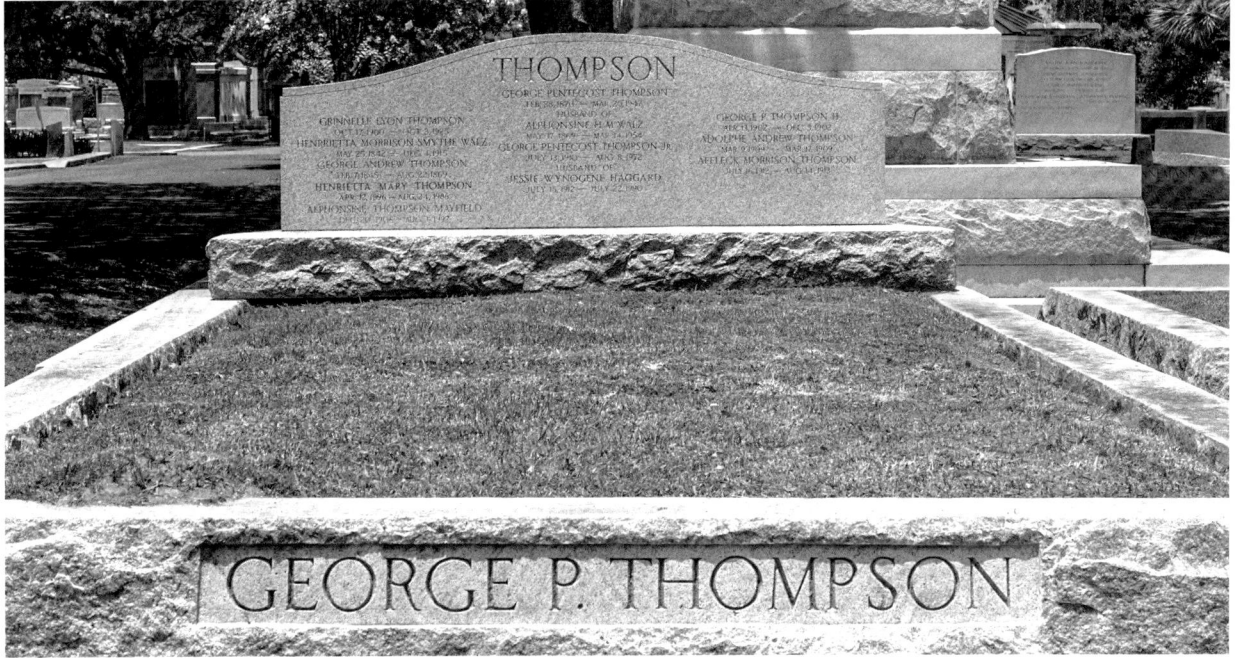

Temporary tomb of Henry Bentin, Metairie Cemetery

moved his shop, from Felicity to downtown Canal Street, then Iberville, followed by two locations on St. Charles Avenue, then North Rampart. He finally settled into 109 South Basin Street (now Elk Place) in 1920, where he remained until his death.

It was in New Orleans that recognition finally came. In the early 1920s, Bentin's hair was beginning to turn gray, yet his blue eyes still sparkled when he spoke of his craft, his English less than perfect and with a heavy accent. The city realized it had a rarity working in its midst, a master violinmaker whose instruments were suddenly sought by virtuoso musicians. The *Times-Picayune* of August 1920 ran a feature article about Bentin that briefly summarized his life and work while concentrating on the process of making a violin. He explained that crafting the instrument required three months, then another three to apply the varnish with great care. He also described the time when someone came into his shop and stole a violin: "It was the best violin I have made. The thief knew the value of it." The reporter observed that Bentin possessed "a strange dogged optimism" about the loss of his prized creation: "I know someone is playing it, that is something after all." The violin was never found.

When Jan Kubelík (1880–1940), the Czech composer considered at the time the finest violinist in the world, came to New Orleans to perform at the Jerusalem Temple on April 13, 1921, he also brought Bentin fame. Bentin was in the audience for the brilliant performance, then went backstage to meet the maestro, where the two men struck up a conversation. Suddenly, Kubelík handed Bentin his 1715 "Emperor" Stradivarius, for which he had paid $10,000 in 1910, at that time the highest amount ever paid for a violin. Bentin stood in disbelief that he was holding one of the world's most famous violins. He carefully examined the burled tiger-stripe maple back, remarkably one piece. The red-tinged varnish seemed to give the instrument a glow. Bentin then asked Kubelík if he could bring him one of his own violins to examine. They agreed to meet the next day at Kubelík's rooms at the St. Charles Hotel.

The humble Bentin later said, "When I stand at the door of his room, I was afraid. I did not know whether

I could go in. I felt like I wanted to run away." When he and Kubelík began a long conversation in German, Bentin relaxed. "At last," he recalled, "I can wait no longer. I take out my fiddle and hand her to Kubelík." What transpired next he would remember the rest of his life. The maestro put the violin under his chin, "he plays a little bit, then he looks like he is surprised and he plays like the devil for ten, twenty minutes." Kubelík put down the instrument and walked across the room and took out his Stradivarius and handed it to Bentin. "I kiss her. I tell you I could not help it." Kubelík played a little on it, then on Bentin's violin. The great man alternately played each violin for about three hours. Stopping, he said, "Mr. Bentin, you have made a fine instrument." So grateful was he, Bentin wanted to give Kubelík the violin, yet paused as he wondered what his wife, Annie, would say after a year's work.

"Why didn't you?" she asked at home. He immediately returned to the hotel and handed the instrument to Kubelík, who offered to buy it. Bentin refused; it was a gift. Kubelík accepted and then asked Bentin to measure his Stradivarius and make an exact copy. The violinmaker crafted a one-piece, striped German maple back with a German spruce top.

Bentin had recently finished the instrument when he lent it to the young and rising violinist Adrien Freiche, who had returned to his hometown of New Orleans in January 1922 to play a series of concerts. Bentin admitted that he wanted "to see if it would stand the test." Freiche's performance and praise, as well as Kubelík's testimonials, brought virtuosos worldwide calling to Bentin's studio, a who's who of the day's finest violinists: Austrian Fritz Kreisler (1875–1962); American Albert Spalding (1888–1953); Polish-born Paul Kochanski (1888–1953); and the finest of all, Russian Jascha Heifetz (1901–1987), among many others.

When Bentin was asked the secret to the highest-quality violins, he answered simply, the varnish. "A good violinmaker must be half chemist: he must know how to make and how to put on varnish if he wants to make a good violin." Like his father, he studied the varnish used by the Italian masters in Cremona—Antonio Stradivari, Andrea Amati, Giuseppe Guarneri, and others. Bentin said that the proper application is what gives the violin its tone. "It must not be too hard or soft. It must be of the proper consistency so that most of it will stay on the surface and will not soak into the wood. This gives the wood a hardness that accentuates the vibrations…allowing the player to have his softest and sweetest notes." According to the leading violinists of the day, Bentin accomplished what few makers have ever done, producing an instrument rivaling the best of the late seventeenth- and early eighteenth-century Italian makers.

At some unknown time, he began numbering his violins and placing his maker's mark inside the instrument. The mark was simple: "H. Bentin," followed by a drawing of a violin, "New Orleans, F. A.," and the year. After he began numbering the instruments, he made more than 225 violins. He chose number 206 as his favorite, believing it to be superior to all others. That one he sold to Kubelík for about $1,200. The back of the violin displayed a small oil portrait of Henry Bentin.

Decades of joy, strife, and hard work with his cherished wife ended for Henry on July 16, 1926, when Annie, his wife of forty-five years, died of cancer at the age of sixty-four. Just a little over two years later, on August 25, 1928, Henry, age seventy-one, died of pneumonia at Touro Infirmary and was buried with his wife in the Thompson family tomb in Metairie Cemetery.

After their son John died in 1943, the family buried him in Garden of Memories Cemetery in Jefferson Parish. They later moved Henry and Anna Bentin's remains from Metairie Cemetery and reinterred them next to their son on February 12, 1944. A modest bronze plaque, level with the ground, is all that marks the grave of one of the finest violinmakers of all time. Yet his legacy is embodied in the instruments he lovingly crafted. They are played still.

Reverend Albert Richard Edbrooke
1870–1925

Set back from Metairie Avenue in Metairie Cemetery is a granite coping tomb with a rough-cut granite monument and rustic cross bearing a Celtic design. In the center of the cross is a chalice with the Host rising from it. It marks the final resting place of the Reverend Albert Richard Edbrooke, rector of Grace Episcopal Church in New Orleans.

Albert was born on December 19, 1870, in Plymouth, Devon, a major port overlooking the English Channel in the southwest corner of England. His mother, Amelia Ann Hannaford Blight (b. 1844), and father, Edwin Pugsley Edbrooke (b. 1840), married at Stoke Damerel, Devon, in 1865. They had three sons, Edwin R. B. (b. 1866) and Frederick (b. 1868), both born in Wimbledon, and Albert (b. 1870). Soon after Albert's birth, the couple appears to have separated, for in the 1871 English census, the boys are boarders with a Dawson family at 25 Wyndham Street in Plymouth, with young Edwin listed as a "scholar," meaning he attended school. Amelia is listed as married, working as a servant and nurse to a family named Alston and living at Waterton Lodge on Milton Road. I have not located Albert's father between 1871 and 1890; he does not appear in the census of 1871 or 1881. He turns up in the 1891 census as unmarried and a licensed liquor salesman in London.

By 1881 Albert's mother was working and living at His Majesty's Men's Prison in Exeter, about seventy miles east of Plymouth. She was employed as an "institution matron & servant," meaning nurse. She remained there well into the 1890s. Her three sons were also living in Exeter in the household of Richard Vodders, perhaps a relative, at 82 Holloway Street Cottages, and all were listed as scholars. Albert would have been eleven years old. During his time in Exeter, he became a choir boy in the Anglican Cathedral Church of St. Peter and was confirmed there by Bishop Frederick Temple. He was studying to become a pharmacist, or "chemist," until he made a life-changing decision.

In mid-September 1889, nineteen-year-old Albert traveled four hundred miles across southern England and the Channel to Antwerp, Belgium, where he boarded the steamer *Bordeaux* bound for New Orleans. His means were no doubt modest, and he traveled in steerage. He sailed into the American port on October 7, 1889, where the ship's manifest listed him, for unknown reasons, as a farmer. He was alone in a new country and strange city.

Soon after, the Episcopal bishop chose Albert for missionary work in Shreveport, Louisiana. At the same time, as he was journeying back and forth between Shreveport and New Orleans, he began working with the YMCA. This may have had a simple beginning: stepping off the *Bordeaux* into a strange land, he would have needed a safe place to live, and he would have been familiar with the YMCA, as Exeter was home to one of the oldest YMCAs in the world, founded in 1848. (In years to come, he became a board member and a leader in the organization.)

In 1891 Albert began preparing for the deaconate in the Episcopal Church with another Englishman, Jessie S. Moore. They studied with the Reverend John W. Moore, Jessie's brother, of St. George's Episcopal Church. In two years' time, on June 18, 1893, Bishop Davis Sessums of St. Paul's Episcopal Church on Camp Street ordained Albert deacon and named him an assistant curate in charge of Christ Episcopal Church in Covington, about twenty miles north of Lake Pontchartrain.[4] It was in this little church that he served as deacon from 1893 to 1895, then rector from early 1896 until April 1900.

His ordination to the priesthood on June 23, 1895, brought Reverend Edbrooke accolades in the local paper the following day: "The cultured know him as a most agreeable companion, the poor and the sick and the lowly as a friend and counselor whom they love. His feeling that the Holy Ghost called him to Christian ministry was no false consciousness." While at Covington, Edbrooke also became cocurate of St. Paul's Church in New Orleans.

He may have scrapped his allegiance to queen and country when he became a naturalized US citizen on March 3, 1897, but he did not feel the same when it came to playing cricket. In August 1900 he served as a bowler, or pitcher, for the Victoria Cricket Club (founded in June 1887 in honor of Queen Victoria's Jubilee), which played regular matches at the Sportsmen's Grounds in Audubon Park. Active in recreation as in work, Albert was kept on the run between St. Paul's and the Covington appointment, a rural church in bad repair. He raised $500 to have the building painted, add a chancel, and remodel the interior. Then, assigned to be rector of the Episcopal Church of the Good Shepherd in Lake Charles, Louisiana, he paid off all its debts, consecrated the church, and took on missionary work in the rural towns of Jennings and Crowley, Louisiana, well west of Baton Rouge.

Albert married Louise McGraw on November 13, 1900. Six years later Albert was recalled to New Orleans, Louise's hometown, to help another failing church, Grace Episcopal Church on South Rampart Street. Louise's parents, proprietors of the Morris McGraw Woodenware Company, lived there. In just two years Albert increased the church's membership by more than half, from 330 to 437, and initiated weekday noon services for businessmen. Under Reverend Edbrooke's stewardship, in June 1908, Caroline Stannard Tilton, a wealthy widow, willed the congregation $20,000 to build a new church to replace the old South Rampart structure. The new site on Canal at Marais Street cost the considerable sum of $27,500 in April 1913. It would be 1920 before construction could begin.

In 1911 Albert was appointed president of the standing committee of the Archdiocese of Louisiana, a position he held twice, from 1911 to 1916 and 1919 to 1925. Albert and Louise had moved into her father's two-story pillared house at 1444 Henry Clay Avenue, near Audubon Park. Yet even amid such comfort, the forty-one-year-old minister suffered a heartbreaking blow in the early afternoon of August 28, 1911, when Louise died at home of uterine cancer. Although he initially kept at his duties, on June 30, 1912, perhaps needing a break from his bereavement, Edbrooke boarded the ship *New York* at the port of New Orleans and sailed for England. Having been too long away from his mother and brothers, and never previously having met his nieces and nephews, Edbrooke remained with his family for about a month before returning on August 3, 1912.

The following year a congregation in Stanton, Virginia, asked him to become rector of their parish, Emmanuel Episcopal Church. The local papers played on the dramatic upheaval; a bold headline of August 17 read, "Rector Edbrooke Decides to Remain Rector of Grace Church Here. Virginia wants Him, But New Orleans Loves Him and Keeps Him." So, he remained in New Orleans. During the winter of 1913 he traveled to Asheville, North Carolina, where he met and fell in love with Margaret Parmalee, a widow from New York. They married in a quiet ceremony at Biltmore, George W.

Vanderbilt's Asheville estate, on January 6, 1914, returning to New Orleans to live at 923 North Solomon Street.

Albert Edbrooke's ongoing spiritual journey deepened his beliefs, both conservative and liberal. He delivered fiery sermons on divorce, going so far as to support an antidivorce legislative bill sponsored by the Democratic US senator Joseph E. Ransdell as well as the women's right to vote (he further said women were fully capable of missionary work, both at home and abroad). The laying of Grace Episcopal's cornerstone for its new home on Sunday afternoon, March 28, 1920, was a moment of great pride for Edbrooke. He had continued to increase the church's membership, now more than doubled from when he had first arrived, to 772 people. The little church was thriving.

The new church was completed that summer with a total outlay of $115,000, leaving about $60,000 of debt. It would be many years before the church was clear of this financial burden. Edbrooke was now fifty, and the pace of his work began to drain him. He and Margaret took a vacation in 1921 to La Ceiba, Honduras, a Caribbean resort town familiar to New Orleanians as the home of their largest importer of bananas, the Standard Fruit Company.

Missionary trips throughout the state in the years that followed maintained the frenetic tempo of Edbrooke's early years in the priesthood. His reappointment as president of the standing committee of the Archdiocese of Louisiana in 1919 meant more responsibility. During the early 1920s he and Margaret began taking trips to Hendersonville, North Carolina, to escape the summer heat, frequently staying at the Kentucky Home Hotel on Fourth Street.

More than twenty years before, Albert's father had died in Somerset, England. Mid-1924 brought him news of the death of his mother, Amelie, at seventy-nine, on June 6, 1924, in Plymouth, England, after a long career as a hospital nurse. She had been a remarkable woman in her day, a single mother (an often-scorned position in British society) with trained employment.

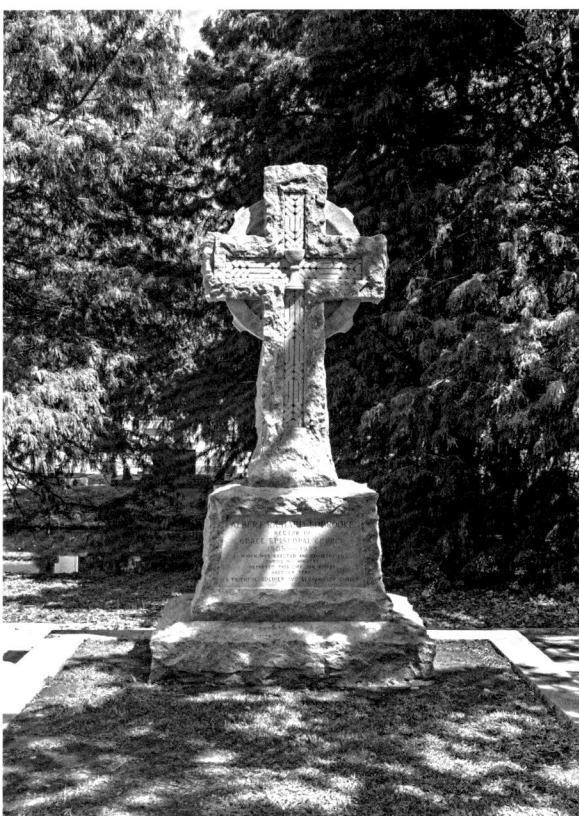

Celtic cross with chalice and Host adorning the center of this rugged granite cross, symbolizing the deceased; tomb of an Episcopalian priest, Albert Richard Edbrooke, Metairie Cemetery

Six months to the day after his mother, Albert died after a short illness on January 6, 1925, from an infection due to chronic renal and cardiac disease. Margaret was by his side, and hundreds of parishioners crowded about his home. He was buried in Metairie Cemetery. The following year, with donations from his congregation, a rugged granite monument rose over his grave. His epitaph reads, "A Faithful Soldier and Servant of Christ." Margaret died September 29, 1932, at sixty-two years old.

Hurricane Katrina on August 29, 2005, devastated New Orleans and pushed several feet of water into Grace Episcopal Church, now farther out on Canal Street, destroying almost everything in the building. The gutted sanctuary and tiny congregation received word from Bishop Morris Thompson on December 5, 2011, that the church would close one month hence. There were fewer than fifteen people present that day.

Virginia Gleaves Lazarus
1871–1897

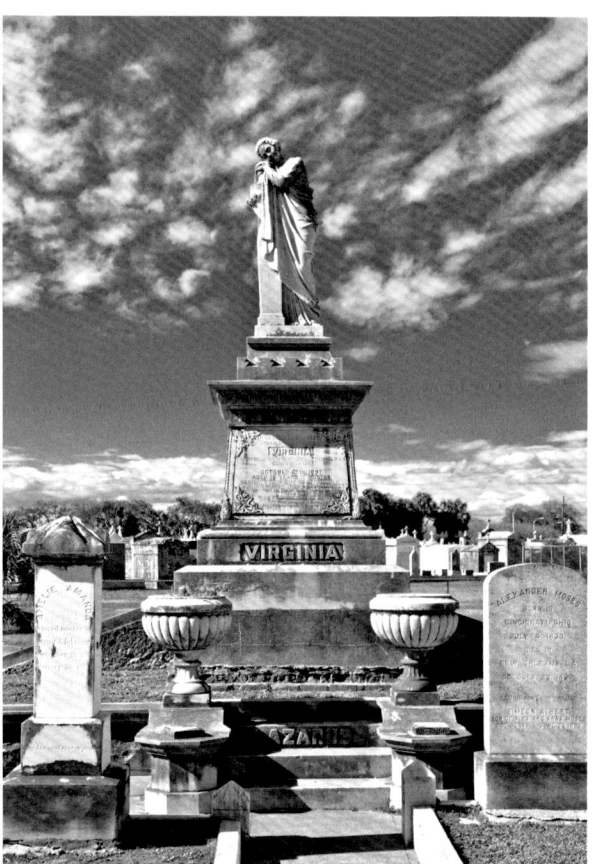

Monument of Virginia Gleaves Lazarus, Dispersed of Judah Cemetery

Near the center of Dispersed of Judah Cemetery stands a high, intricate monument. Atop two large pedestals, the statue of a woman draped in robes leans against an urn topping a column, her right cheek resting on her hand, her eyes closed. In a recessed panel, in bas-relief, is a single name, Virginia. Above the name a white marble pedestal bears a lengthy inscription placed by Virginia Gleaves Lazarus's distraught parents, Henry L. and Sallie Solomon Lazarus.

Virginia's father, born in New York City, had come to New Orleans in 1871. He was a prominent attorney and judge in the civil district court. Virginia, born that same year, was the oldest of their six children. She was a brilliant student, entering Newcomb College in 1896. A photograph of Virginia shows a beautiful young woman with dark hair and piercing brown eyes, her face kind and caring. She was a member of the class of 1899 and listed as "Special" along with several other young women in the 1897 Newcomb College yearbook, the *Jambalaya*. She excelled in poetry and prose, showing great promise and determination; she wanted to be a writer.

The first effective vaccine against typhoid had been developed by the British doctor Almroth Edward Wright at the Army Medical School in Netley, Hampshire, England, in 1896, for military use, but it would not be available in the United States until 1909. It is not known how Virginia contracted the disease, but within days of its appearance, she was bedridden. She suffered for a month or more with what her father described as a long illness. She died on October 27, 1897, four days shy of her nineteenth birthday. Part of her epitaph states, "Her presence filled our home with sunshine, her absence leaves it in gloom."

Shortly after Virginia's death, her mother honored her excellence in English by establishing the Virginia Gleaves Lazarus Award at Newcomb College (now part of Tulane University) and also at Temple Sinai. In 2016 Temple Sinai suspended the presentation of the award that had been given for more than one hundred years for outstanding achievement in its confirmation class. Tulane University's English department has continued to present the award annually for the best essay written by a junior or senior since its conception in 1901, inspiring beginning writers and ensuring that Virginia is not forgotten.

Charles Ferdinand Vorbusch

1891–1915

Just inside the front gate of the Valence Street Cemetery, there is a sizable coping tomb. A substantial headstone at the rear of the tomb bears one of the most unusual inscriptions in all New Orleans's cemeteries. It is simple and shocking:

CORPORAL CHAS. FERDINAND VORBUSCH
NATIVE OF NEW ORLEANS
MURDERED AT GRETNA, LA
SEPT. 1, 1915, AGED 24 YRS. 5 MOS.

To his family and friends, he was called Fred. His family ran a grocery and bakery at the corner of South Rampart and Second Streets. He worked there as a baker and then tried his hand at carpentry. In 1915 he responded to recruiting ads for the police department of Gretna, which at the time had a reputation as a place lawless and dangerous; drunken brawls, shootings, gambling, and corruption seemed to be the only constant. One police officer left for the war in Europe, declaring it safer.

Early on the morning of September 1, 1915, Vorbusch walked several blocks to the Jackson Avenue streetcar, got off at the ferry landing, and crossed the river to Gretna. He was assigned a partner who, like himself, was a rookie. A short time later, as they were walking on what is today Huey P. Long Avenue, at the corner of Third Street, a group of young men stood about drinking. The officers told them to move on. Vorbusch and his partner continued for about a half block when one of the men in the group began yelling and challenging them to leave. When they turned to walk back, a shot rang out, hitting Vorbusch and knocking him to the pavement. His partner and one member of the group began a gunfight. The lone policeman emptied his two revolvers, then took cover around the corner.

The other gunman, severely wounded, walked over to Vorbusch and shot him two more times, once in the head. He was a known thug named Frank "Ike" Burke, an off-duty "special policeman." He was arrested later that day and charged with murder. A public outcry for law and order followed, but little to nothing was done. In November 1915 a grand jury reduced the charge to manslaughter, and Burke was released on bail. After delays he was finally tried in November 1916. The jury found him not guilty, and he was free.

A year later, on December 22, 1917, Burke sat drinking at the bar with a friend in the Sportsmen's Café near the Jackson Avenue ferry landing. At the other end of the bar, he noticed ex–chief of police Joseph Fisher, the man responsible for Burke spending two years in the state penitentiary for an assault in 1909. Burke's friend asked Fisher if he could talk with him alone; Fisher agreed. Both men went into the storeroom to talk, and within moments Burke entered and shot Fisher in the head from about three feet, killing him instantly. Burke

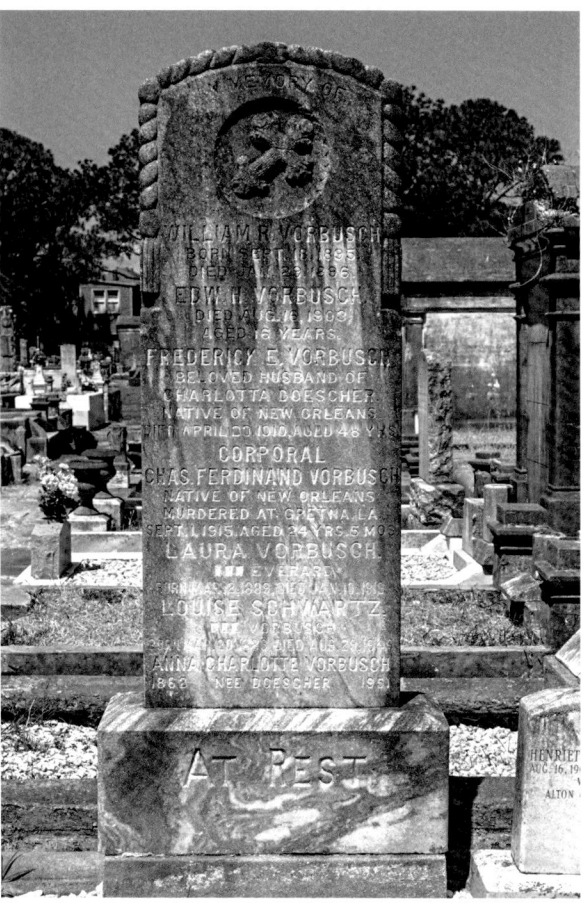

Monument of Corporal Charles Ferdinand Vorbusch, Valence Street Cemetery

was tried for murder and sentenced to life in prison. In the courtroom the day of Burke's trial sat the mother and two sisters of Fred Vorbusch. Burke was released from prison after five years and given a full pardon in 1924. Within the year, his lifestyle caught up with him. He and several companions were drinking in a bar when one accused Burke of taking a fifty-dollar bill. He denied it and placed his pistol on the bar, inviting the others to search him. No bill was found, but the argument continued. Pistols were pulled and shots fired, with one hitting Burke in the head. His assailant was hit and fell to the floor. Burke walked over and shot the man three more times, then he too collapsed. He died in Charity Hospital several hours later, pleading to see his wife. Too late, justice was finally served for the killing of Fred Vorbusch.

Leslie Philip Backes
1897–1918

On the main aisle in Carrollton Cemetery #1 stands a granite tomb topped by a marble-draped urn with marble tablets on all sides. One of these is devoted to Leslie Philip Backes, born in 1897. At the top of the tablet in bas-relief is the Marine Corps coat of arms above the crossed flags of the United States and the City of New Orleans, the latter with its three fleurs-de-lis.

He was the youngest son of Victor J. A. Backes from Germany and Margaret Barbara Buchel from Baton Rouge. Victor Backes was a marble and granite supplier and carver with a shop on Washington Avenue. He and Margaret had eight children, with seven surviving to adulthood. Victor was in competition with numerous other marble cutters, including the large firms of Albert Weiblen and James Reynolds. Whatever success he may have had would have been moderate compared with the established companies. He was forced to advertise in other cities in hopes of increasing his work. This striving for income may have led him to send Leslie to Baton Rouge in 1910 to live with his aunt, Minnie Buchel, his mother's sister. It would have alleviated some of the financial burden.

Leslie enrolled in that city's St. Louis Street elementary school, graduating in June 1911. In November 1910 Reverend T. M. Hunter of the First Presbyterian Church organized the first Boy Scout troop in Baton Rouge, with over twenty boys. Only ten months since its founding, the popular Boy Scouts of America was sweeping across the nation. Backes joined shortly after the start of Troop 3 and eventually rose to scoutmaster. The scouts' early emphasis on tracking, reconnaissance, signaling, mapping, and first aid provided valuable training for potential soldiers.

In August 1912 the Baton Rouge and New Orleans scouts met in Mandeville, Louisiana, and Backes participated in what later was called a Jamboree. In an exercise perhaps inspired by H. G. Wells's 1910 book *War Games for Boy Scouts*, the two scout groups divided into several units and practiced sending dispatches through each other's lines without being detected. Late the next year, Backes was one of a group of boys who undertook a three-day hiking trek from Baton Rouge to New Orleans, a distance of about ninety miles.

In February 1916 Backes graduated from high school and prepared for college. He entered Louisiana State University that fall, majoring in agriculture. He also joined the newly formed Army Reserve Officers' Training Corps, or ROTC, and was assigned as a private in Company D. He played offense on the football team, as he had in high school. The following spring, he was one of about one hundred athletes chosen to take a trip to Fort Logan H. Roots at Little Rock, Arkansas. A newspaper article gave no clues as to the purpose of the outing, yet with the country on the verge of war and a government agency, the Committee on Public Information, constantly spreading prowar sentiments, along with his membership in the ROTC, it may well have been for military training.

On April 6, 1917, the United States declared war on Germany. Had the country paid homage to the Boy Scout motto of "Be Prepared," it would have been better fit to fight a war. A national recruiting campaign called men to join the fight, and on June 5, 1918, Backes registered for the draft. He did not wait to be called up. On June 24 he signed enlistment papers and joined the United States Marines. He was sent to Parris Island, South Carolina, for basic training, then assigned to

Company A, Third Separate Machine Gun Battalion, with the rank of private. He remained at Parris Island, no doubt awaiting his orders to join the Expeditionary Forces fighting in Europe.

Another deadly war was raging in the United States. The first known case of what would be called the Spanish flu was recorded on March 4, 1918, at Camp Funston, at Fort Riley, Kansas. Within weeks, an estimated 1,100 soldiers were hospitalized and several thousand lay sick in their barracks. As soldiers transferred to other forts and to the European front, they carried the virus with them. It was the beginning of a pandemic more deadly than the Black Plague in the fourteenth century. The virus arrived at Parris Island in early autumn and quickly spread through the camp. The most seriously ill men were transferred to Quantico, Virginia, where numerous barracks were turned into hospitals filled with ill and dying men.

Backes arrived at Quantico on November 12 and was placed in one of the hospital barracks. The virus began with chills, fever, nausea, coughing, aches, and diarrhea. Backes's symptoms worsened into a viral and bacterial pneumonia. He developed dark spots on his cheeks. The pneumonia slowly progressed so that every breath was a struggle as his lungs slowly filled with fluid. As the disease advanced, his face began to turn blue with cyanosis. This young man of great promise died on November 19 in the barracks. Before the pandemic was over, it would kill between thirty million and one hundred million people worldwide. More US servicemen died from the flu than in combat.

Leslie Backes's death is not the end of the story. His father and brother carved an intricate white marble settee

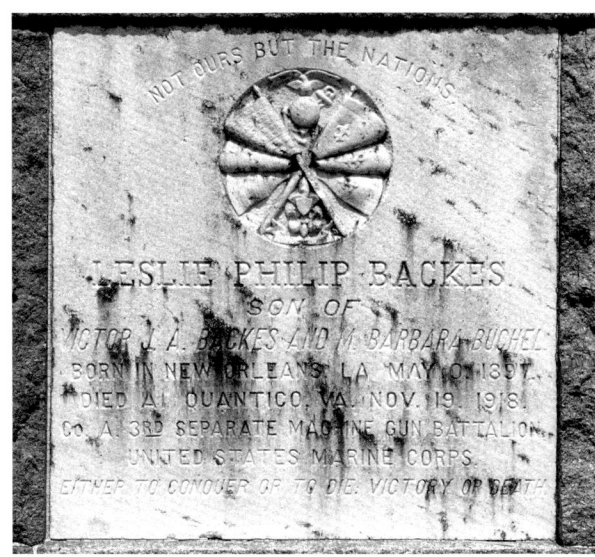

White marble tablet of Leslie Philip Backes, Carrollton Cemetery #1

as a memorial. The seat is supported by carved lions, and the back and arms are adorned with a grapevine motif. The dedication to the twenty-one-year-old son and sibling is engraved with the motto and insignia of the Boy Scouts of America. The bench was placed in the vestibule of the First Presbyterian Church in Baton Rouge in May 1919. The Memorial Tower at Louisiana State University was built in 1923. Inside, a bronze plaque lists the names of the thirty students who gave their lives in World War I. (Today there are four such plaques, with the names of 1,447 students who lost their lives in succeeding wars.) In 1926 the university planted thirty live oaks in memory of the students who died in the "War to End All Wars." Today it is known as the Memorial Oak Grove. Beneath each sprawling tree is a concrete marker featuring a bronze plaque bearing a name. One reads:

**THIS TREE IS DEDICATED TO THE MEMORY
OF LESLIE PHILIP BACKES
MAR. 5, 1897
NOV. 19, 1918.**

We are reminded of the adage "Freedom is never free."

Indigent Burial
unknown–2018

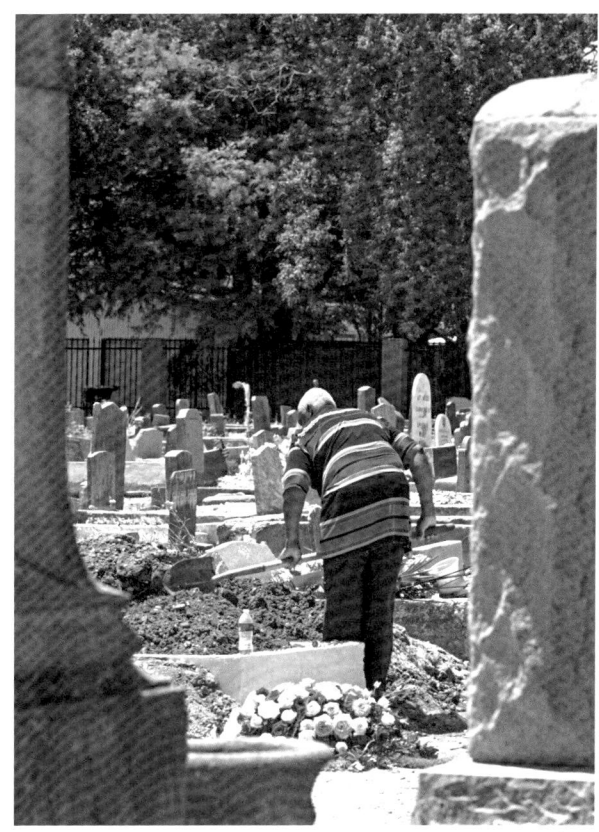

Indigent burial, Carrollton Cemetery #1

The day was clear, with a few clouds drifting overhead. A lone figure stood leaning on his shovel in front of a coping tomb in the Indigent Square 218 of Carrollton Cemetery #1. He was quiet, and the lines on his weathered face seemed to say that he had dug many of these hollows. In the distance a hearse approached slowly, escorted by two police officers on motorcycles, blue lights flashing. Behind the hearse a lone black car followed. The small cortege turned down the aisle as the man with the shovel walked away. Standing next to a tomb, he watched, expressionless, as the undertakers removed the coffin from the hearse and several people stepped out of the black car. They approached the grave and stood silent as the men from the hearse lowered the casket four feet into the coping tomb. One figure stepped forward, holding a small book. He read a few lines from it, barely audible to those standing near him. He closed the book, turned, and walked back to the car, followed by everyone except the man with the shovel. The police departed without turning on their lights. The hearse and car slowly followed until they reached the exit; they went in one direction, the police motorcycles in the other. The entire event had lasted less than fifteen minutes.

The lone man walked over to the grave and began shoveling dirt on the casket, the silence broken only by another groundskeeper's leaf blower on the other side of the cemetery. Later, the lone man stood leaning against his shovel, looking down at the now covered grave, his head bowed. He appeared to be praying.

PART TWO

Plates

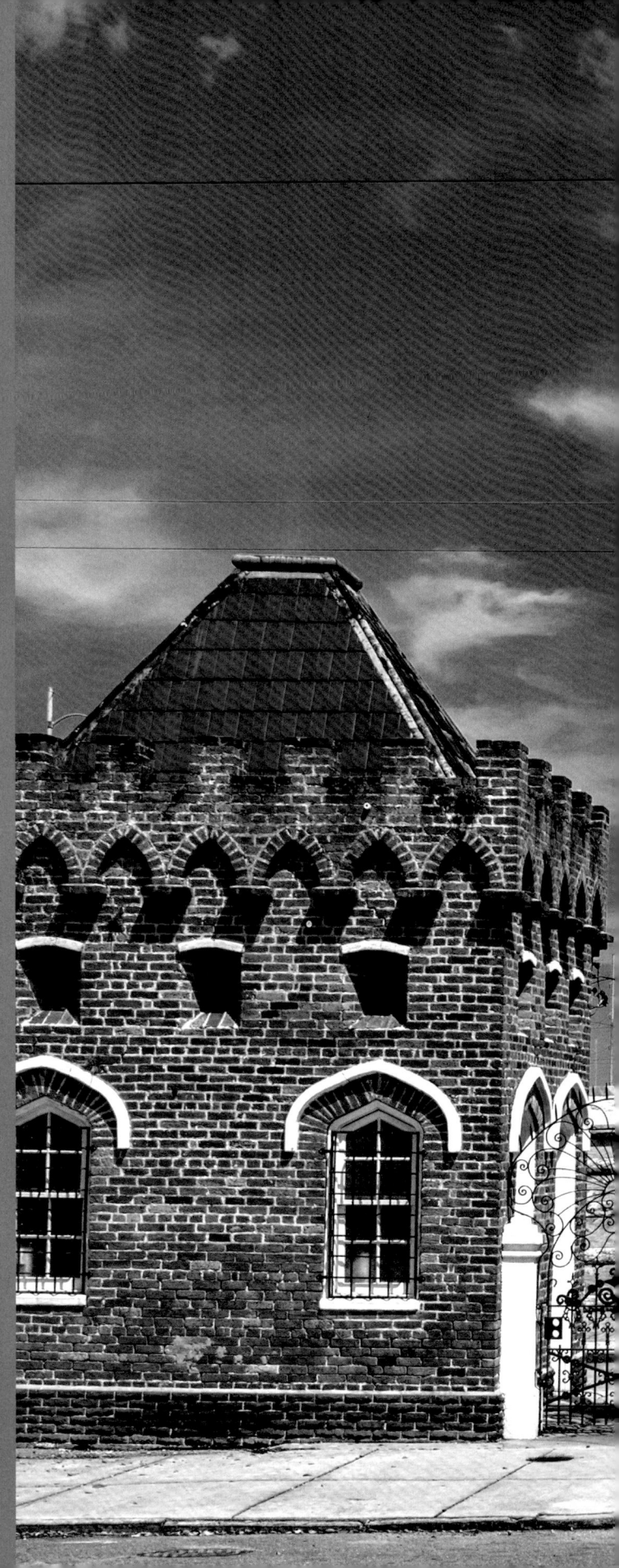

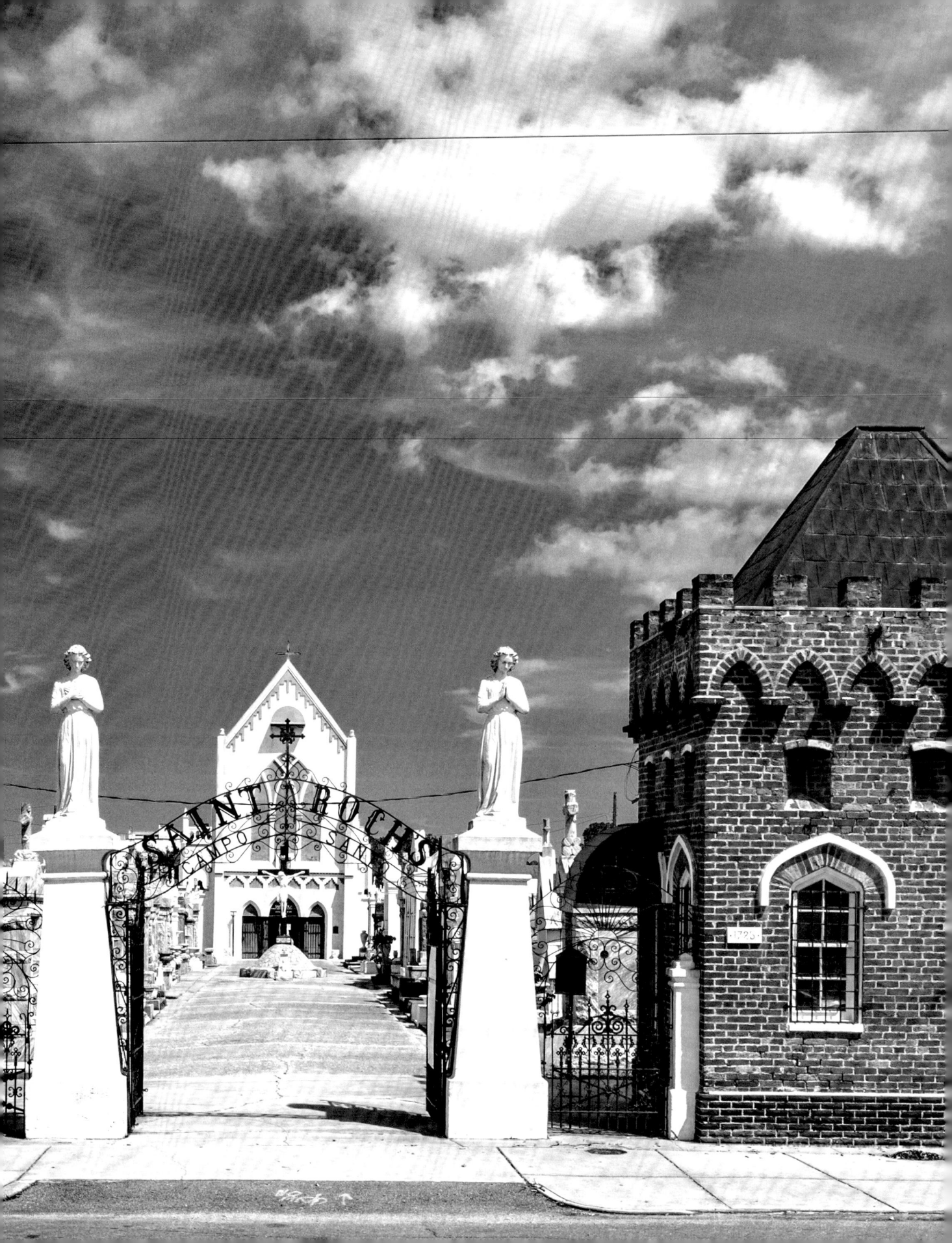

Cypress Grove Cemetery

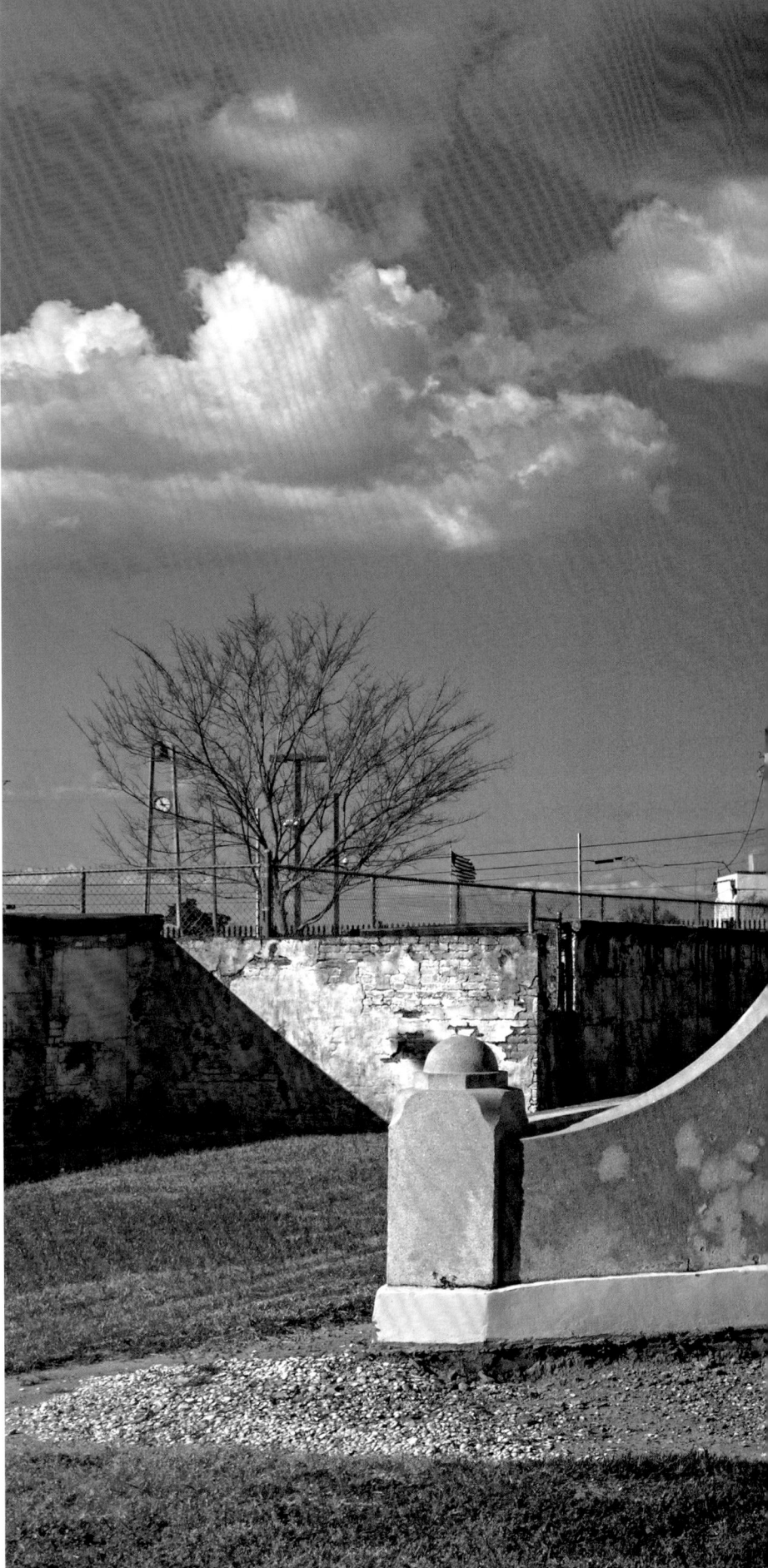

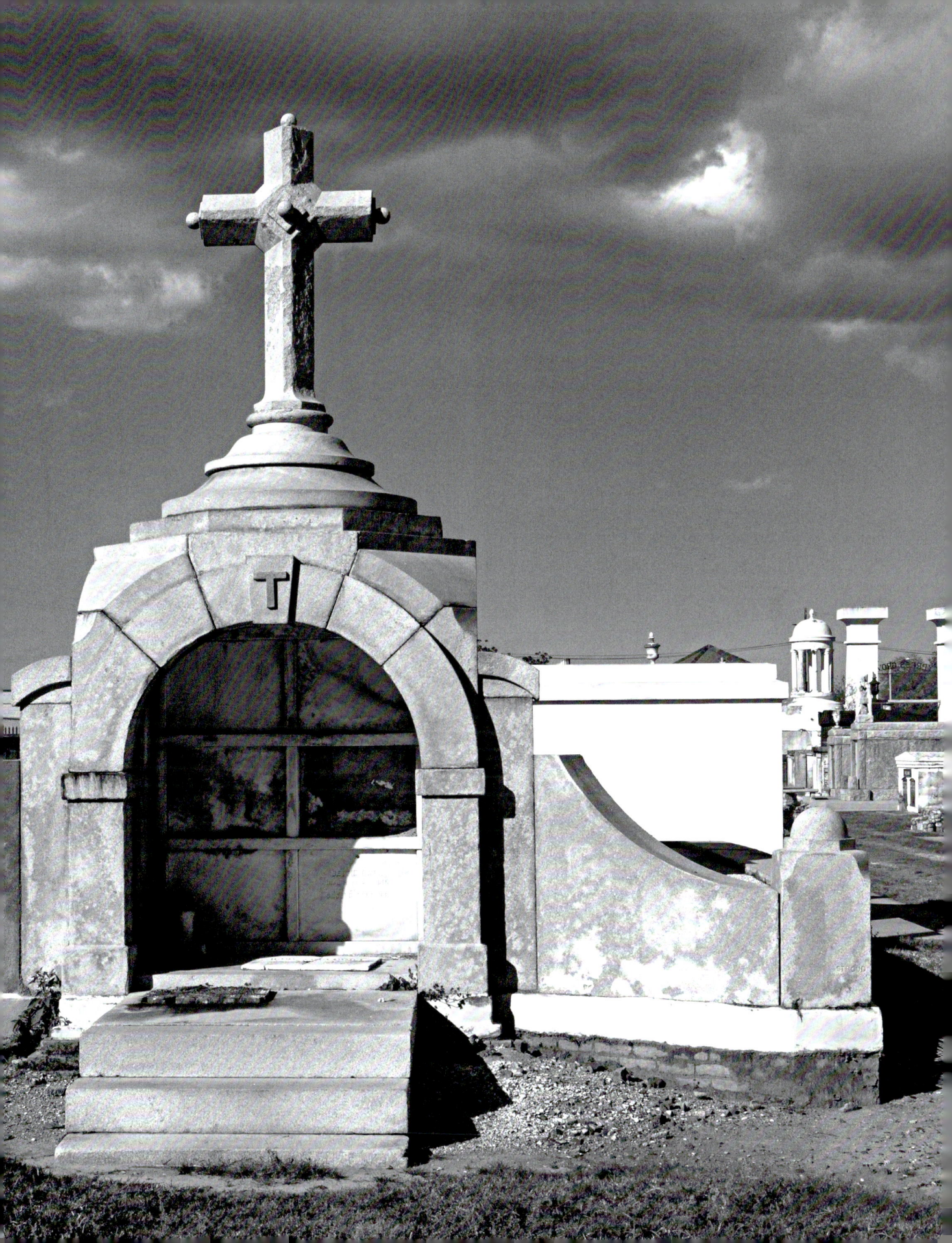

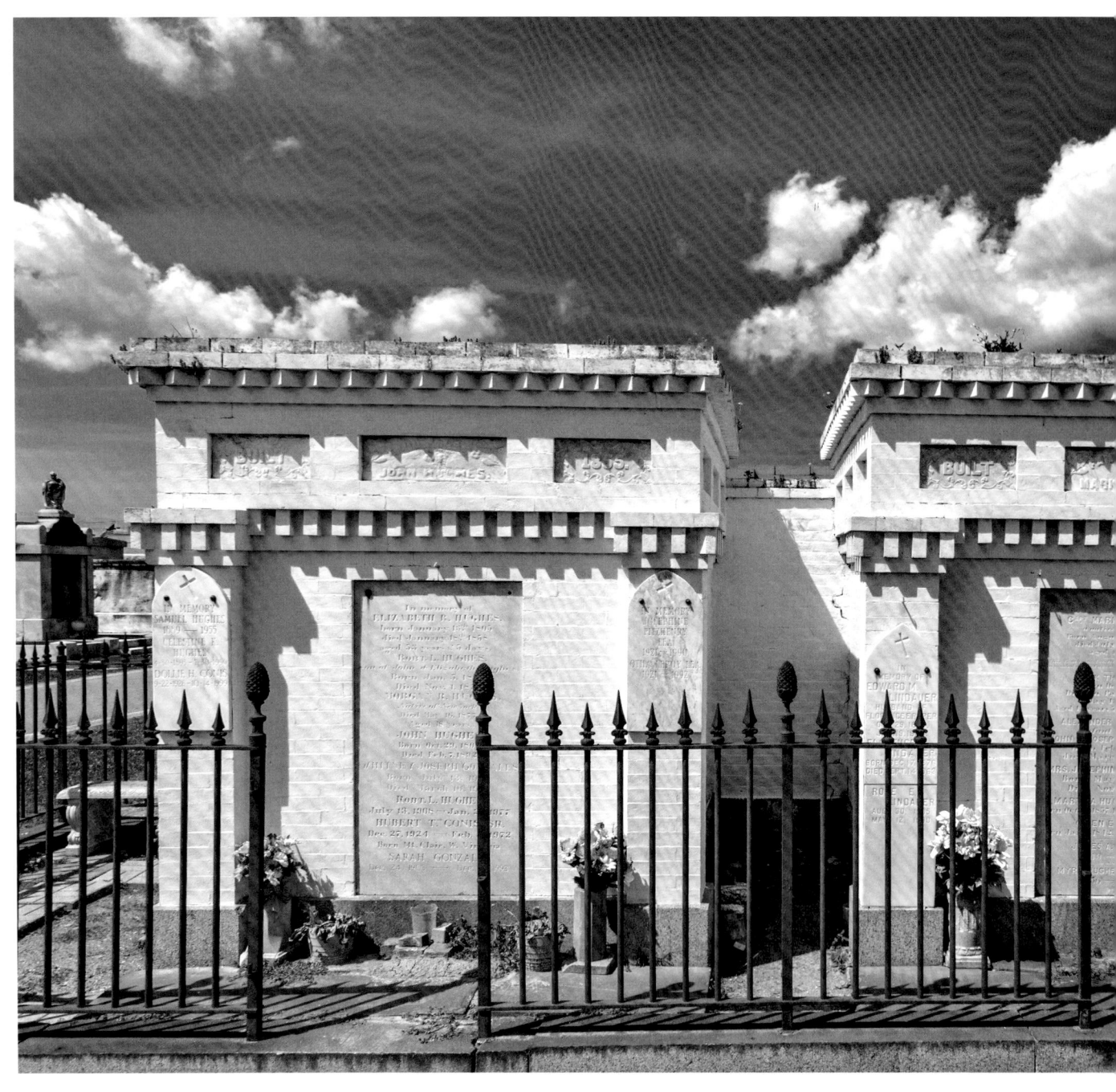

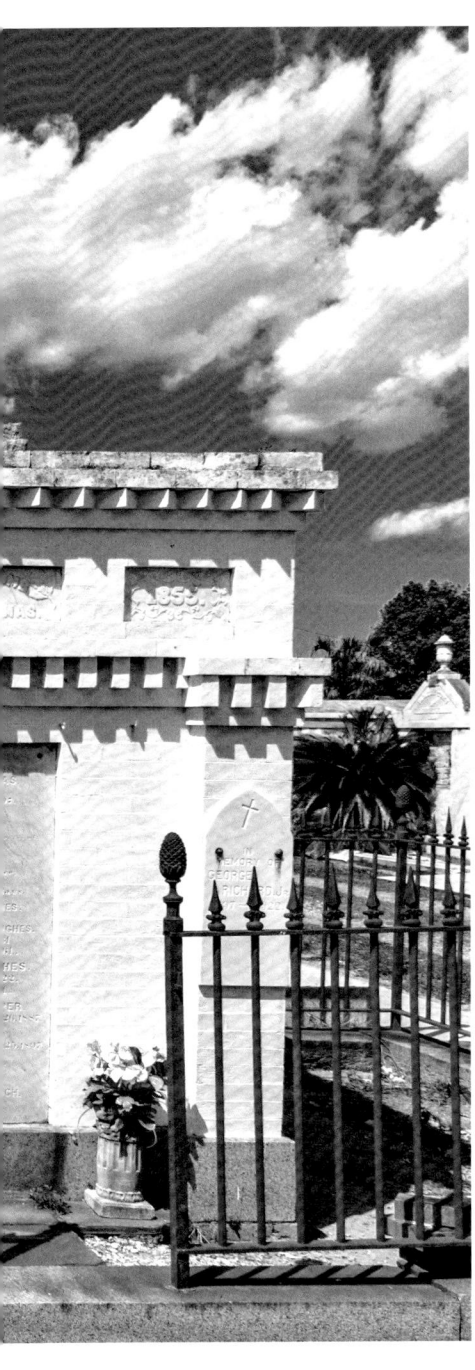
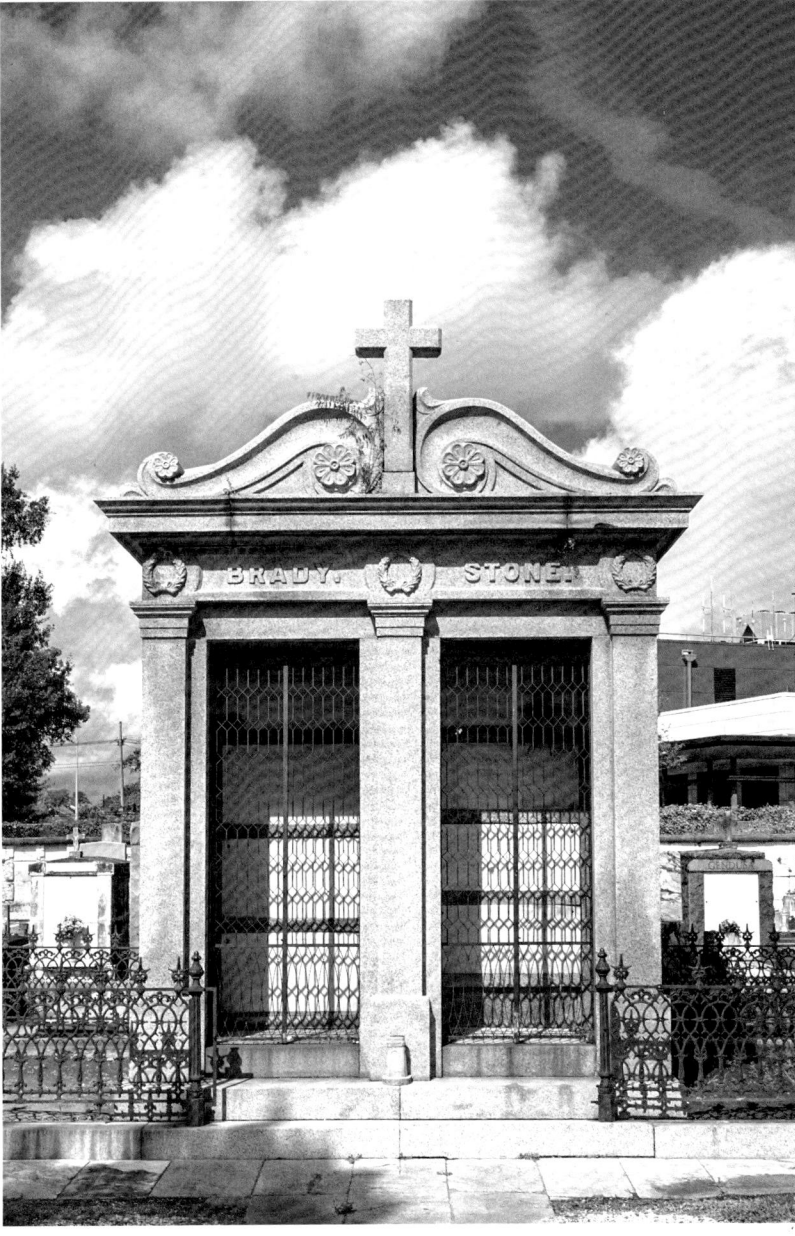

Cypress Grove Cemetery

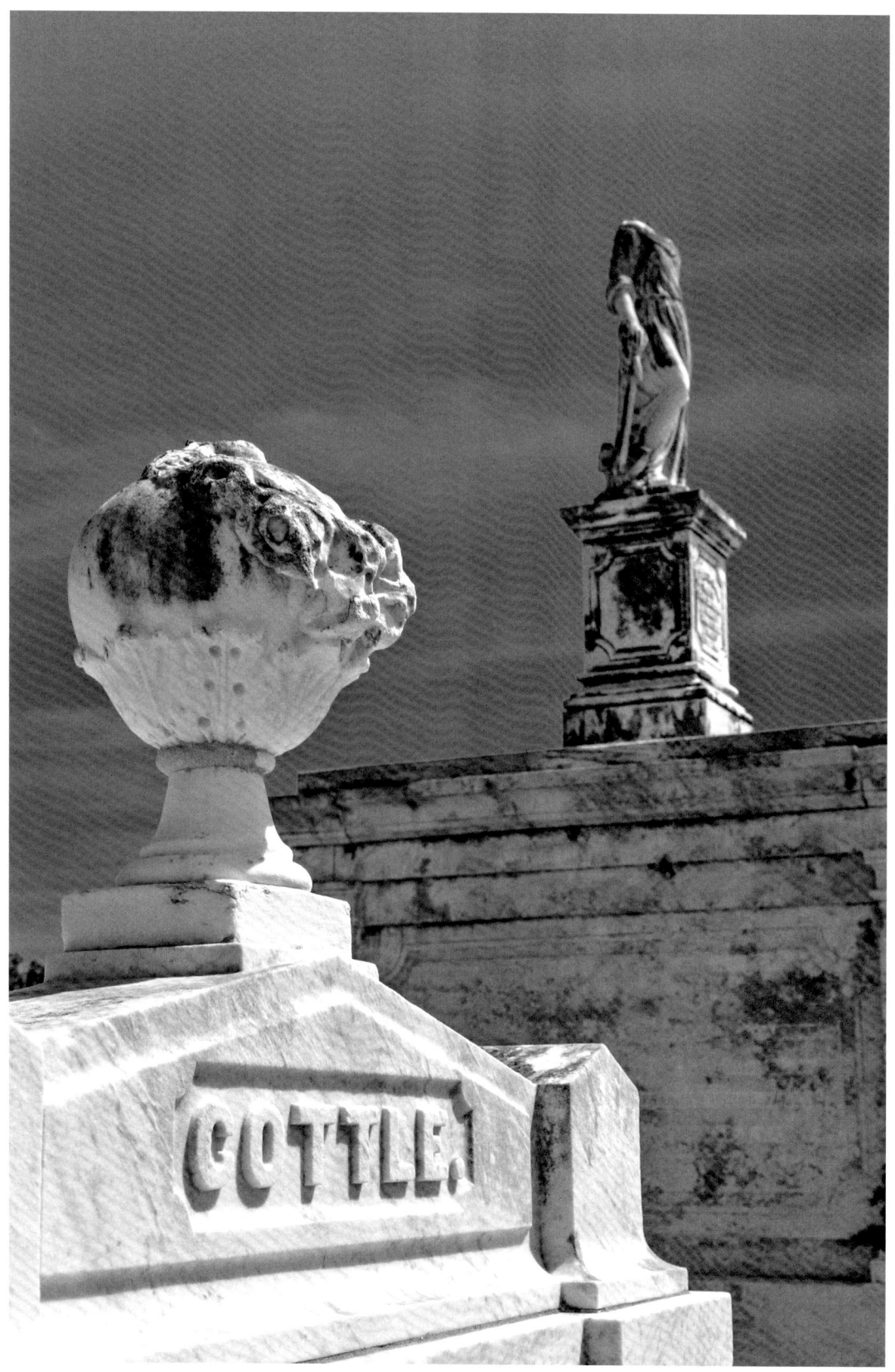

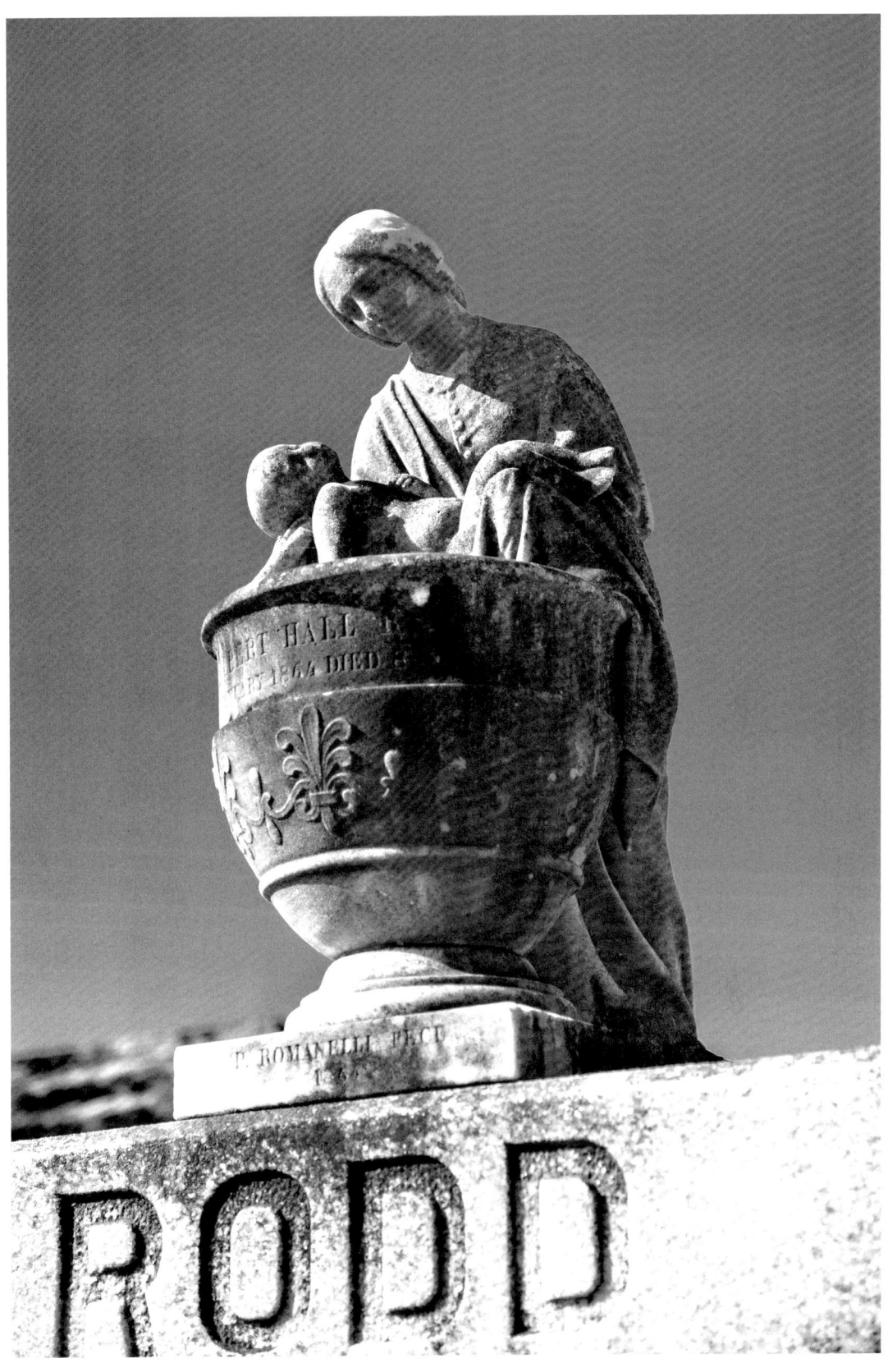

Cypress Grove Cemetery

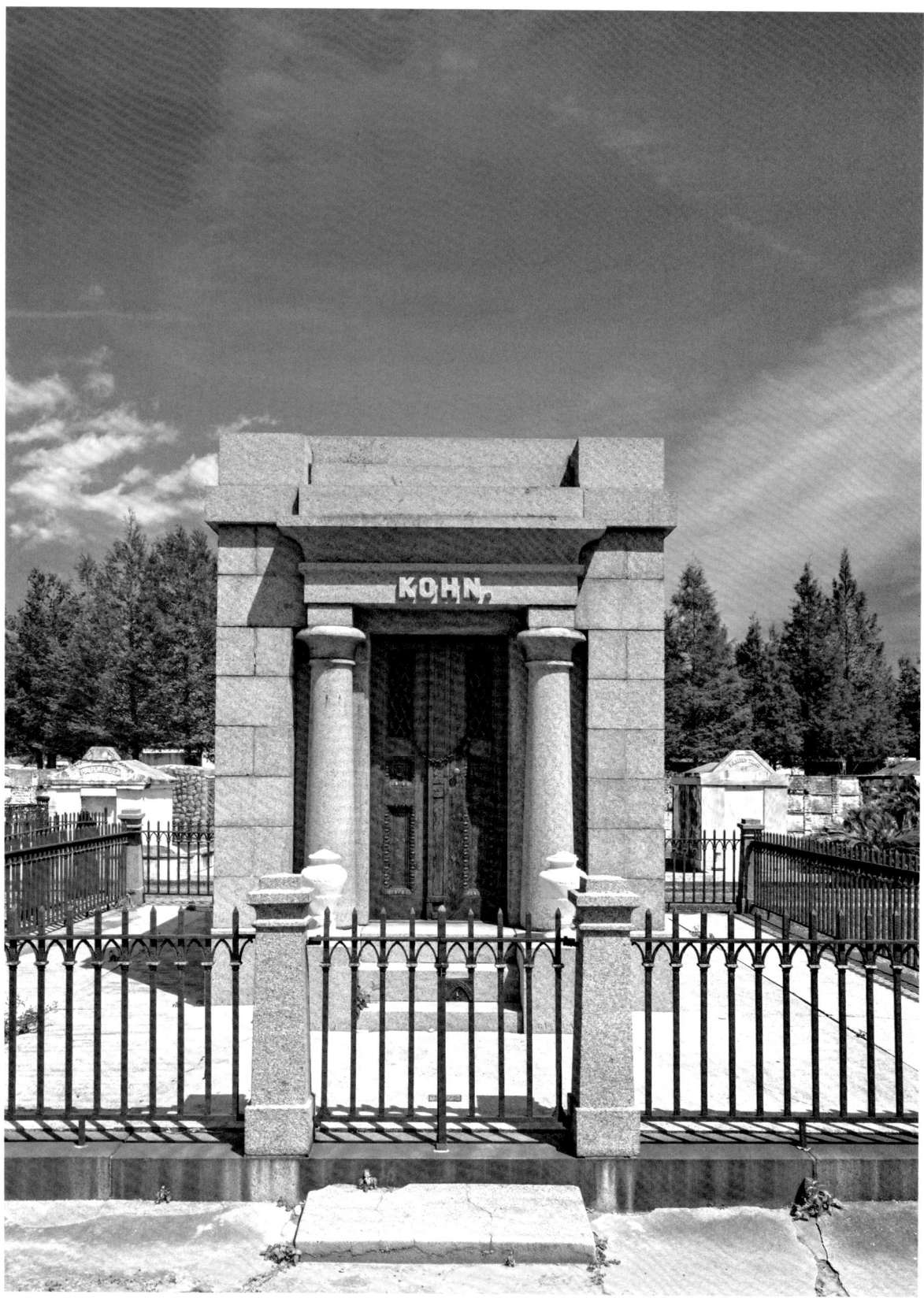

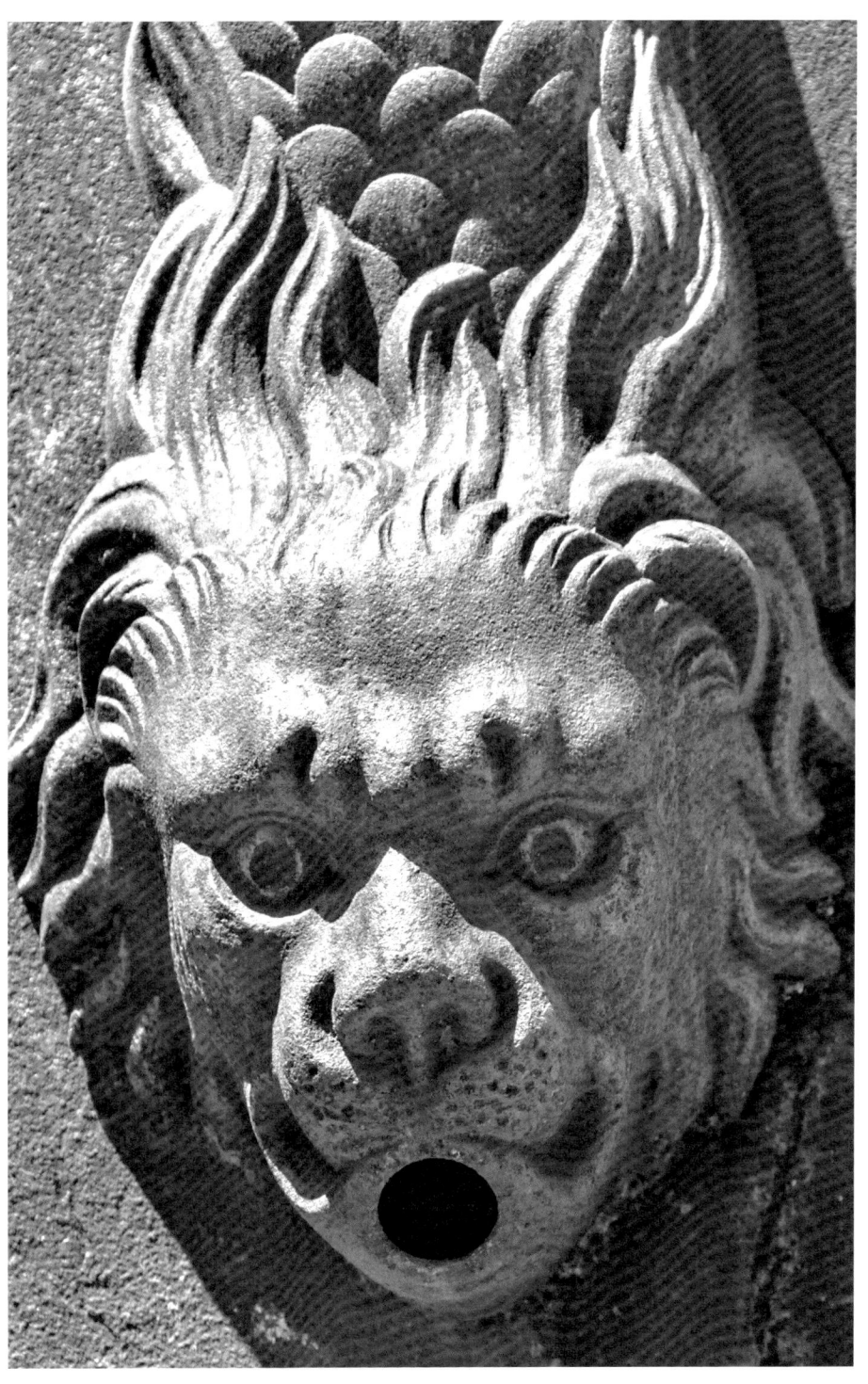

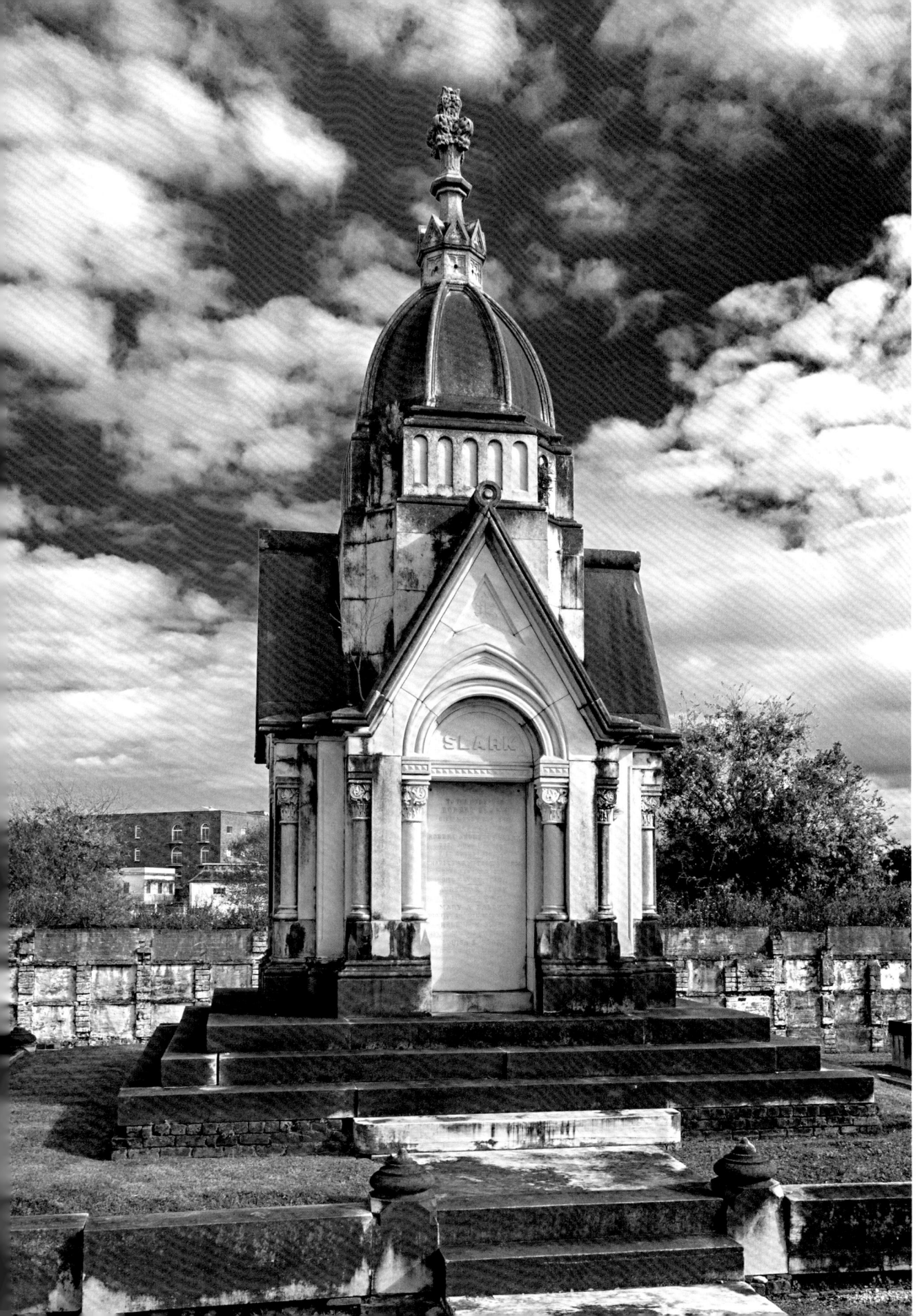

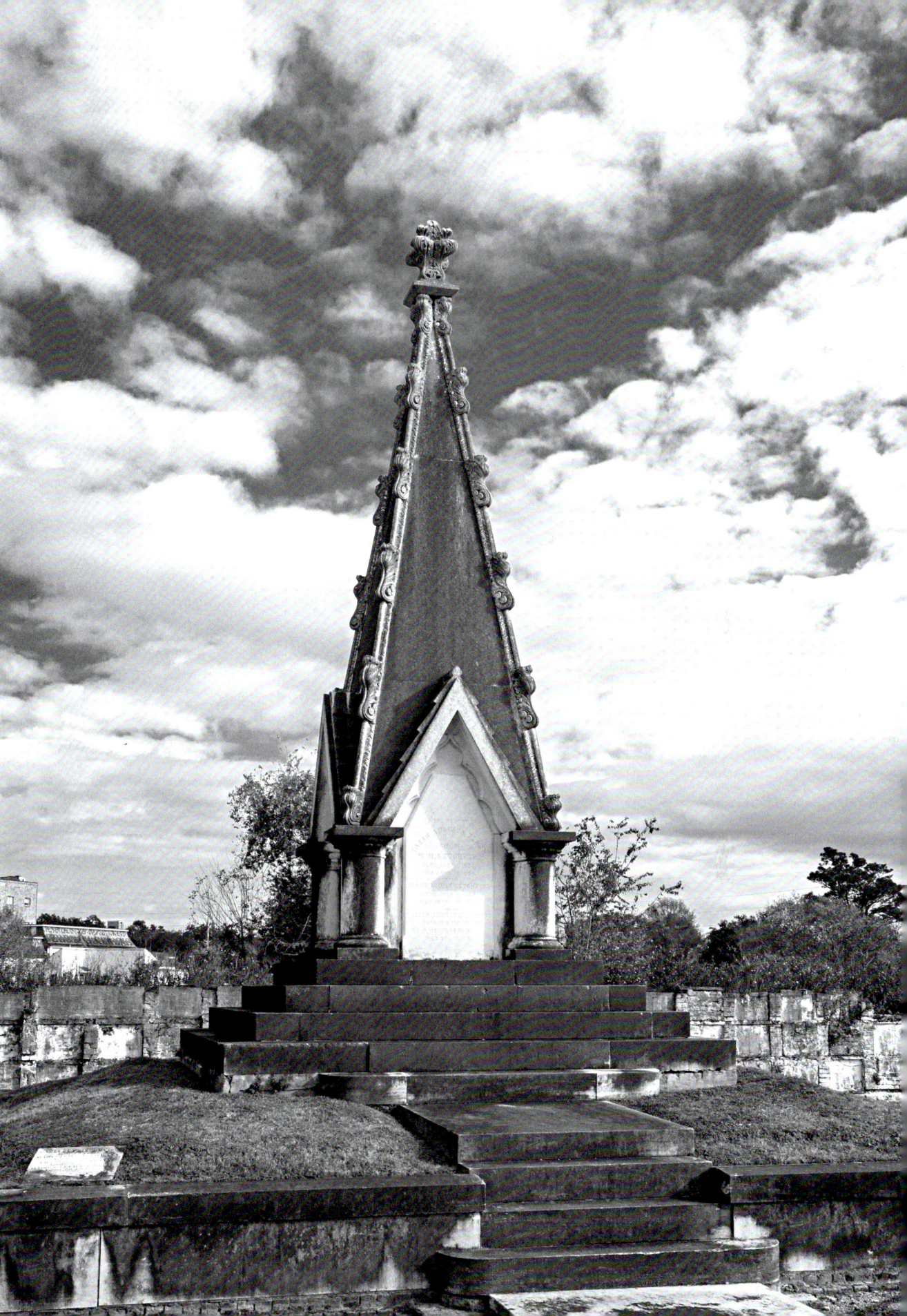

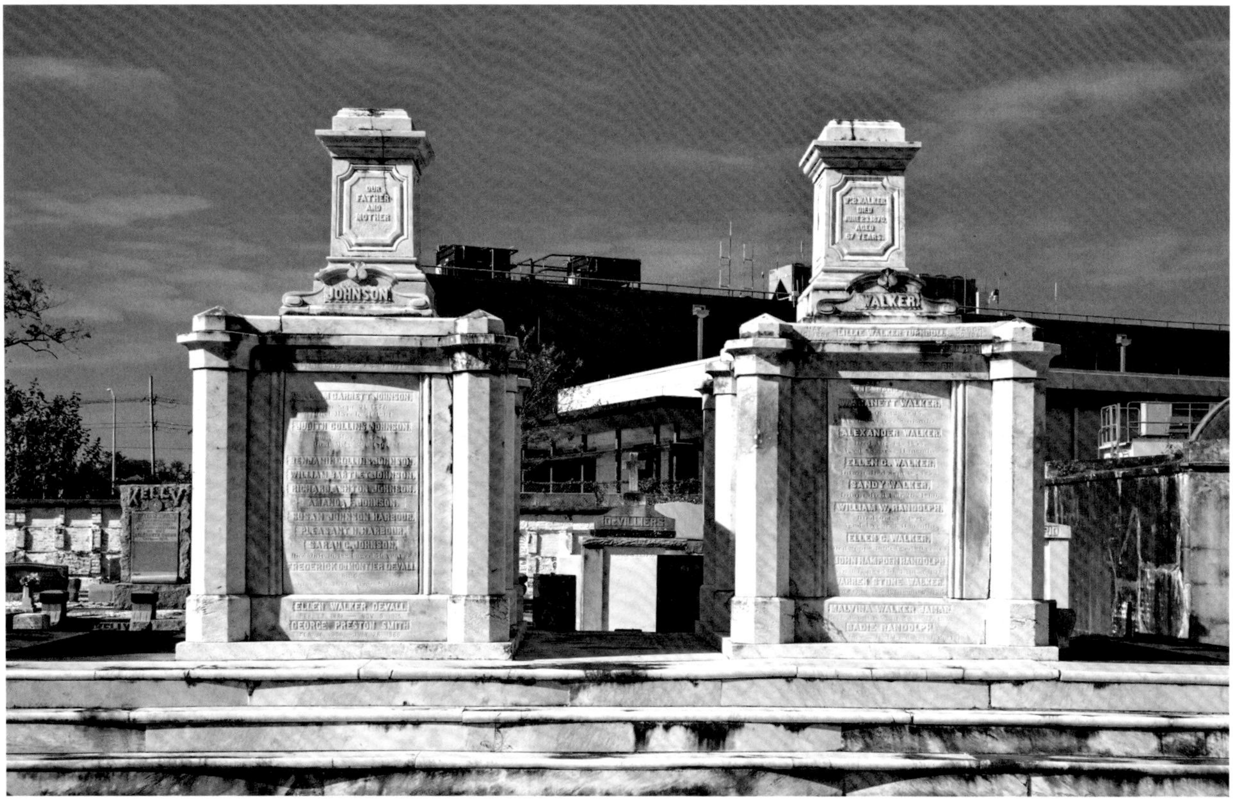

80 *Cypress Grove Cemetery*

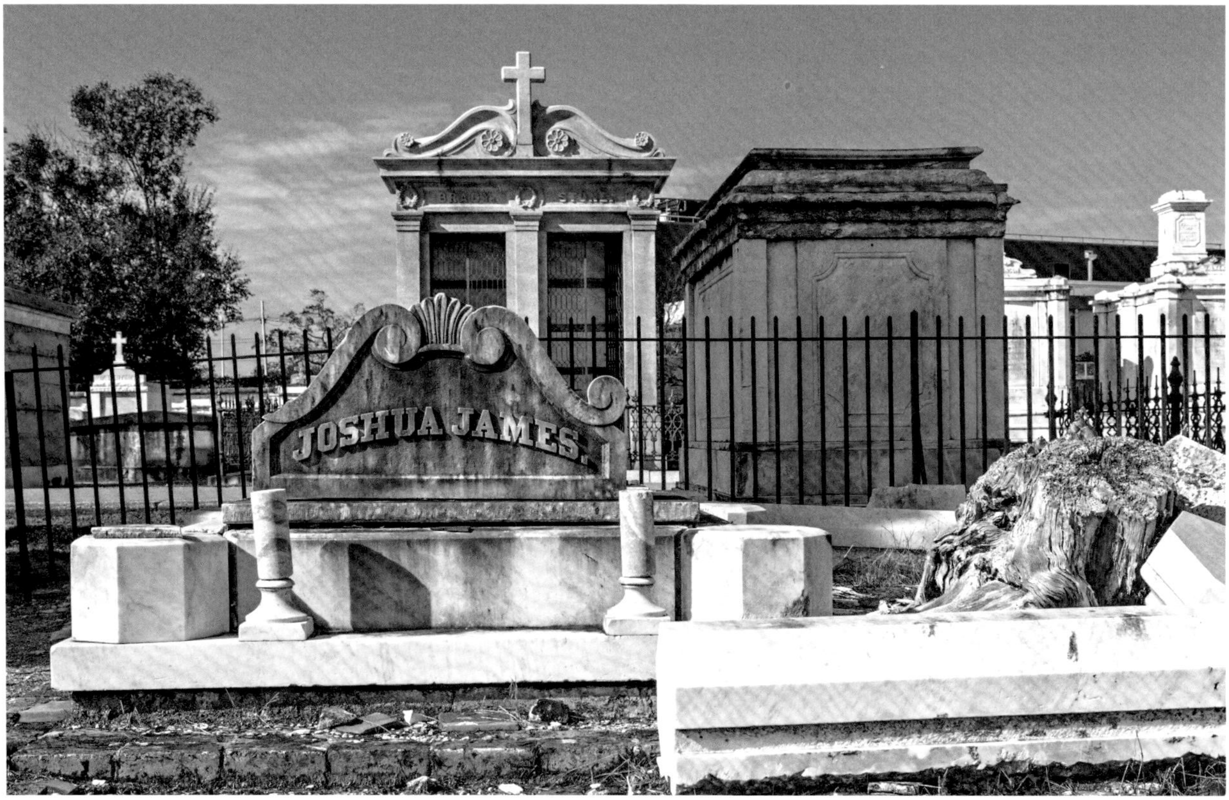

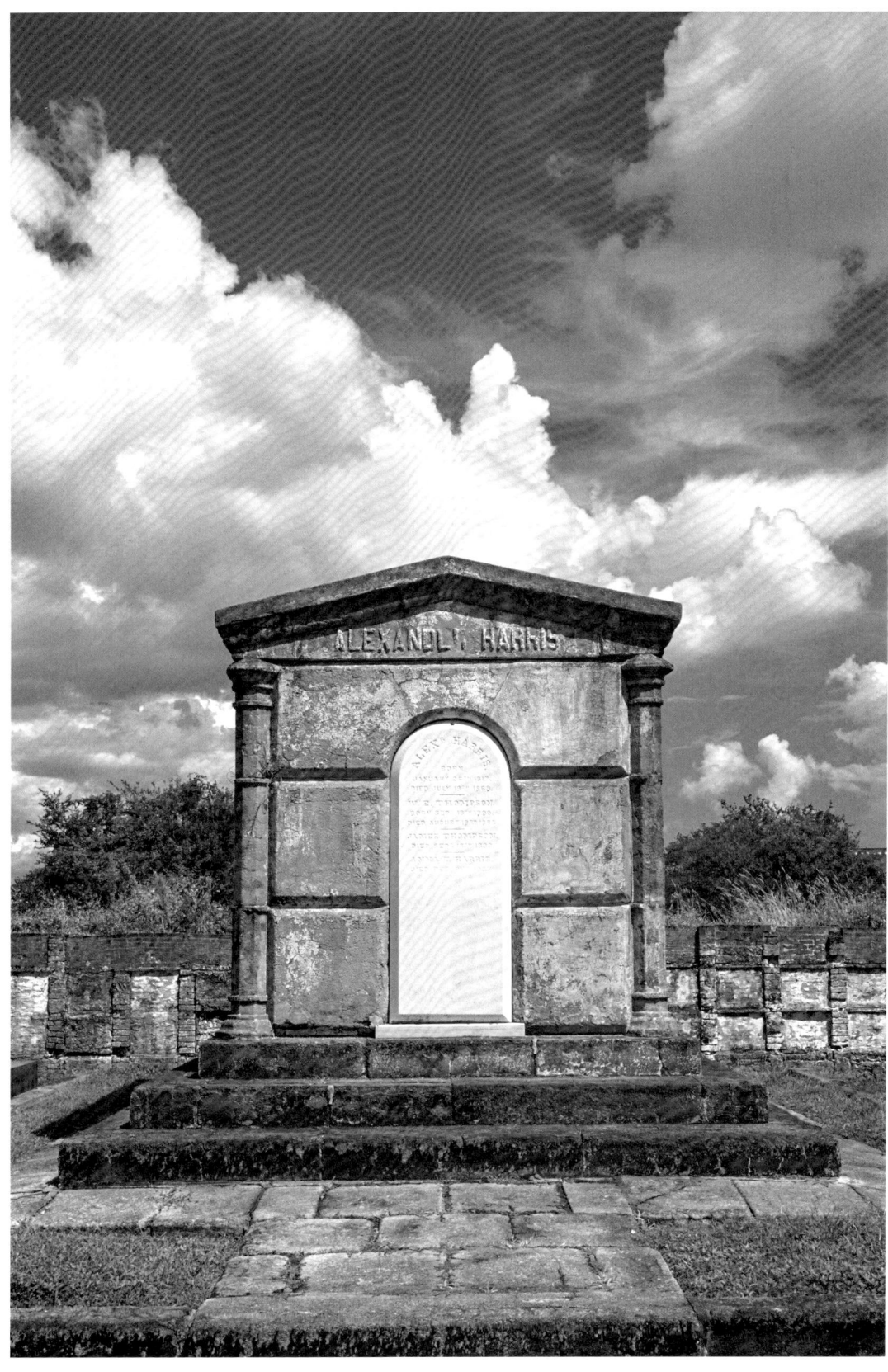

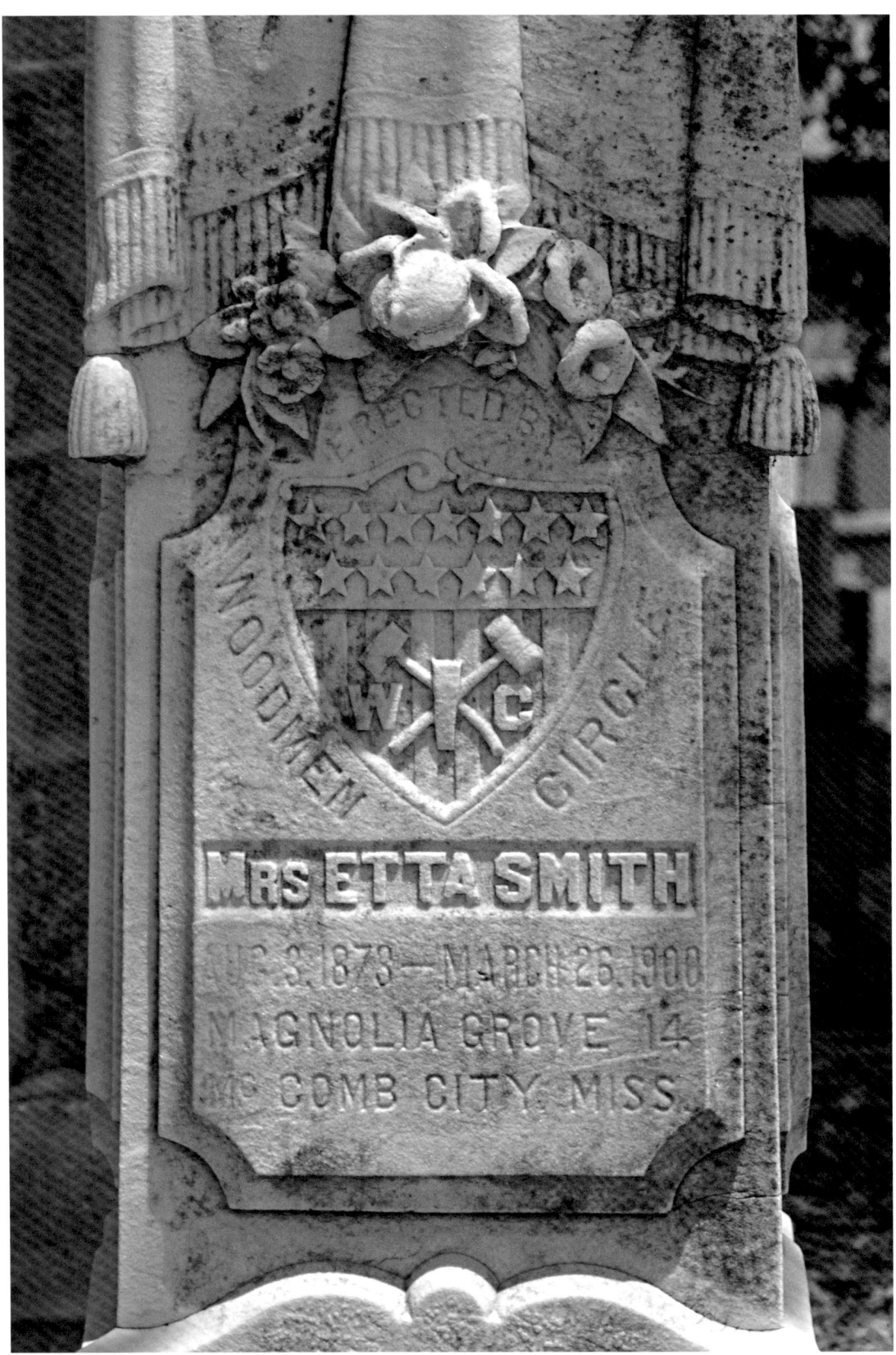

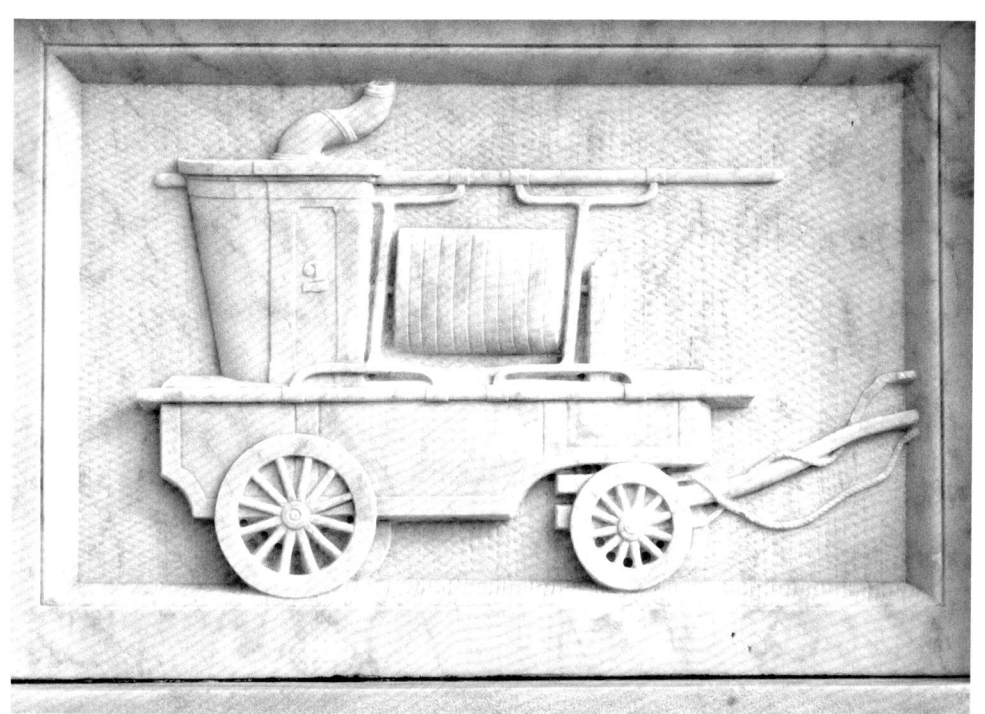

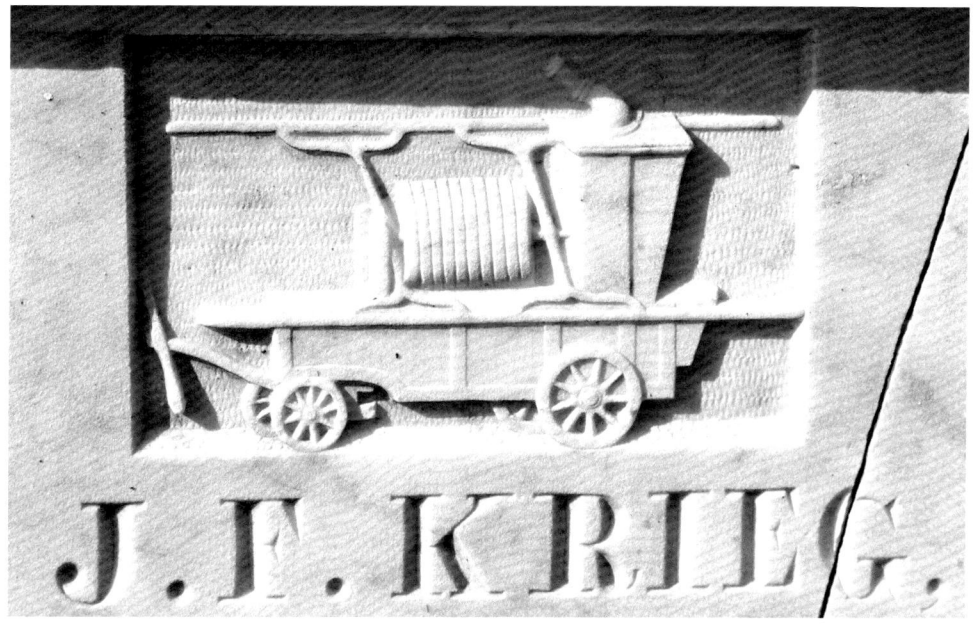

J. F. KRIEG.

Dispersed of Judah Cemetery

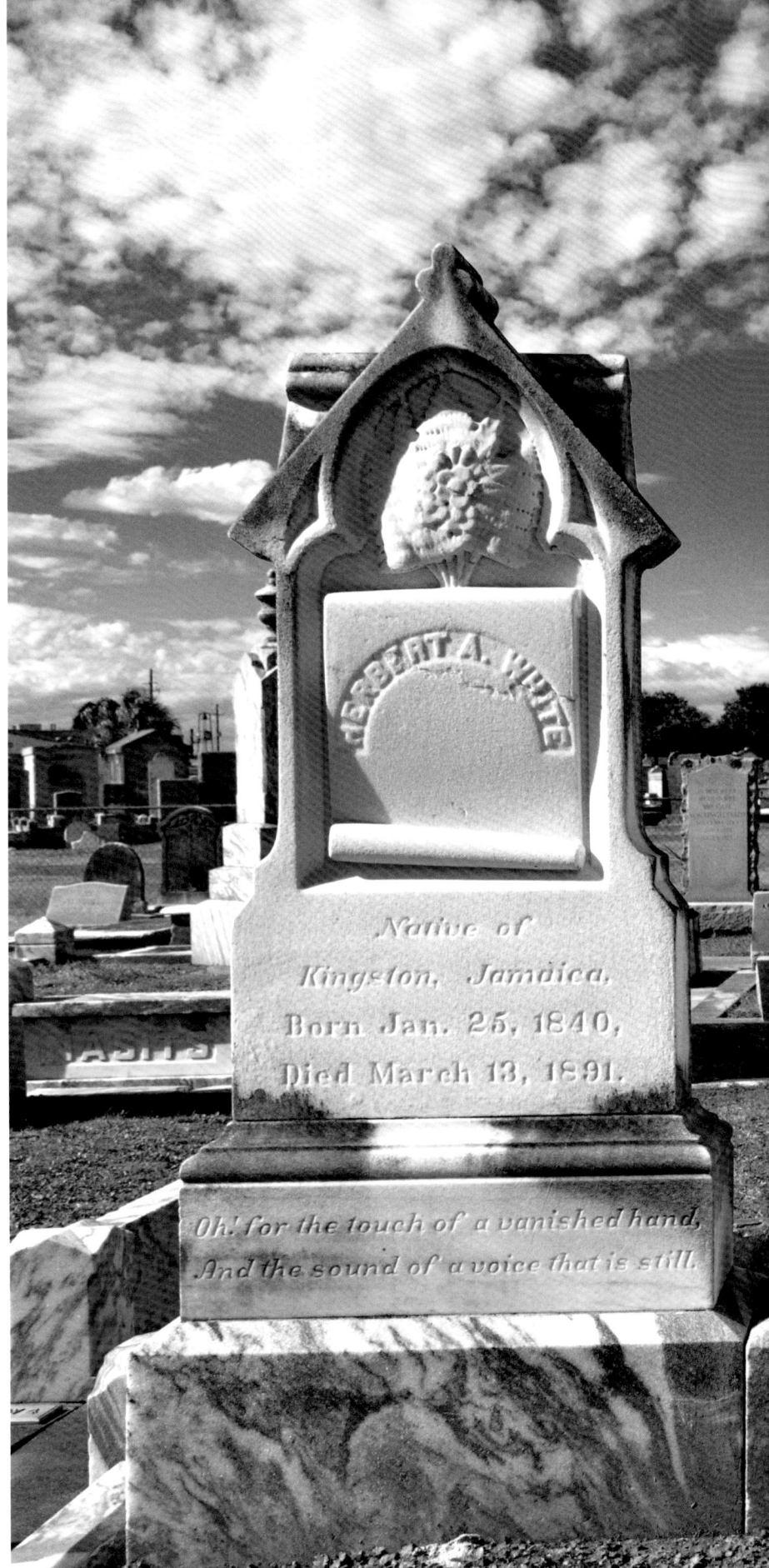

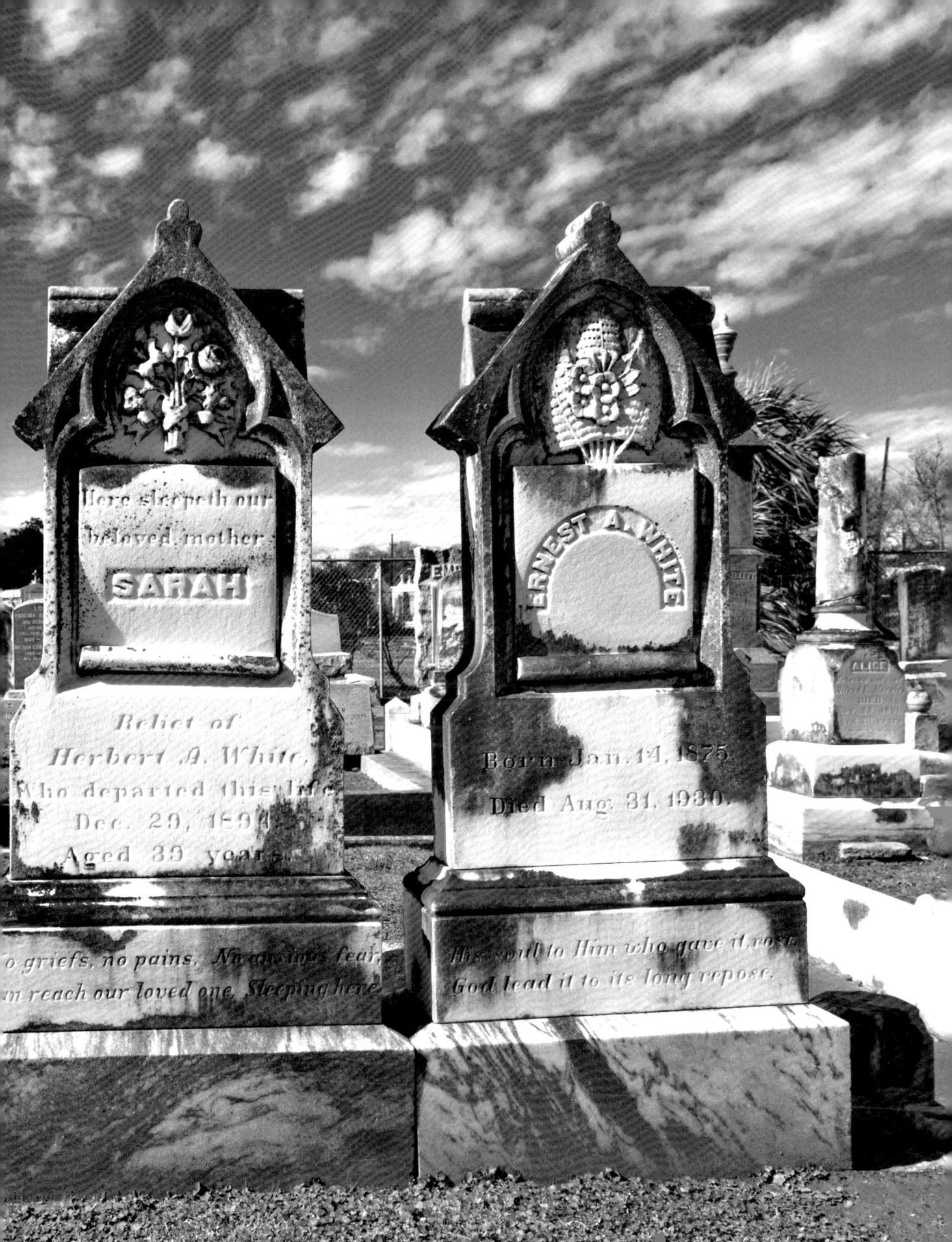

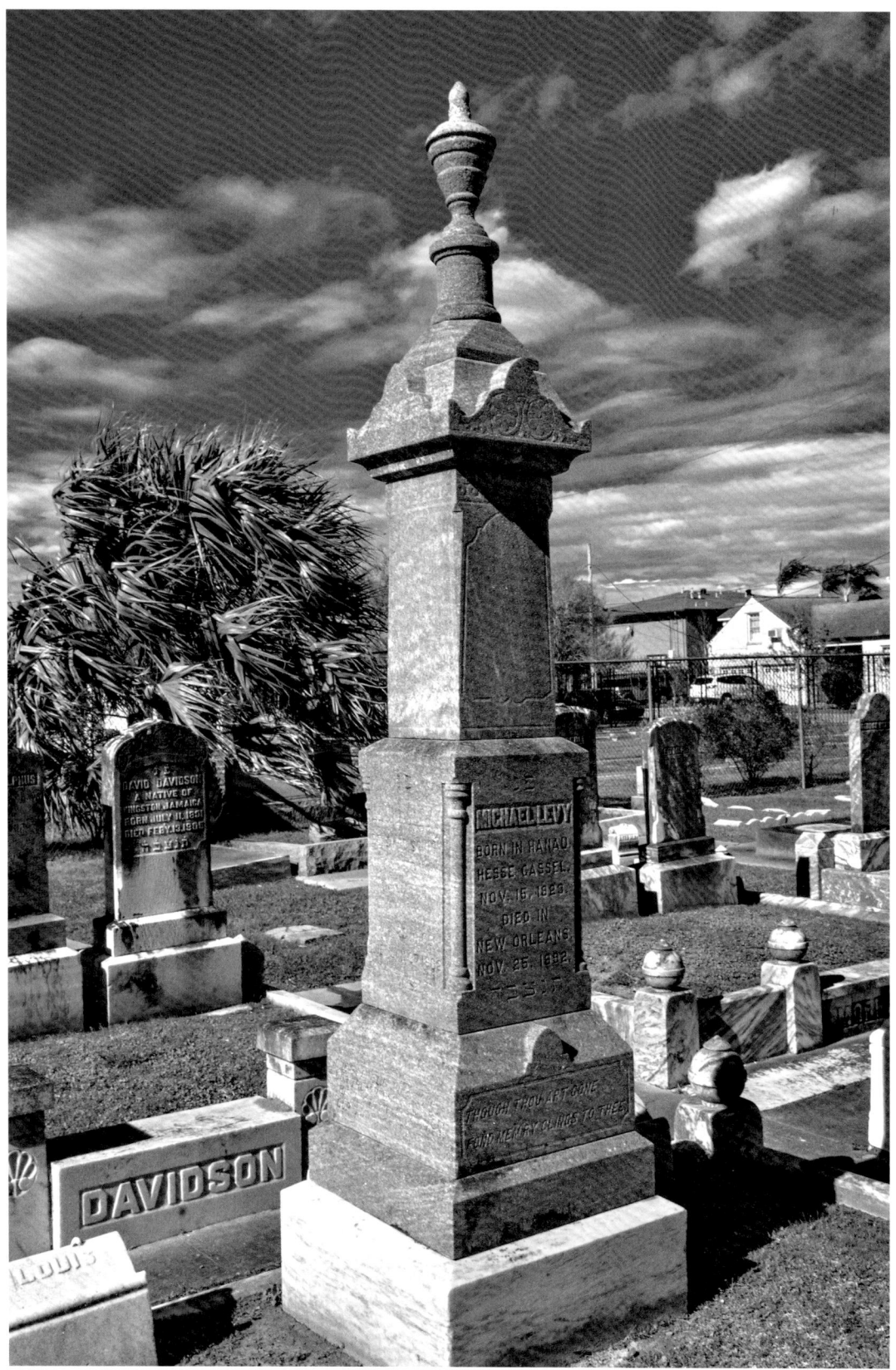

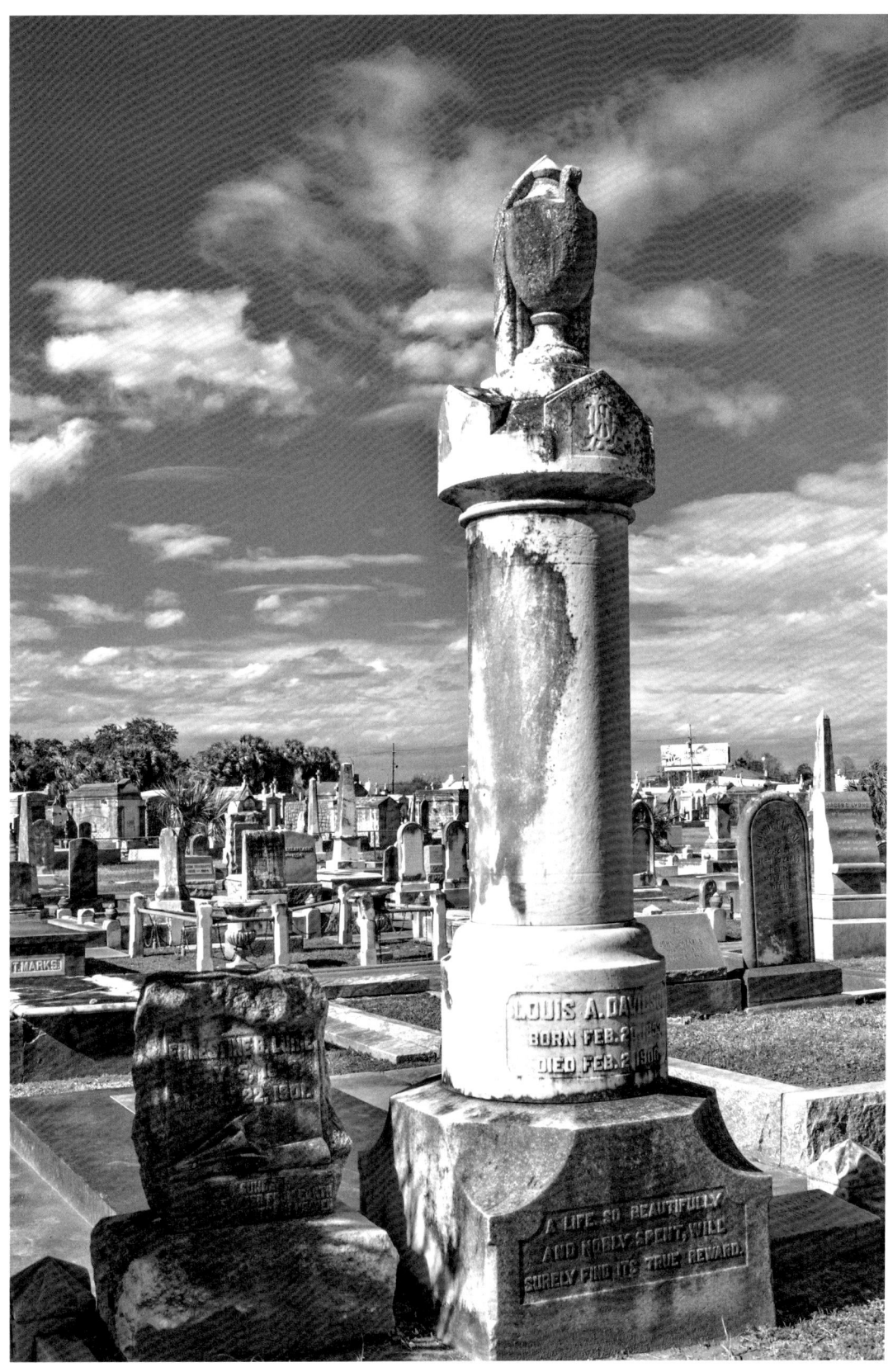

Dispersed of Judah Cemetery 87

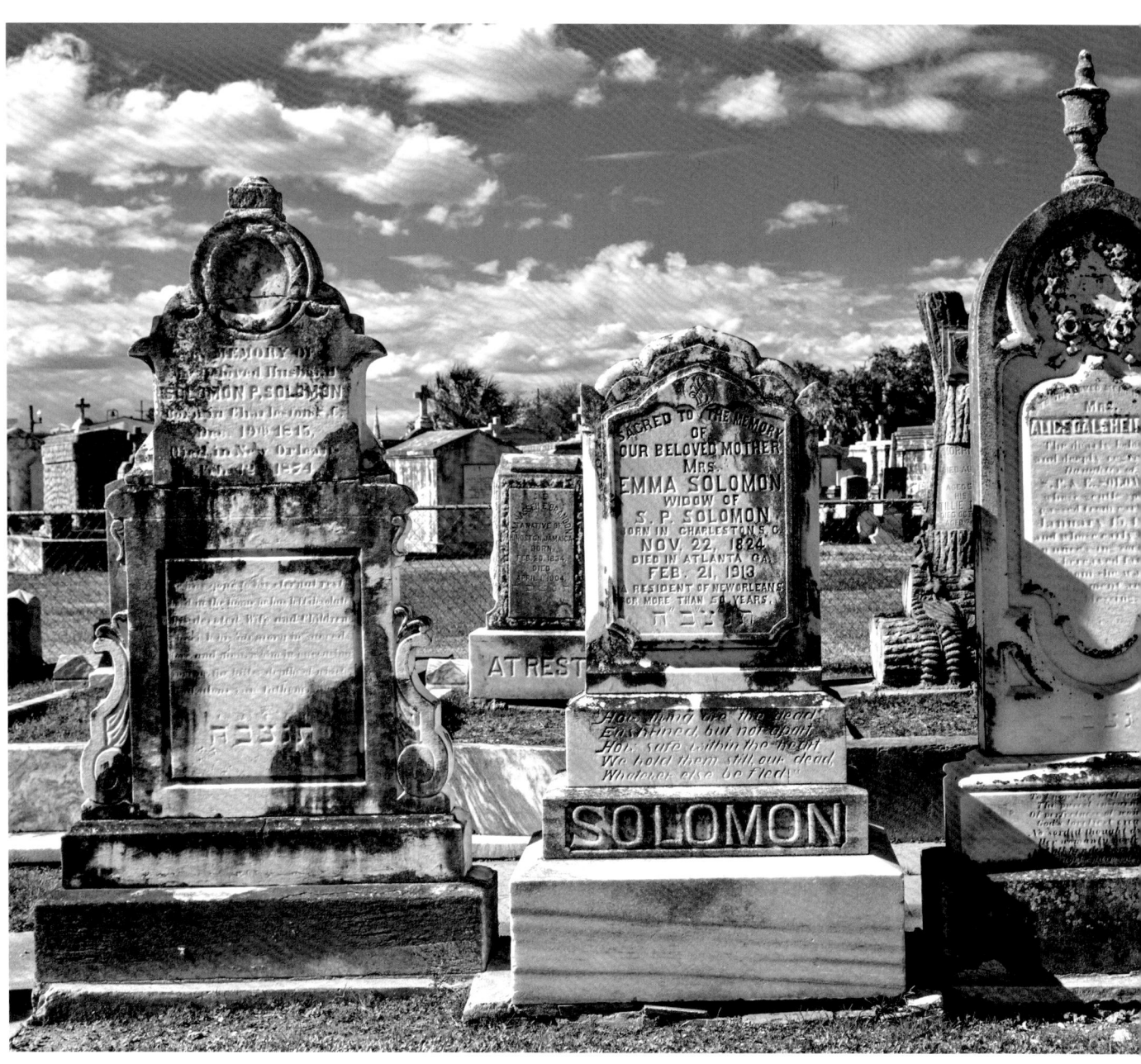

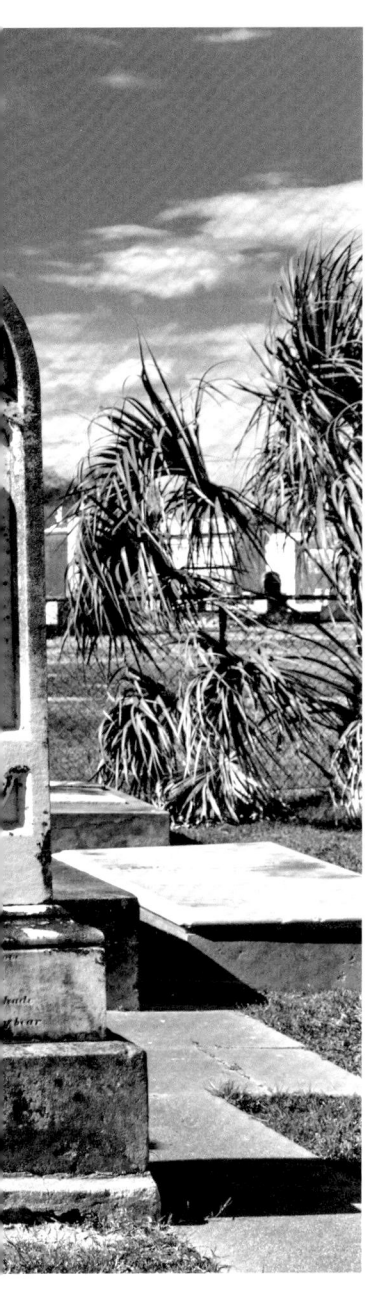
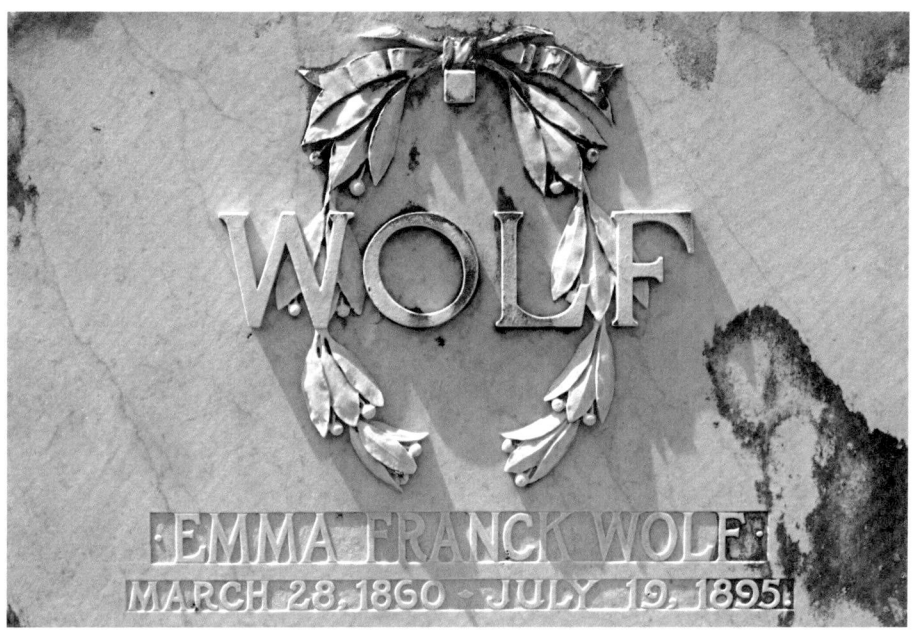
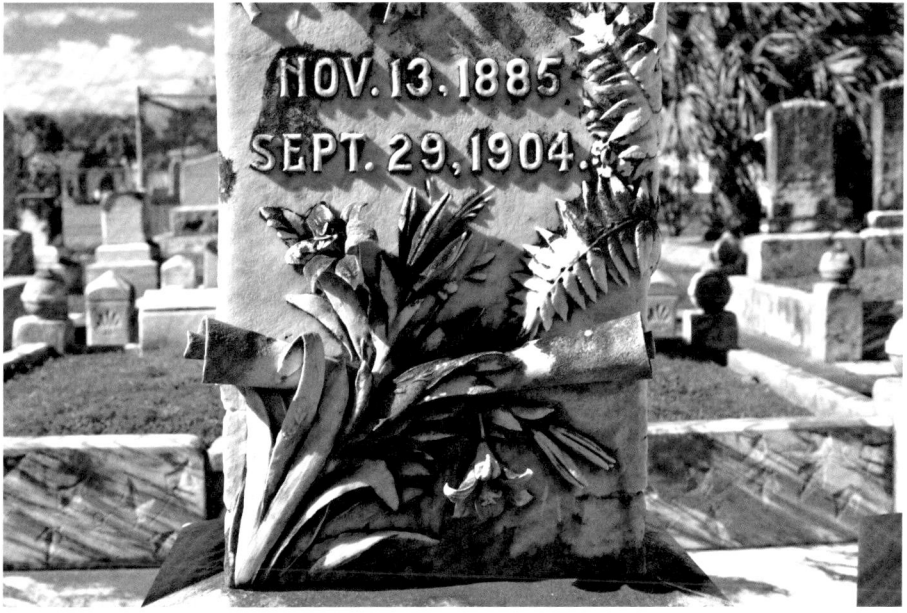

Dispersed of Judah Cemetery   89

Greenwood Cemetery

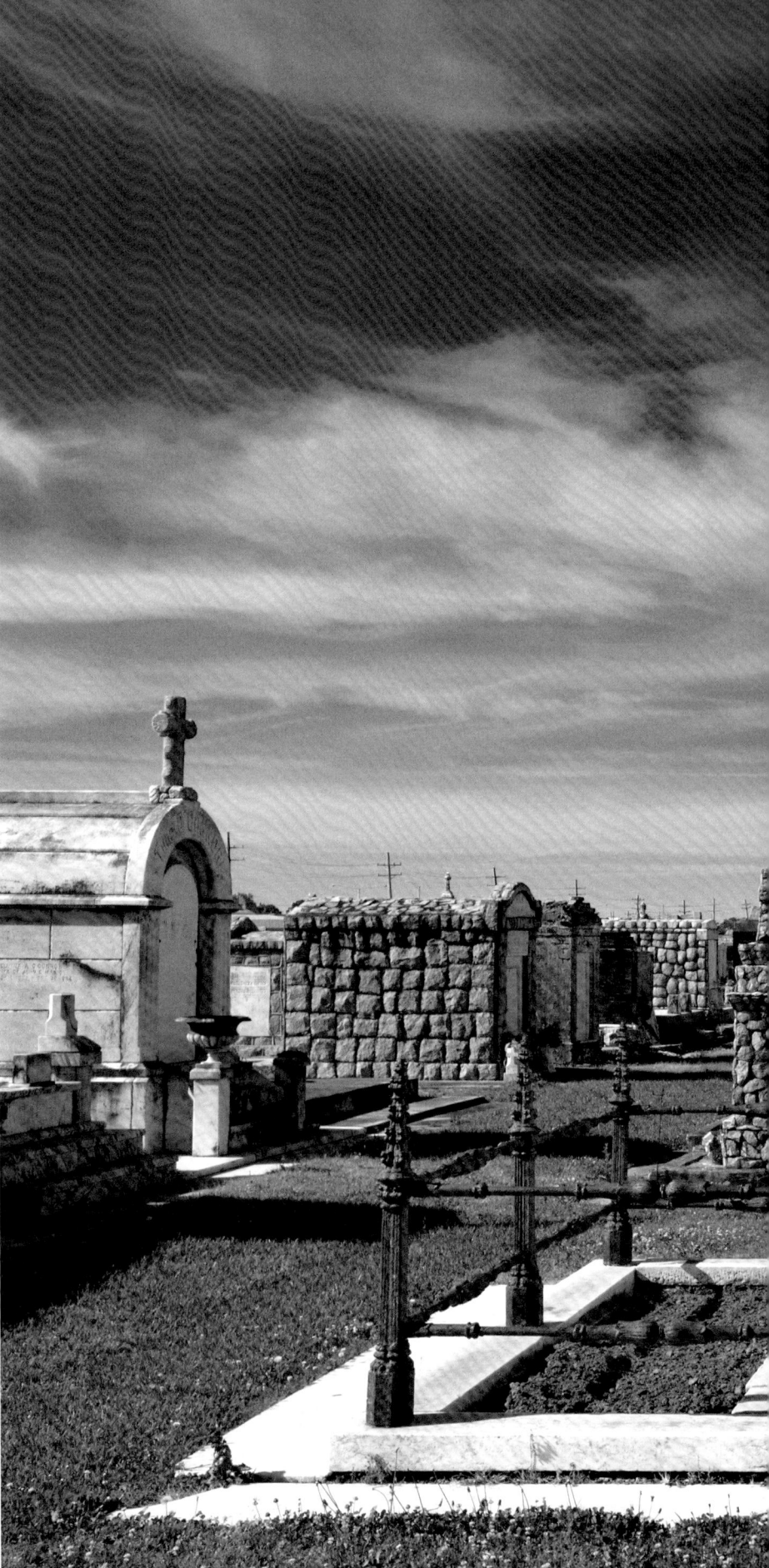

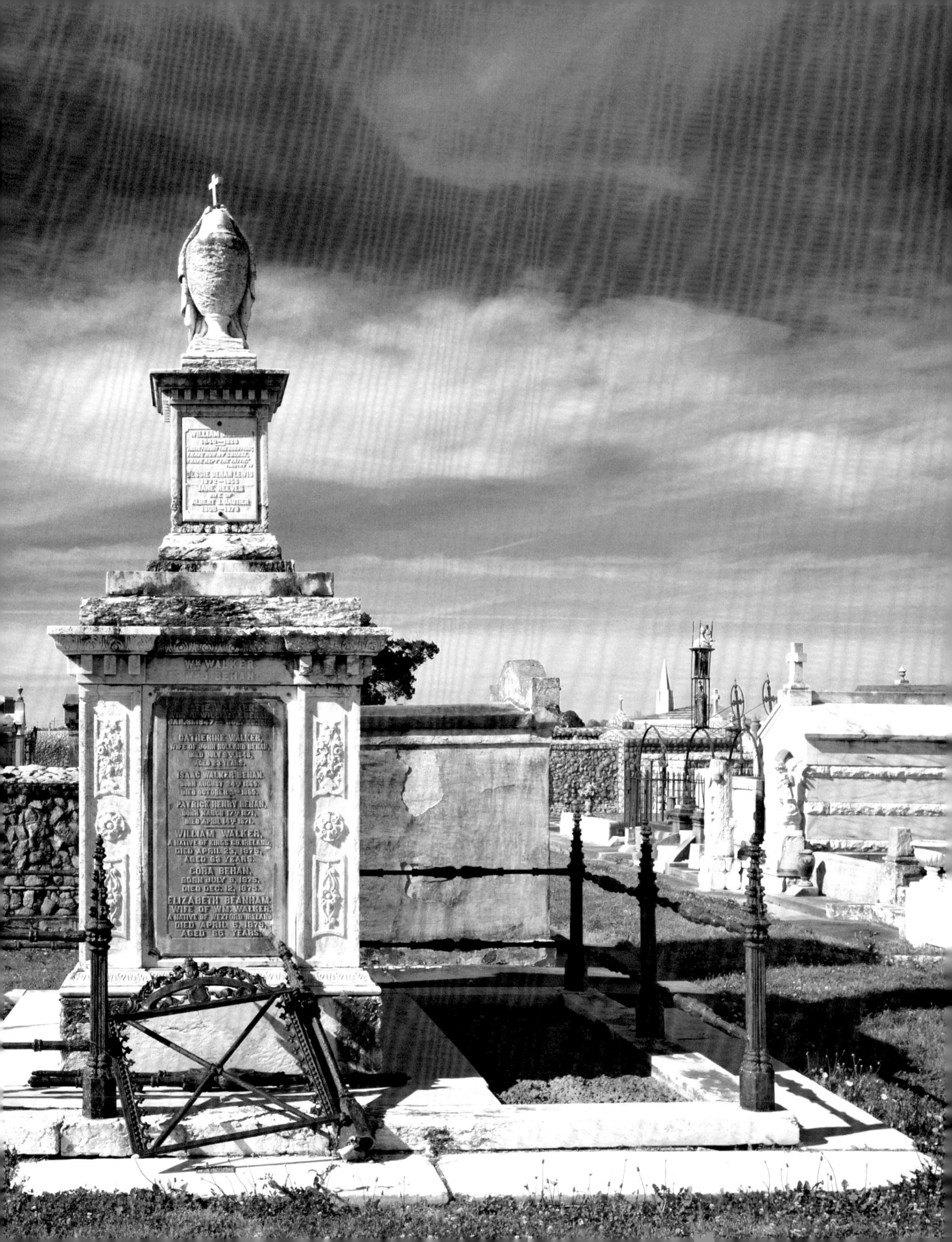

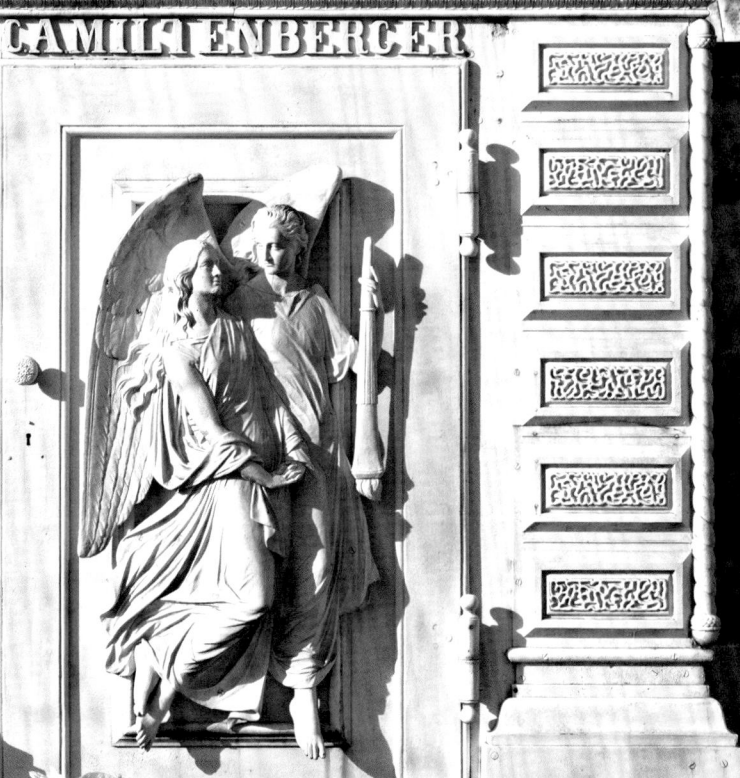

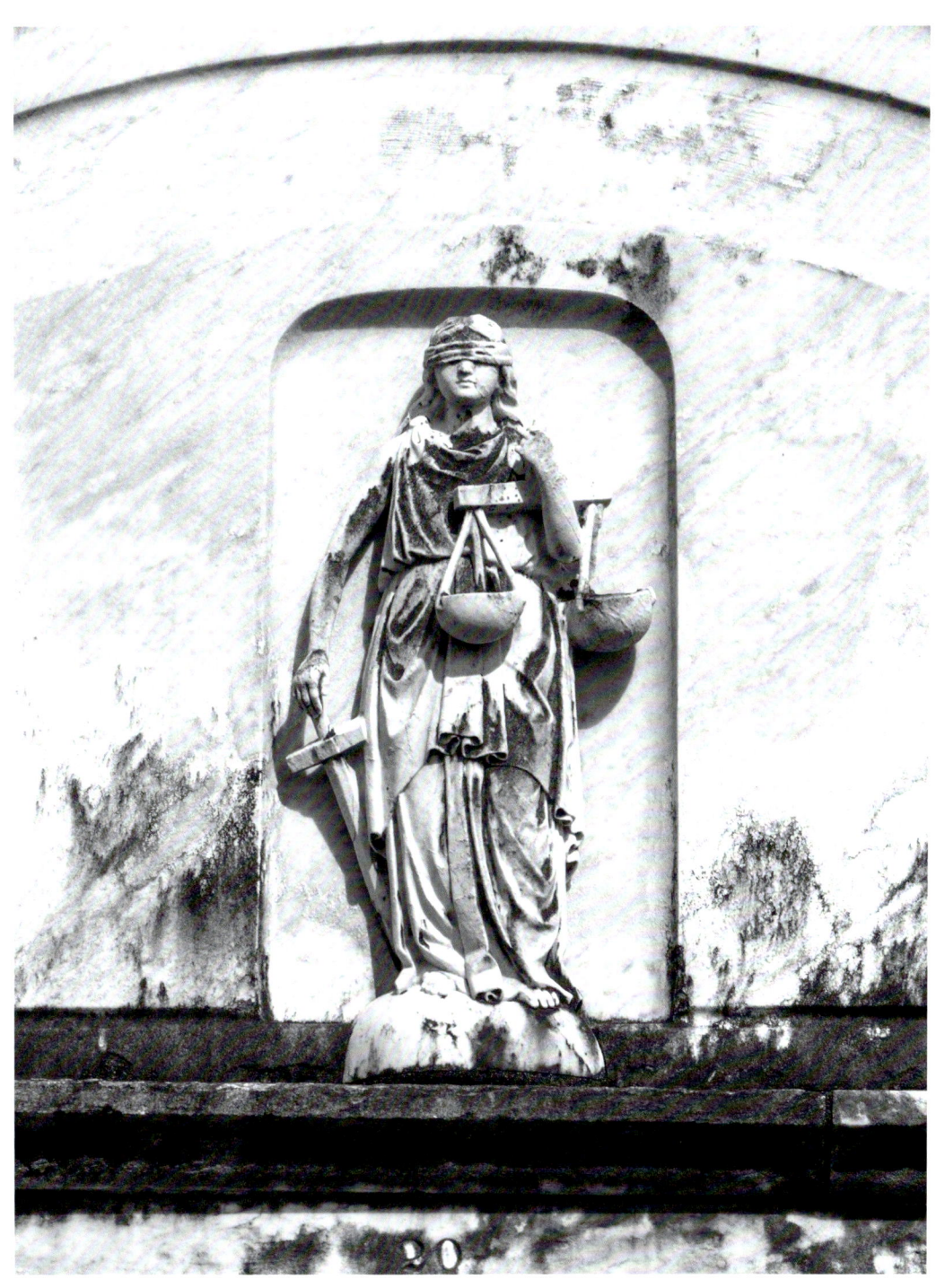

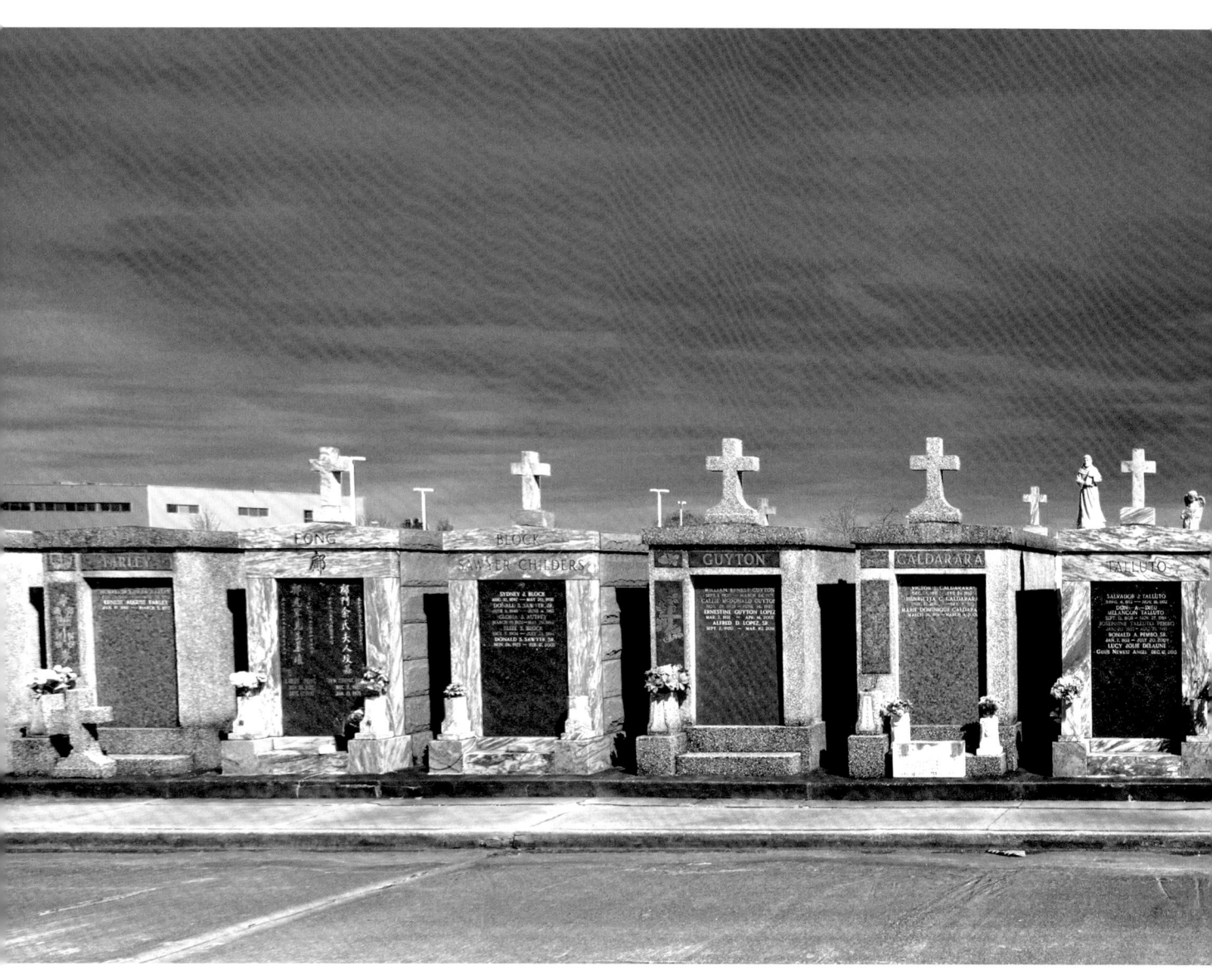

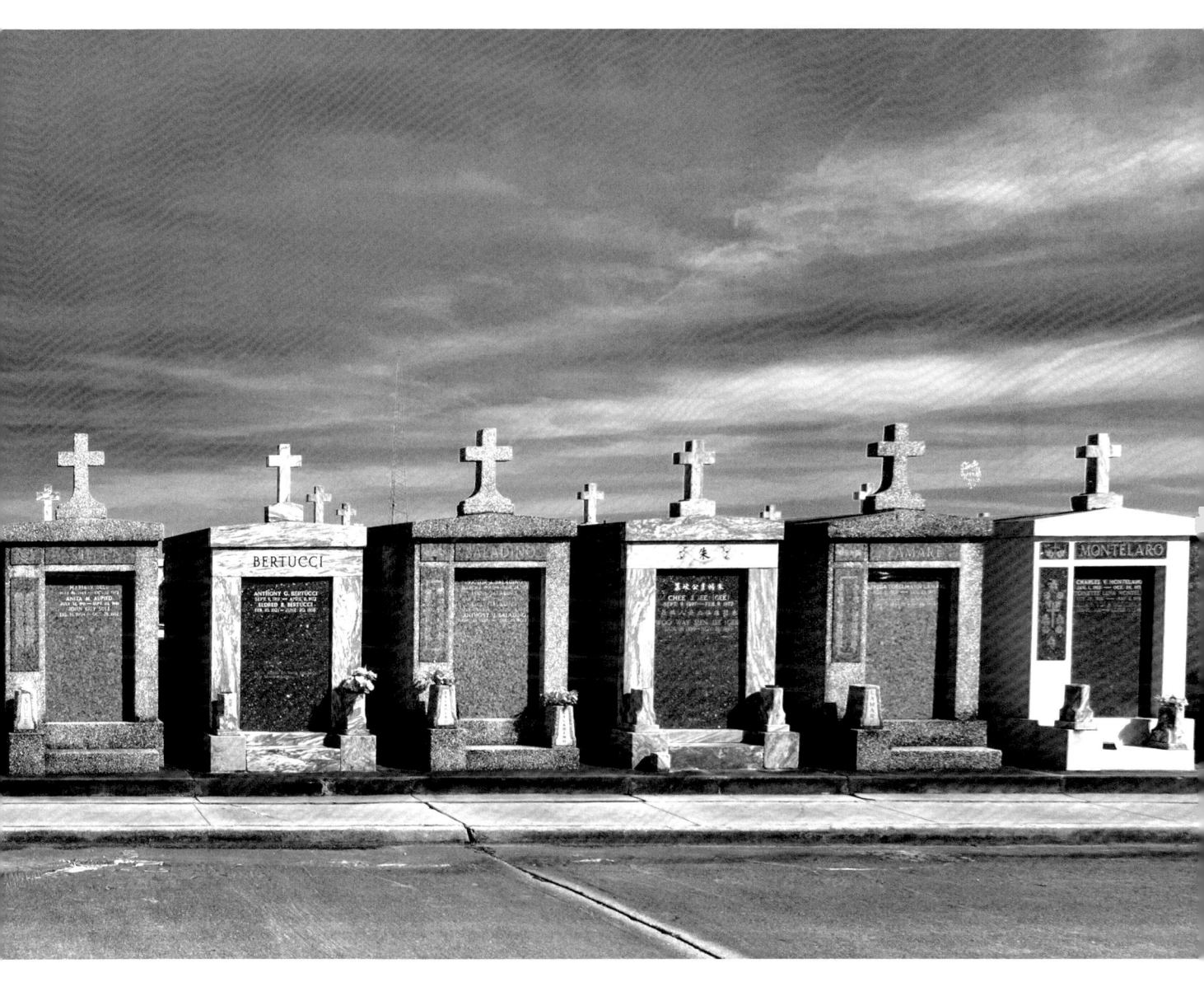

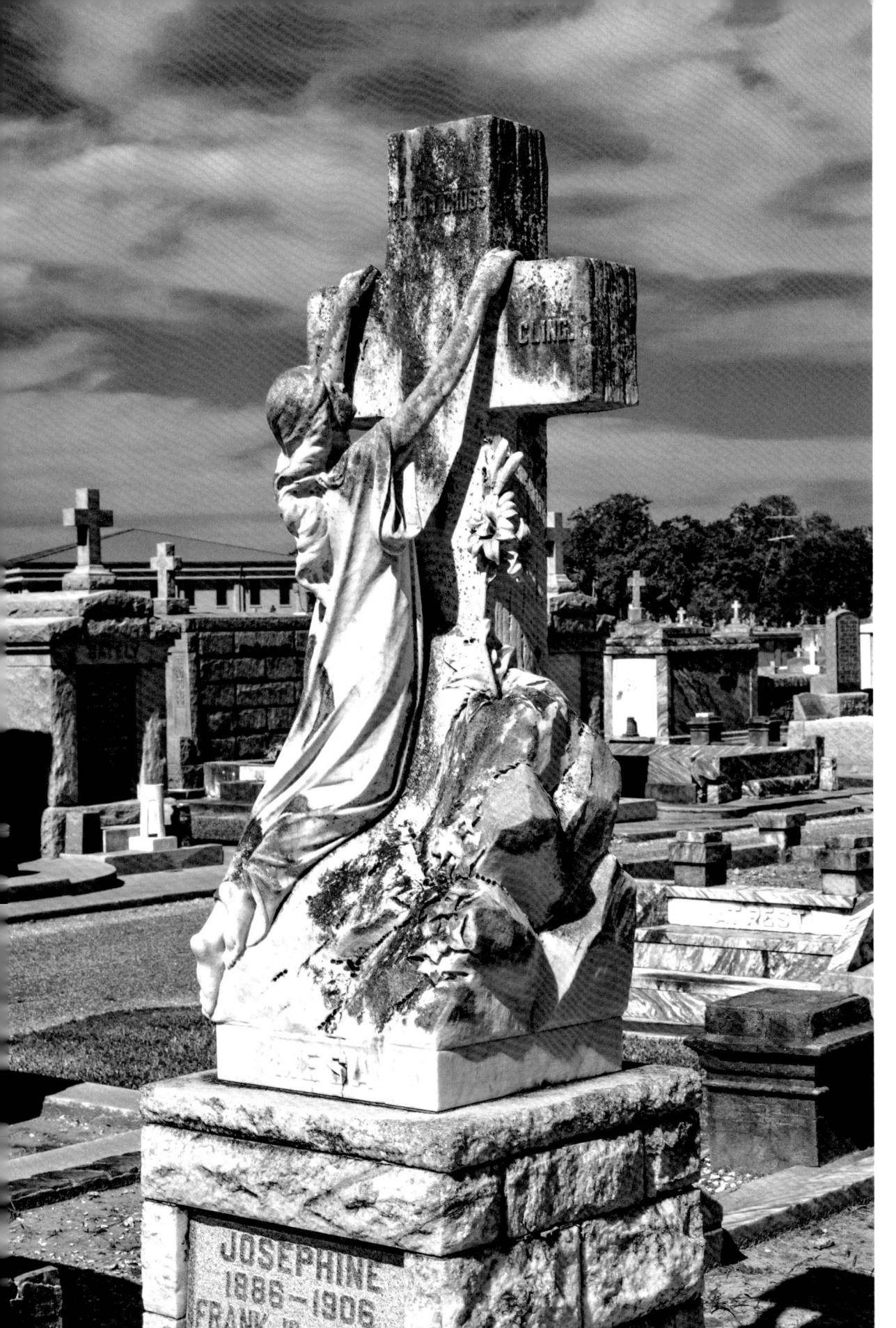

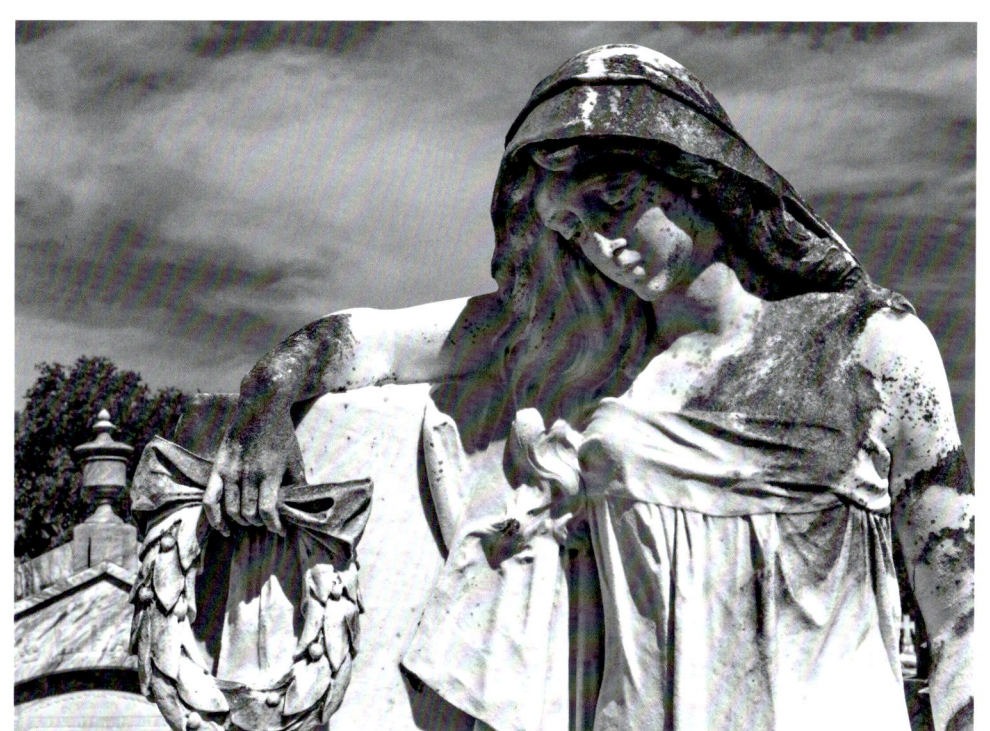

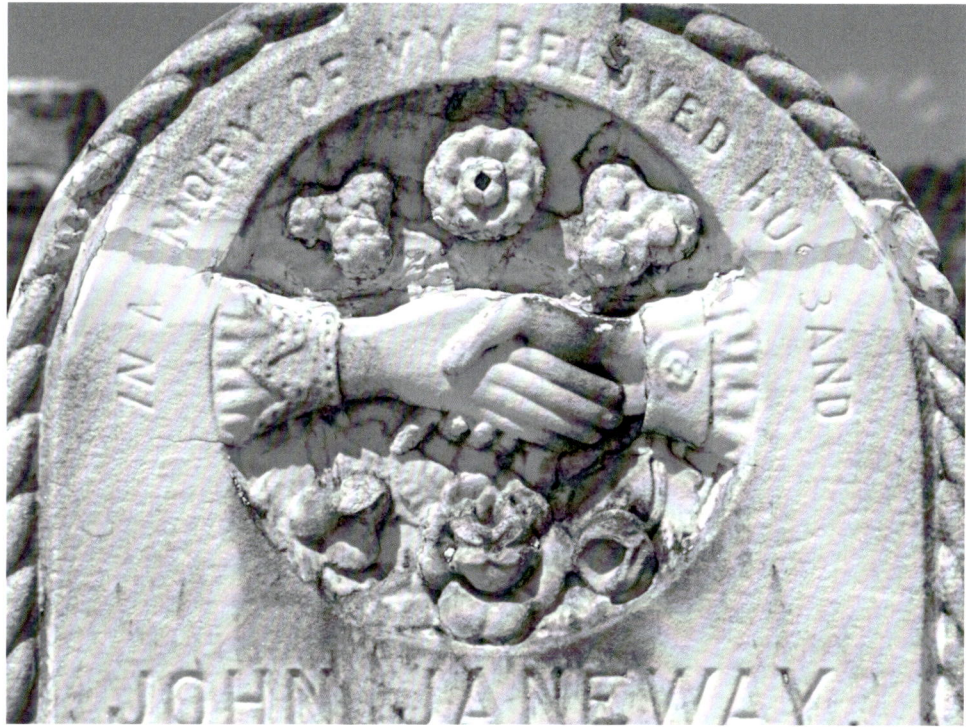

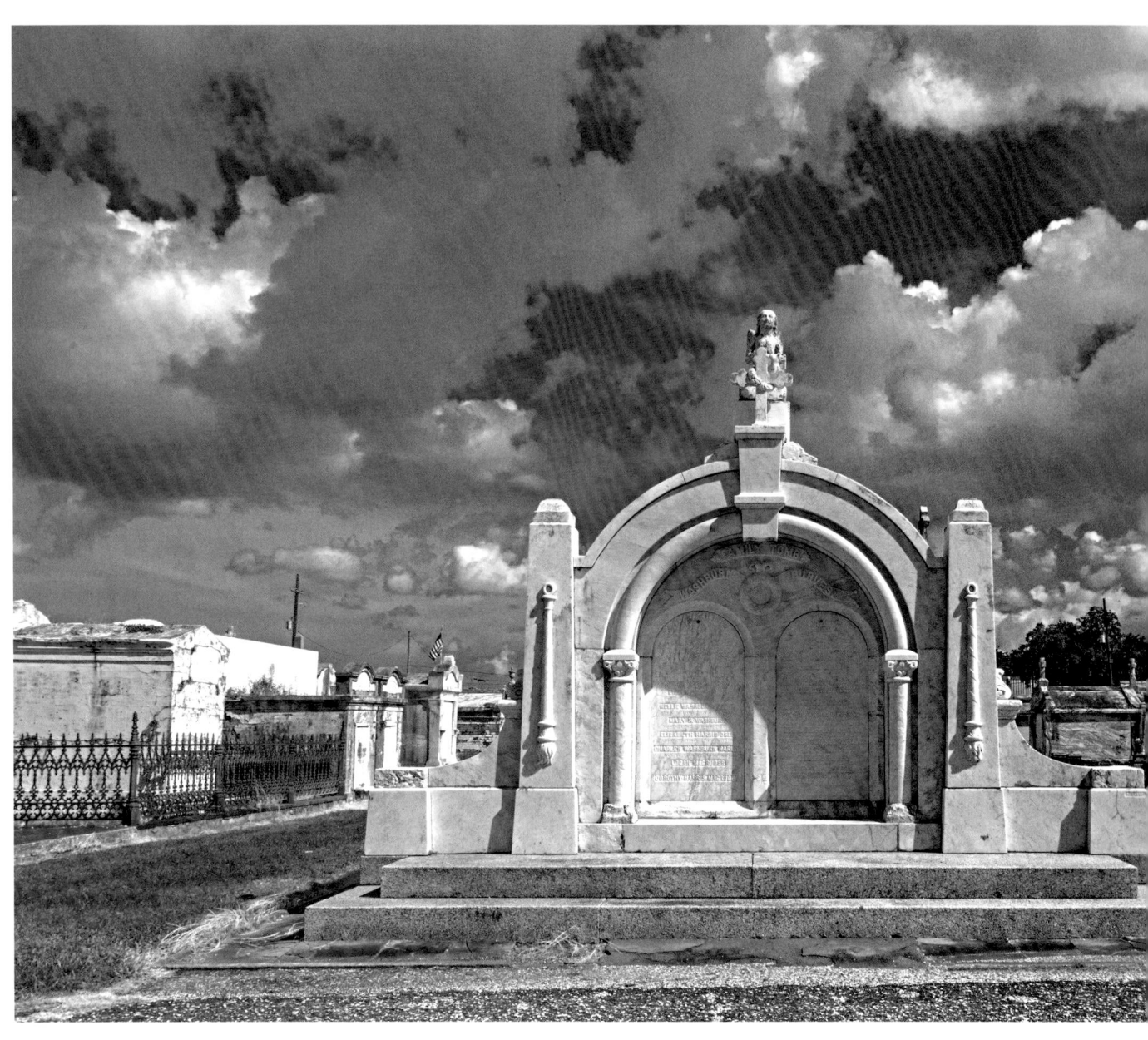

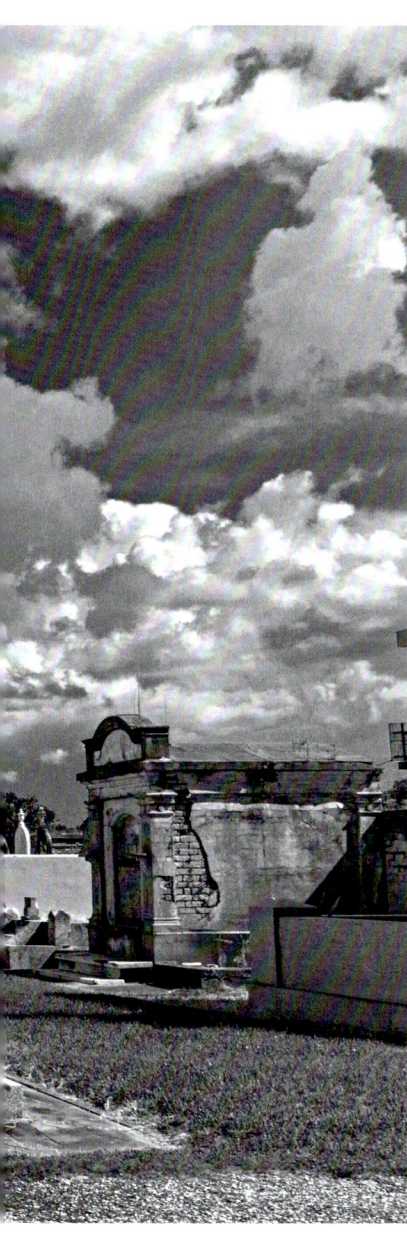

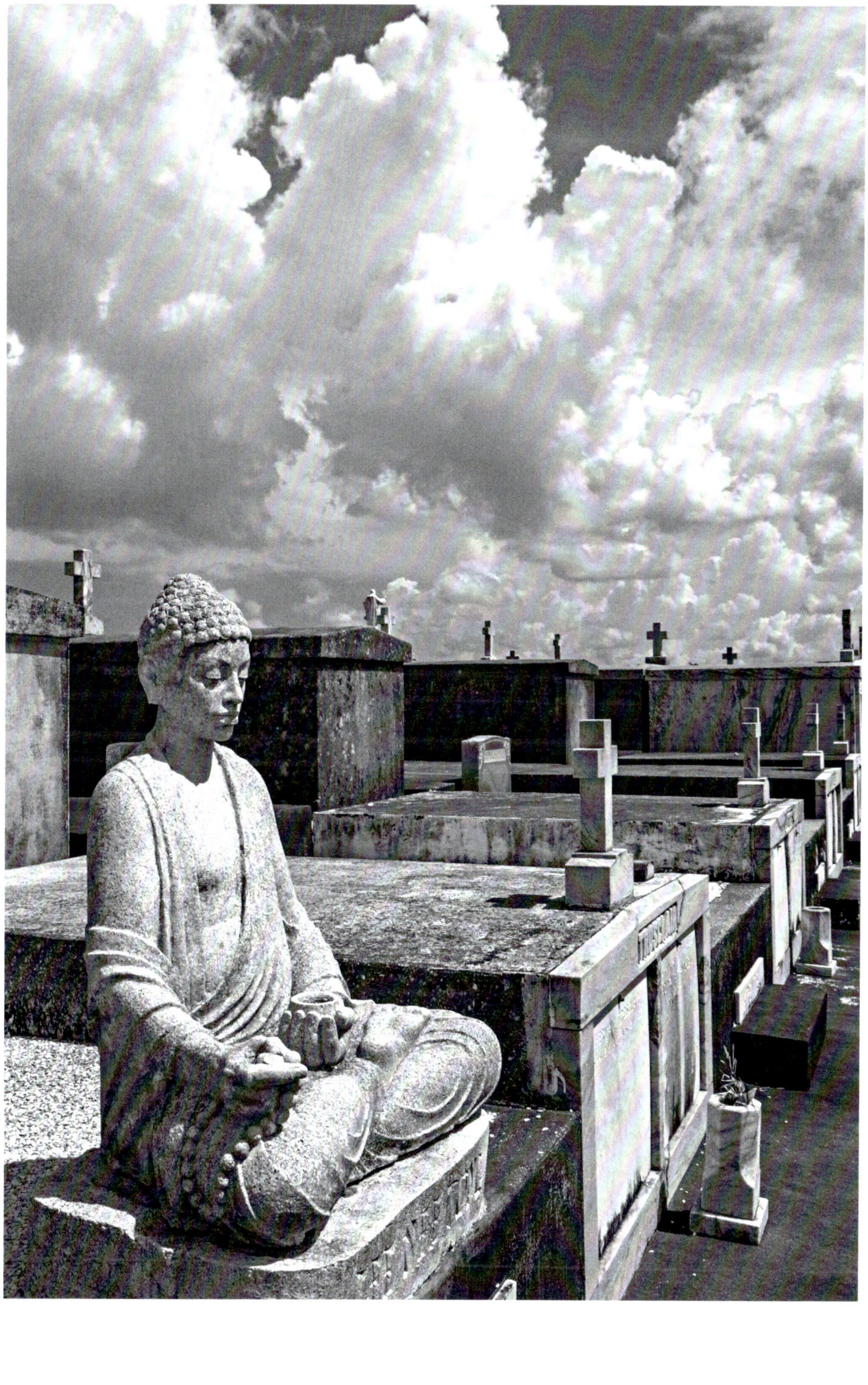

Greenwood Cemetery

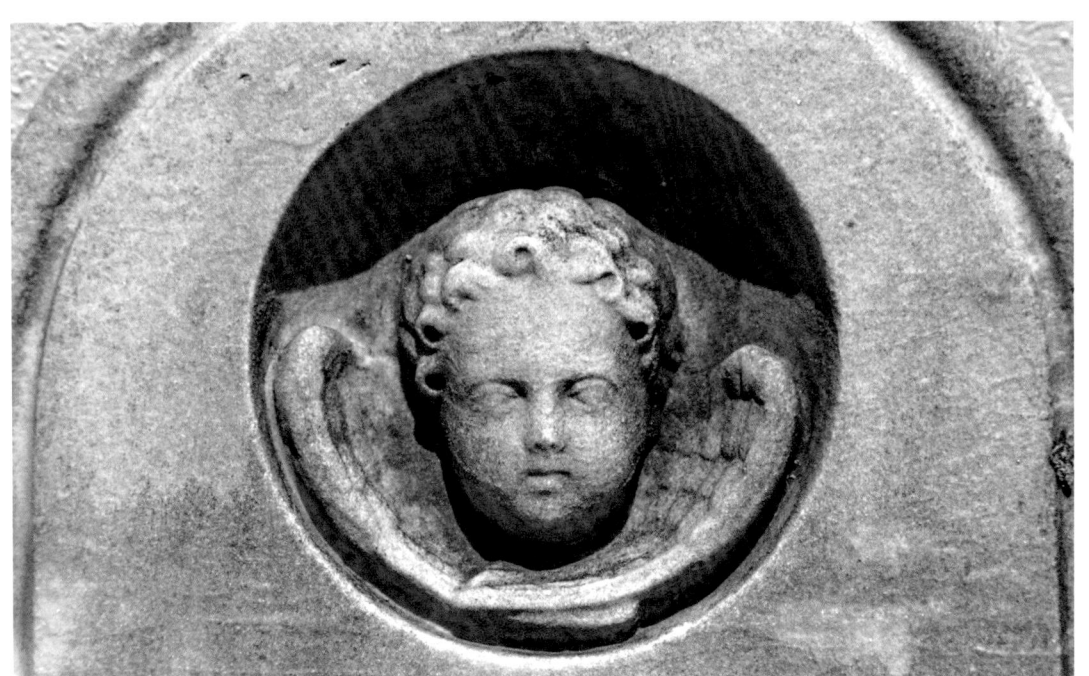

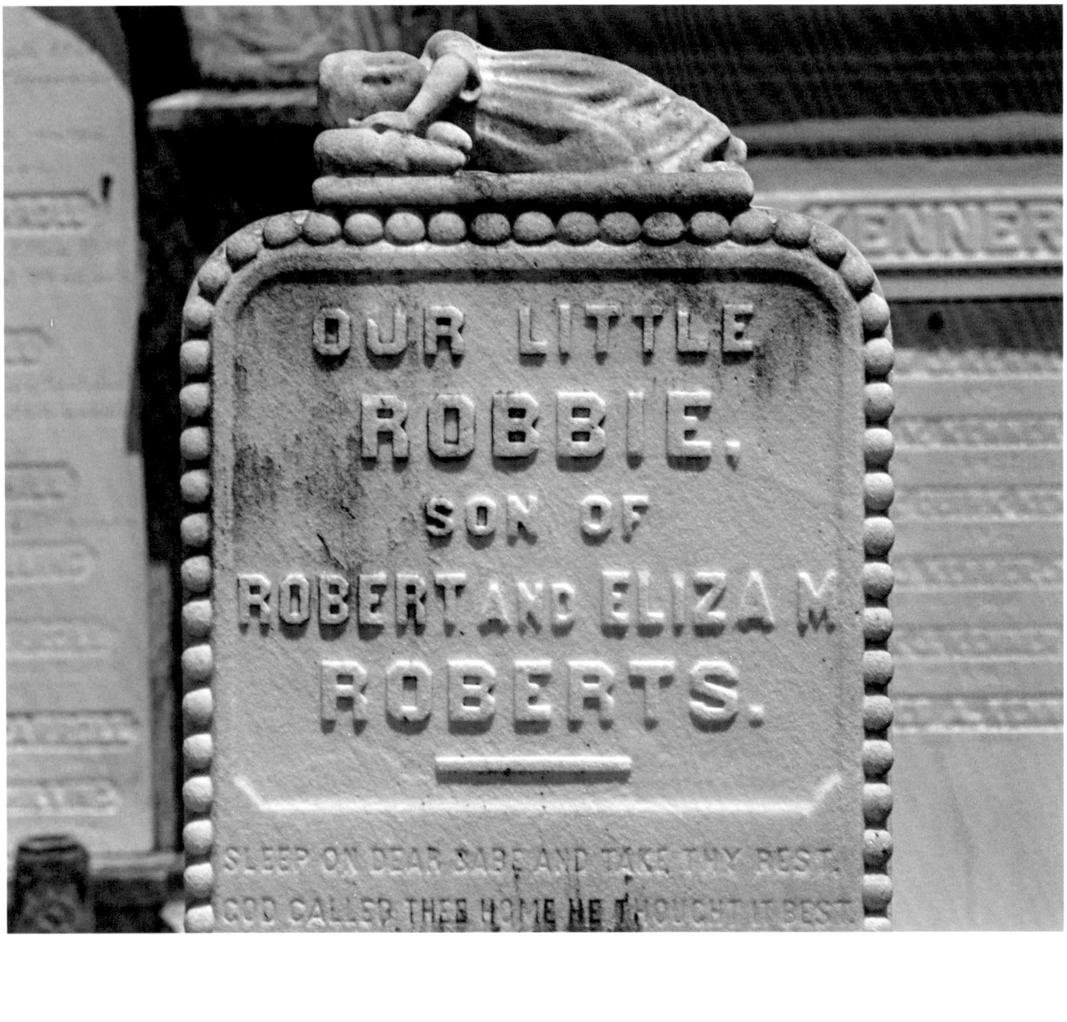

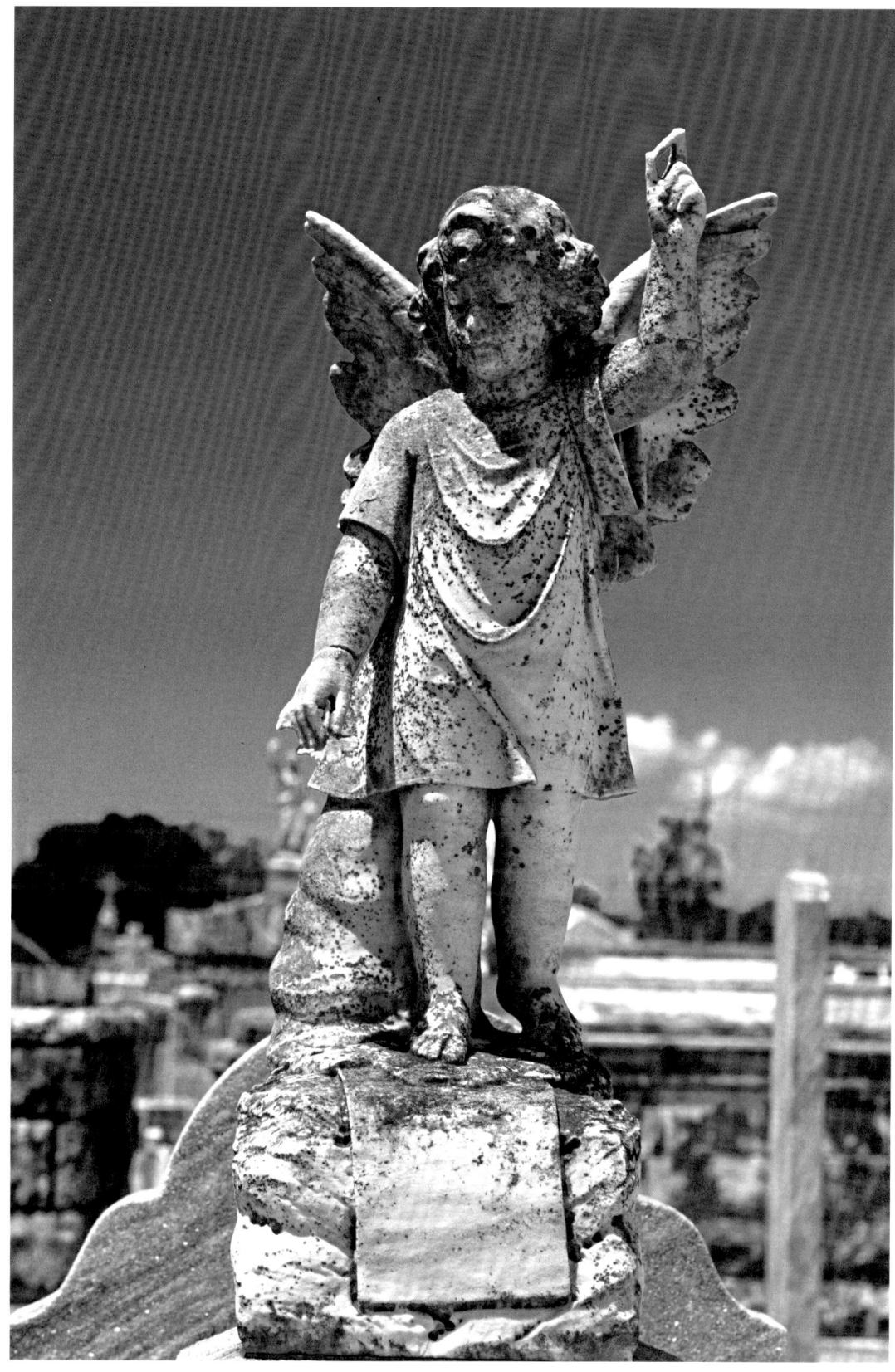

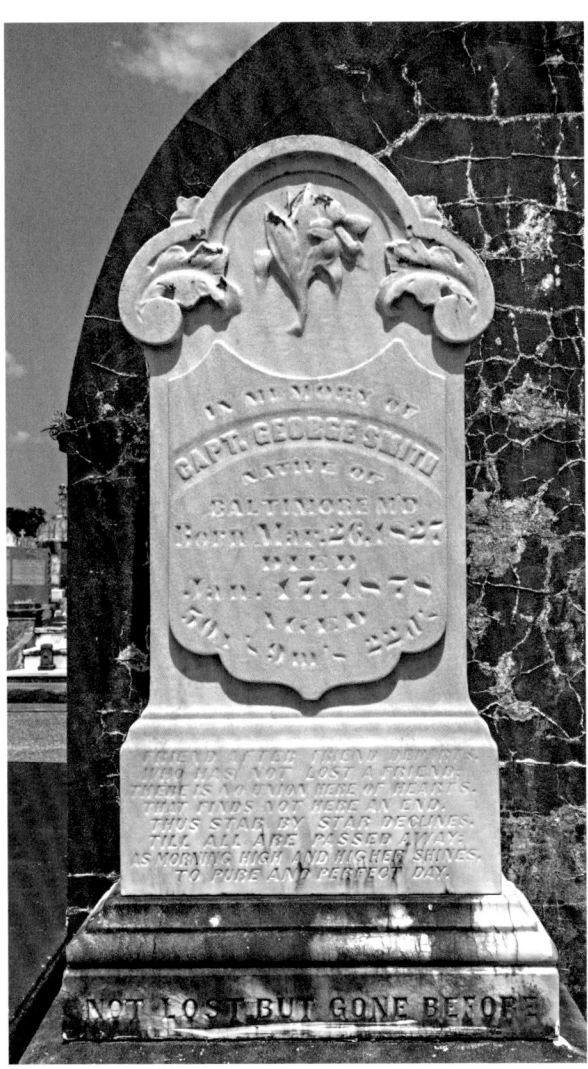
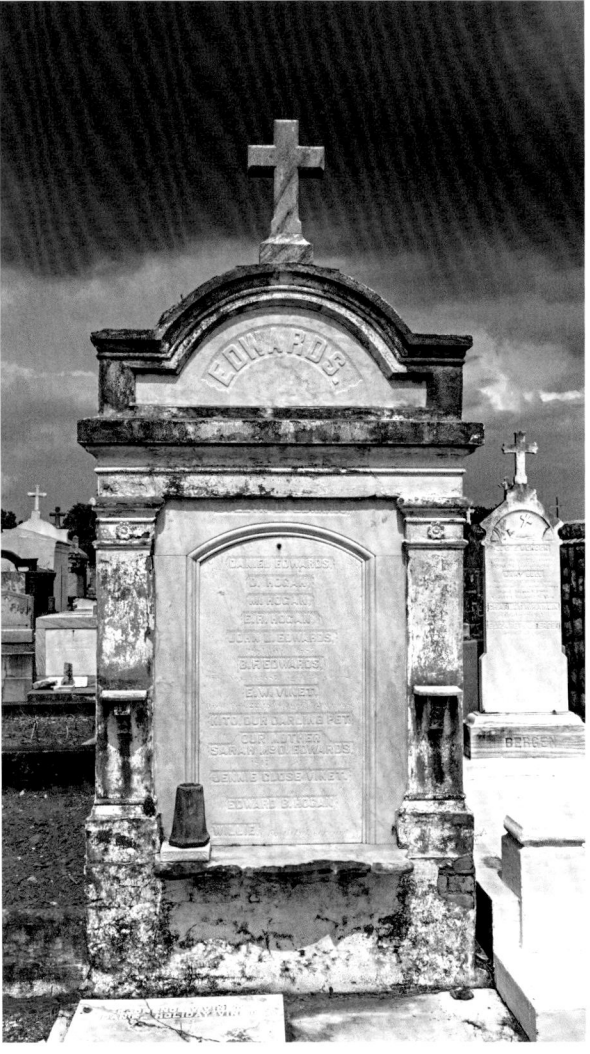

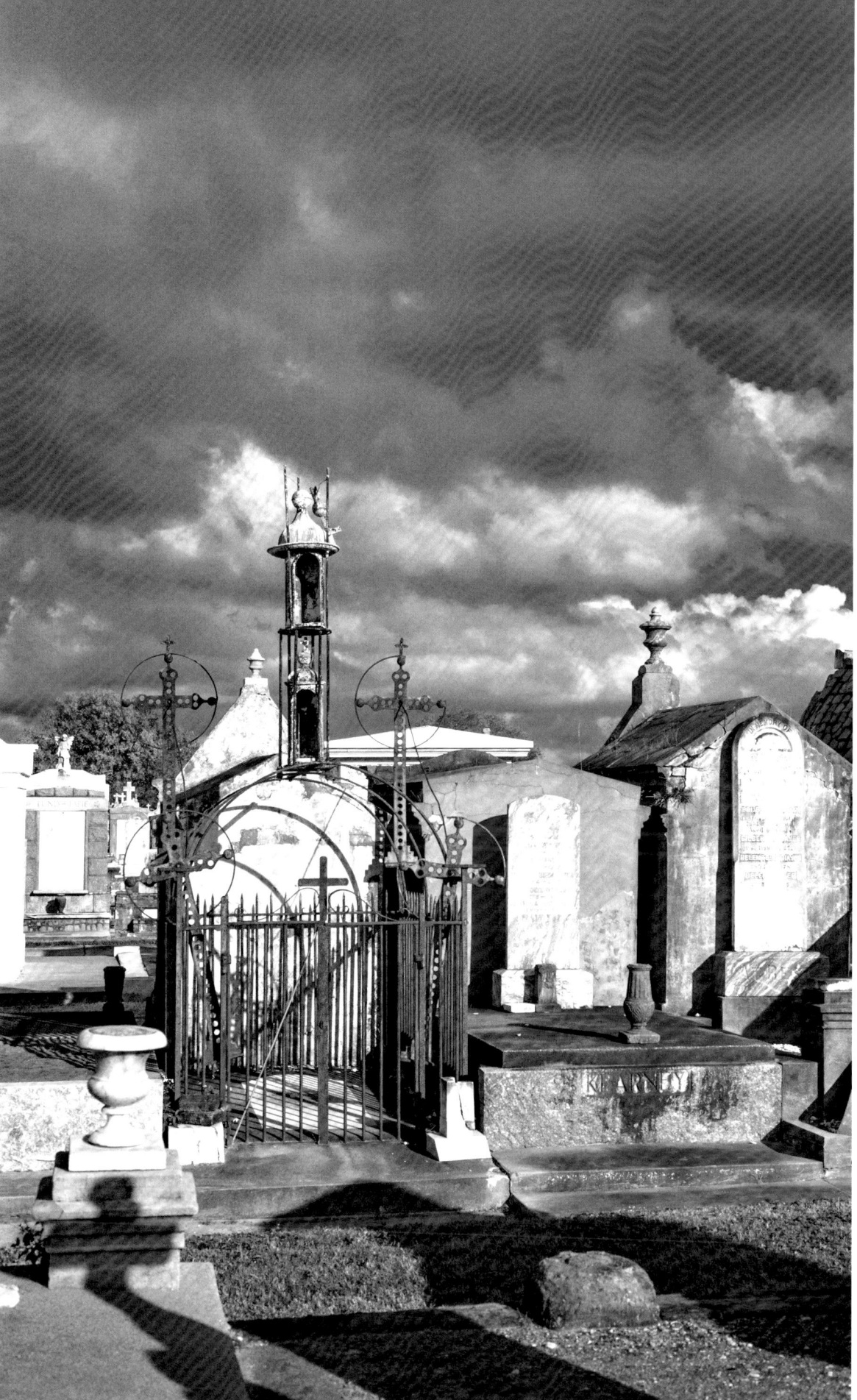

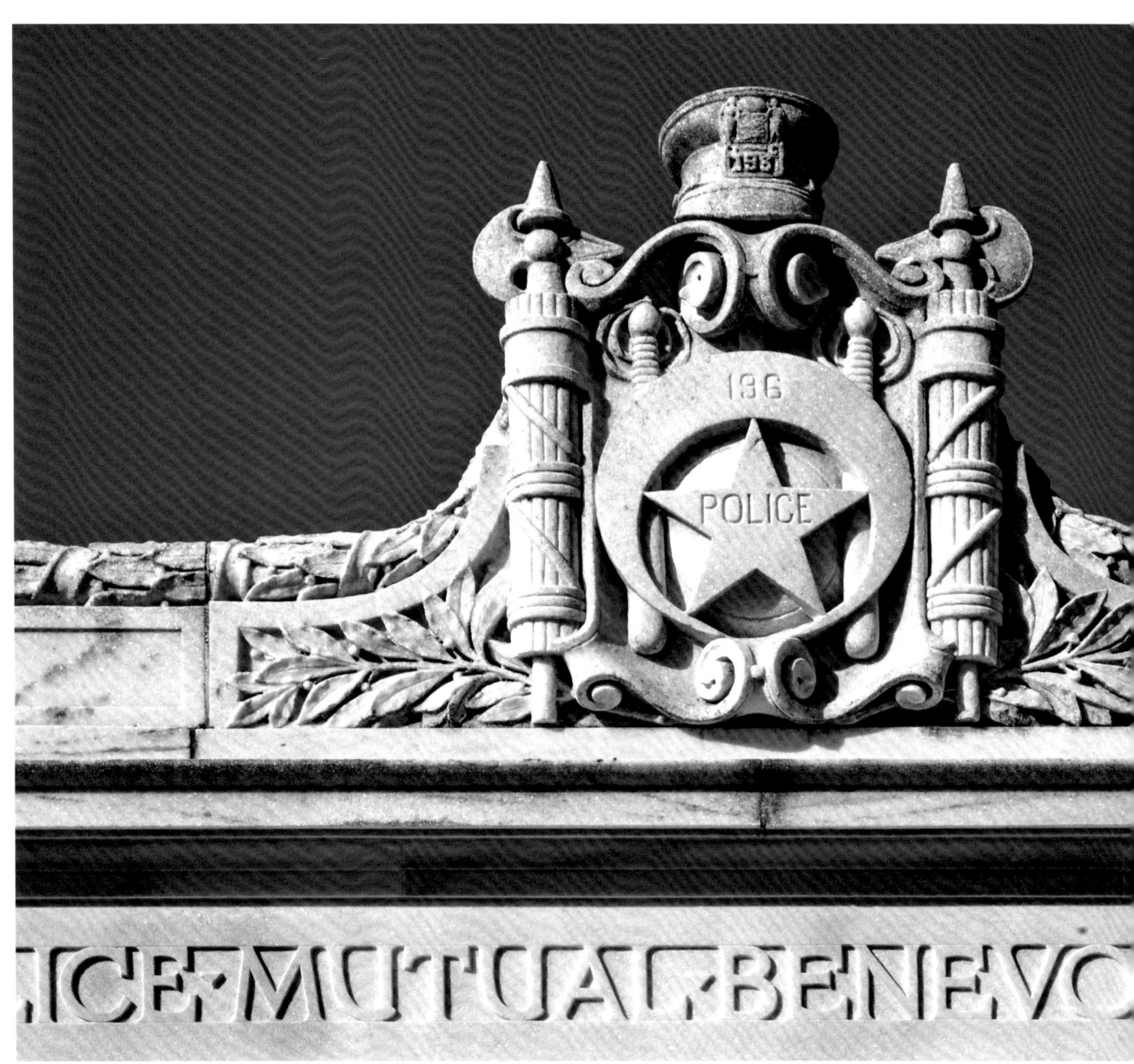

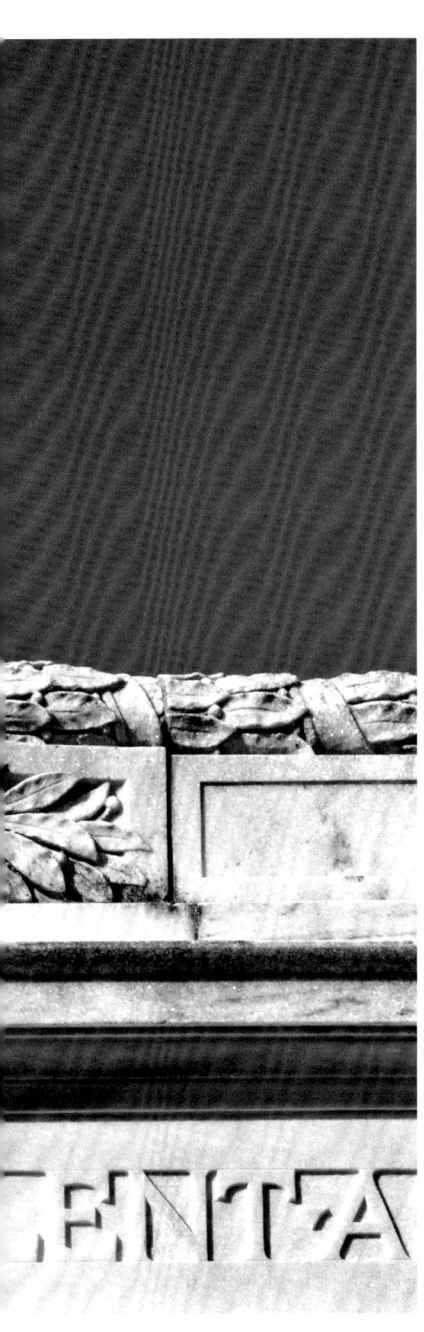

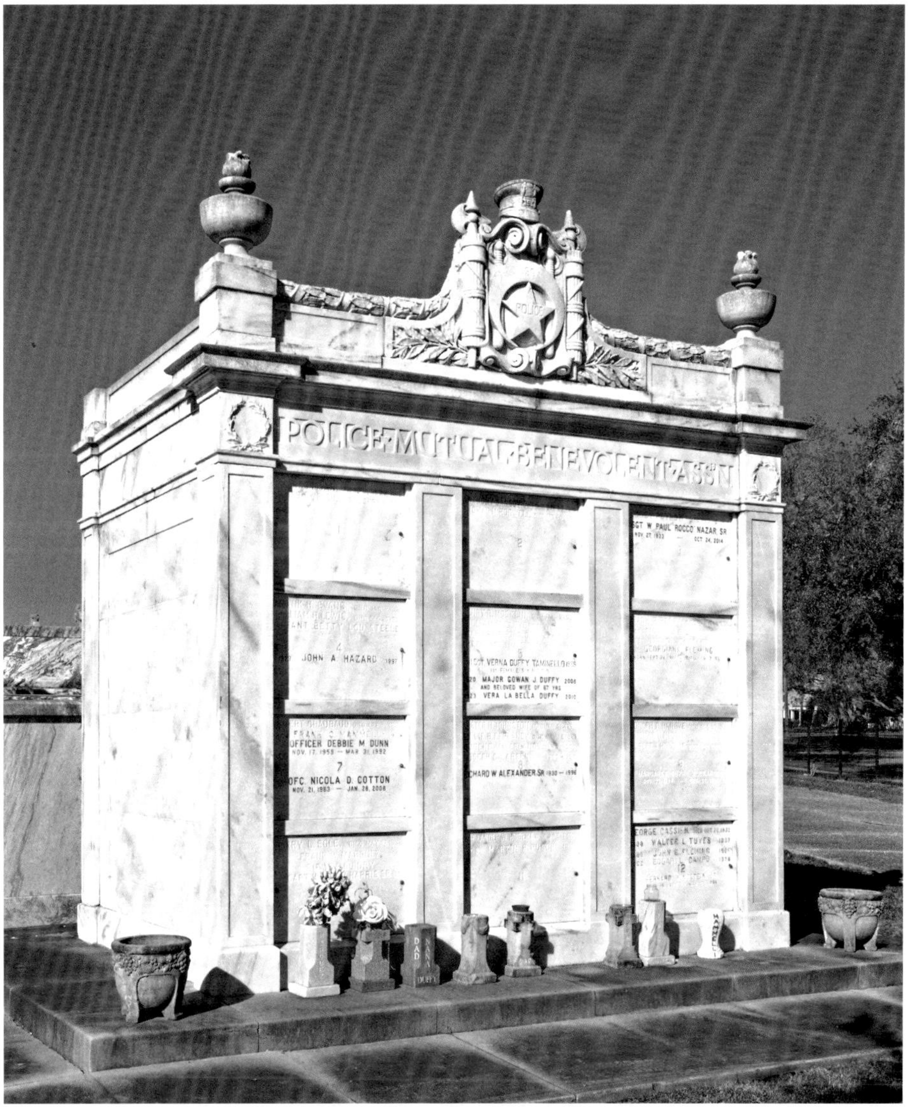

Greenwood Cemetery

Lafayette Cemetery #1 & #2

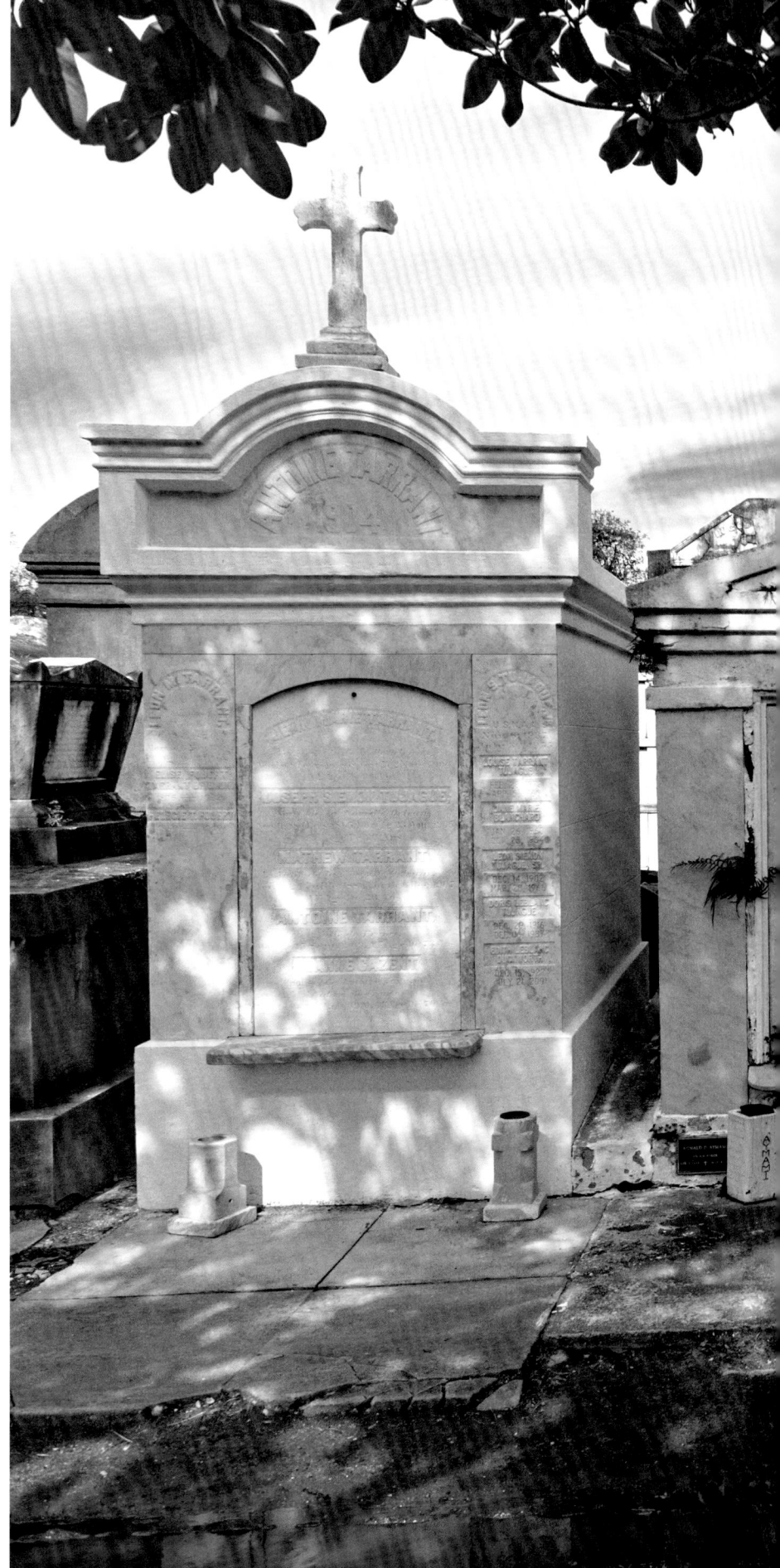

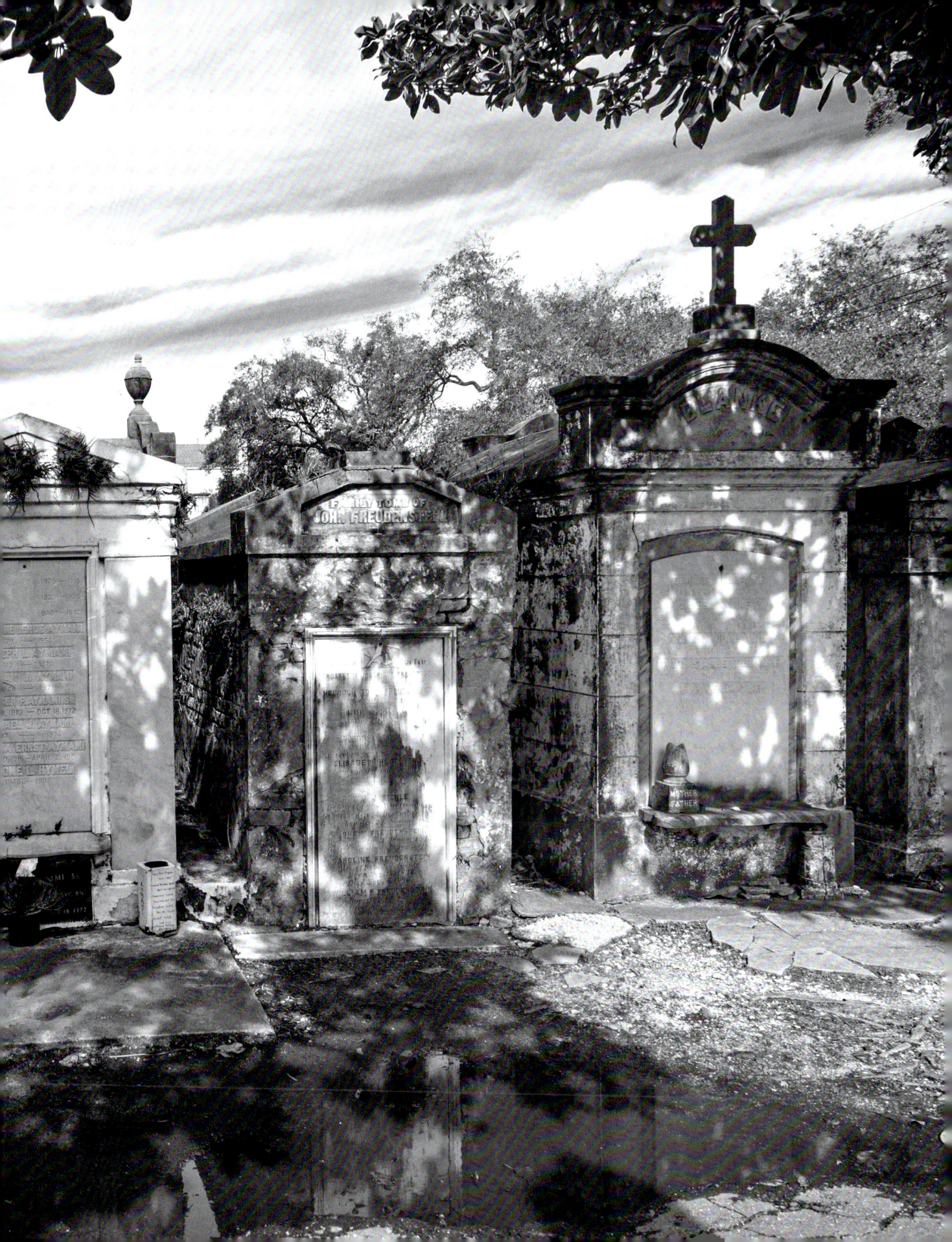

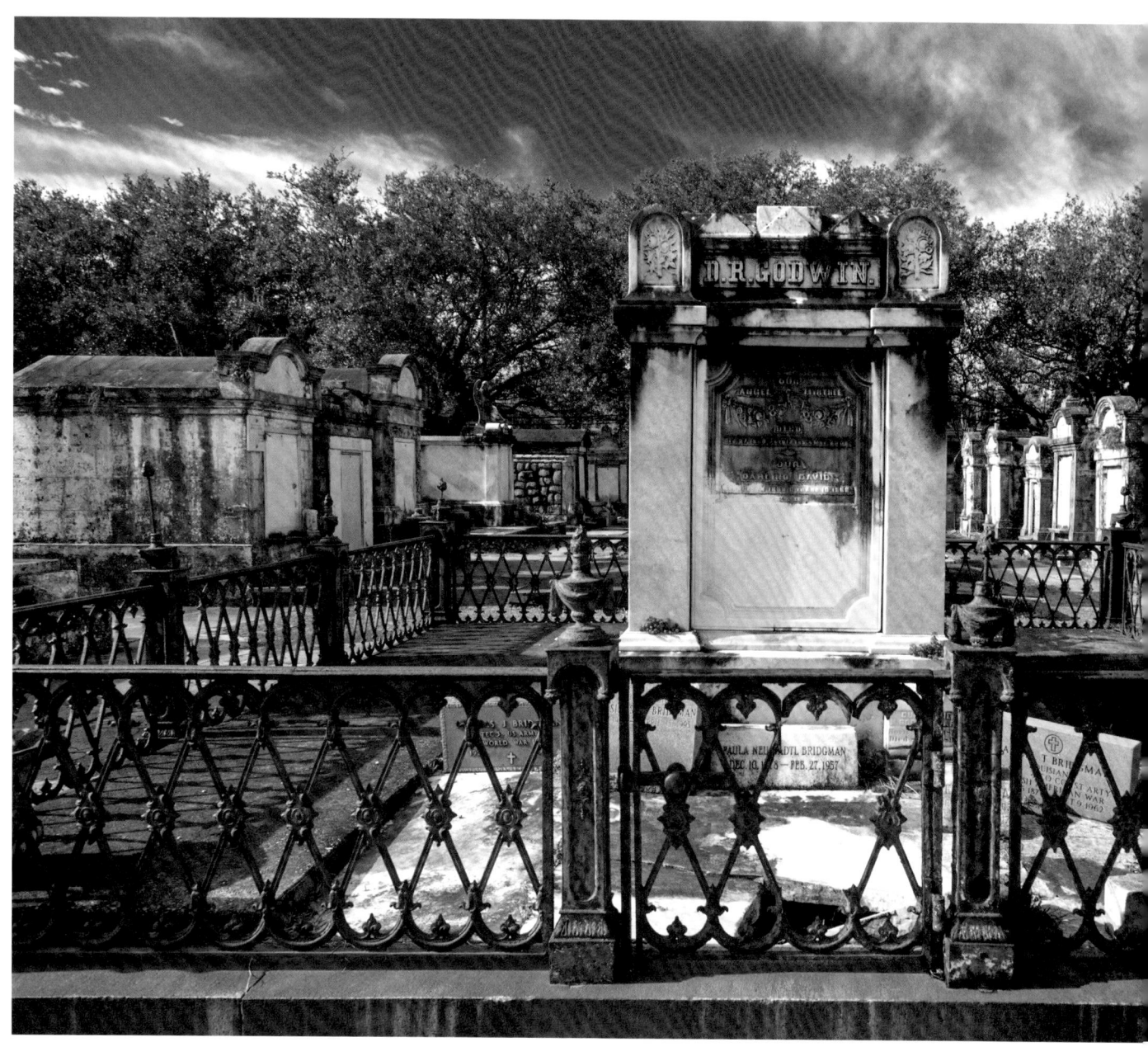

Lafayette Cemetery #1

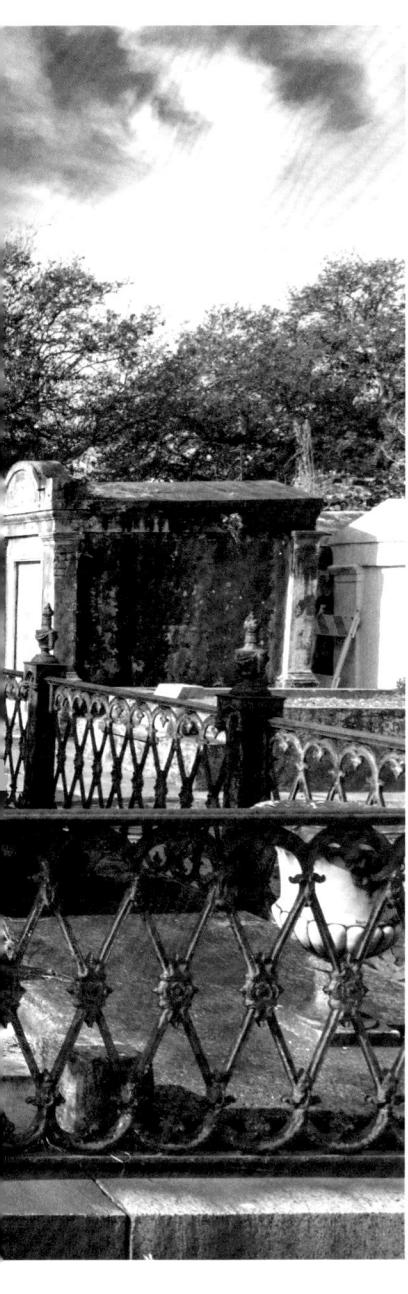
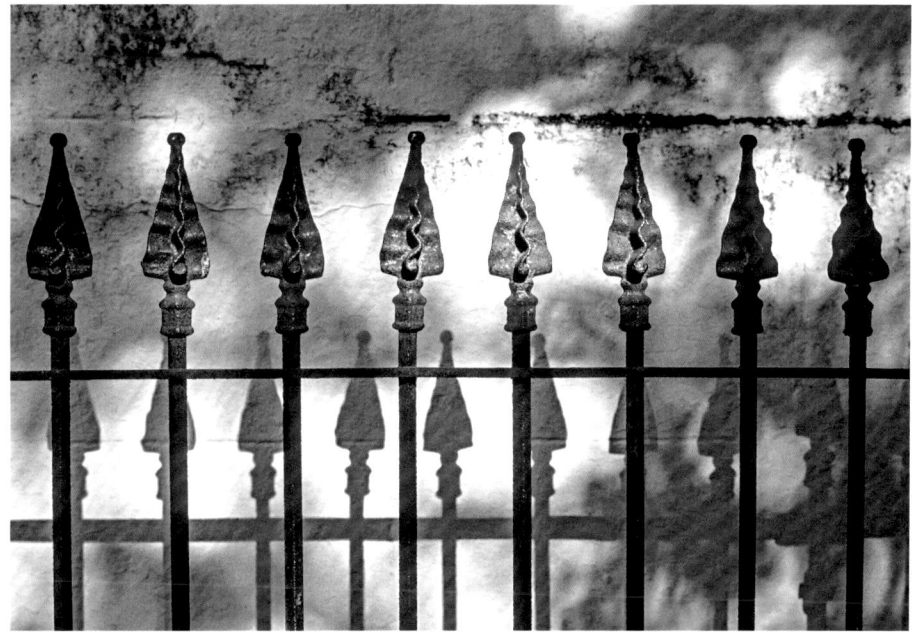

Lafayette Cemetery #1   109

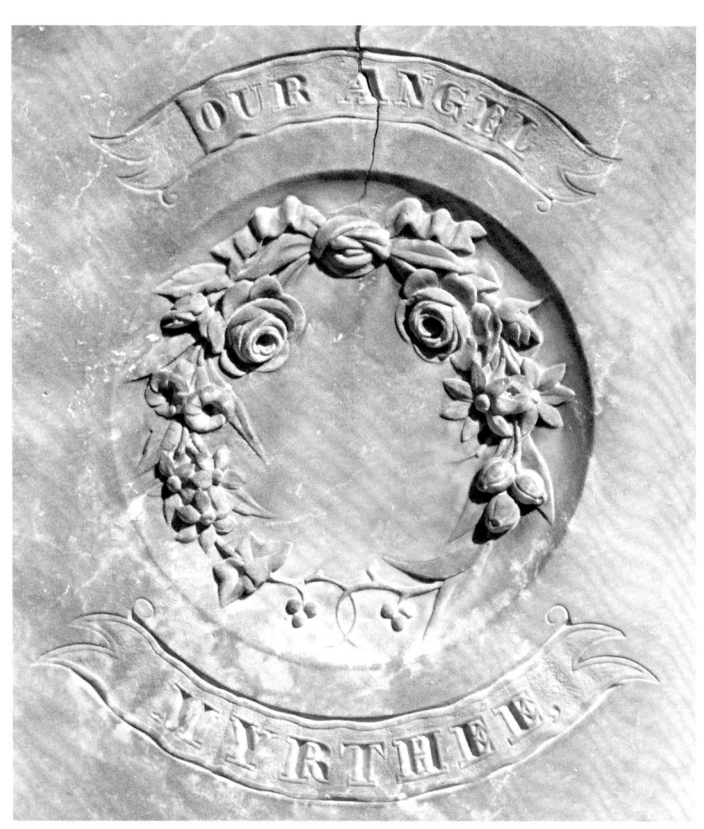

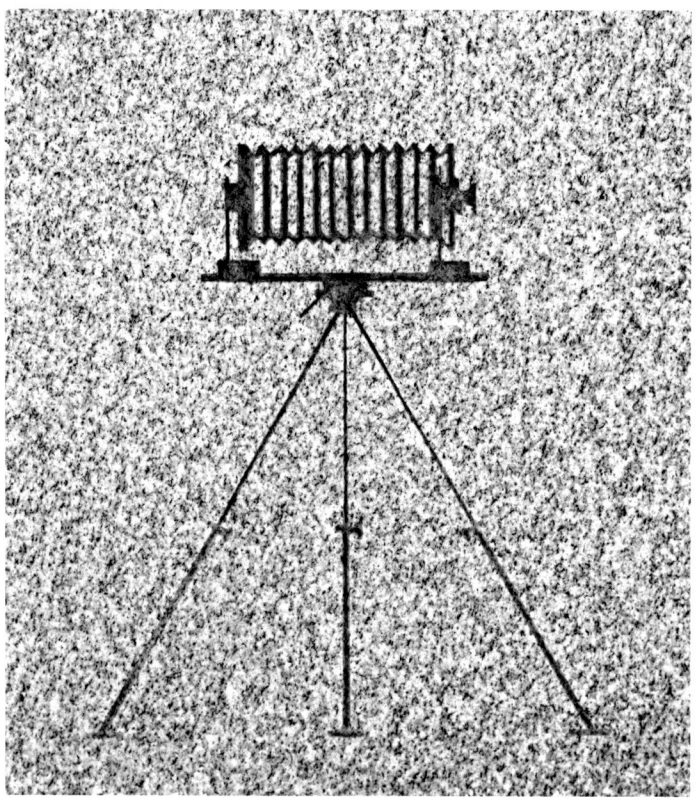

110 *Lafayette Cemetery #1*

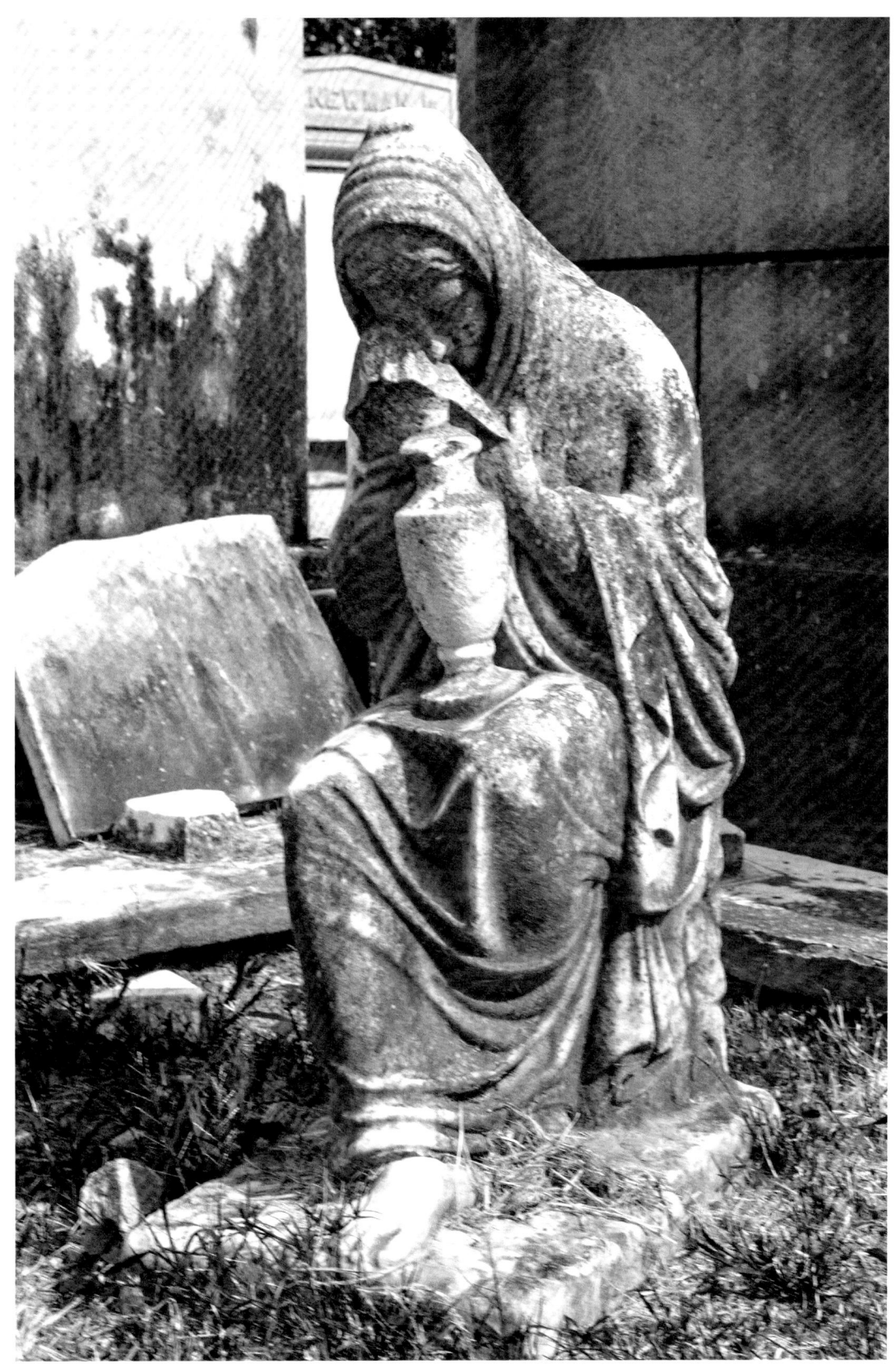

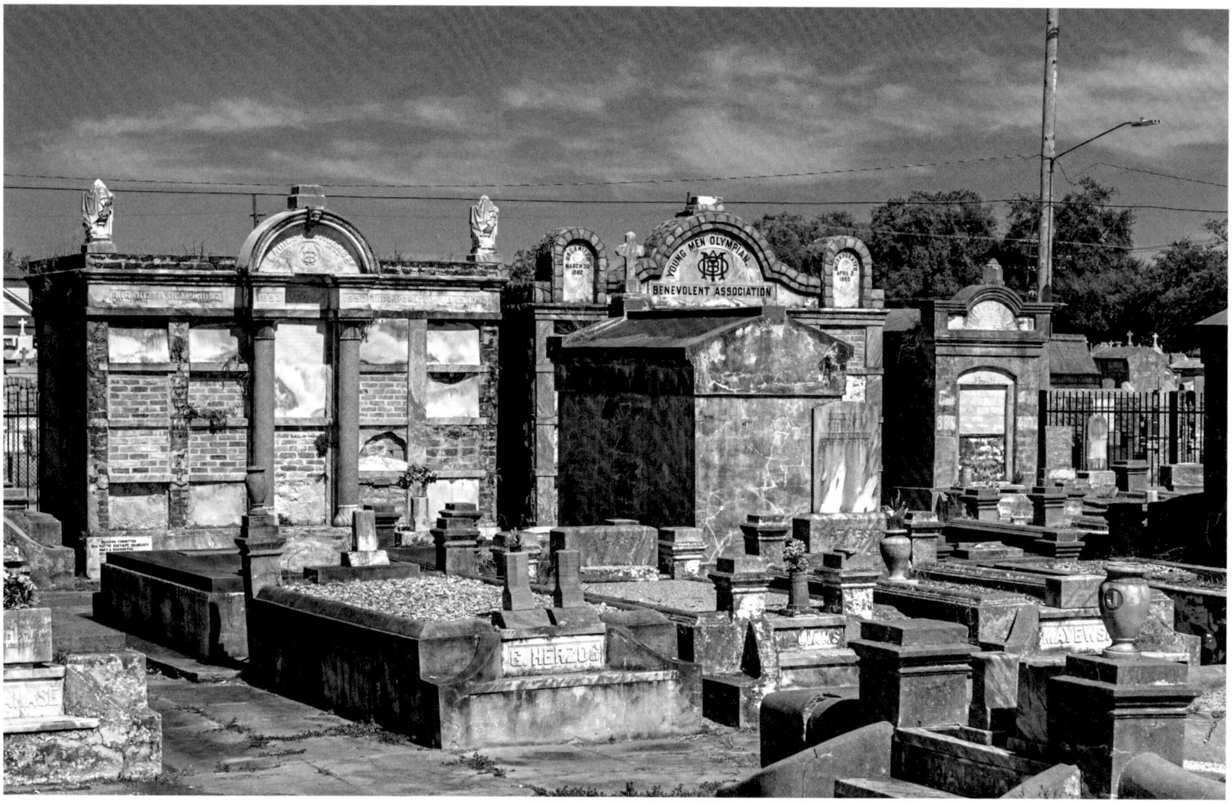

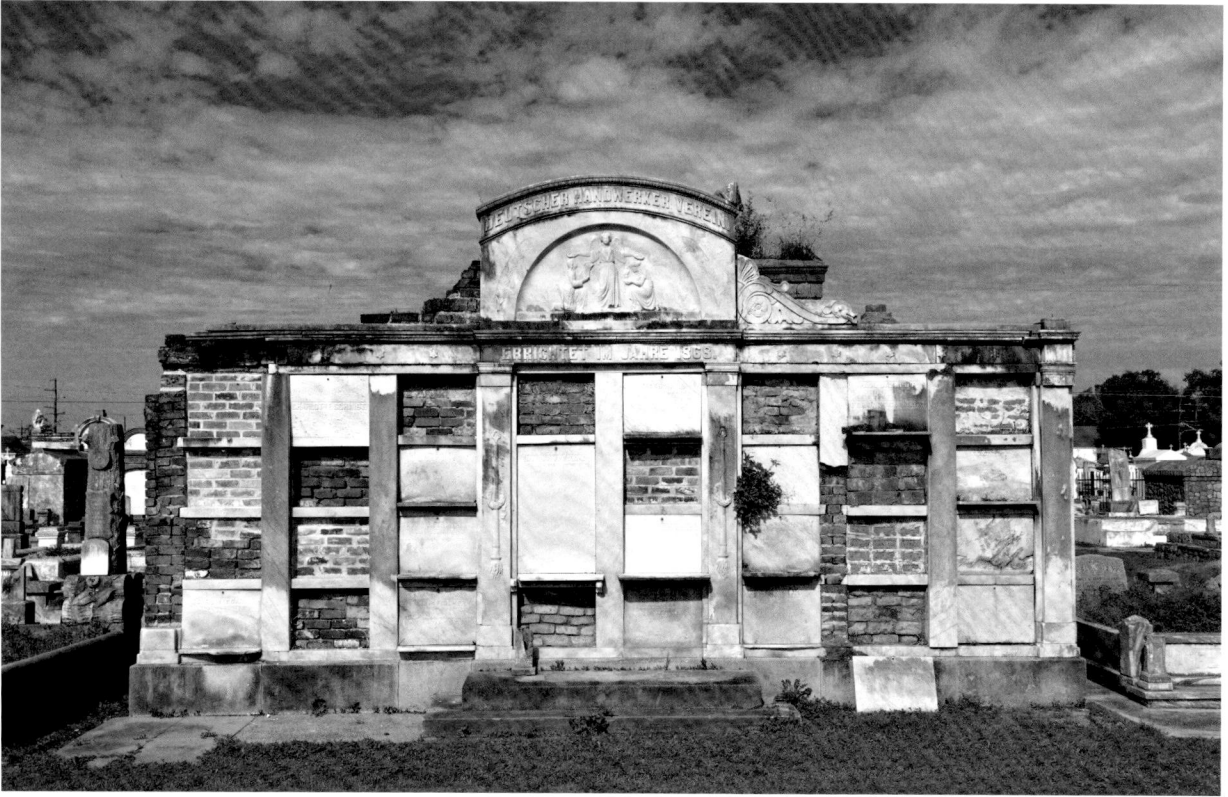

Lafayette Cemetery #2

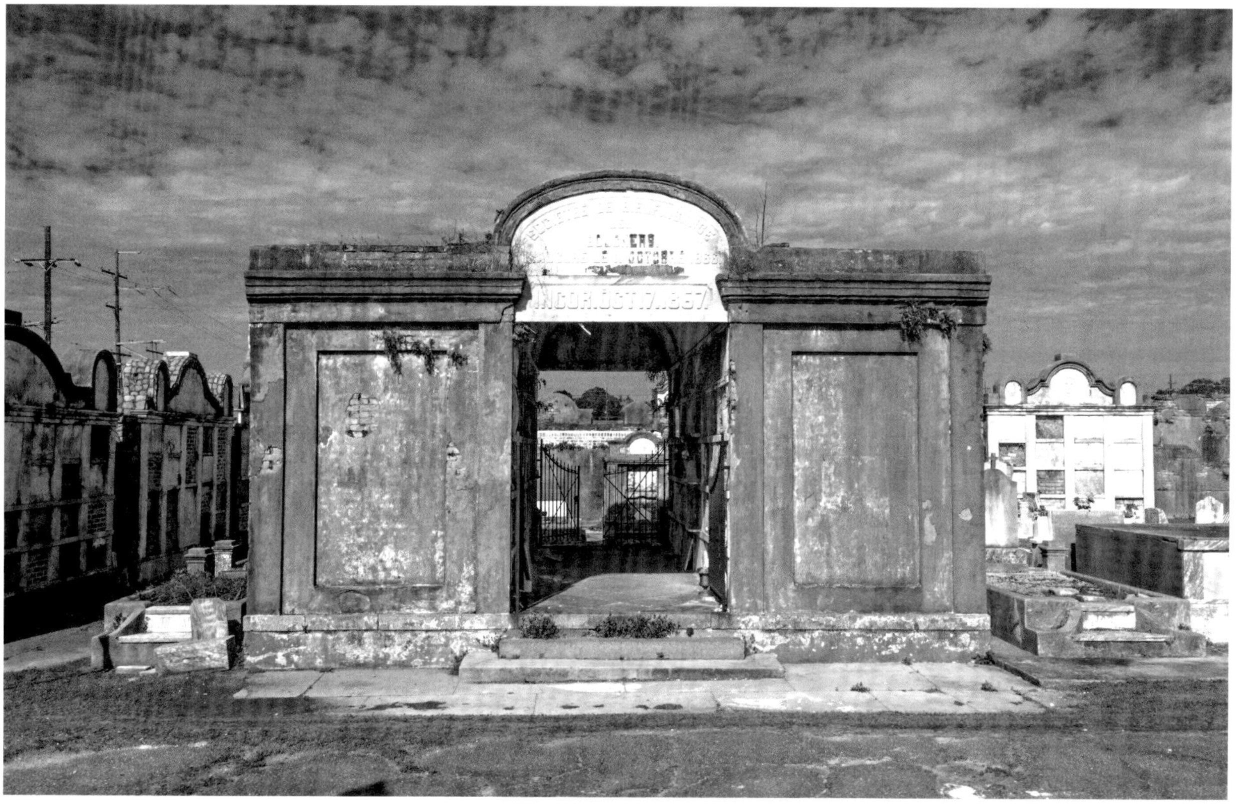

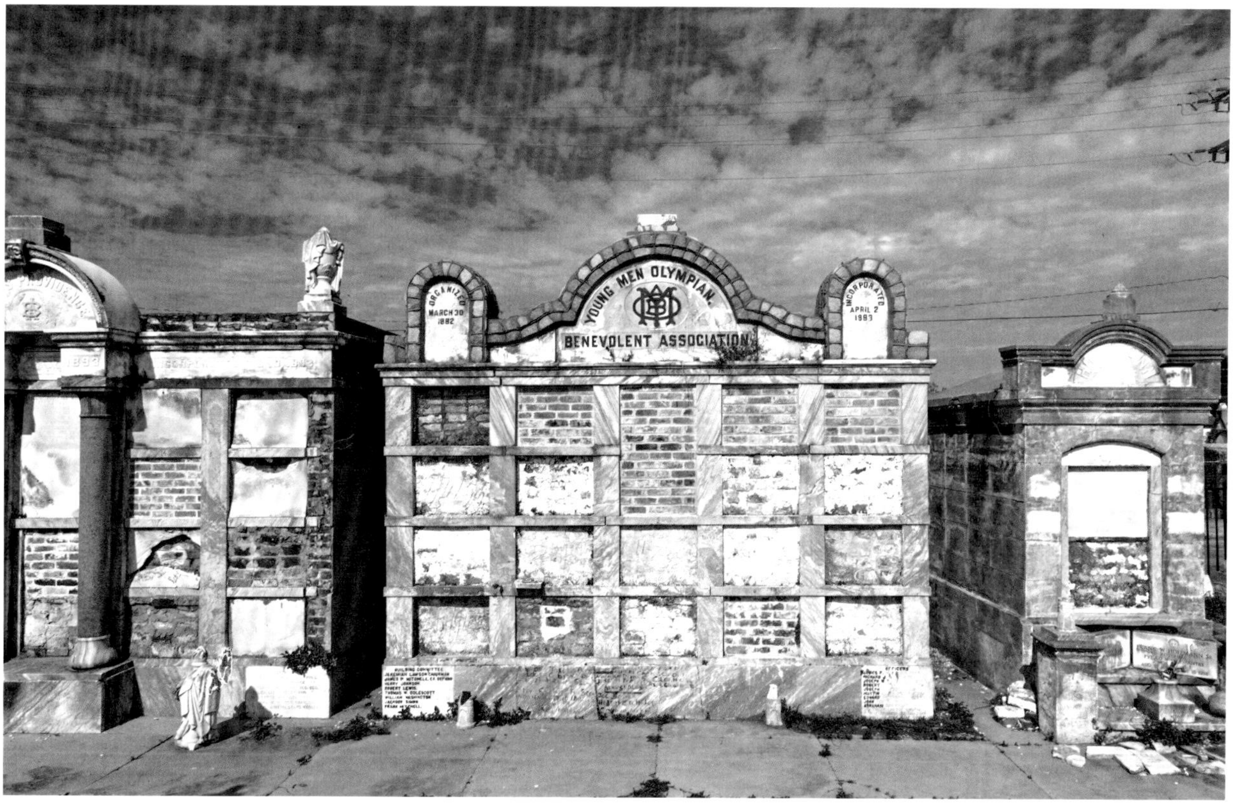

Lafayette Cemetery #2

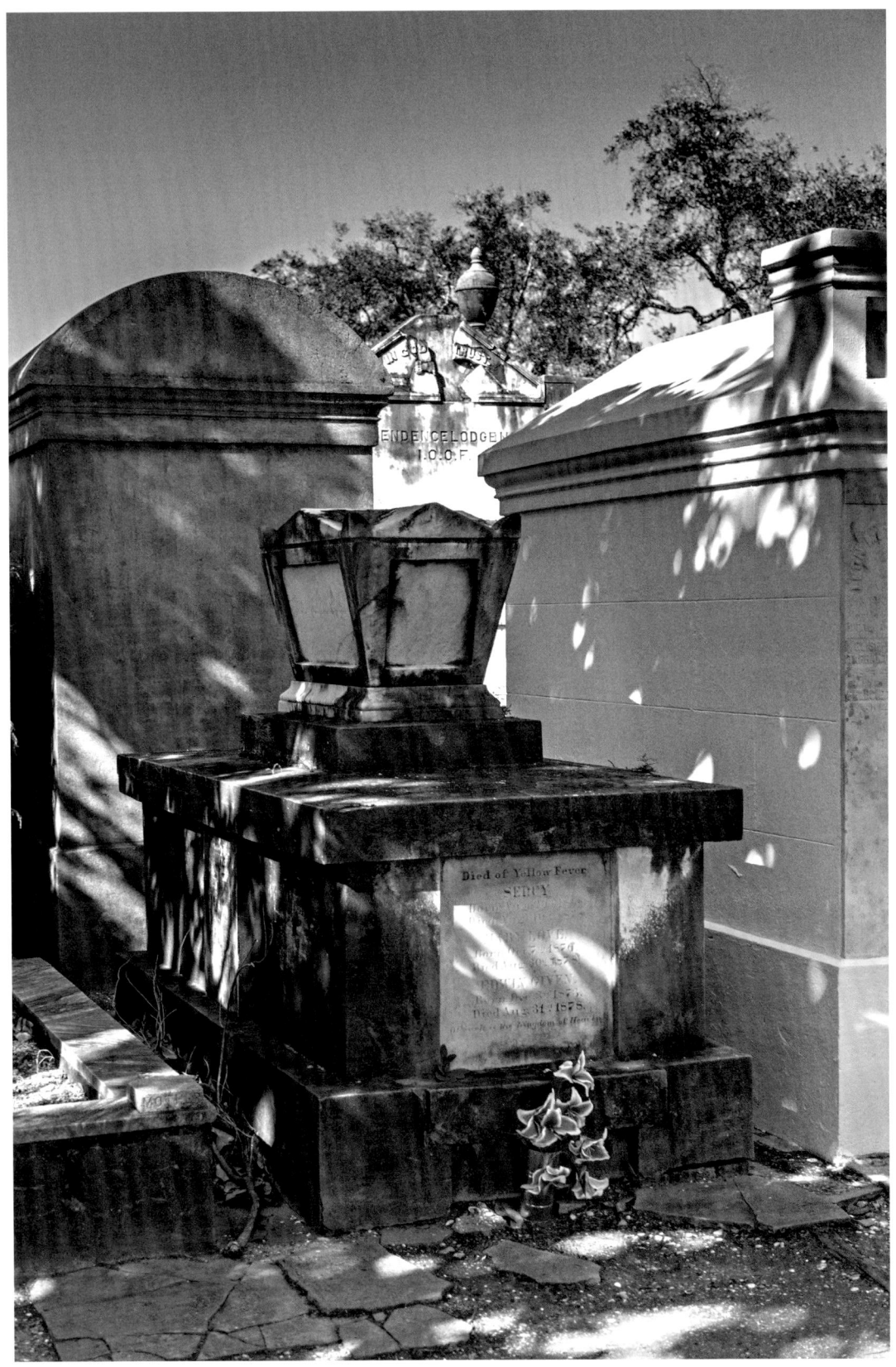

Lafayette Cemetery #1

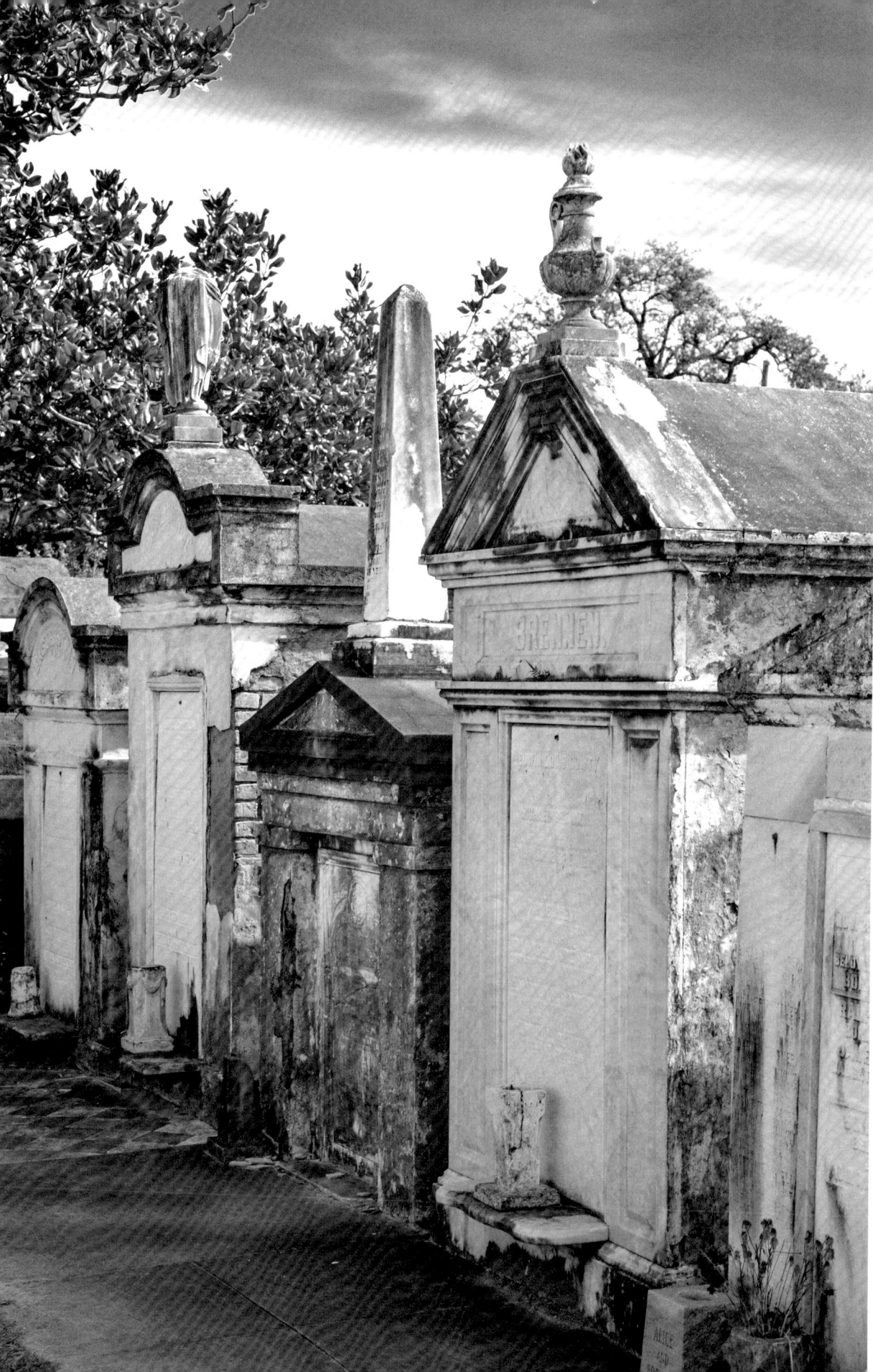

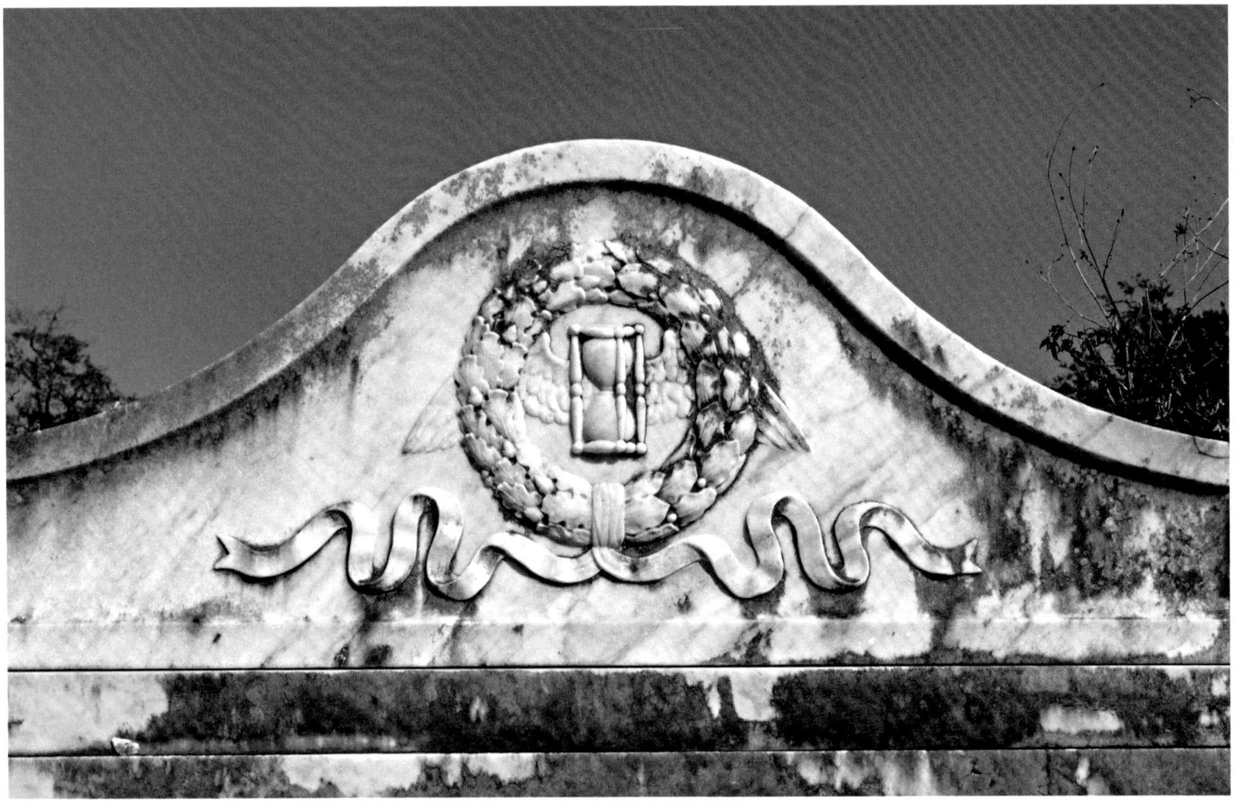

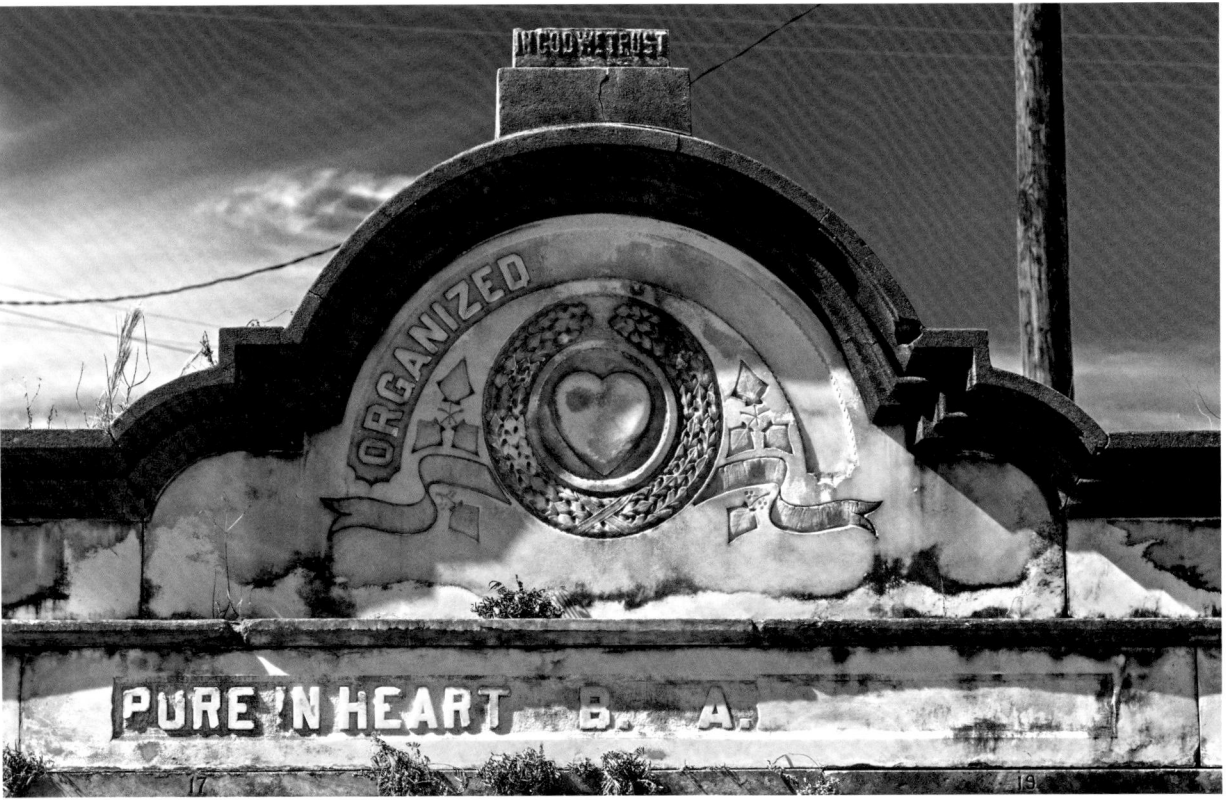

116   *Lafayette Cemetery #1 & #2*

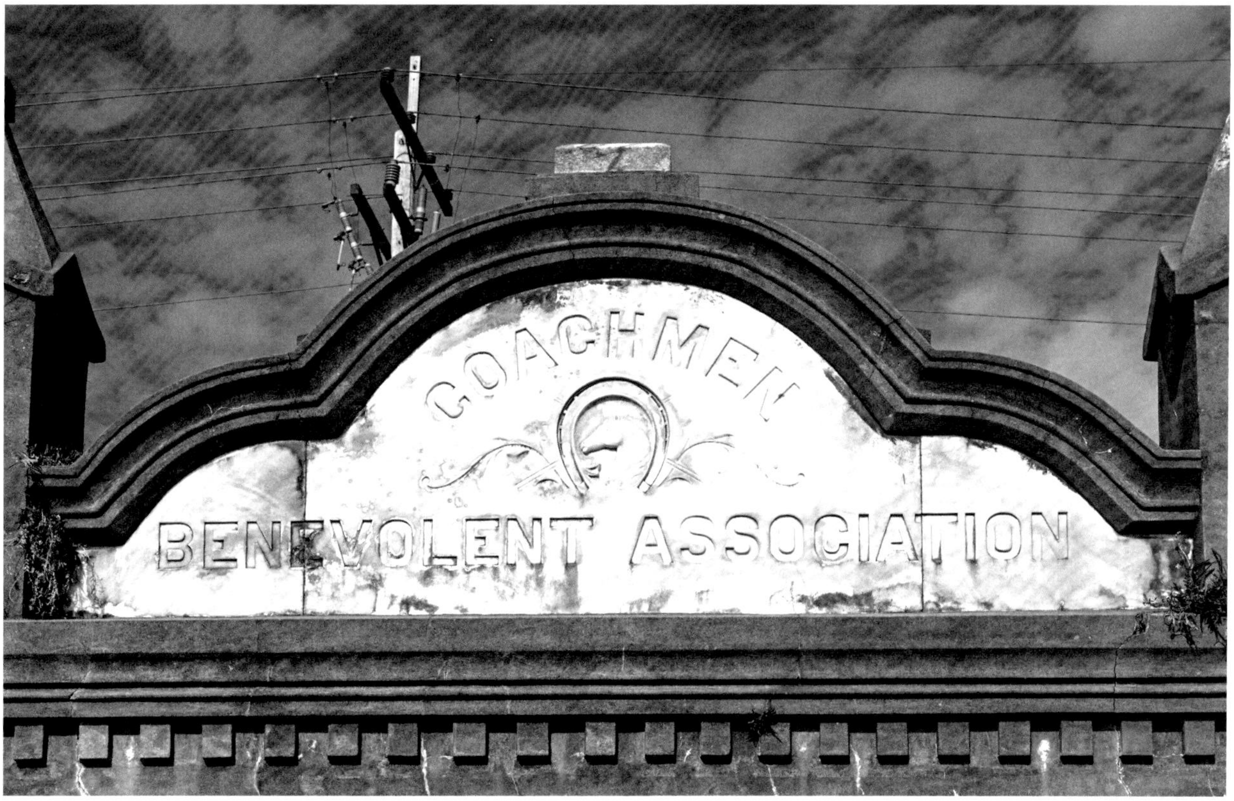

Lafayette Cemetery #2

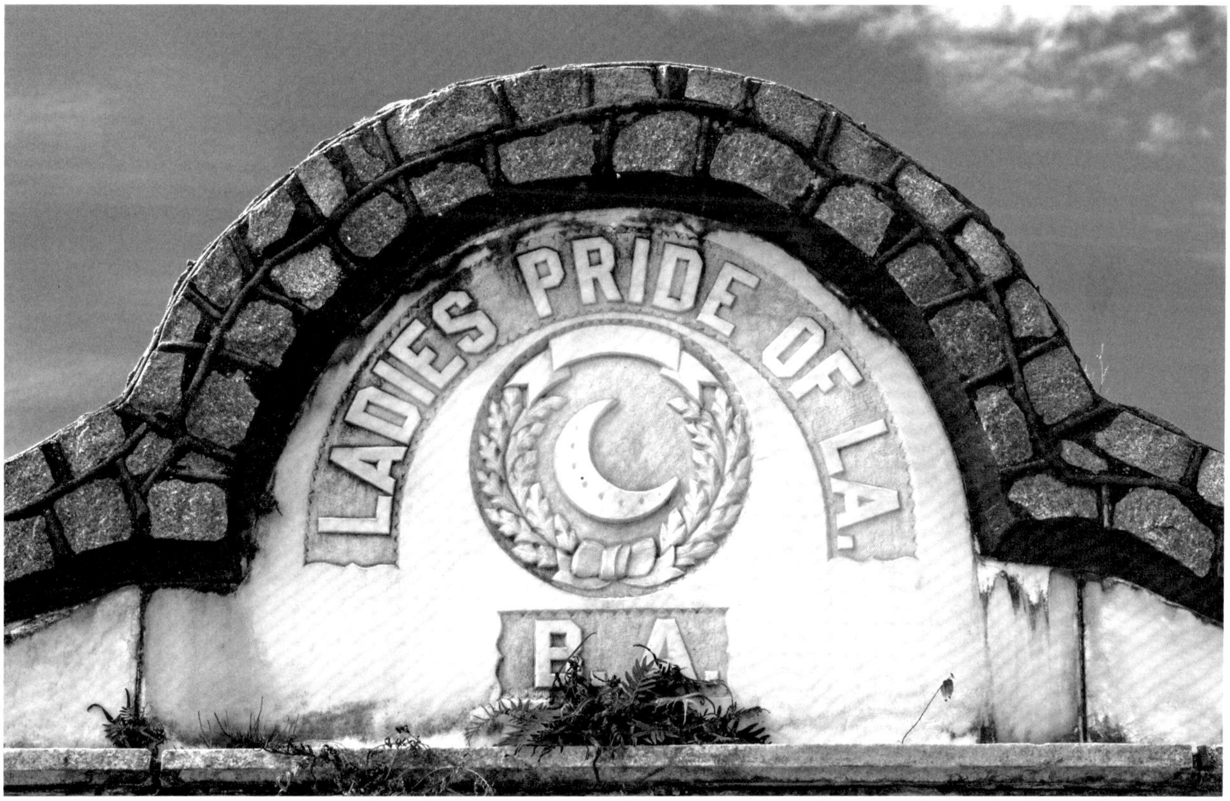

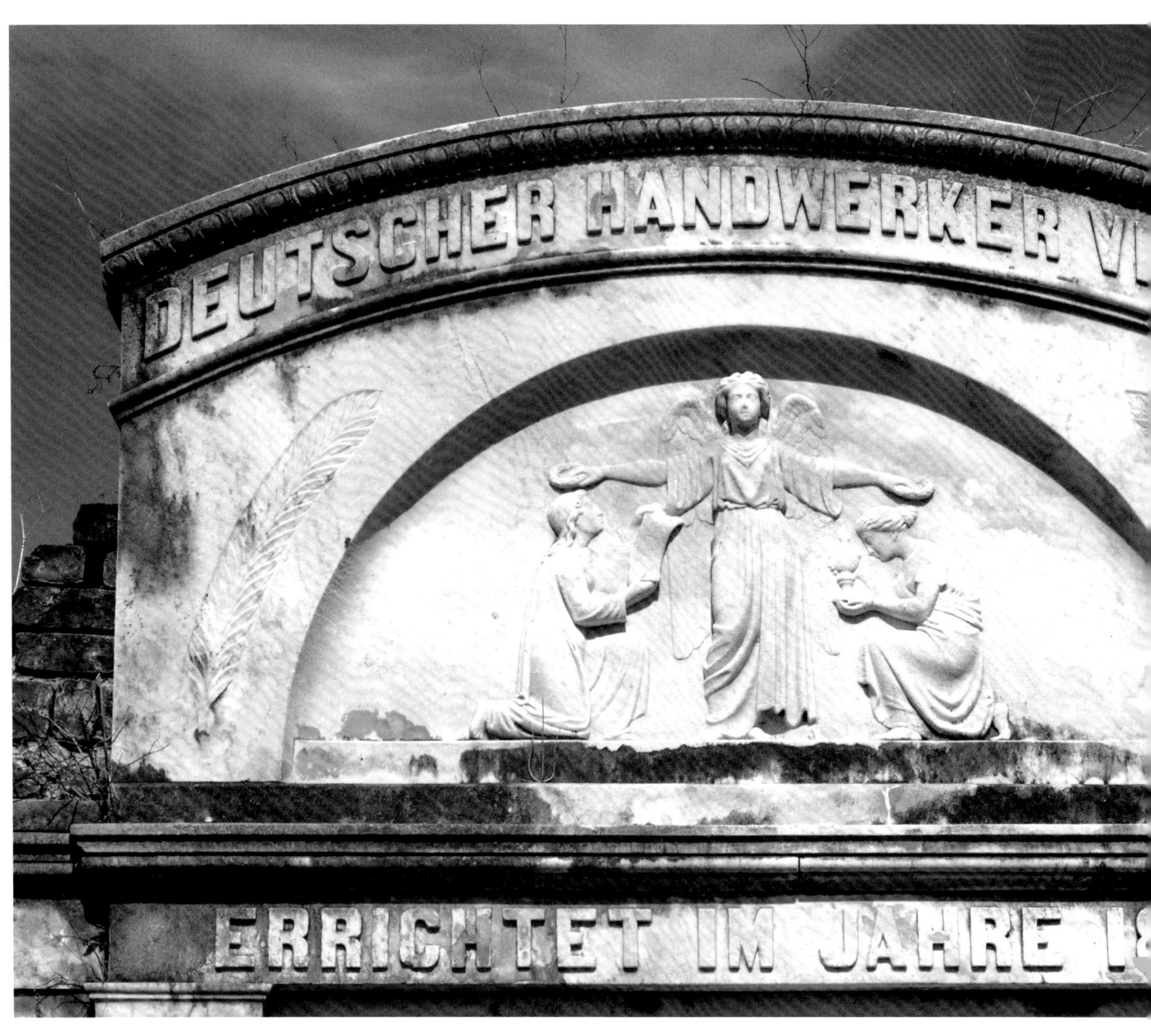

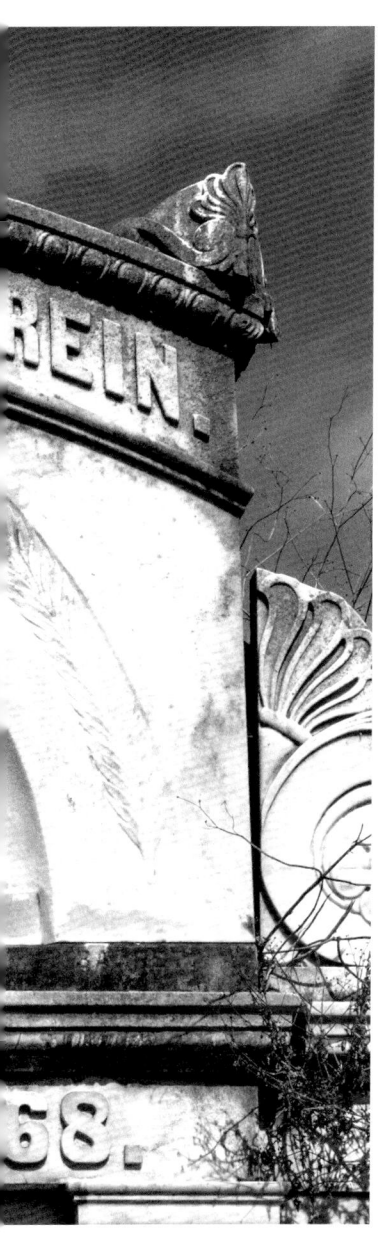
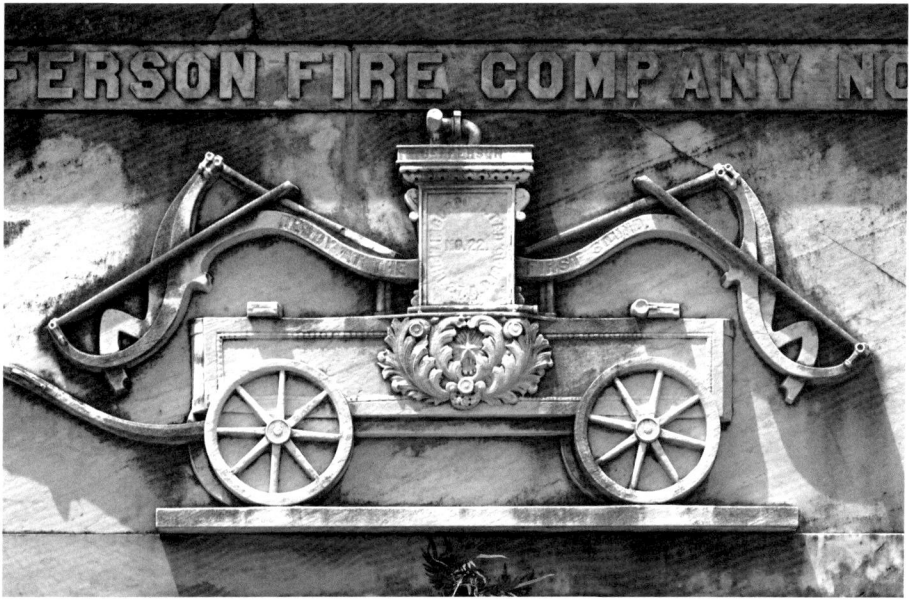
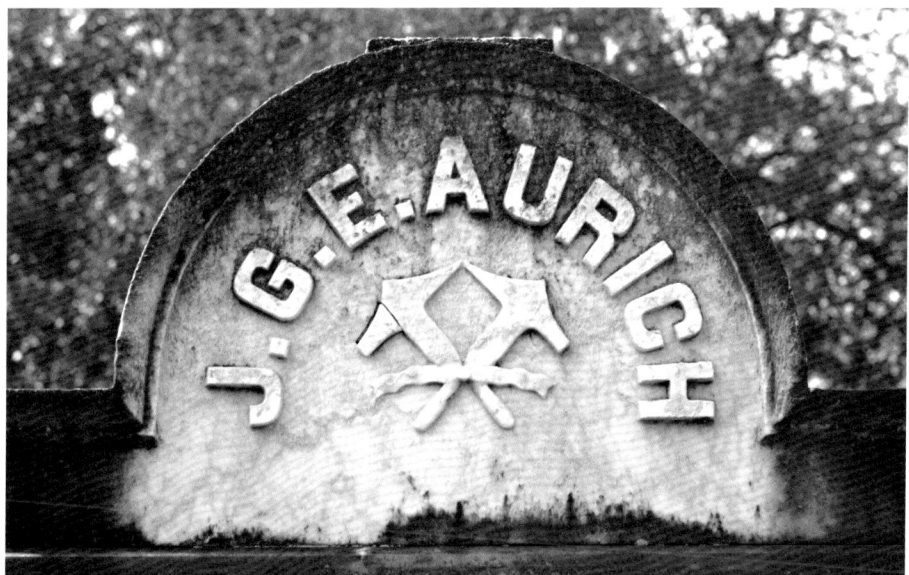

Lafayette Cemetery #1   119

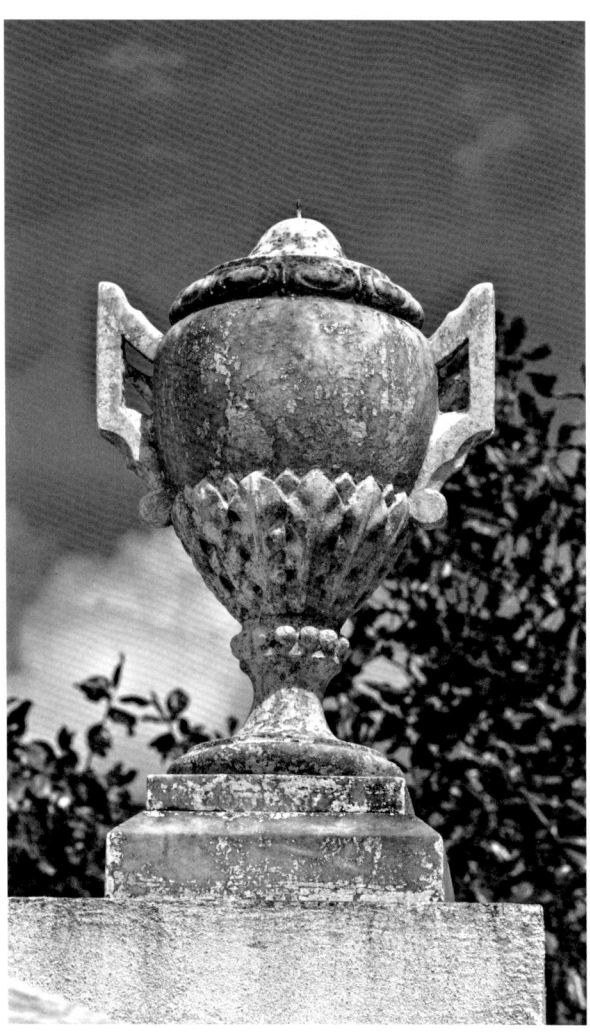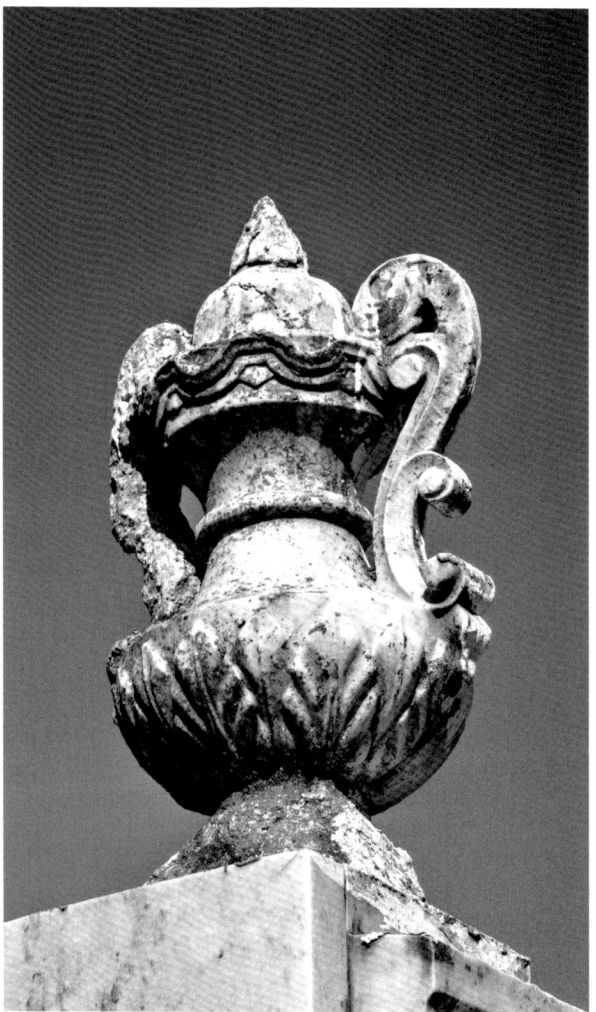

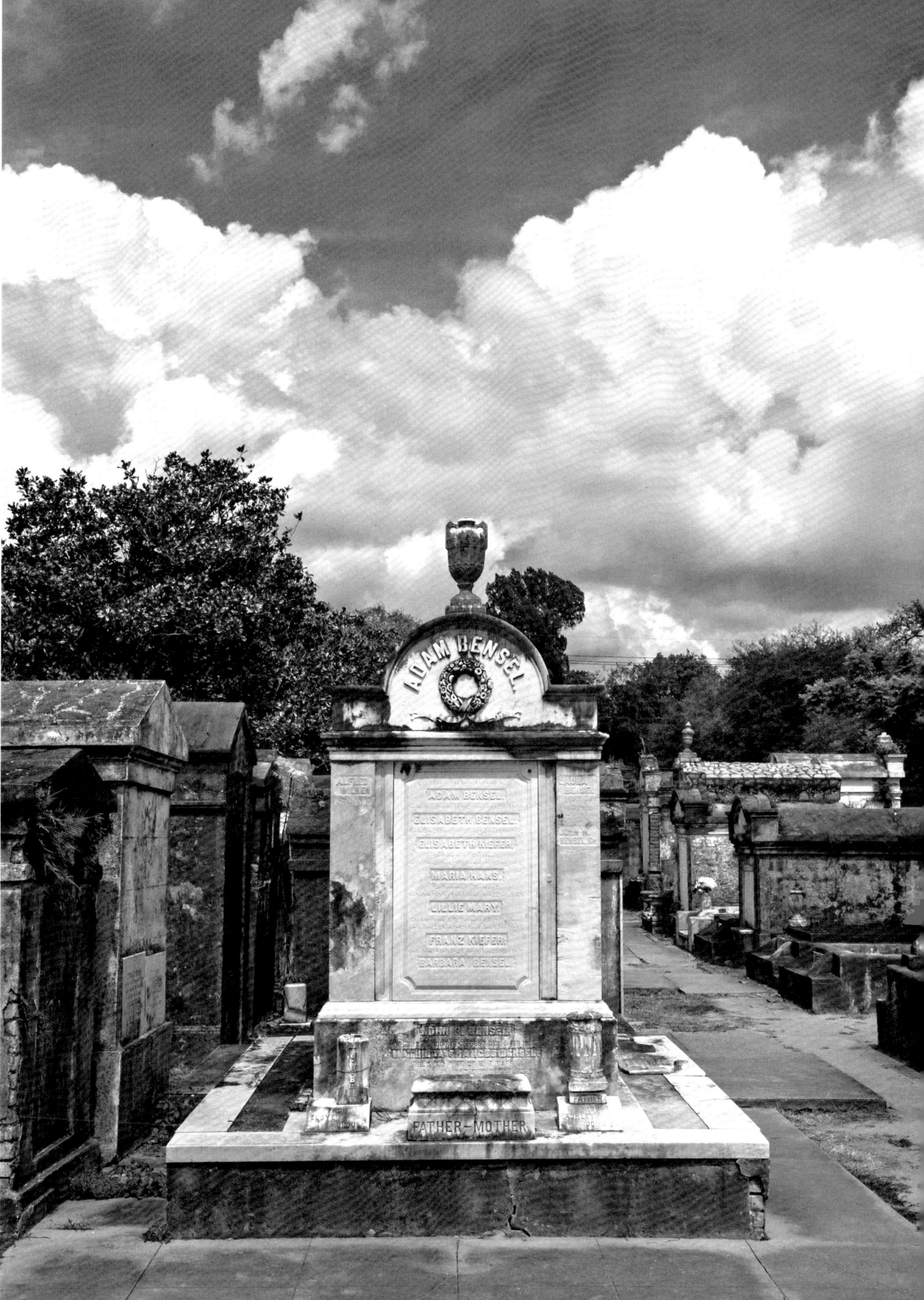

Metairie Cemetery

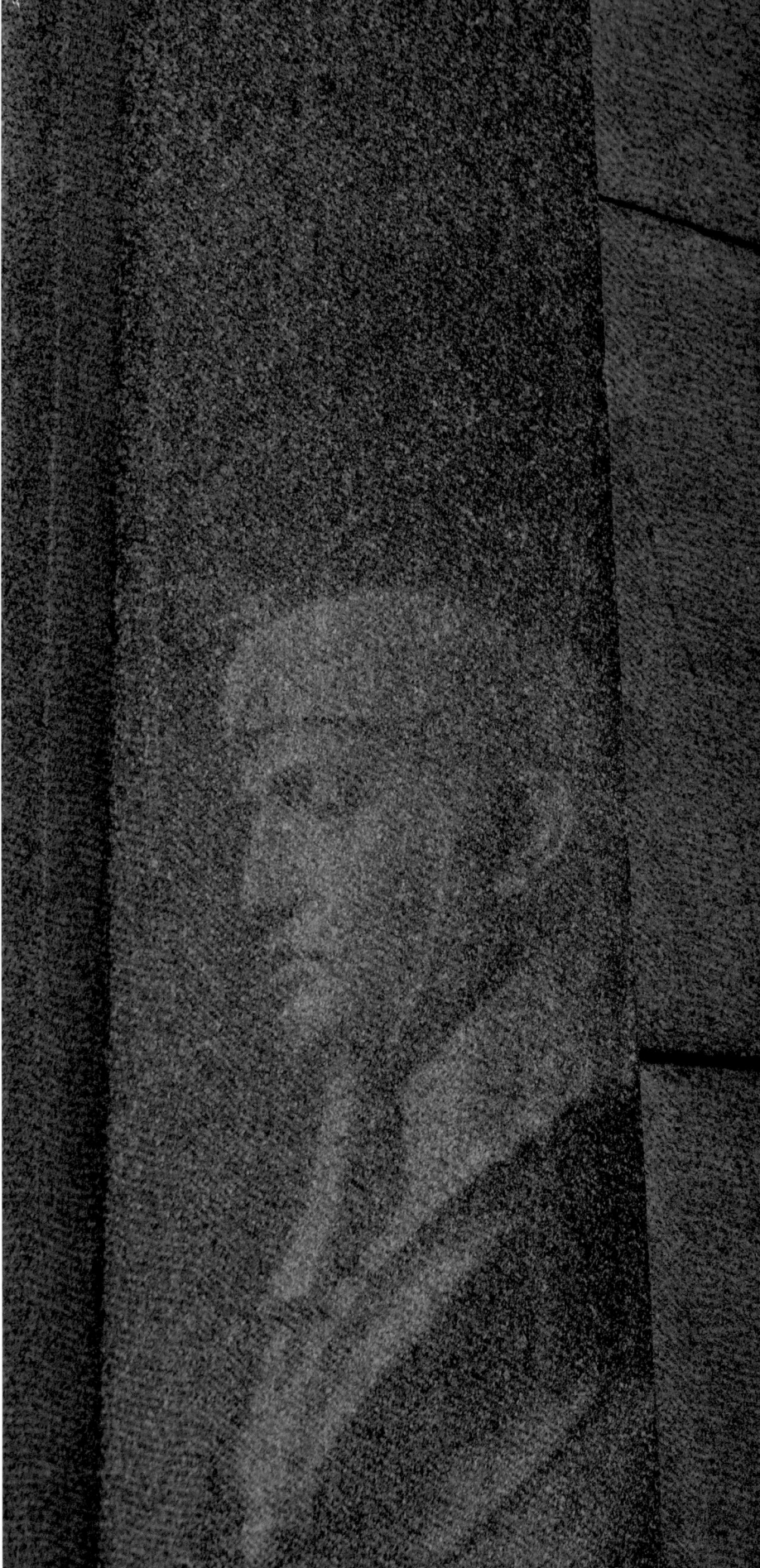

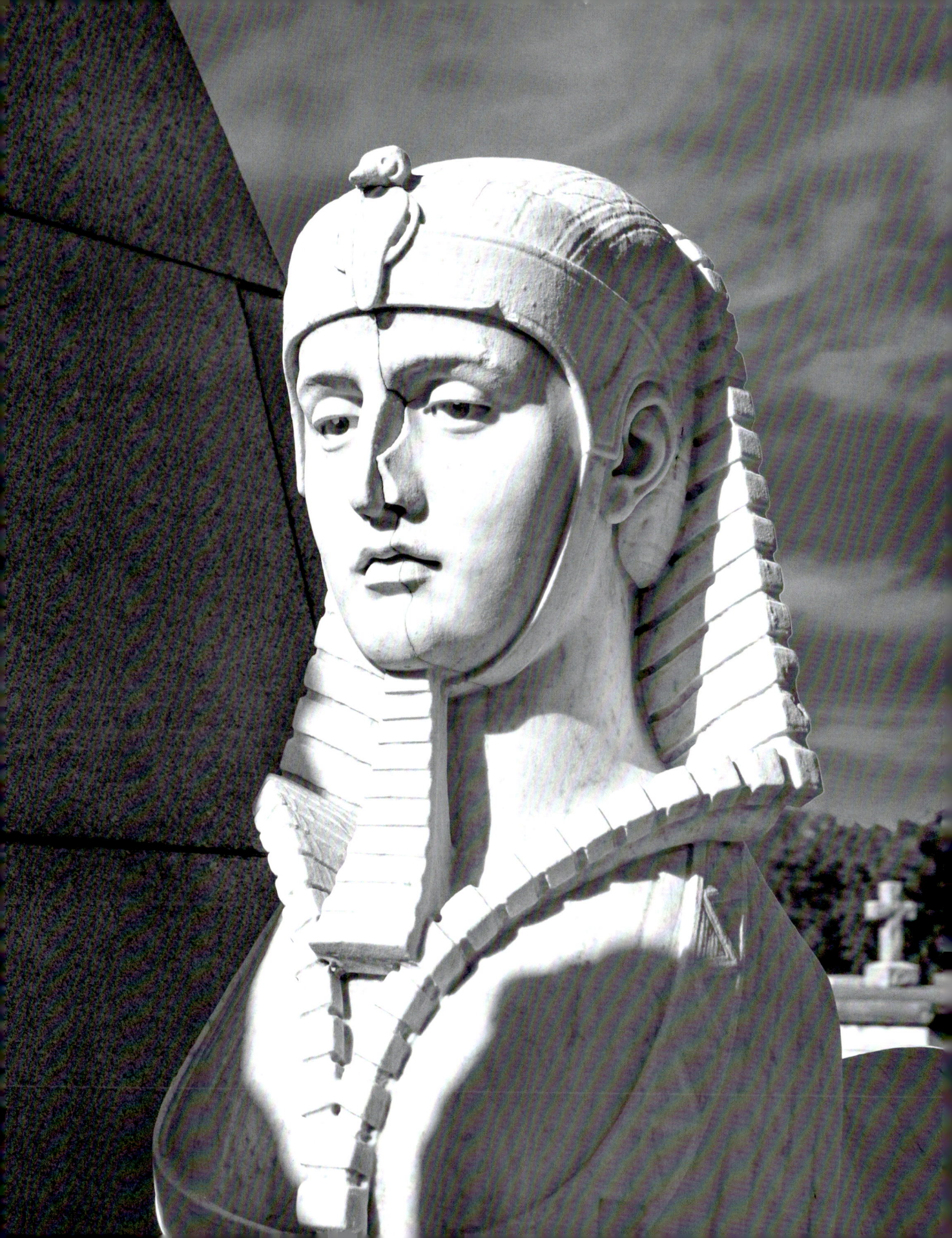

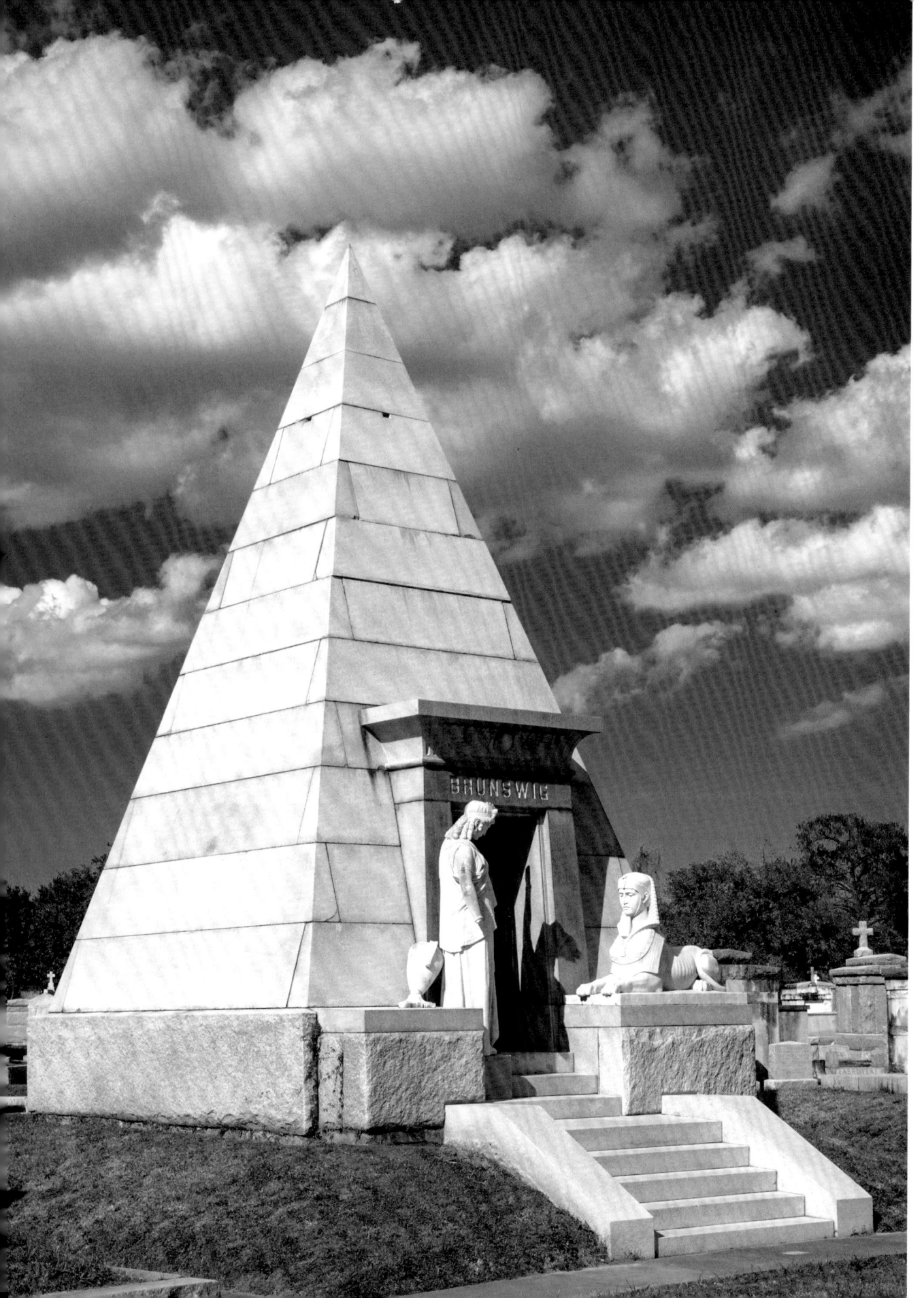

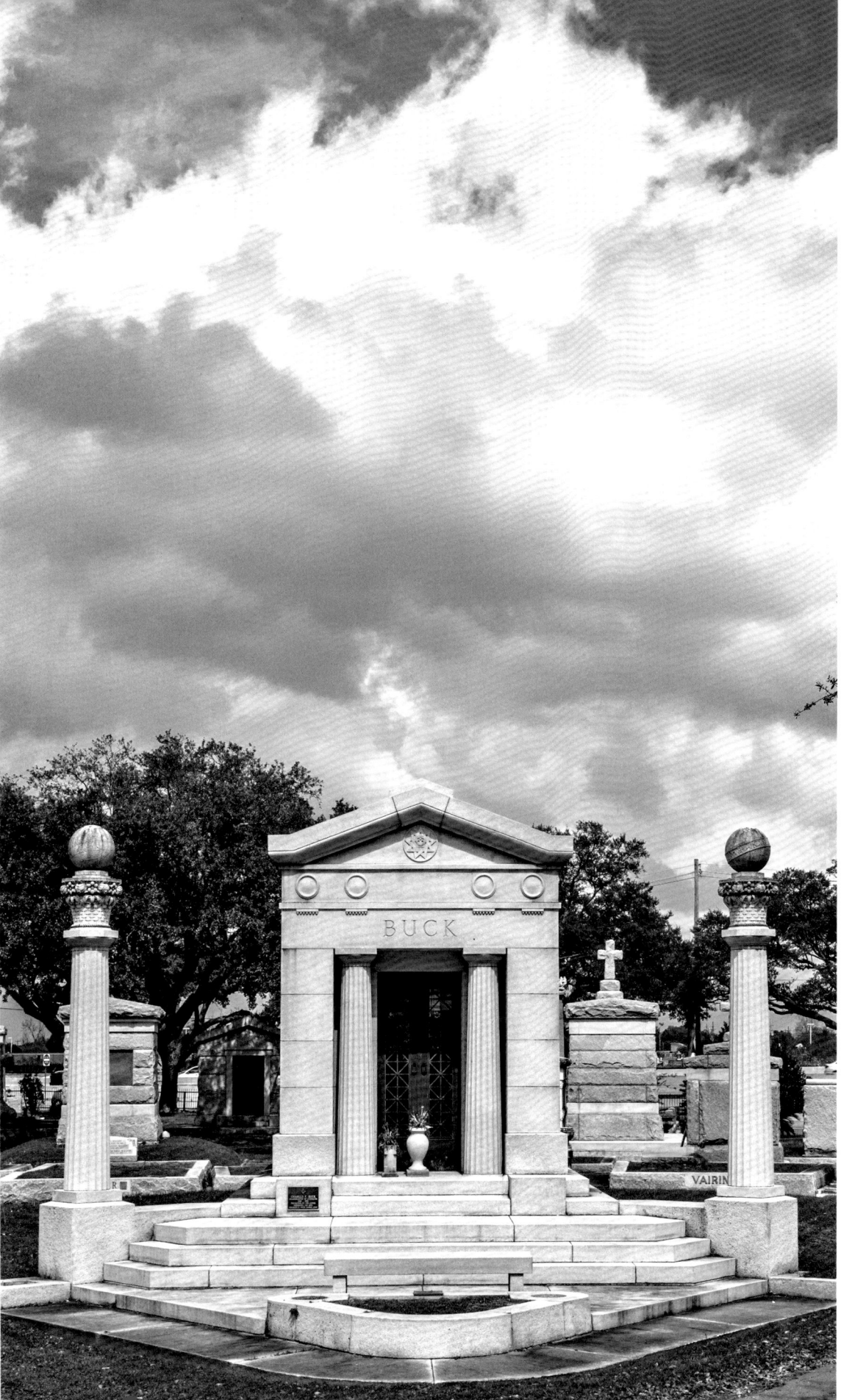

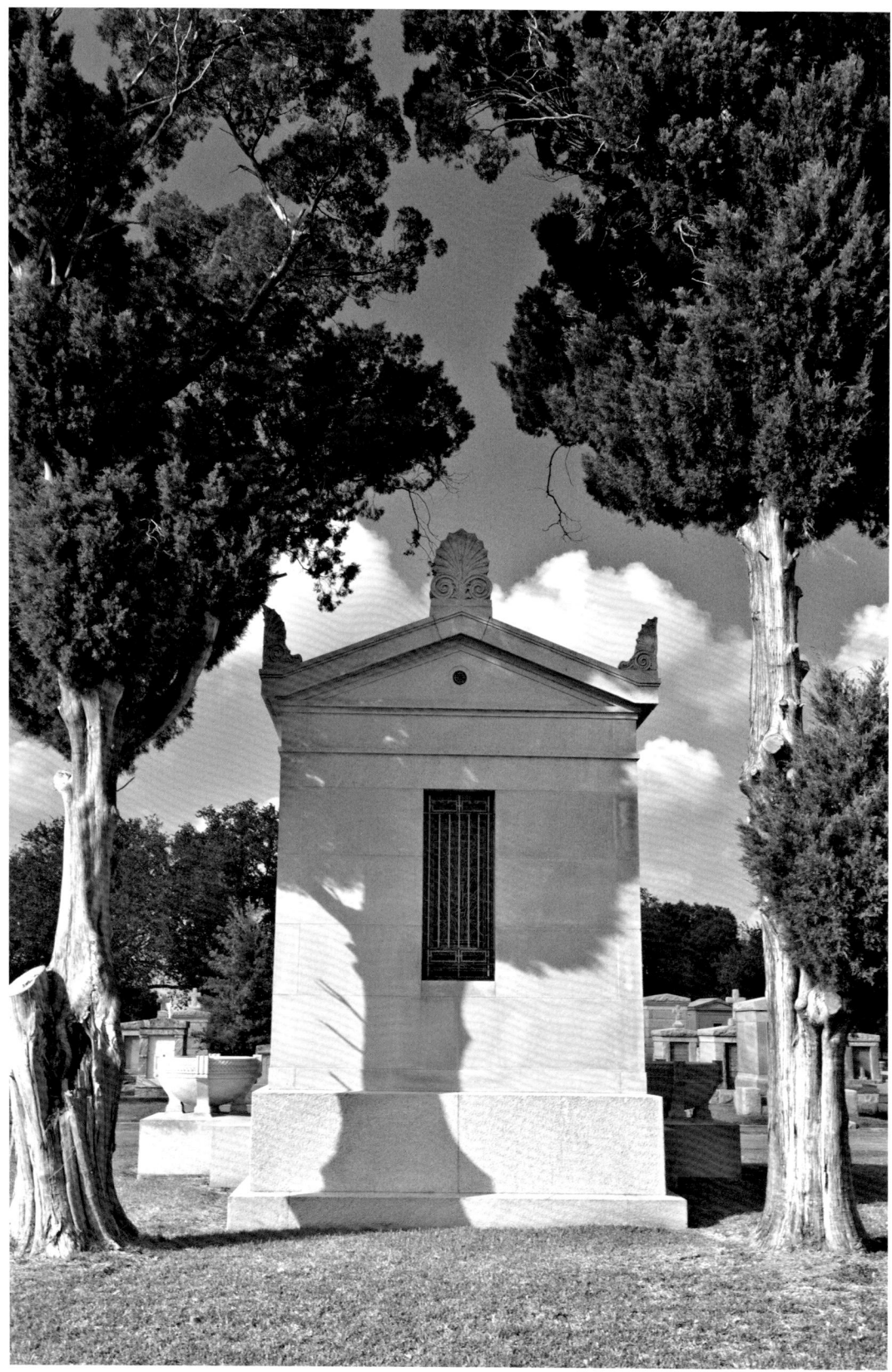

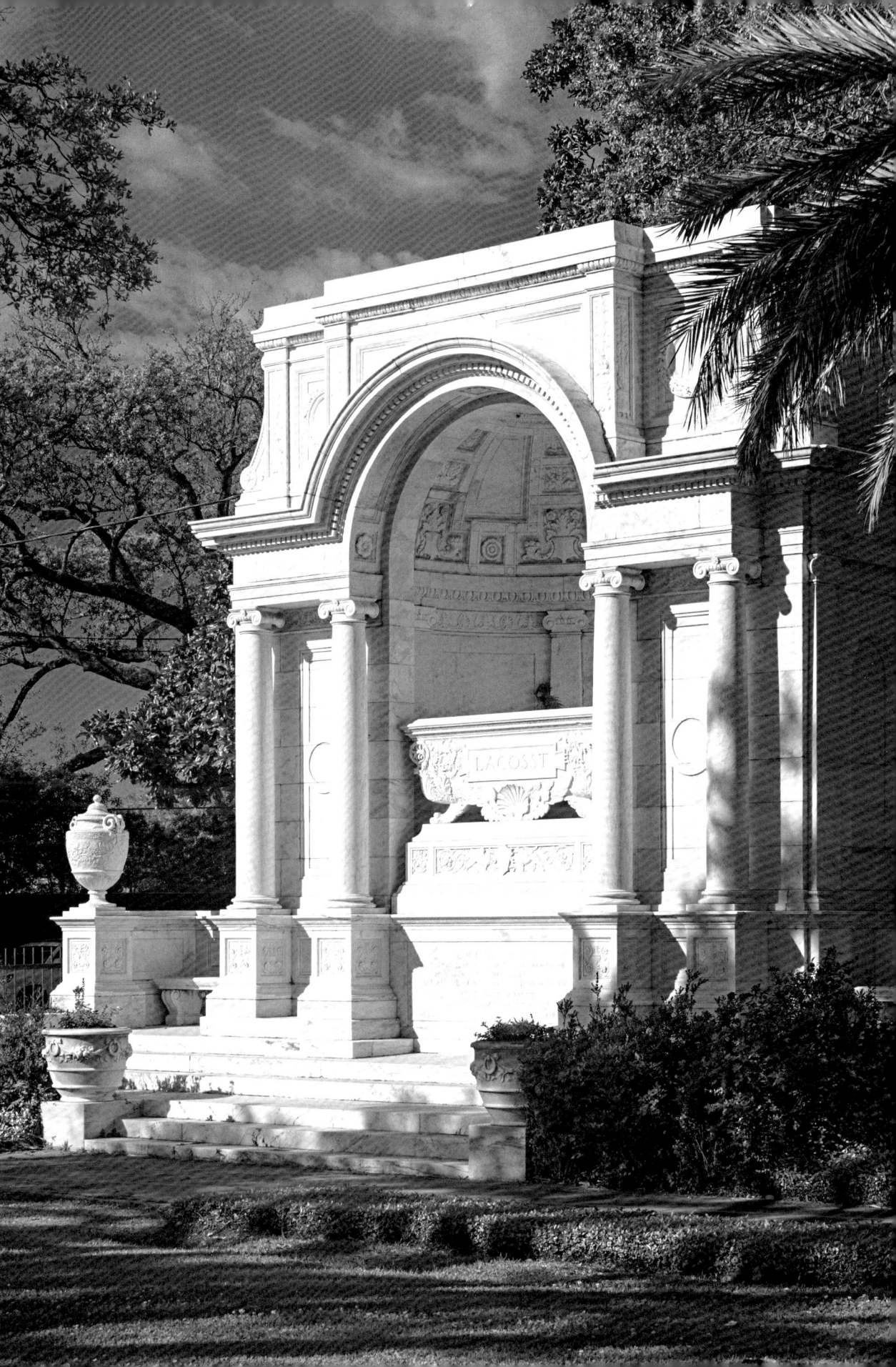

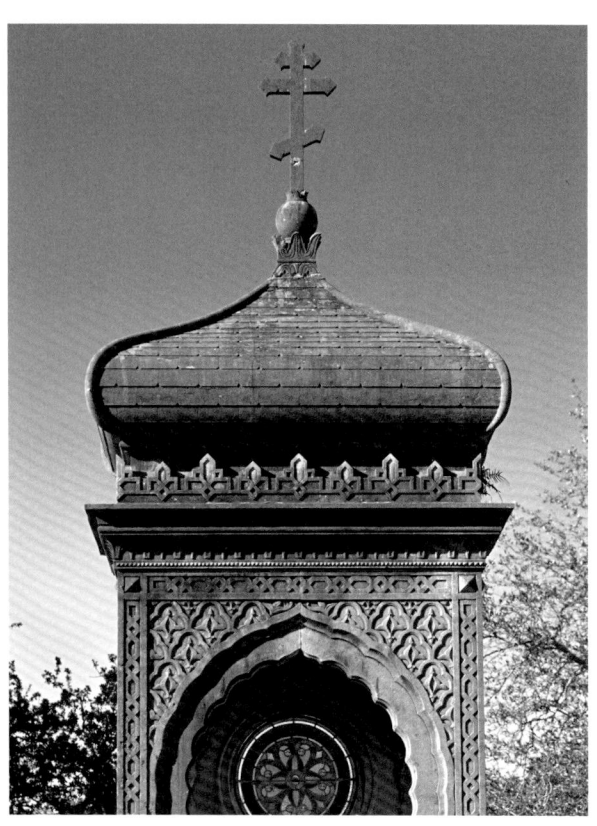
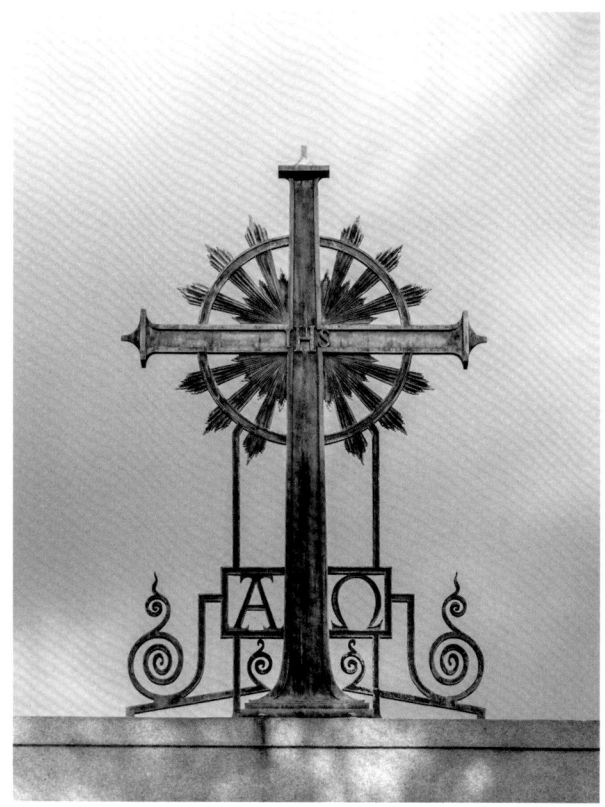
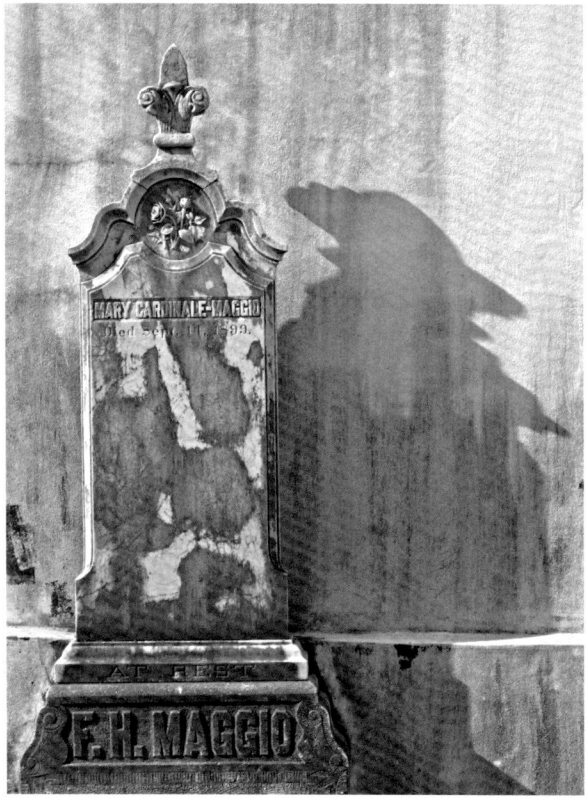
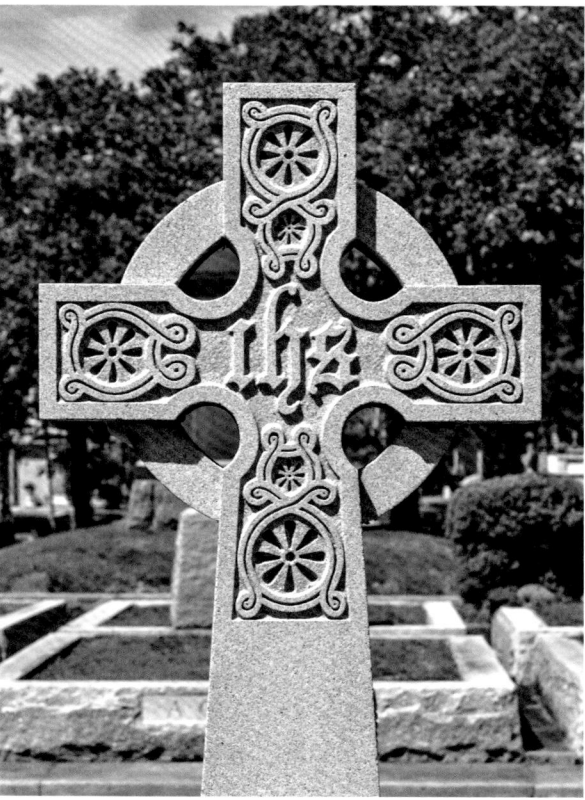

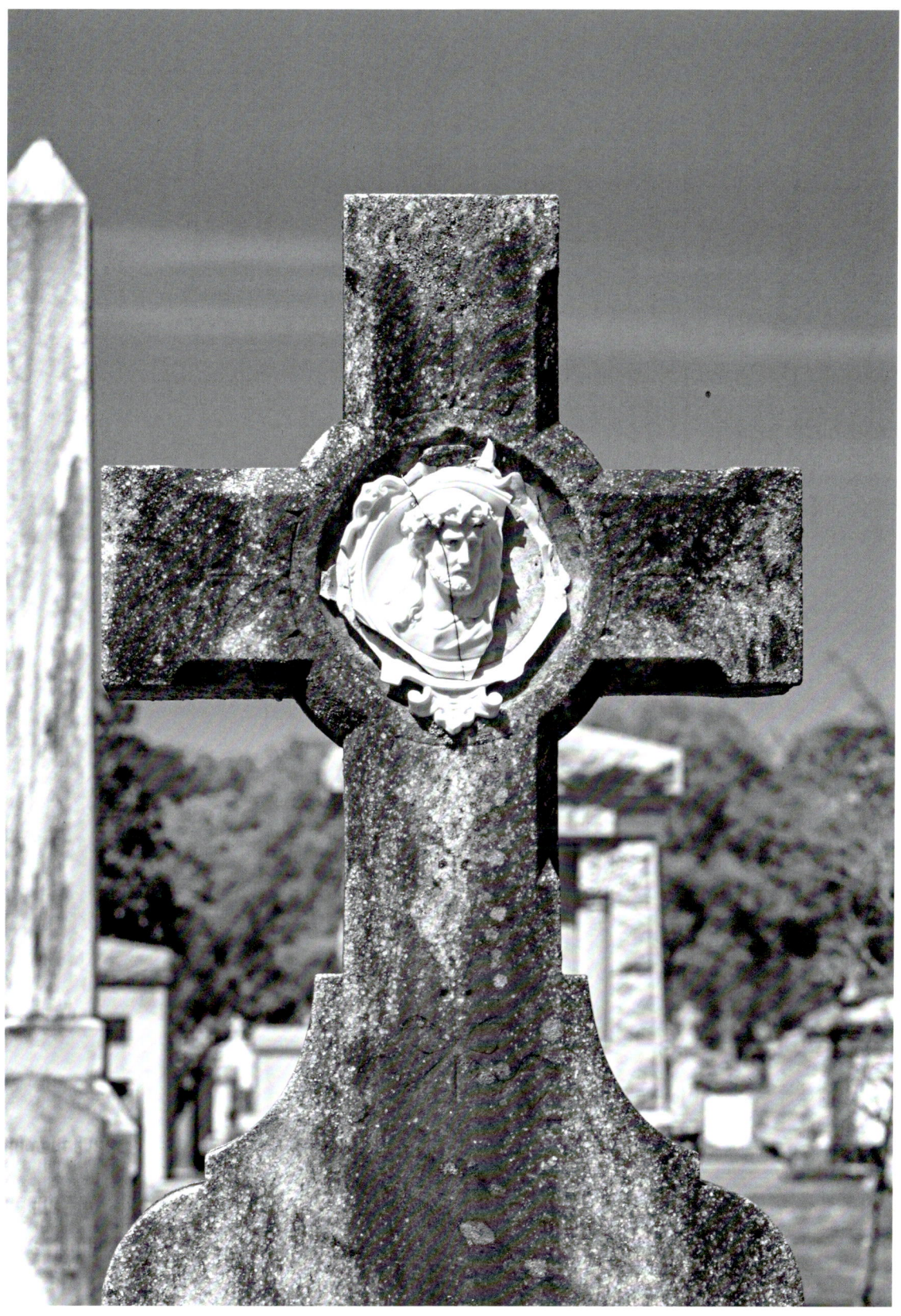

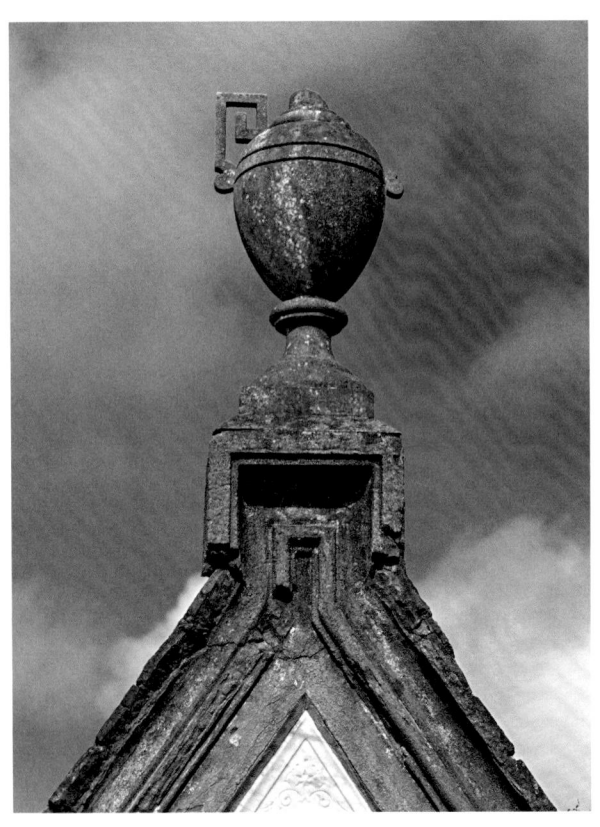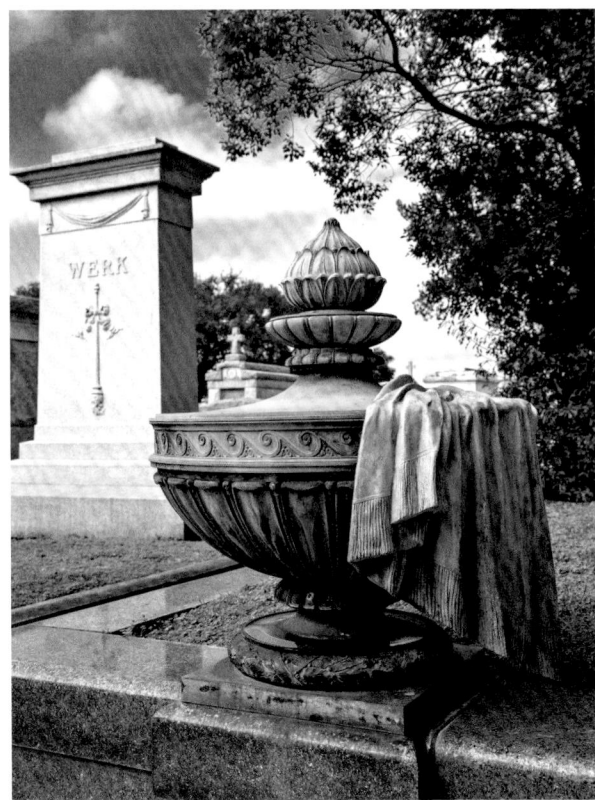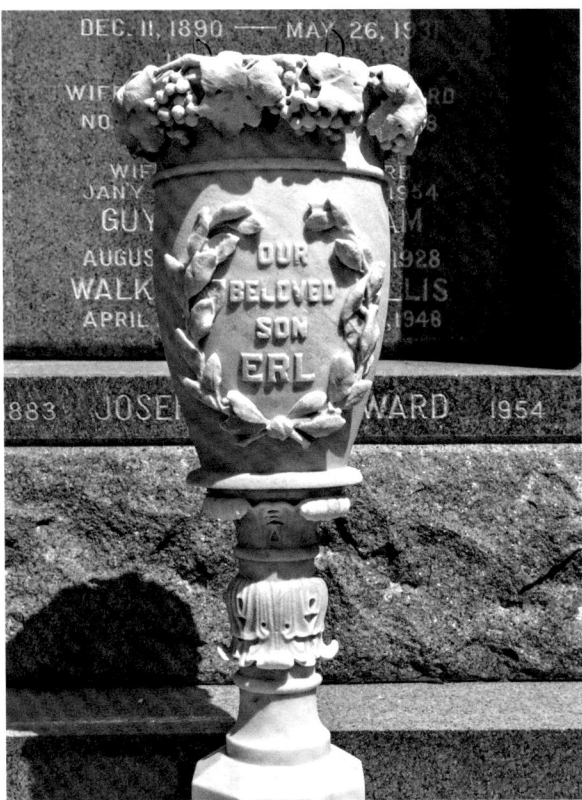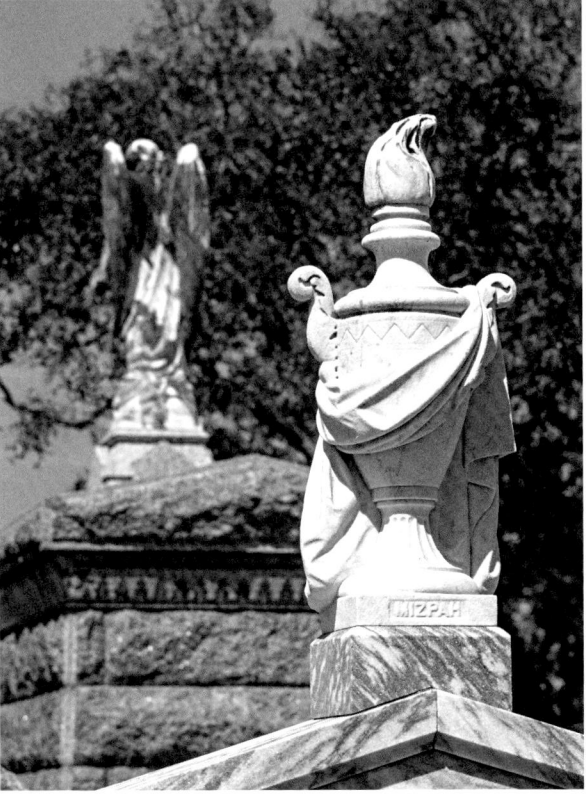

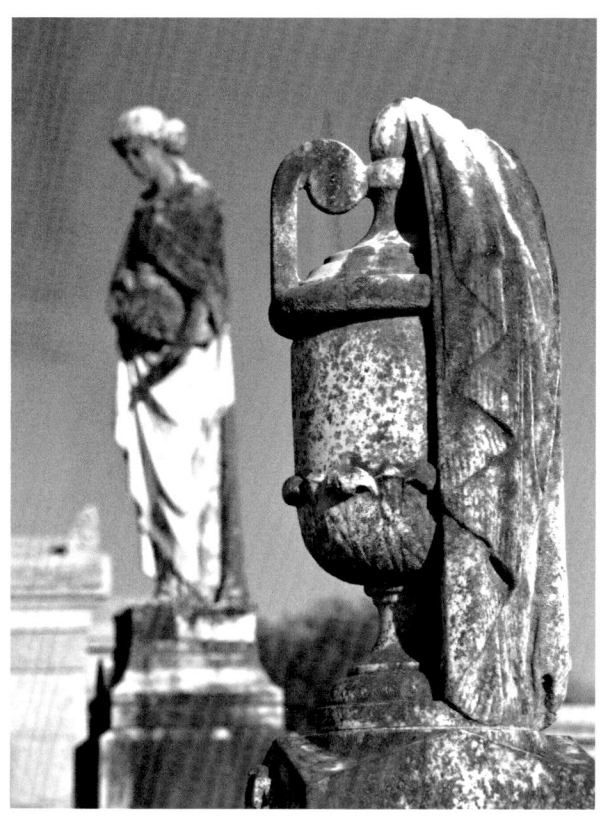 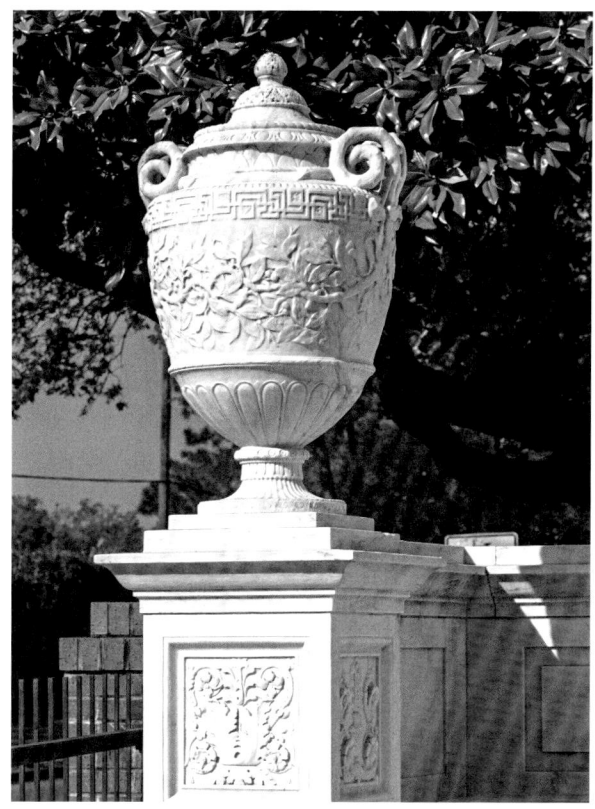
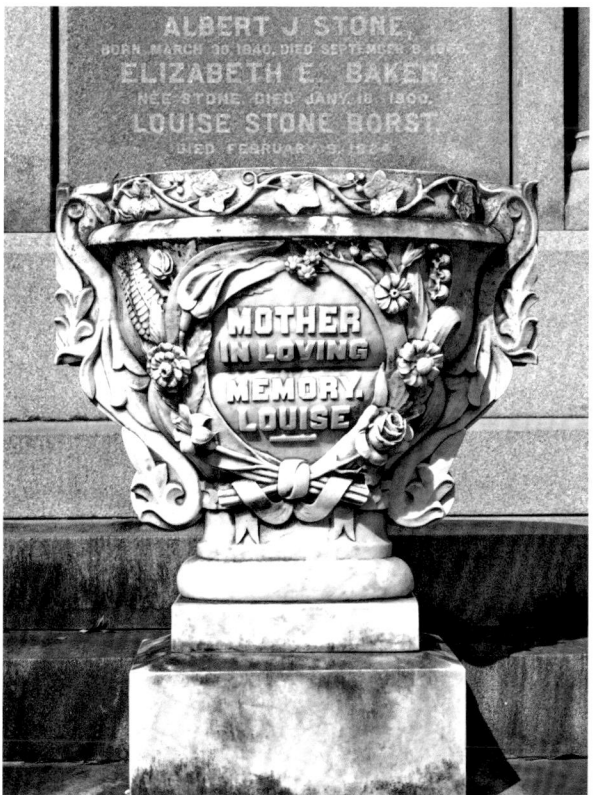 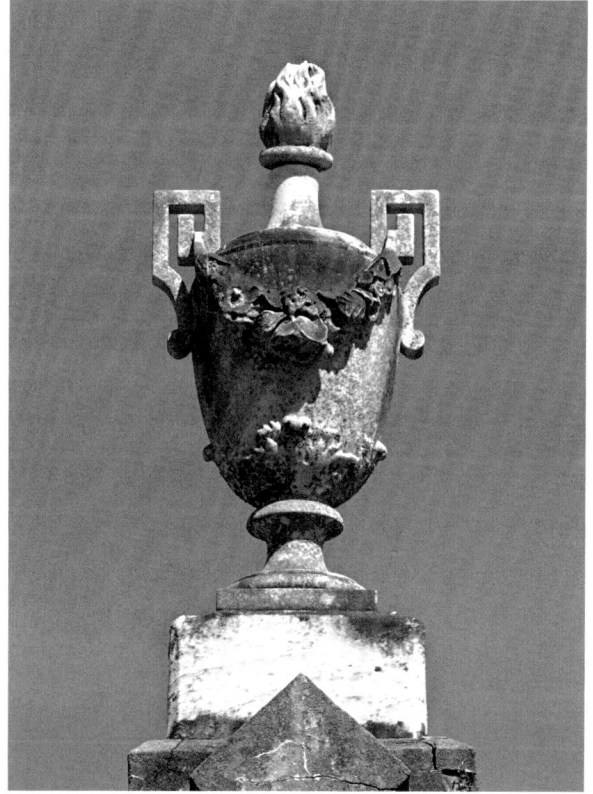

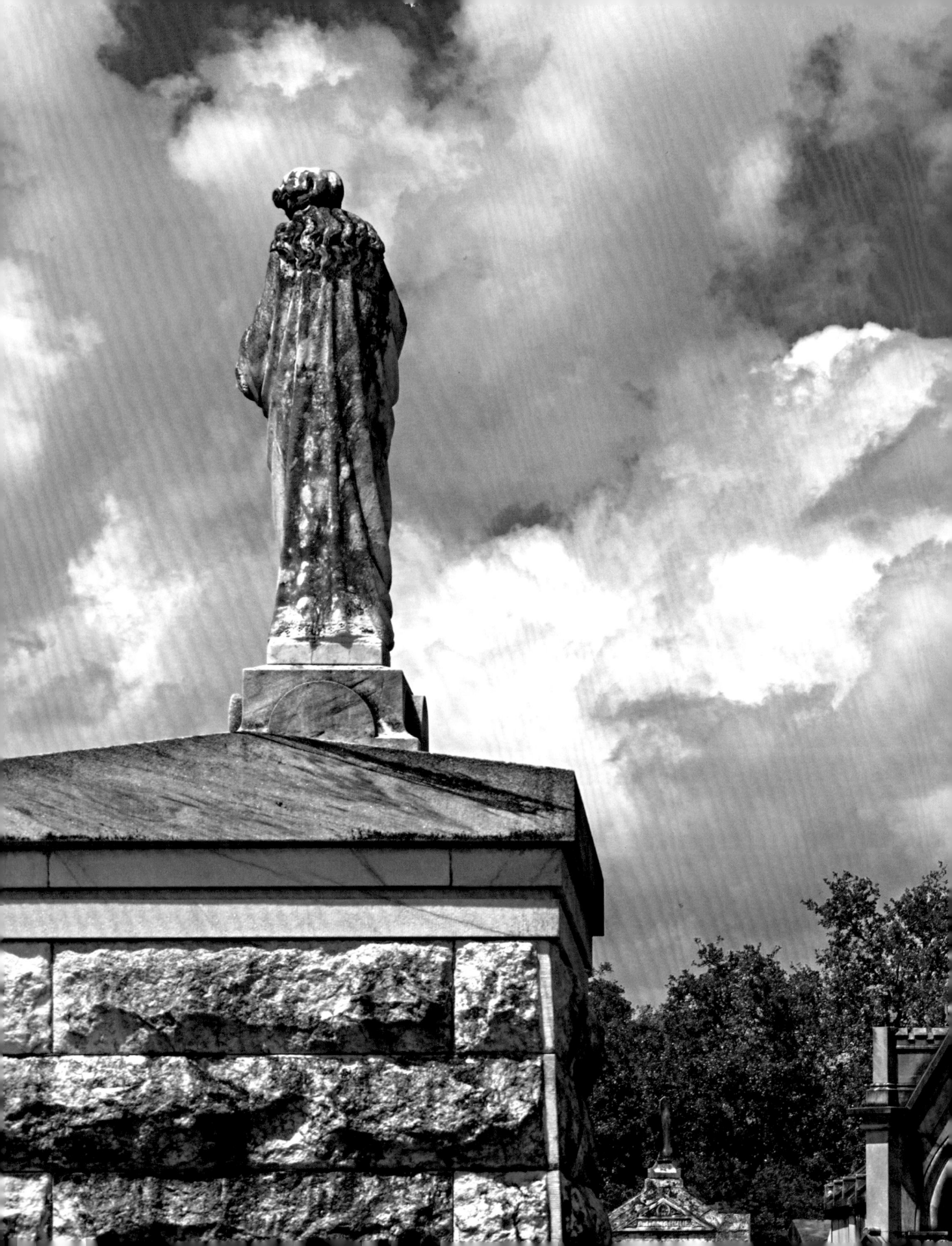

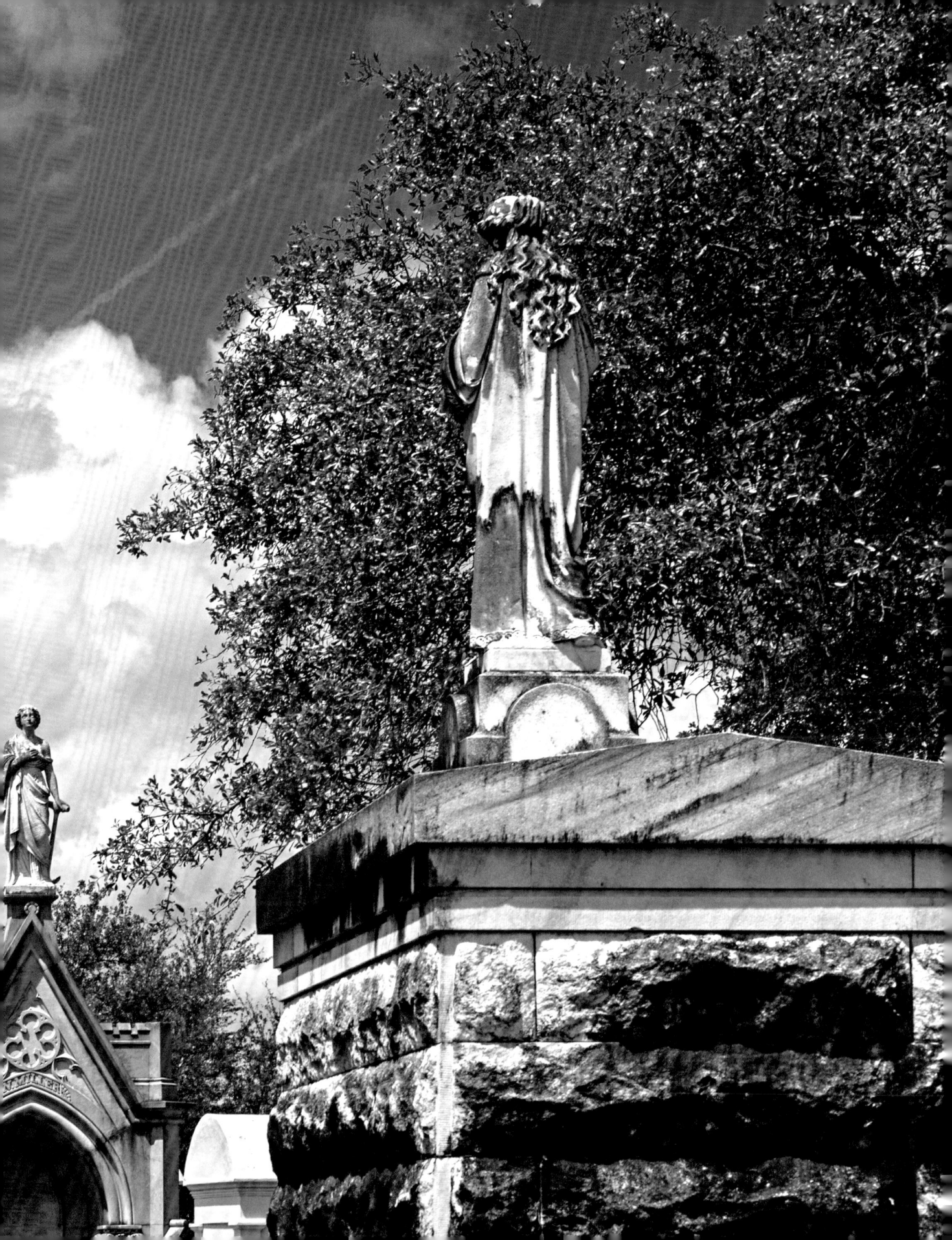

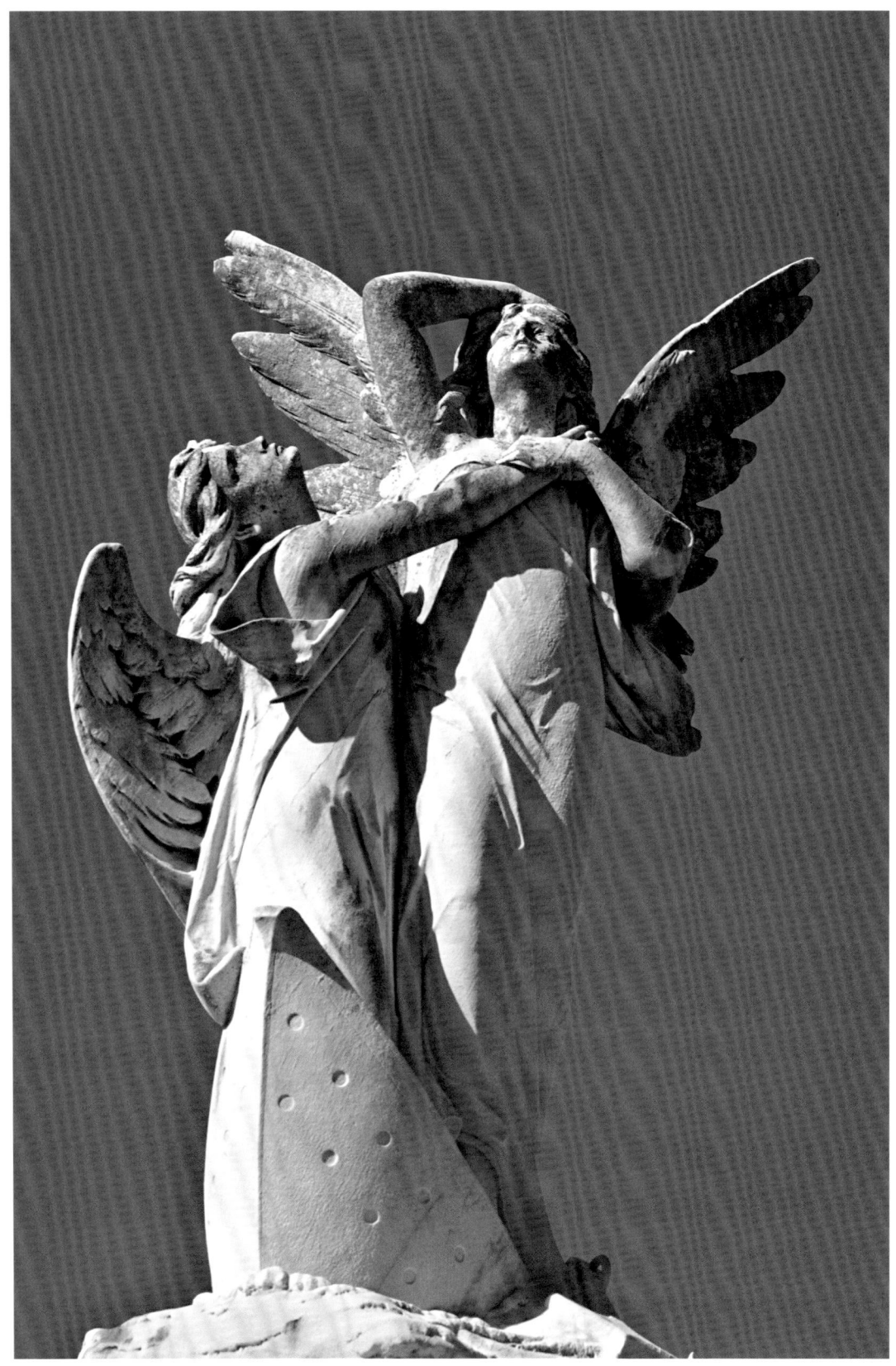

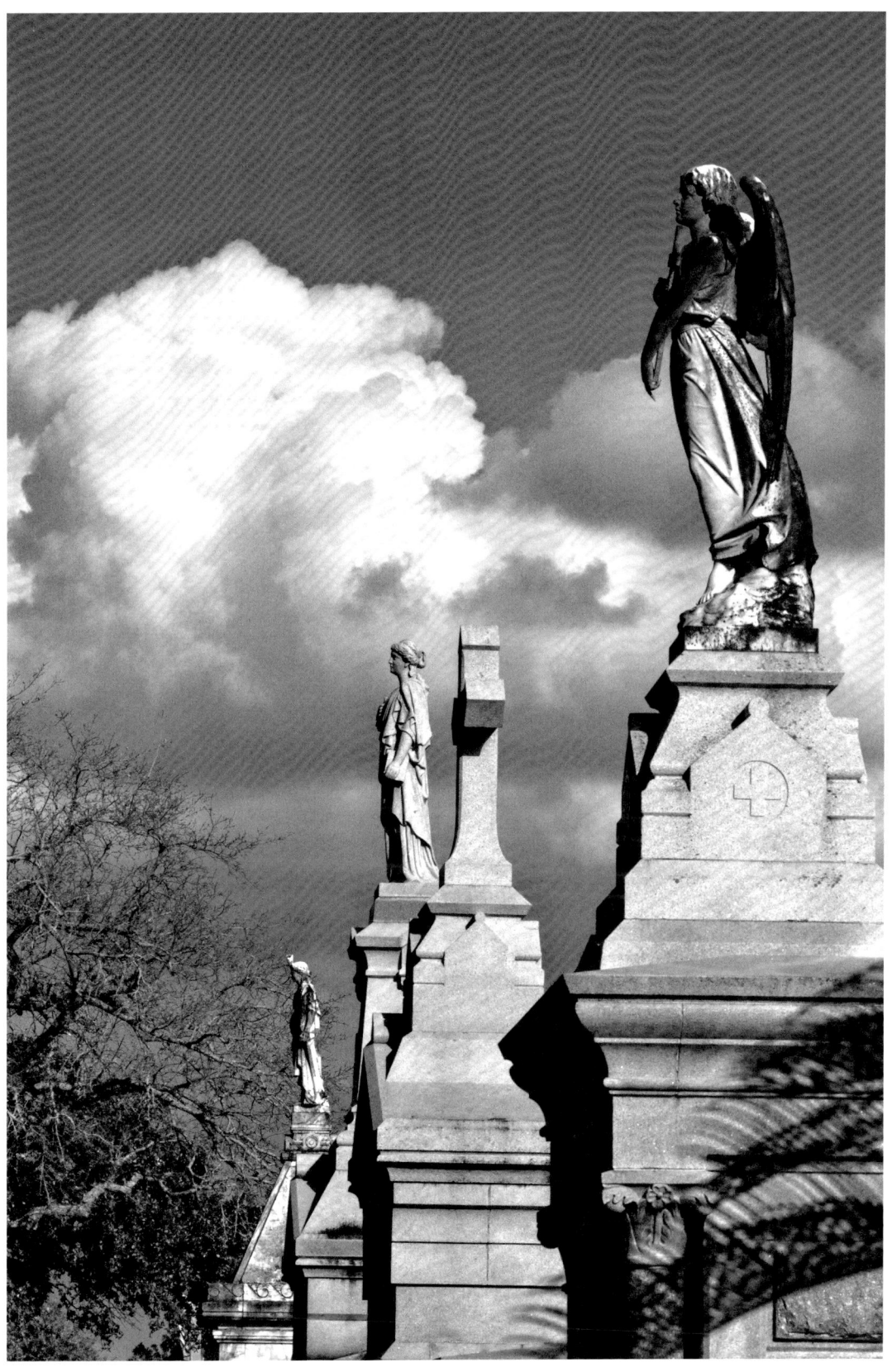

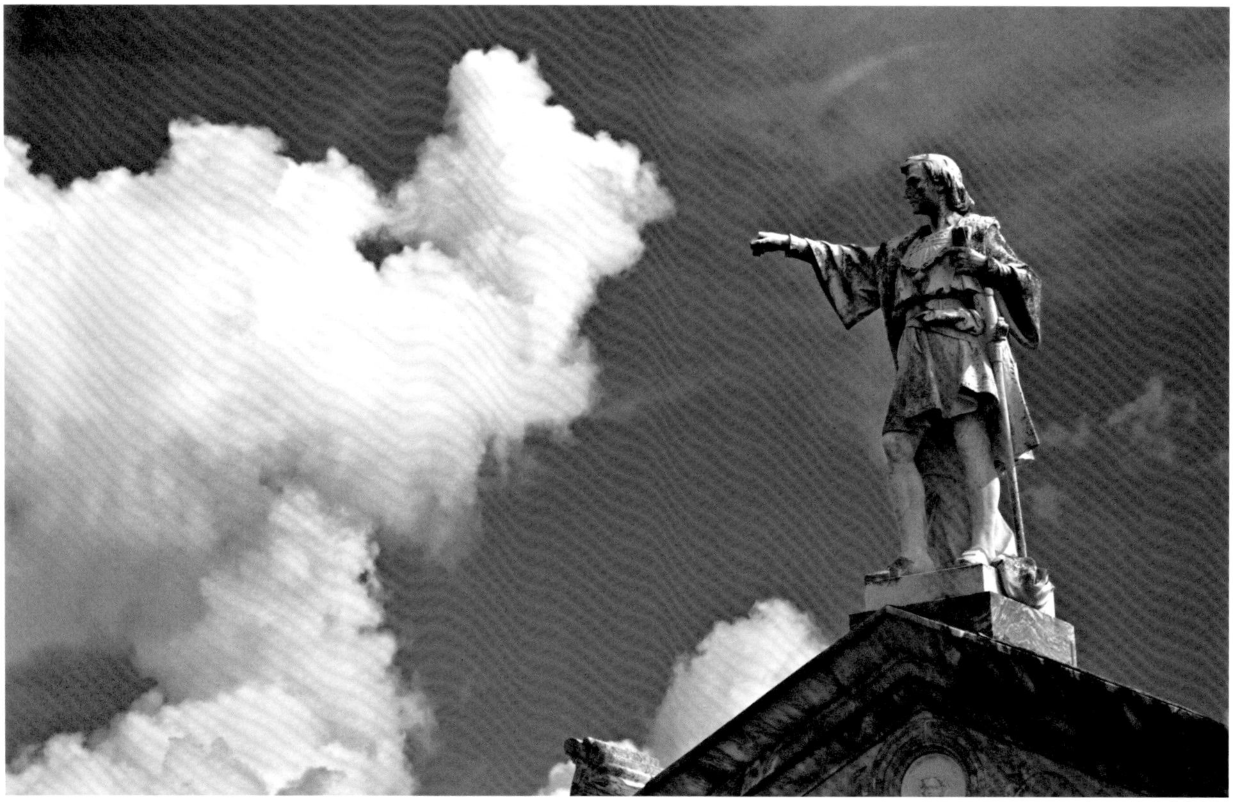

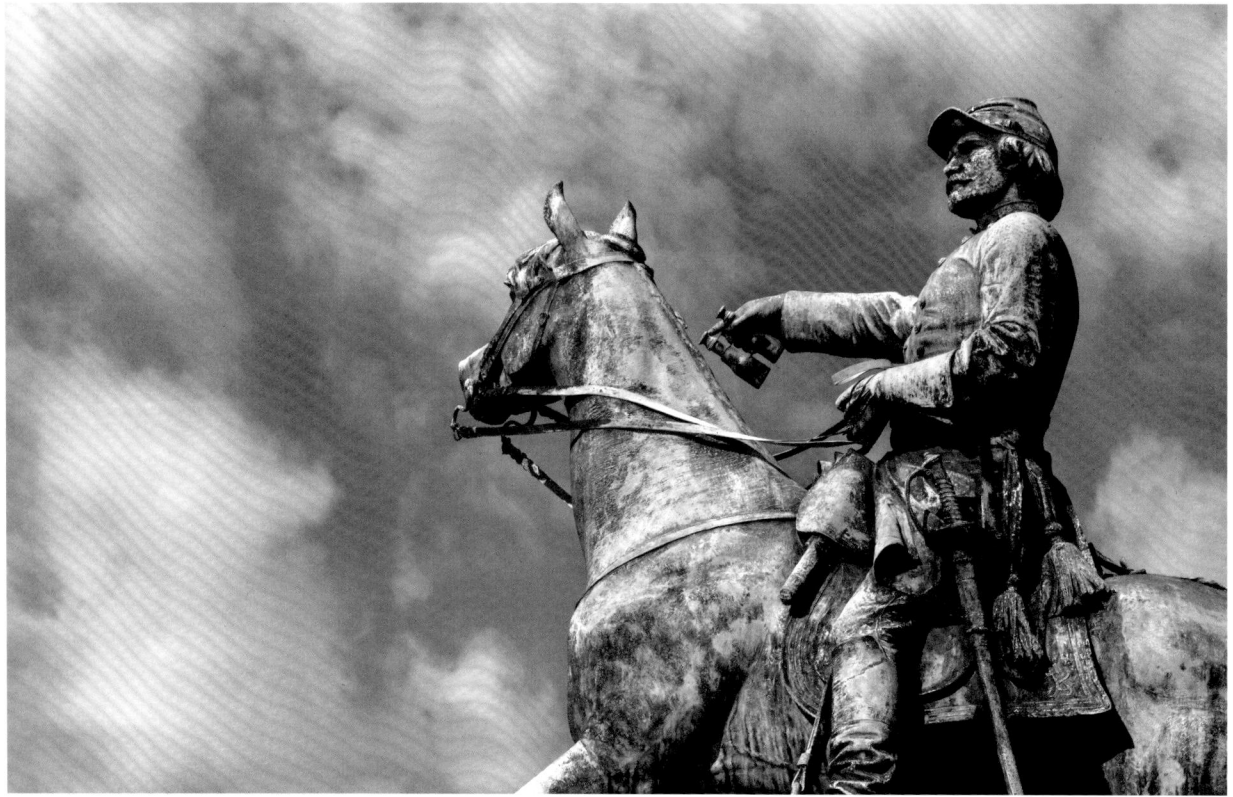

136   *Metairie Cemetery*

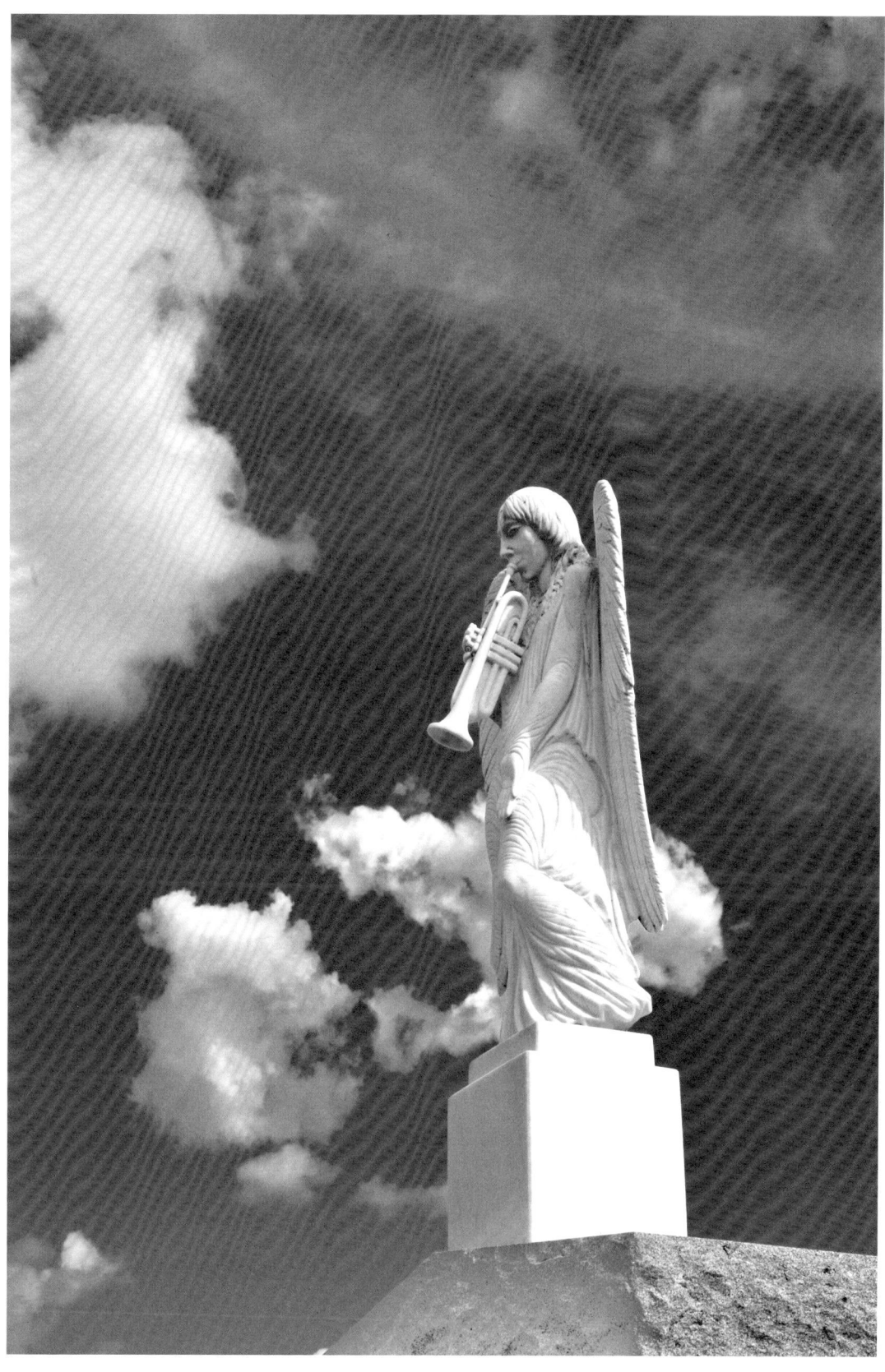

Metairie Cemetery

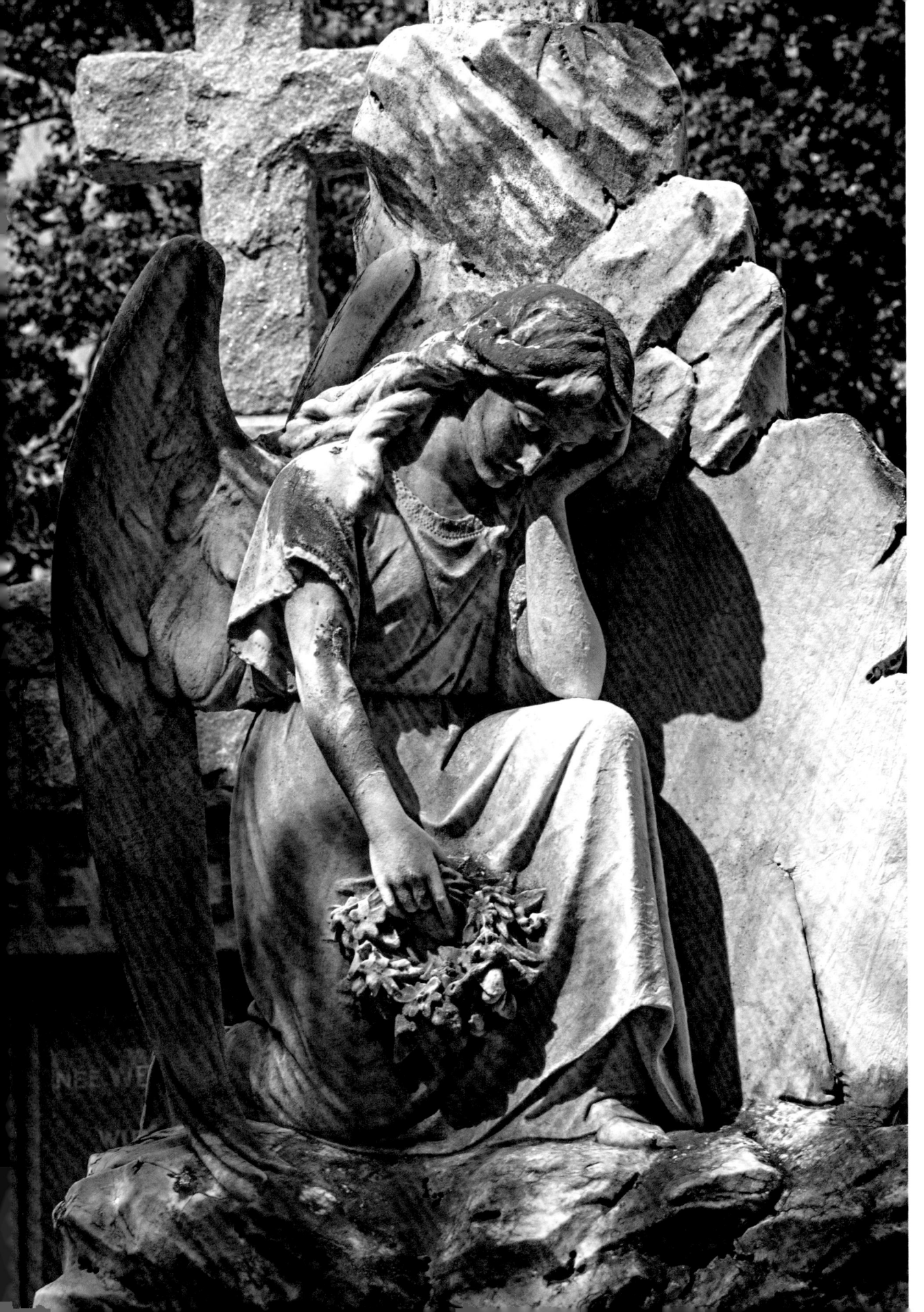

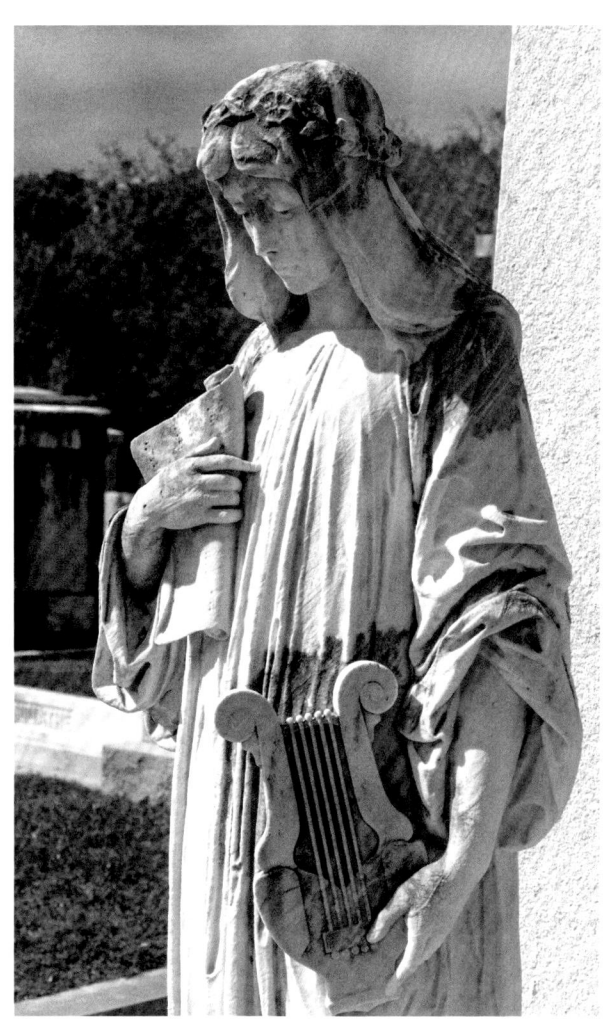
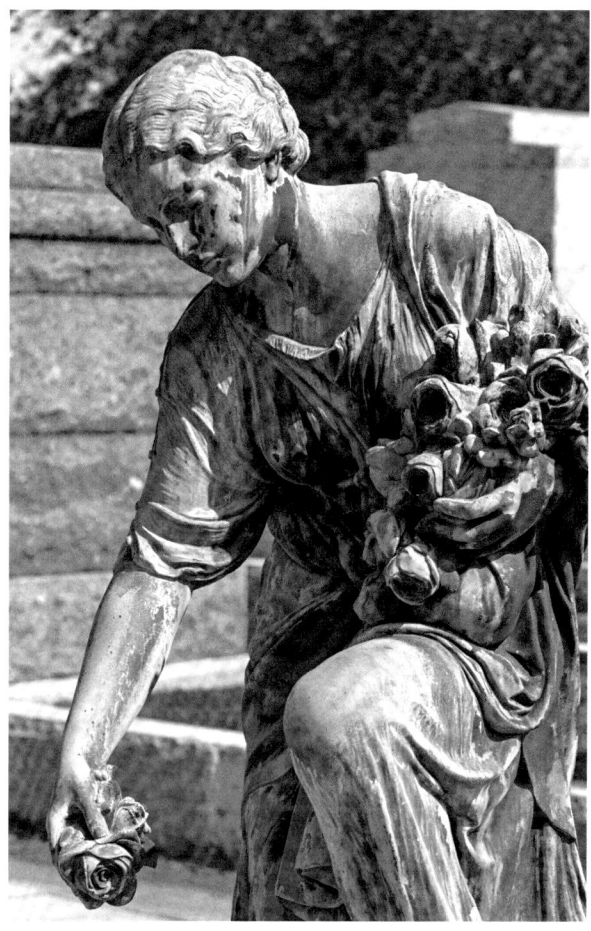

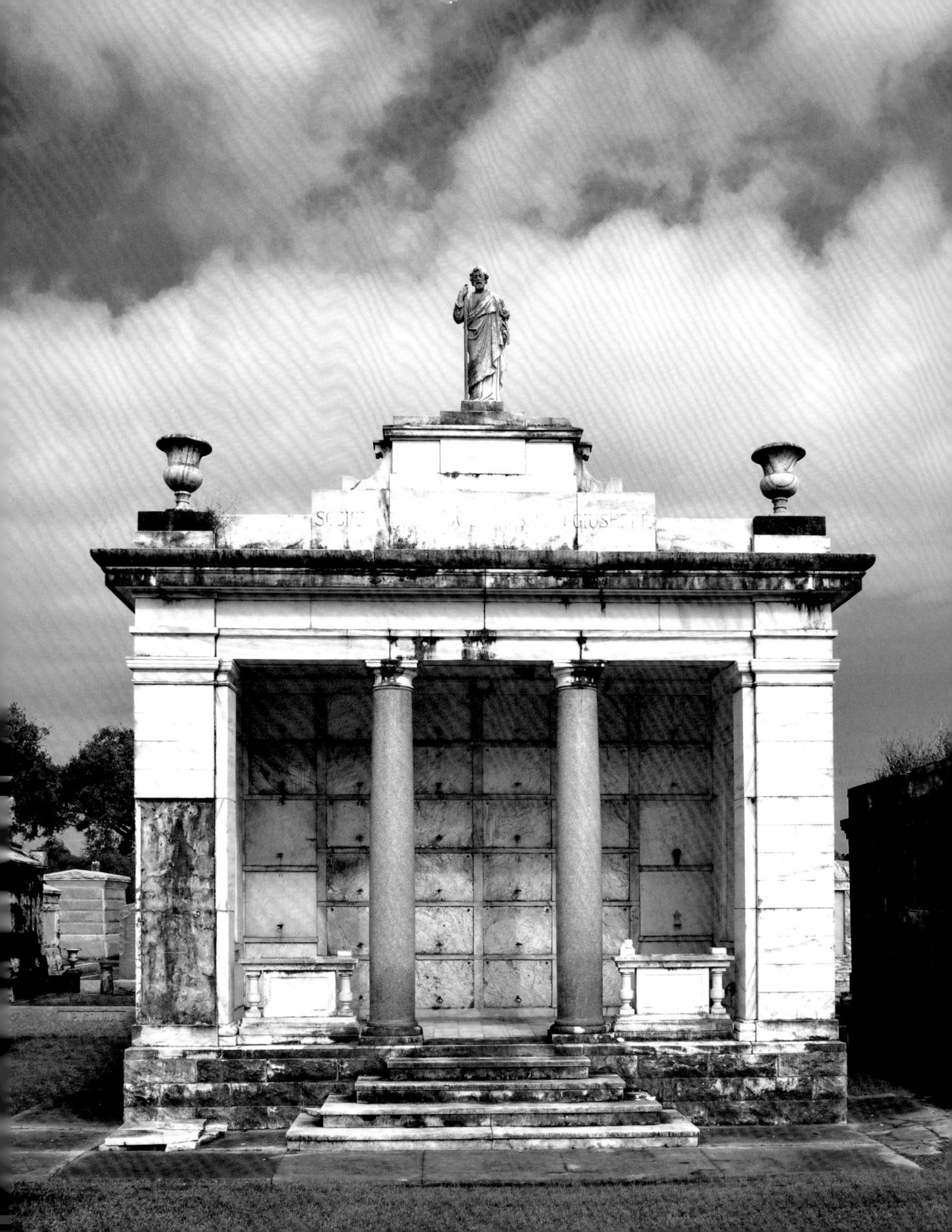

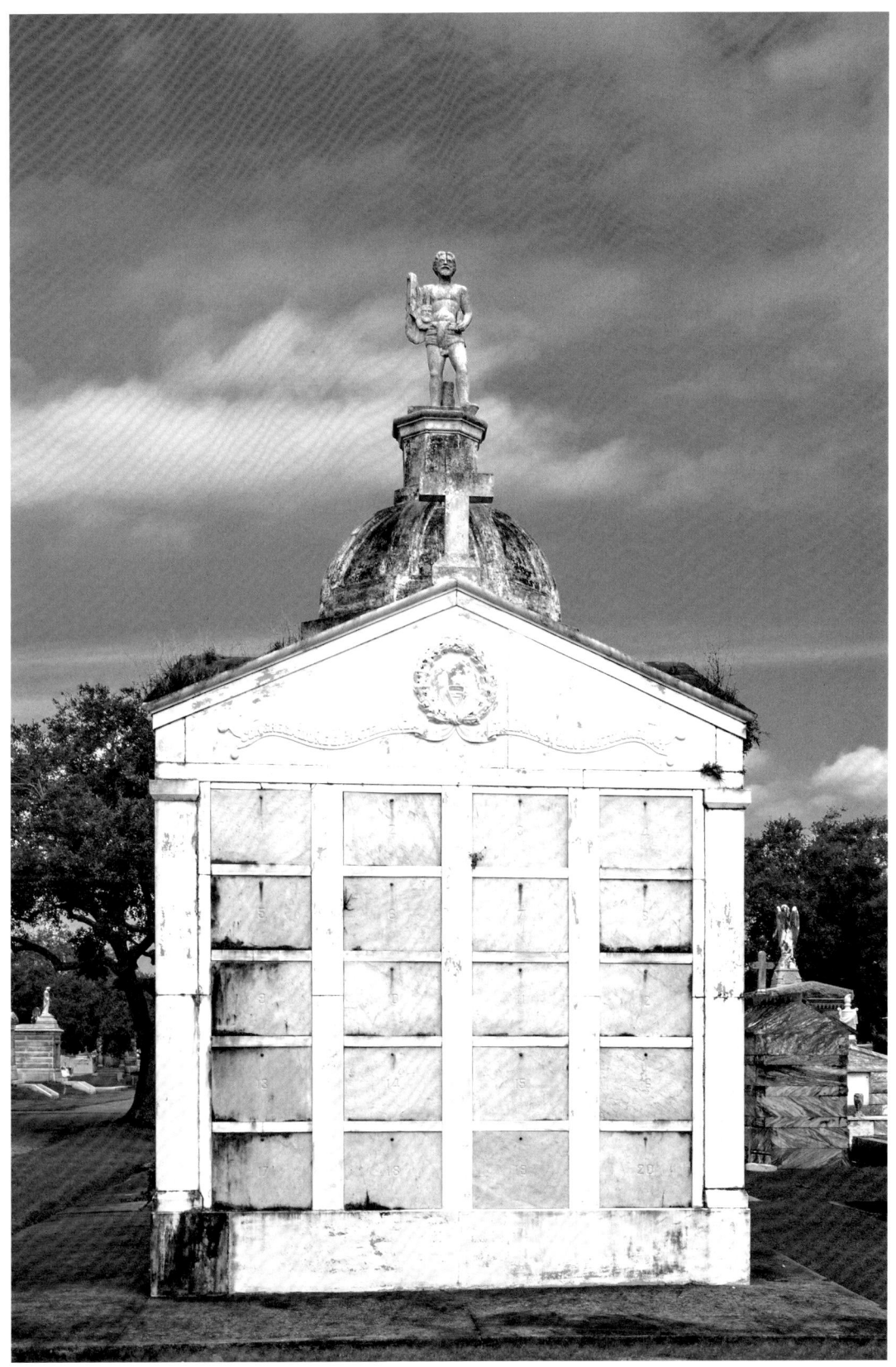

Metairie Cemetery

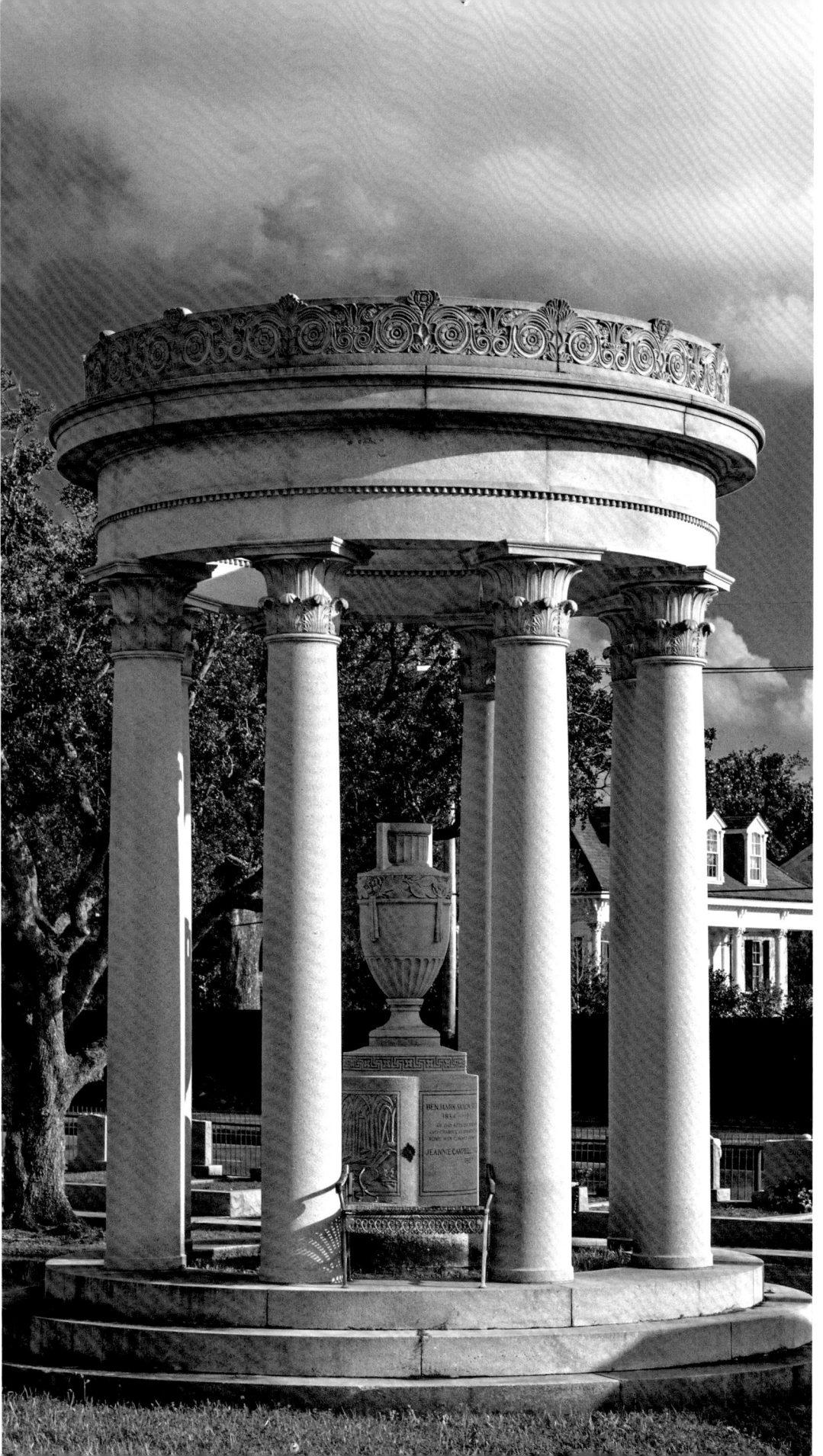

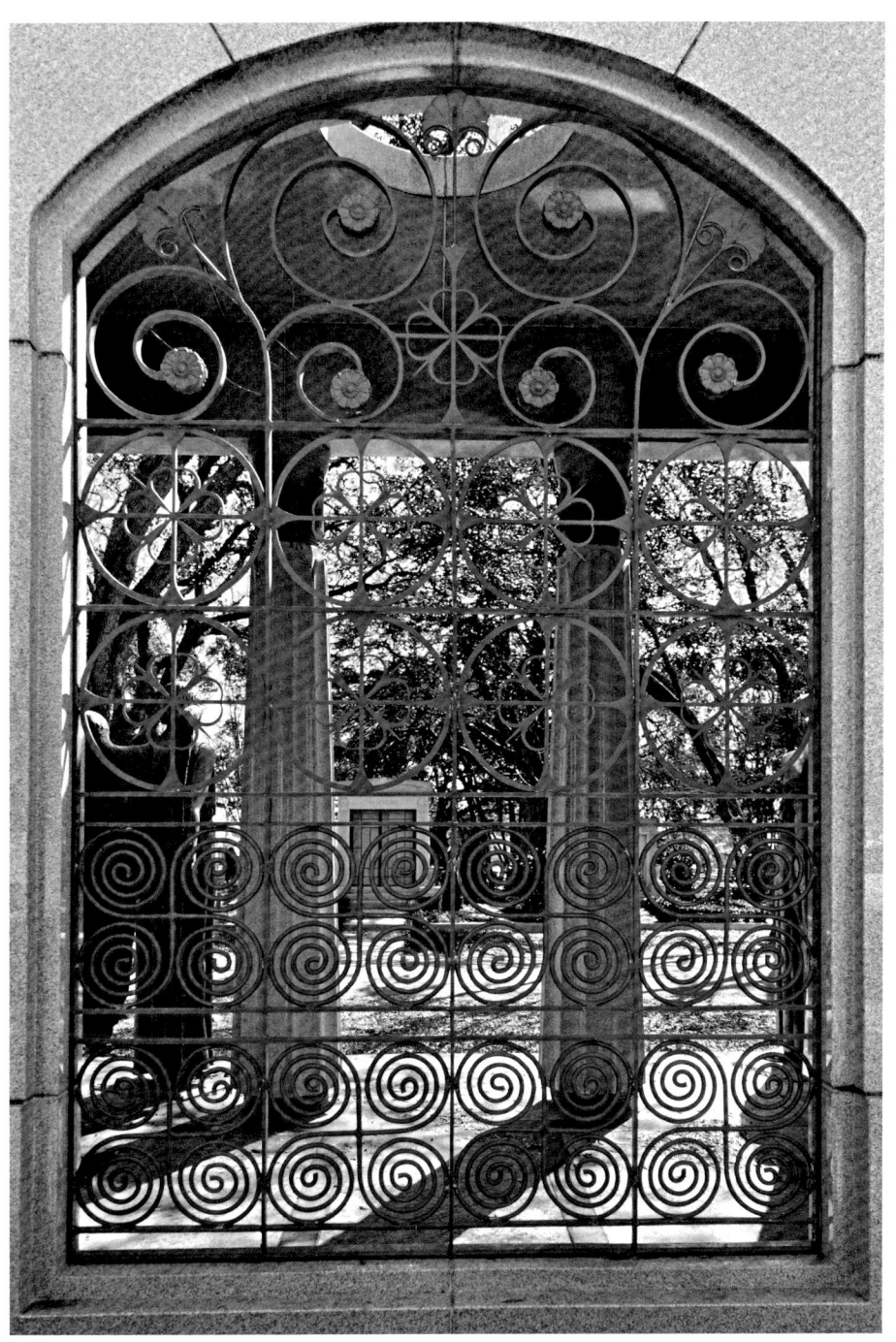

St. Louis Cemetery #1, #2 & #3

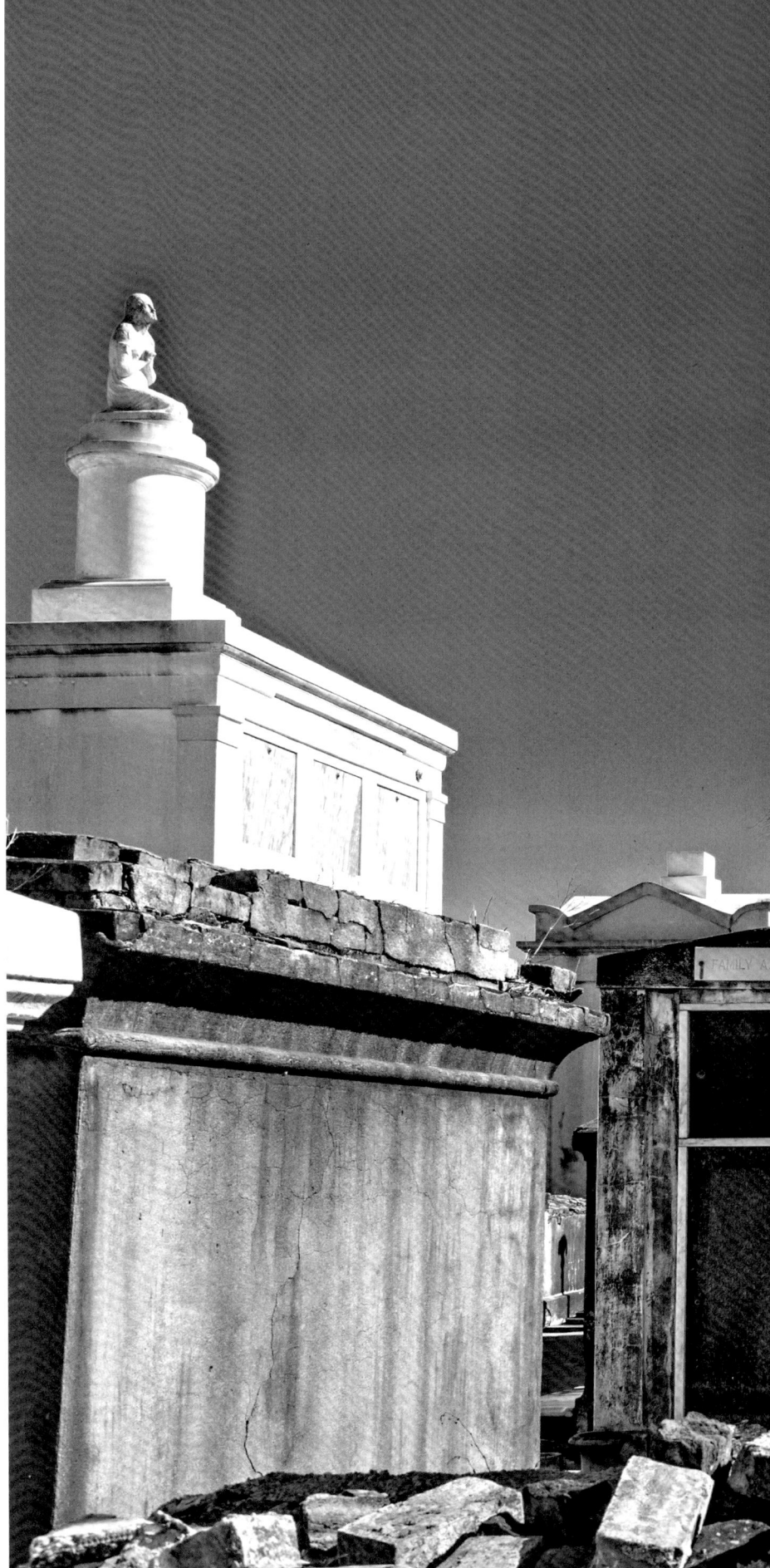

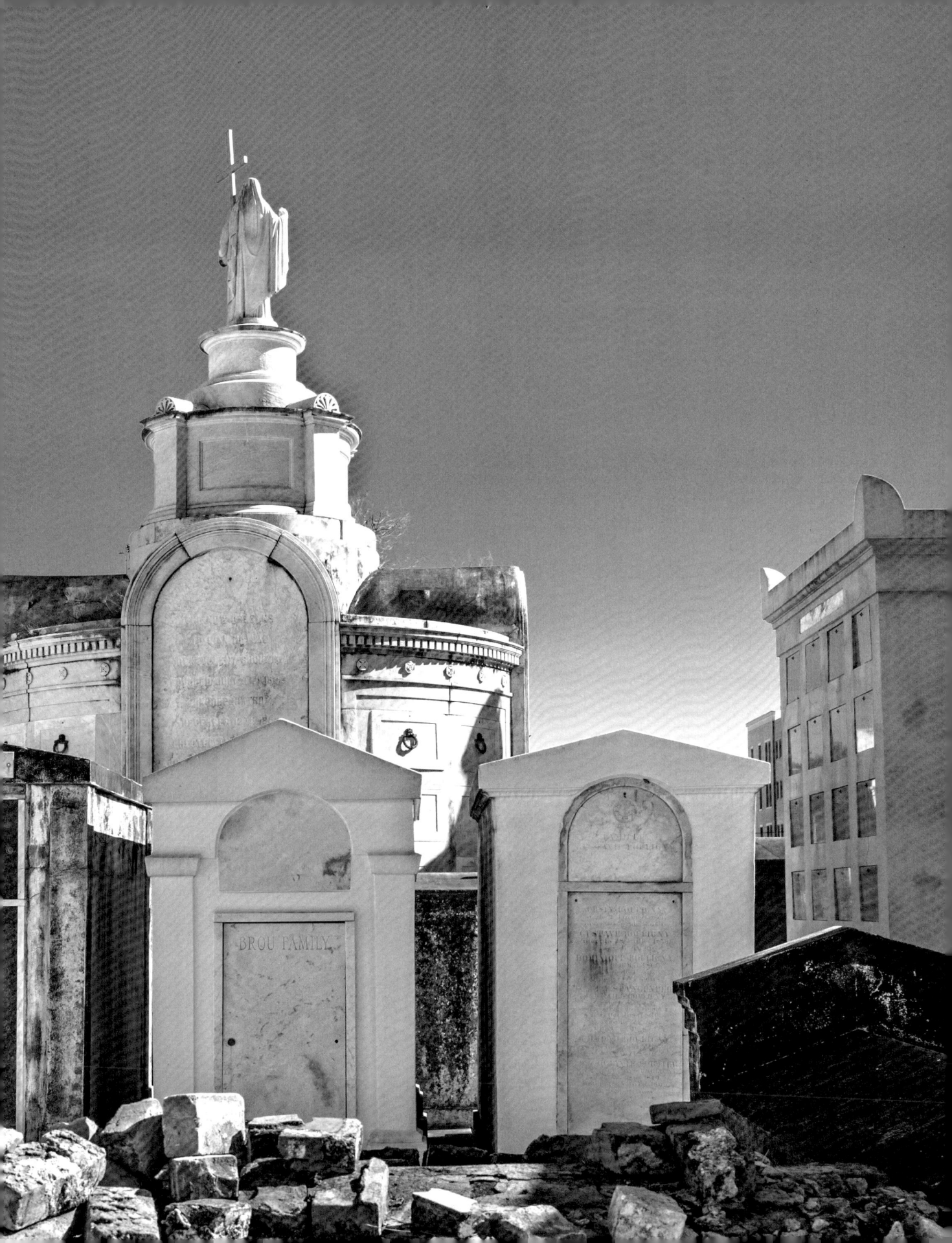

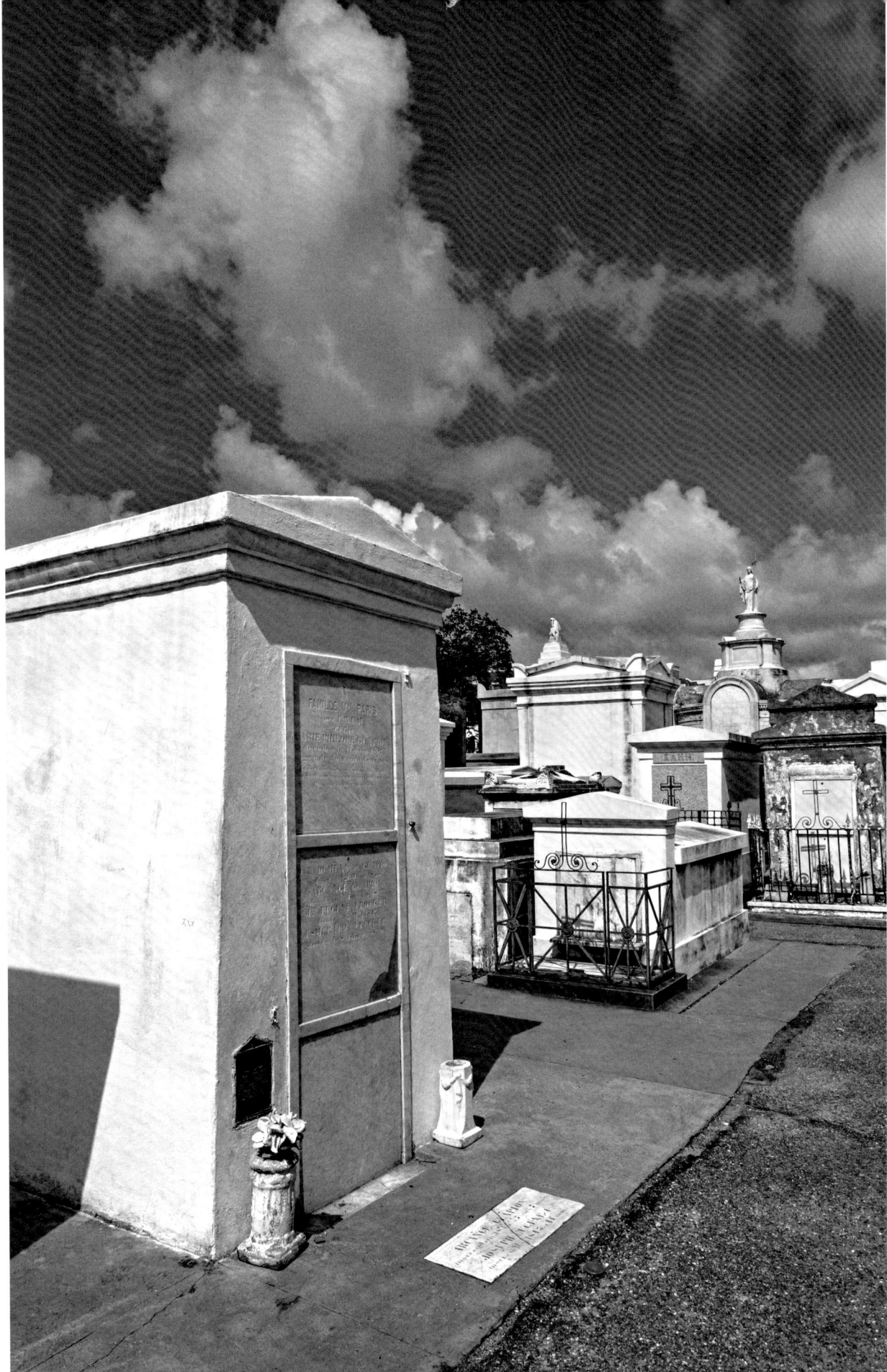

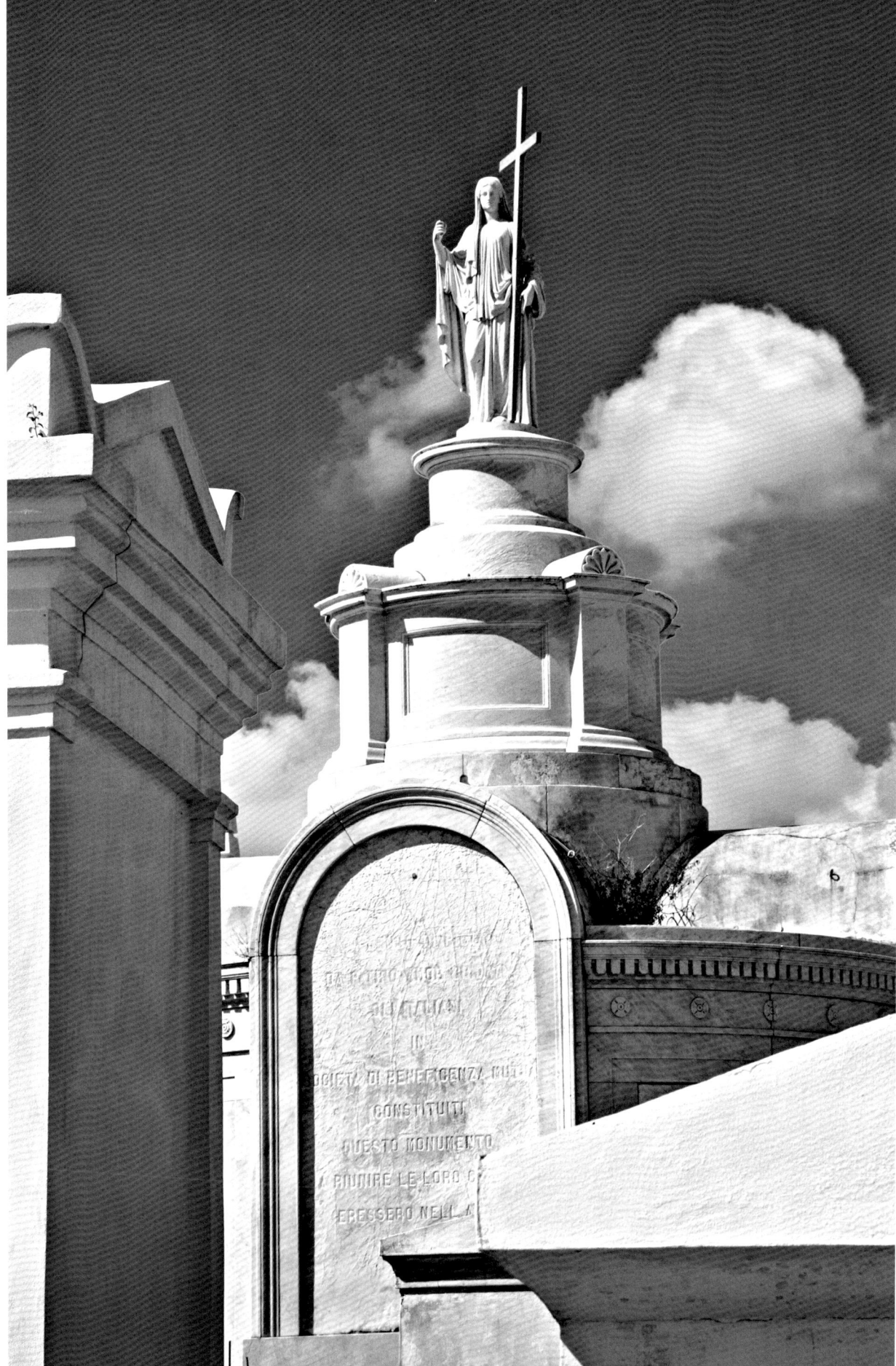

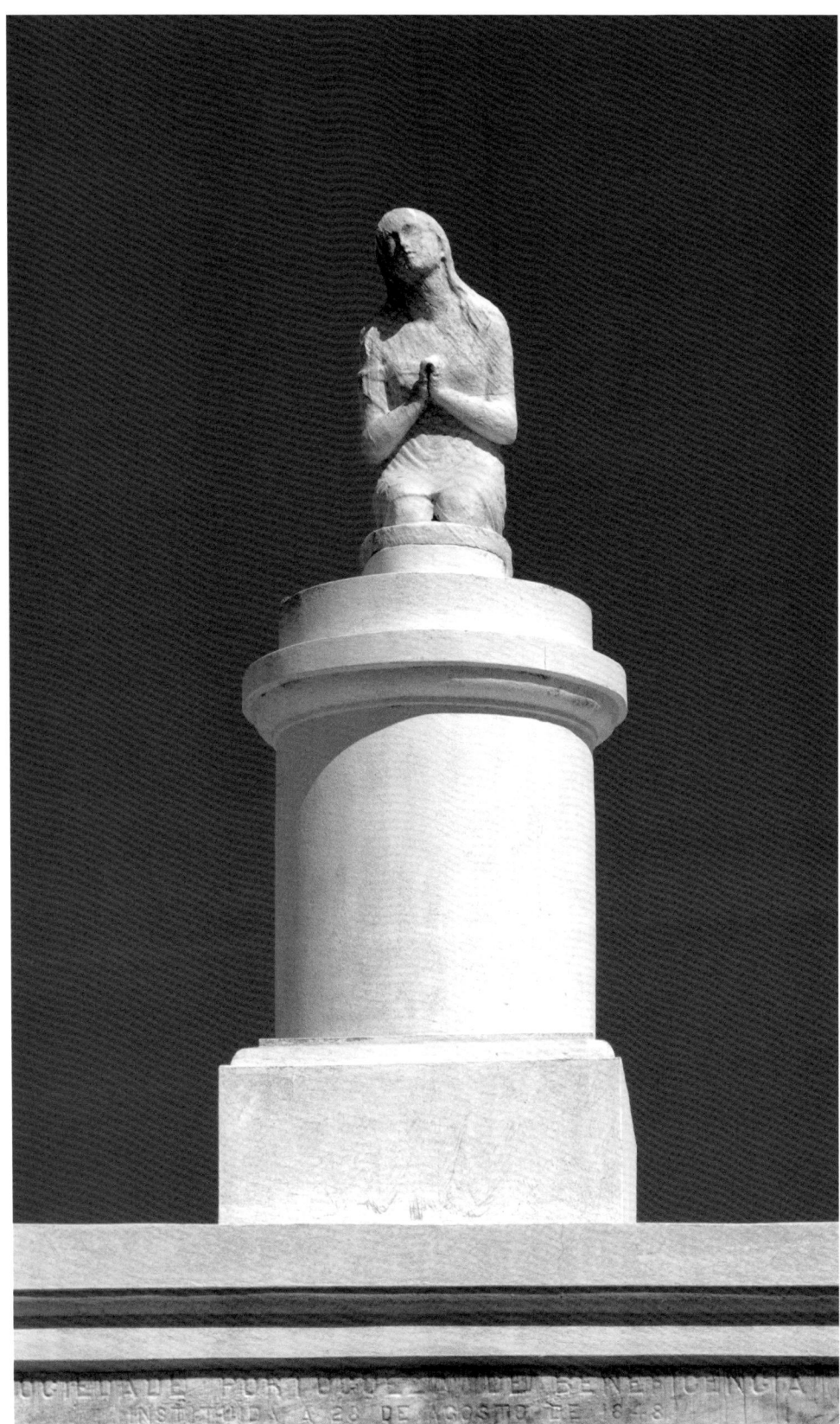

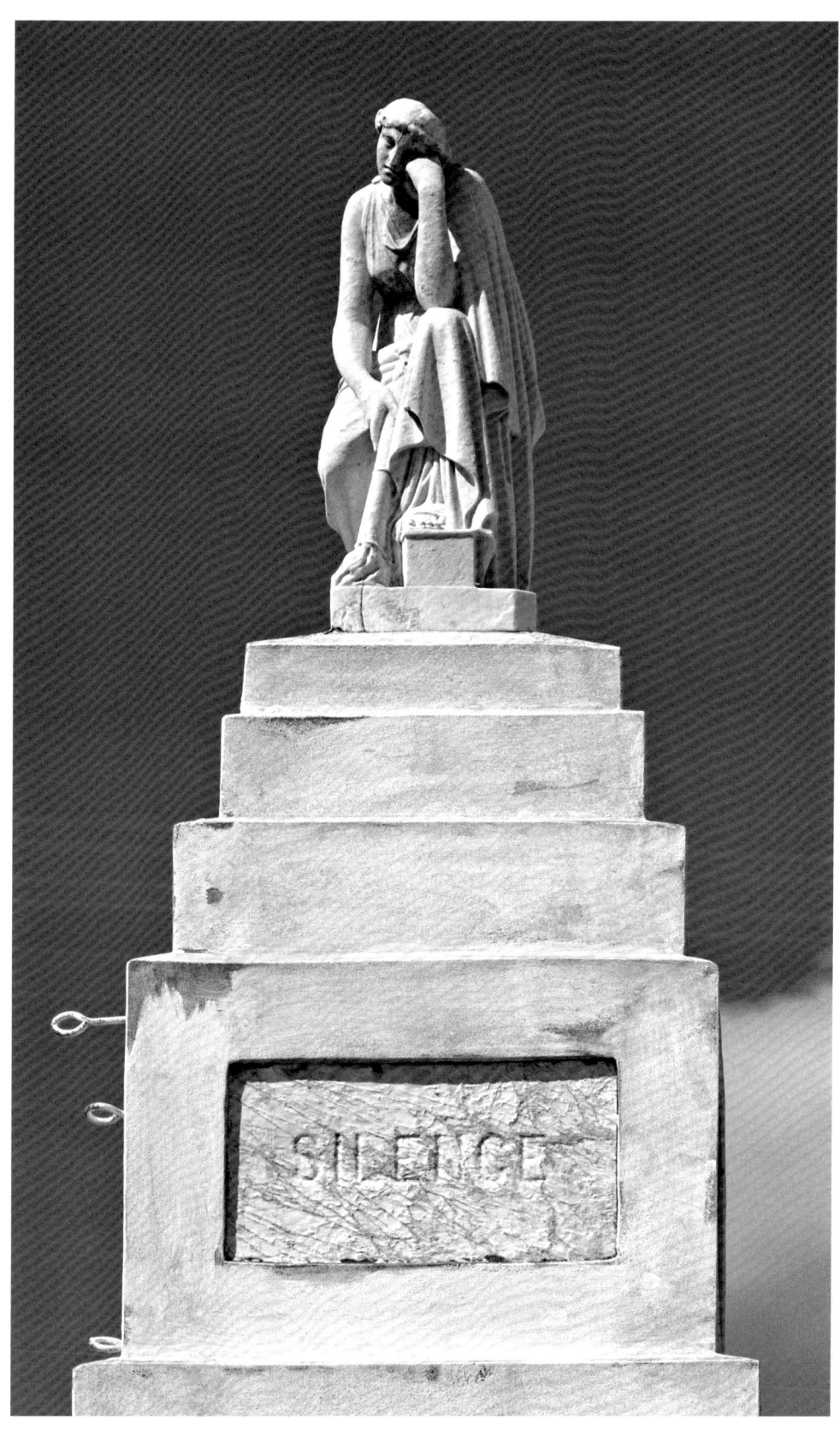

St. Louis Cemetery #1

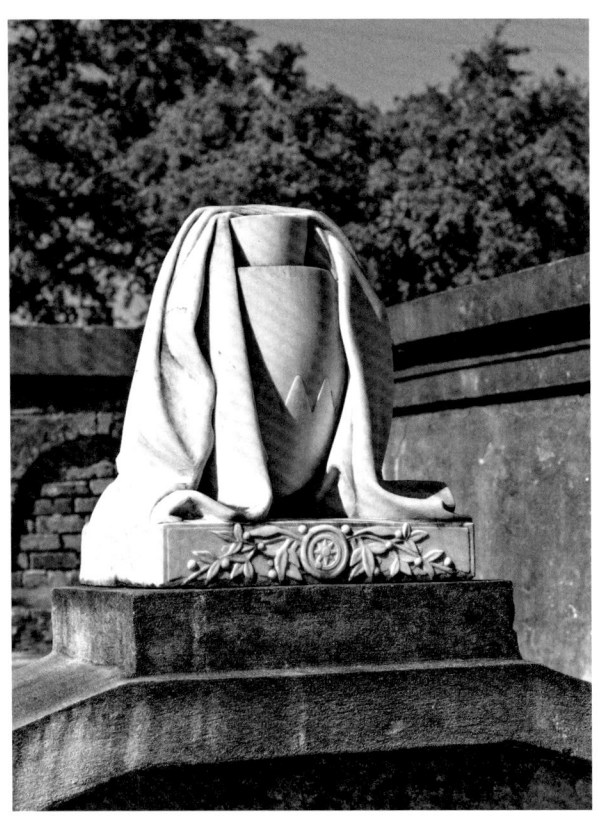
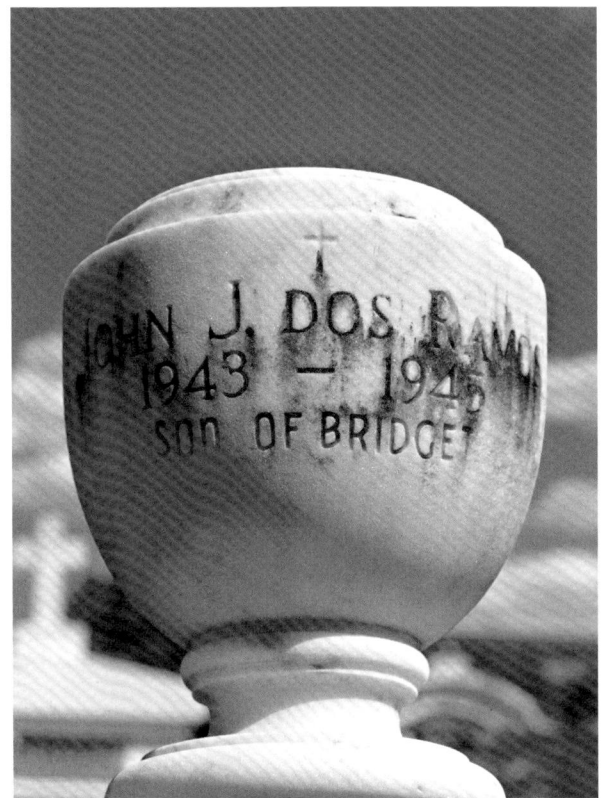
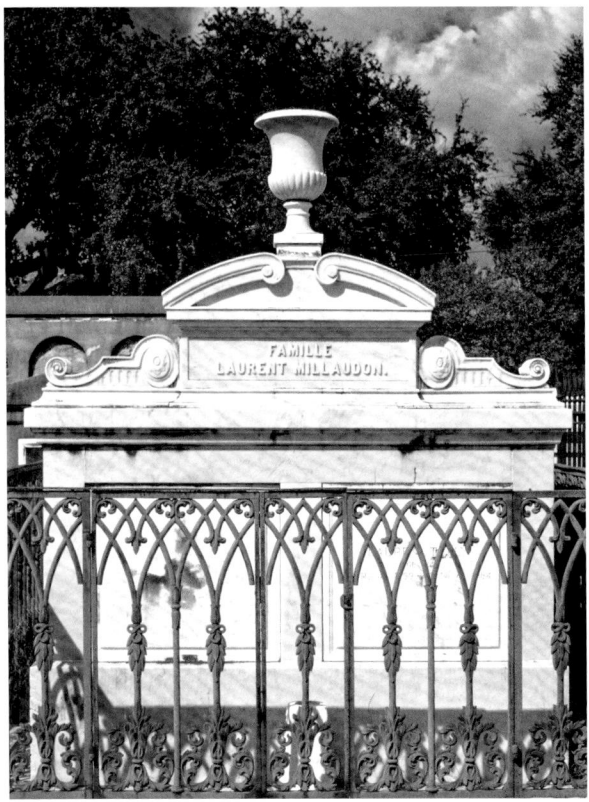
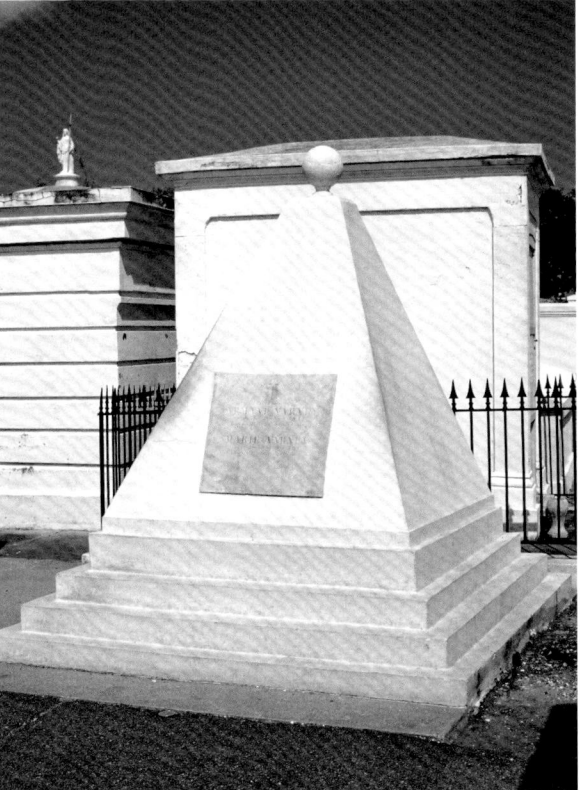

150   *St. Louis Cemetery #1*

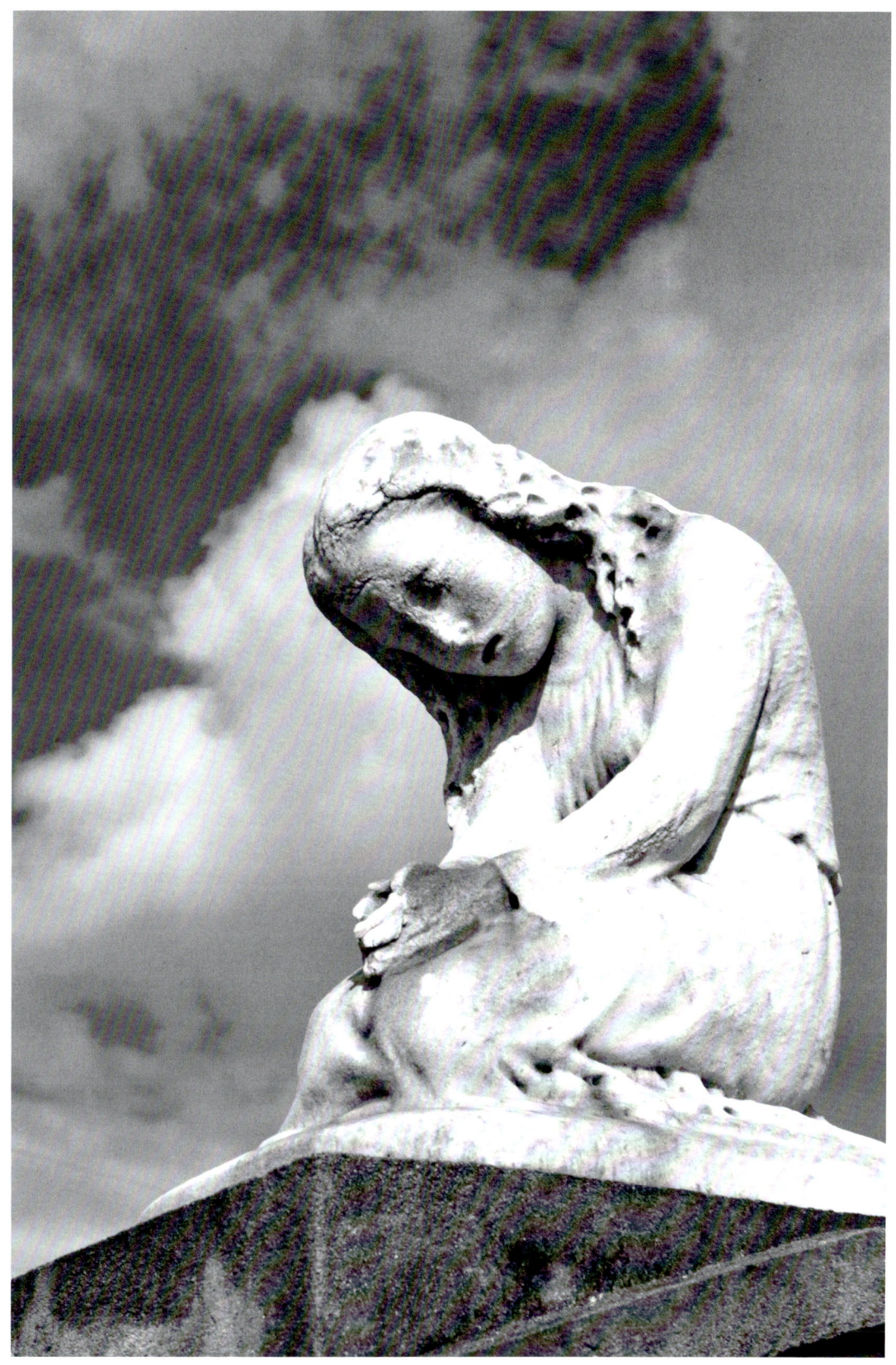

St. Louis Cemetery #1   151

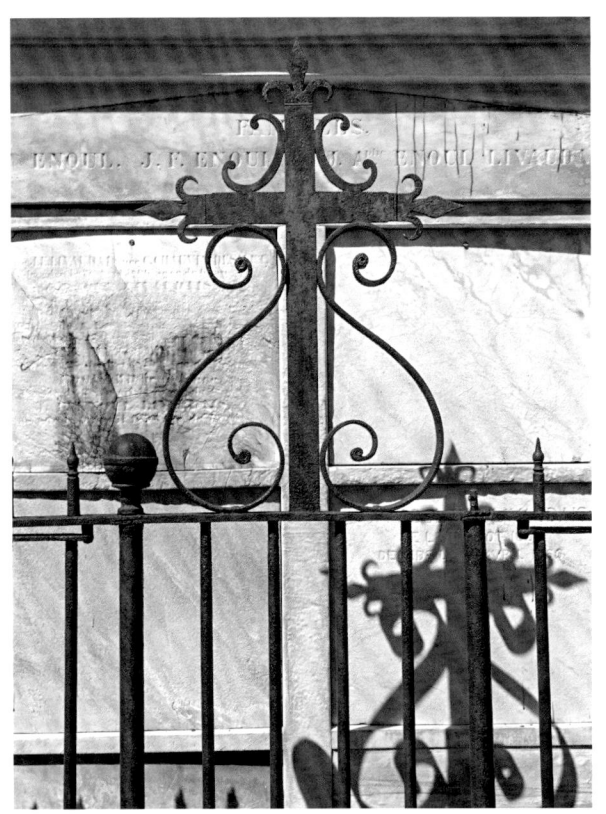
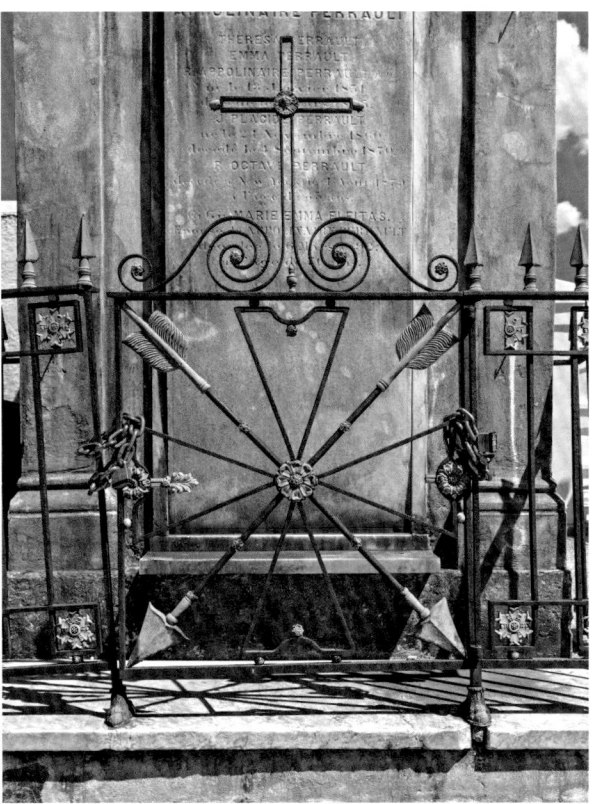
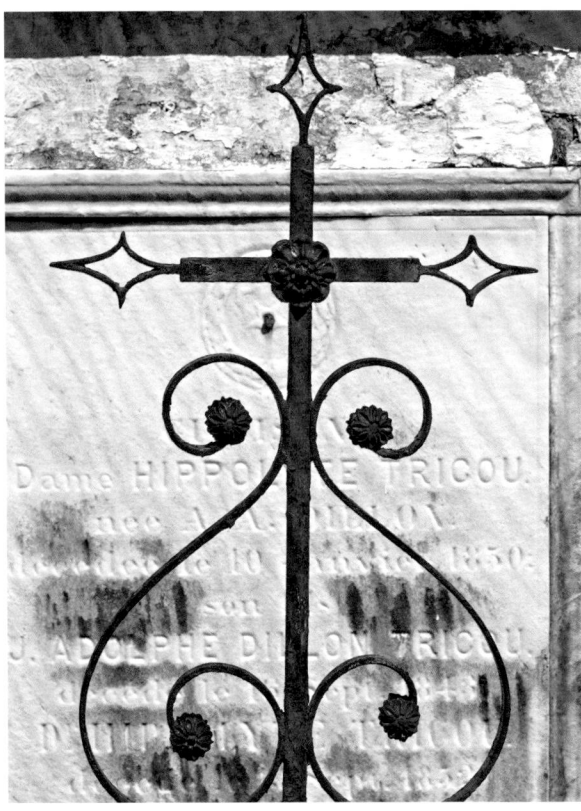
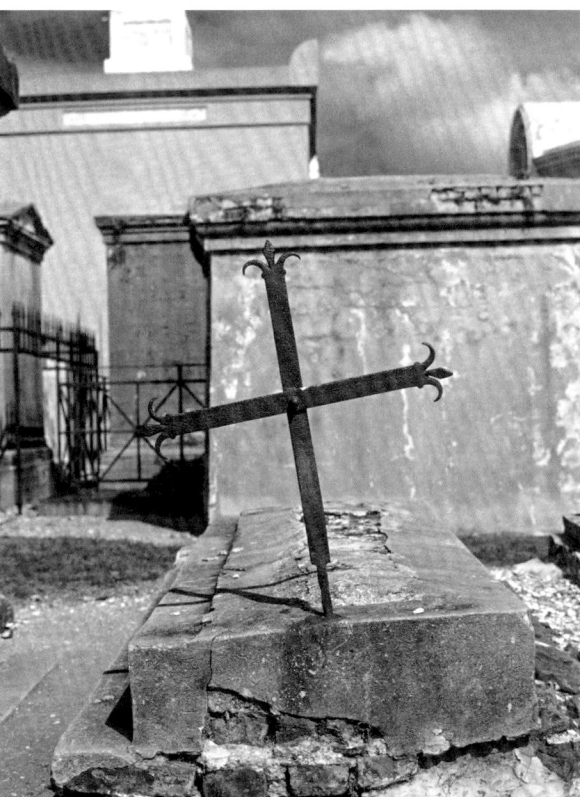

St. Louis Cemetery #1

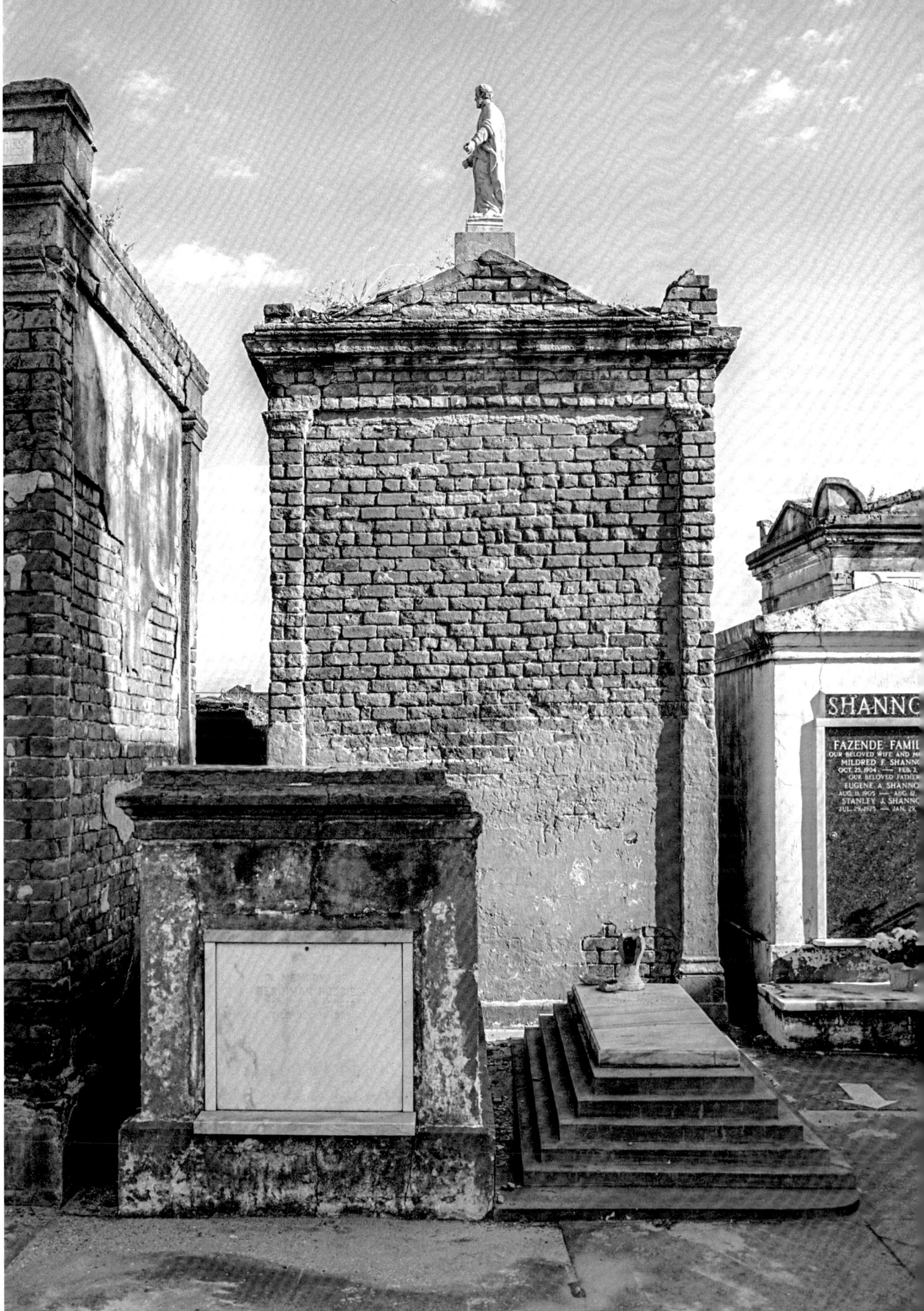

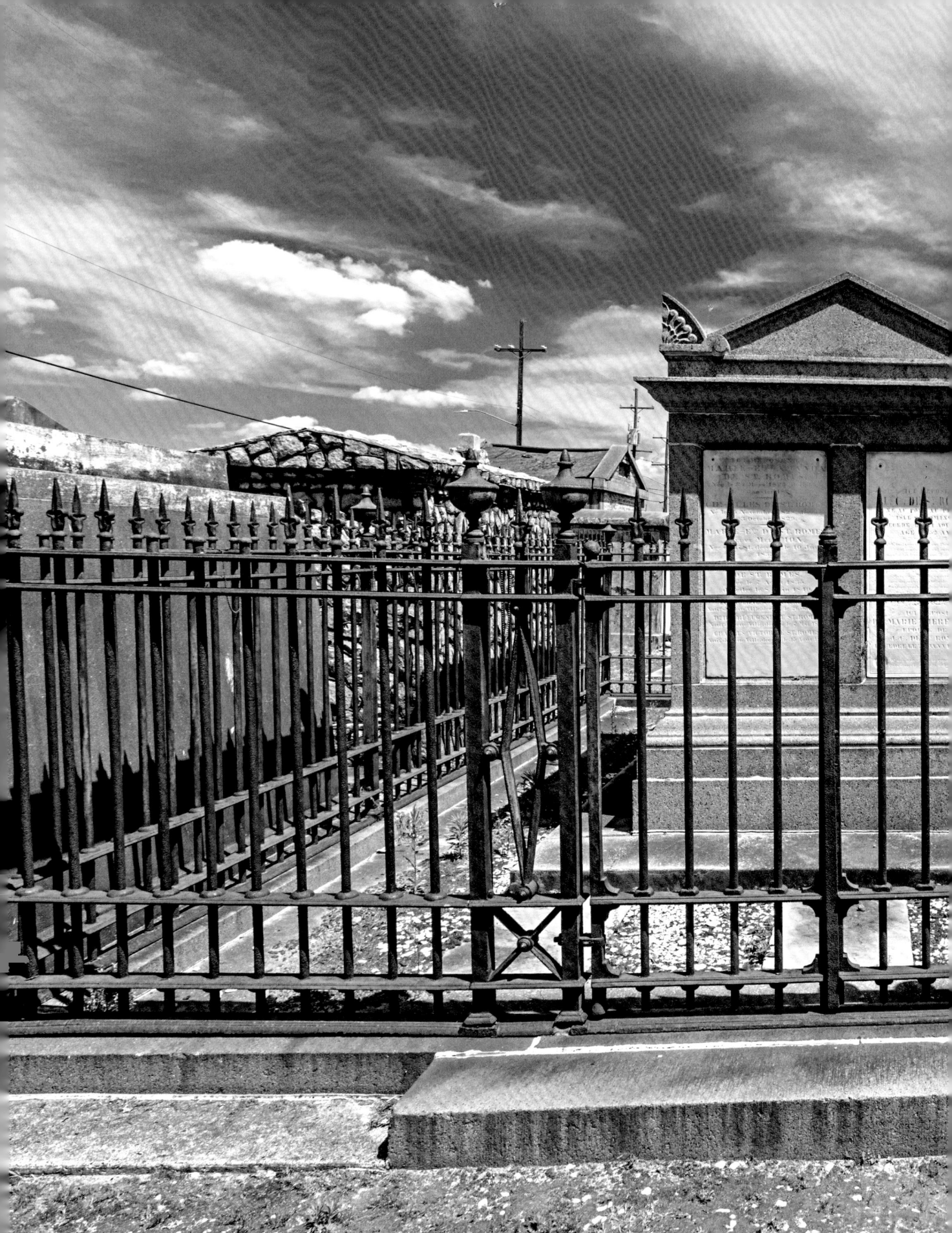

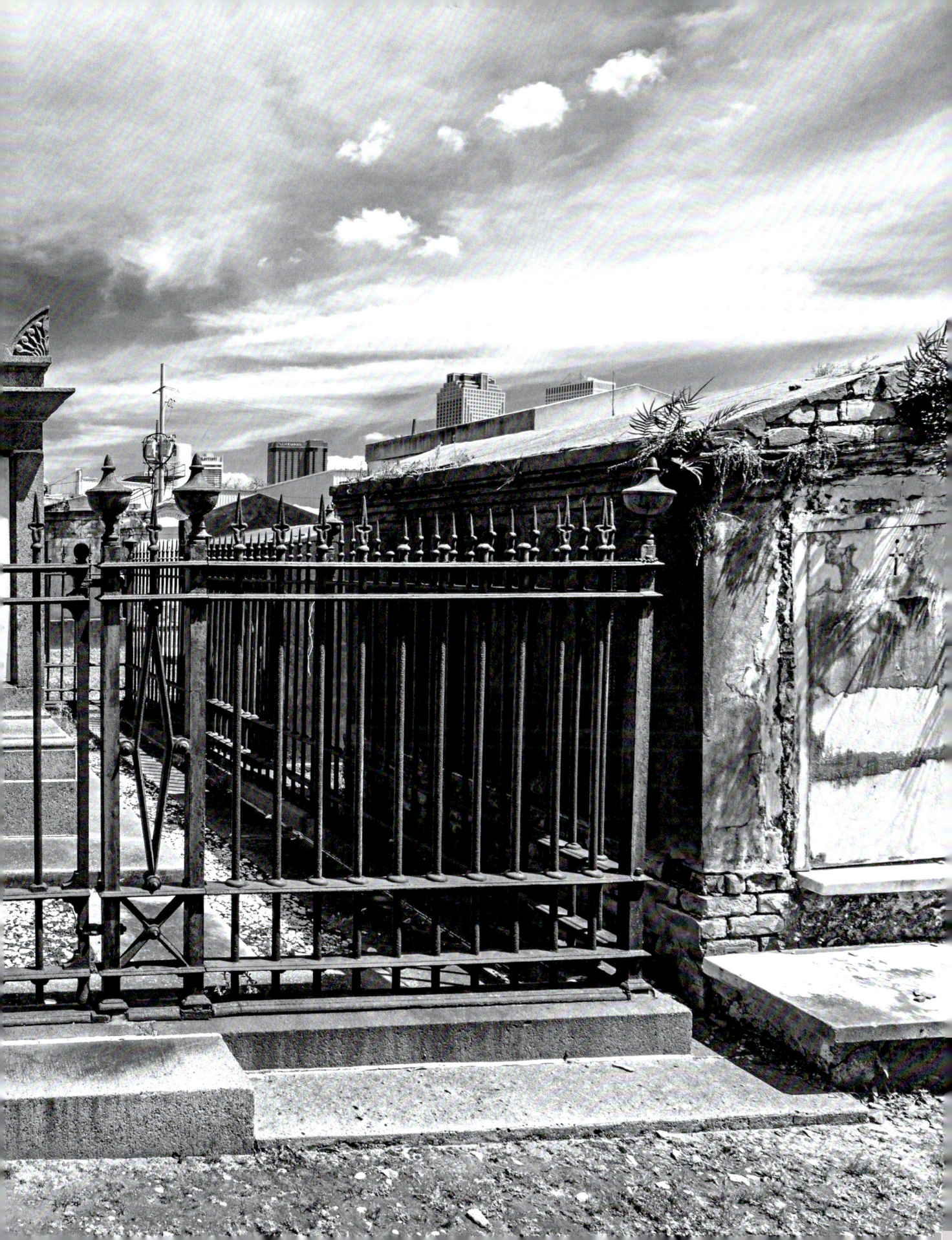

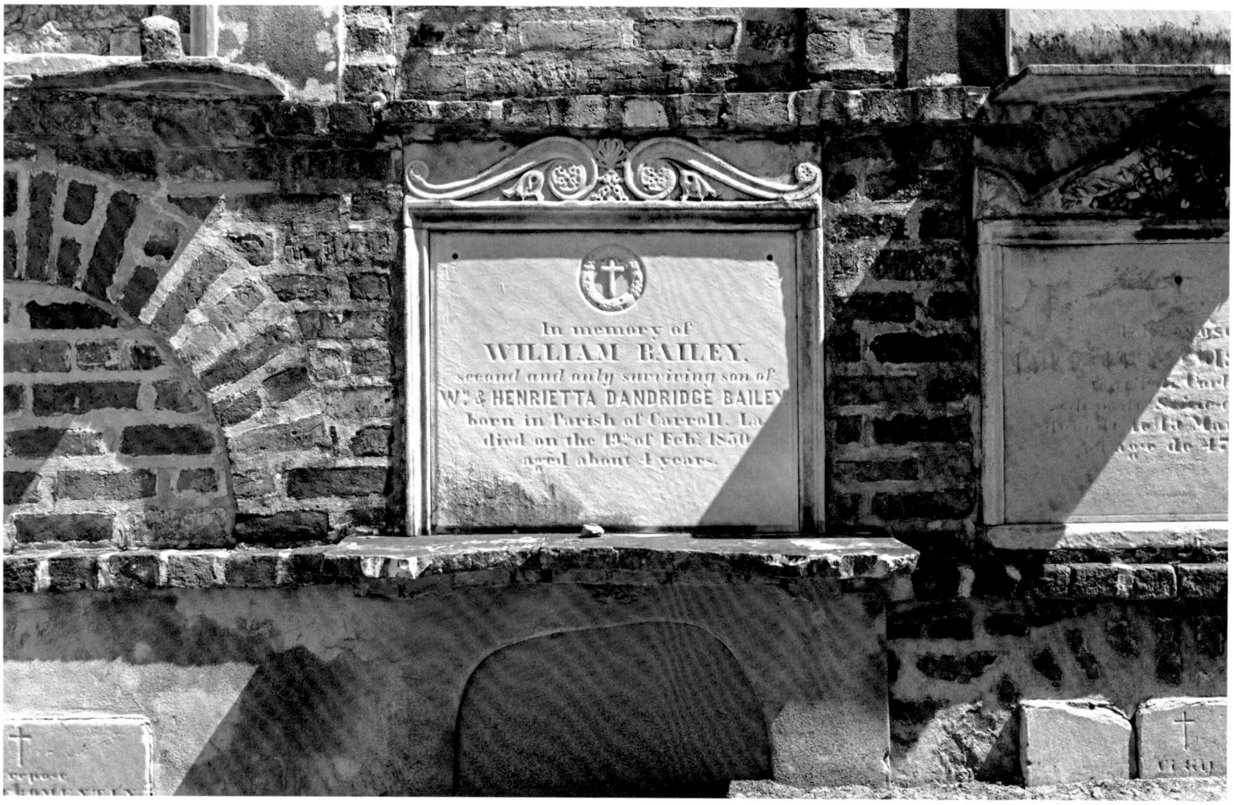

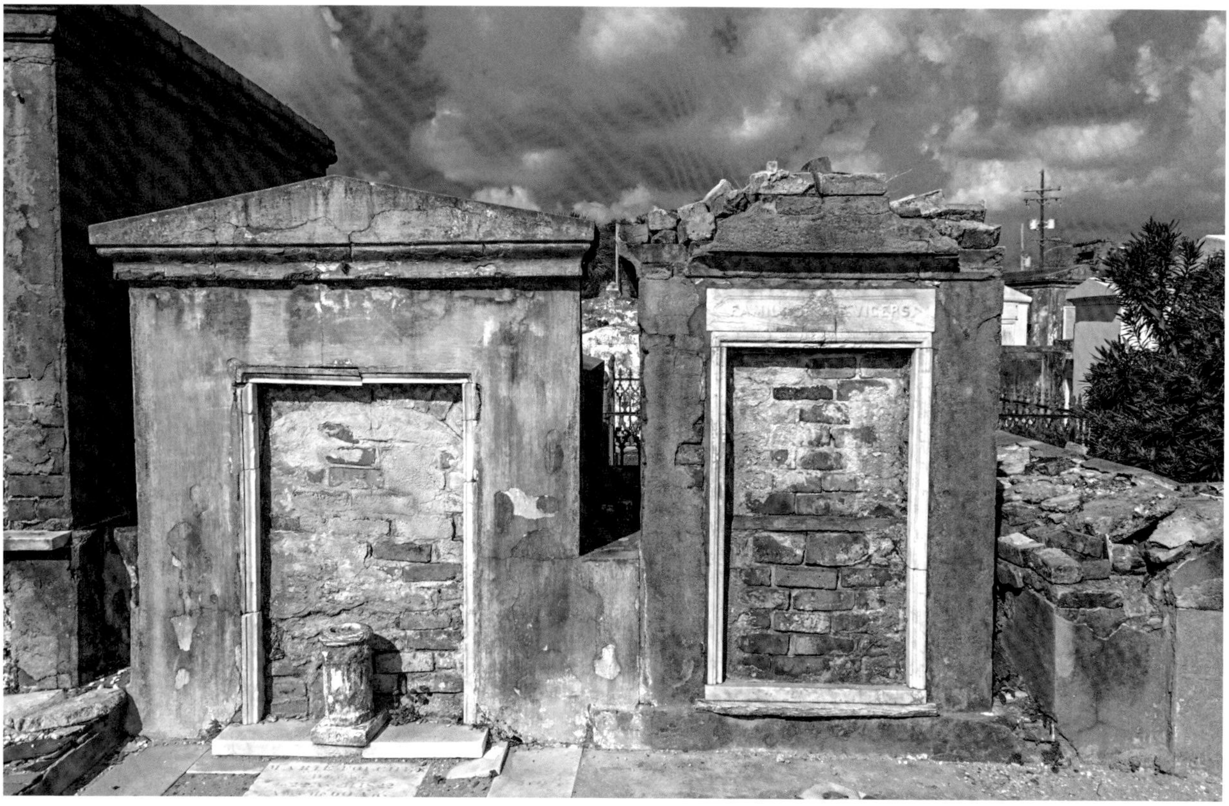

In memory of
WILLIAM BAILEY,
second and only surviving son of
W^m & HENRIETTA DANDRIDGE BAILEY
born in Parish of Carroll, La
died on the 12th of Feby 1850
aged about 4 years.

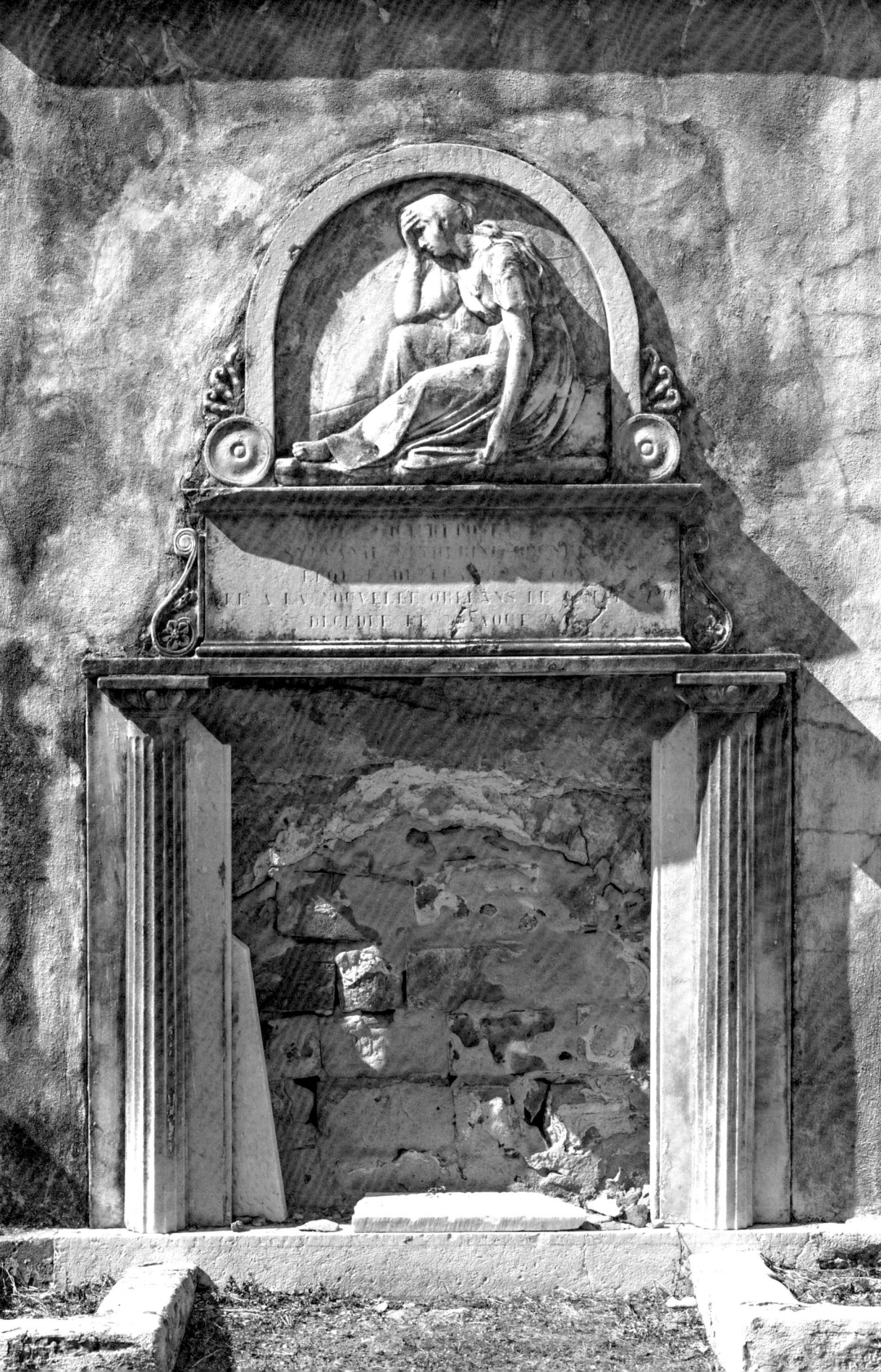

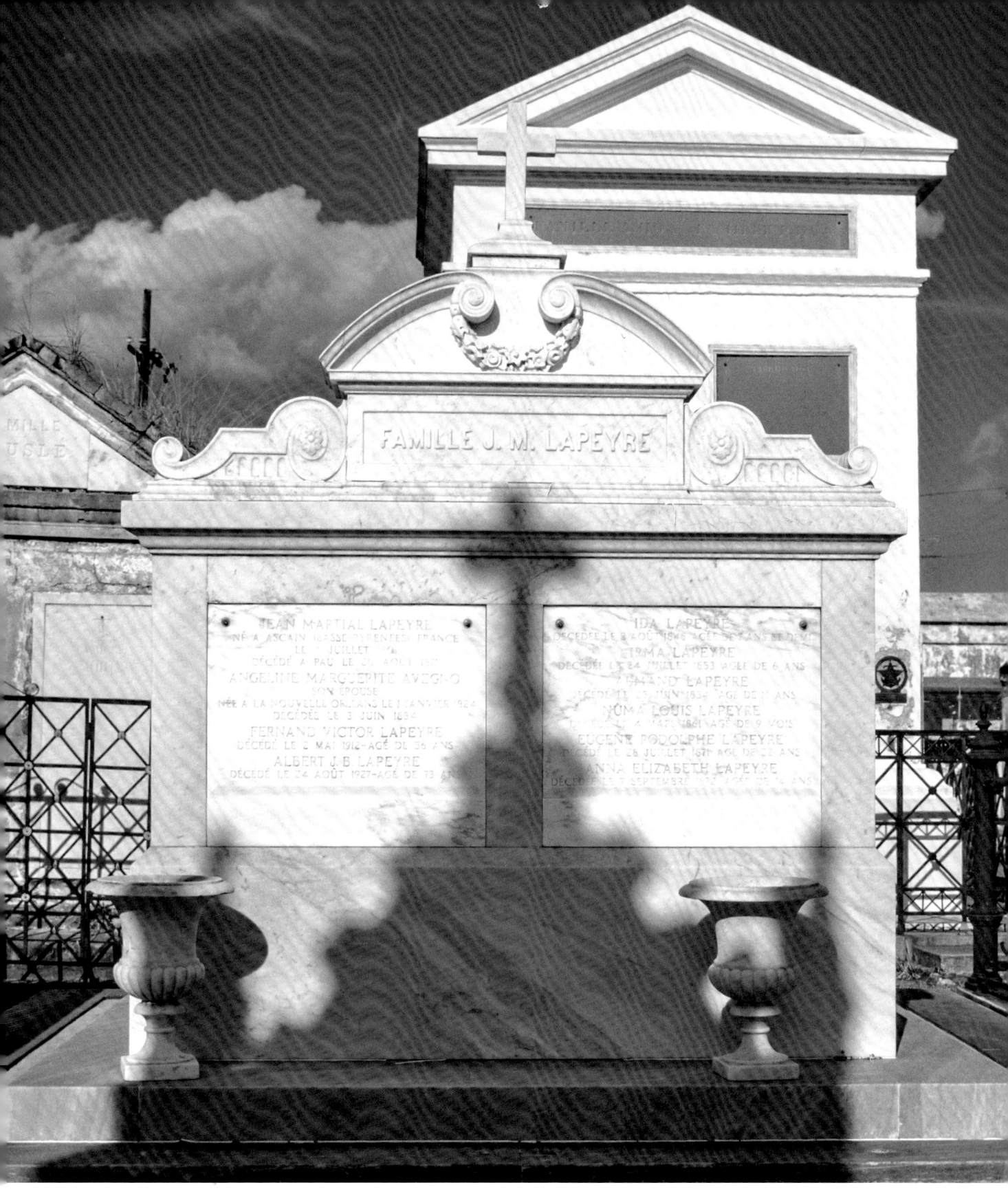

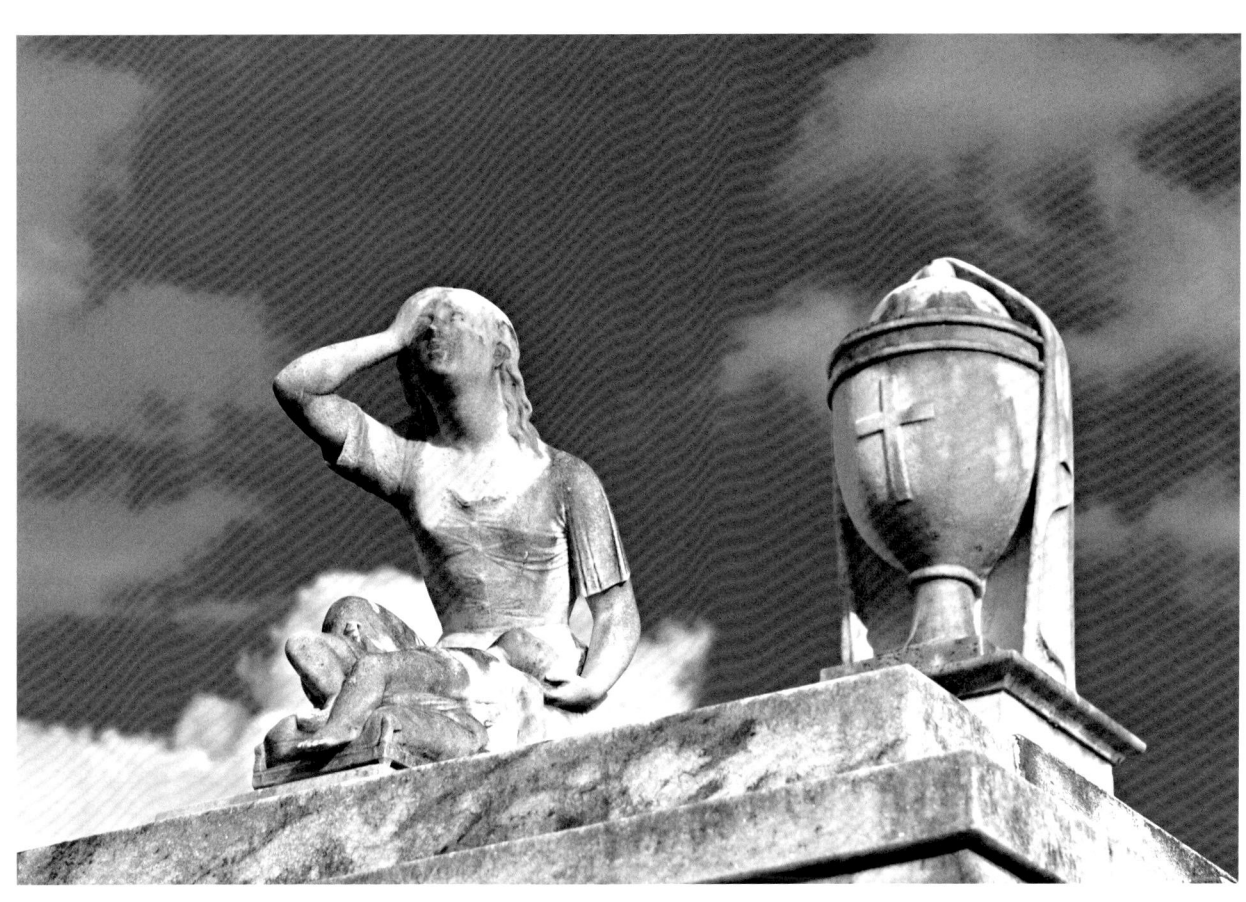

St. Louis Cemetery #3 159

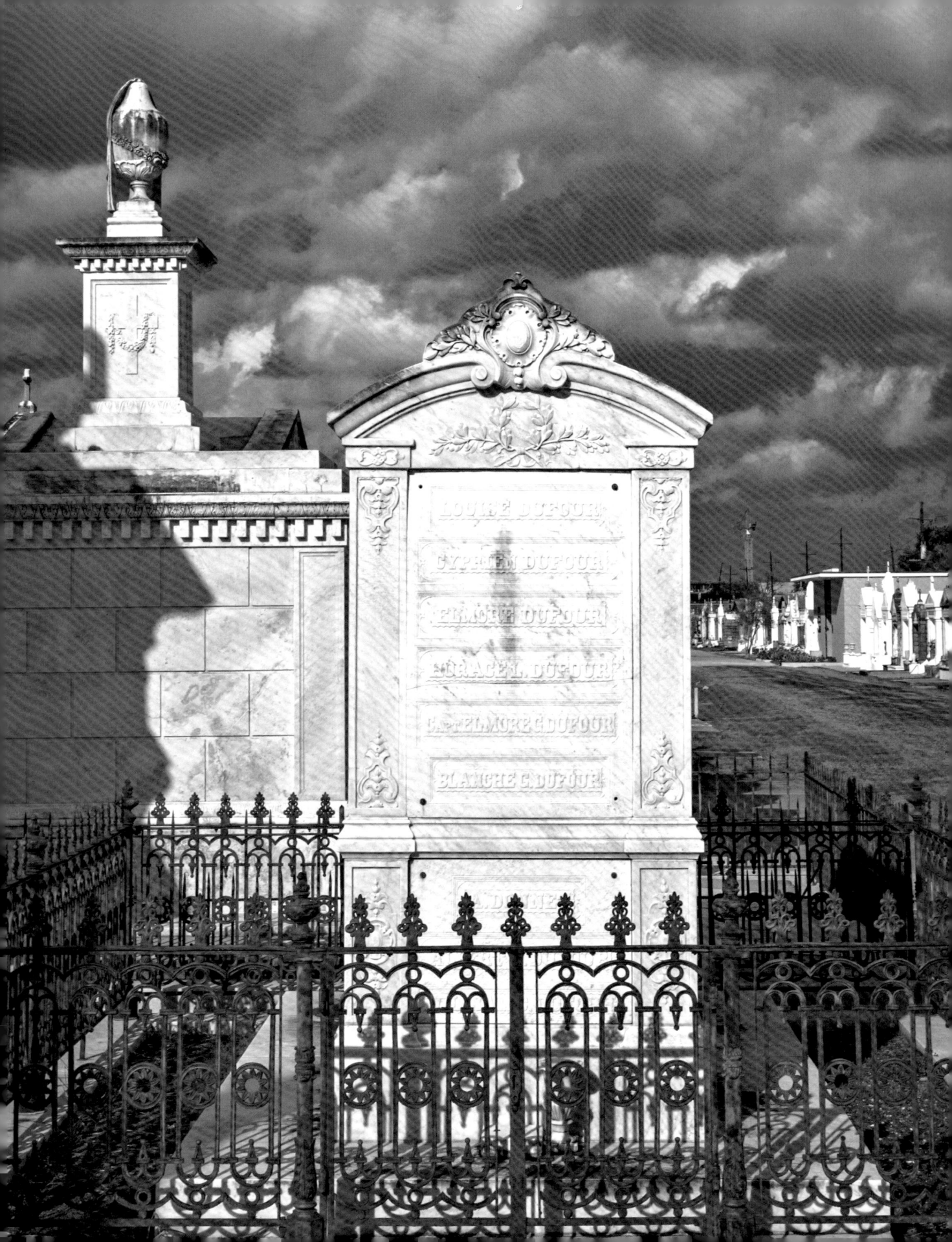

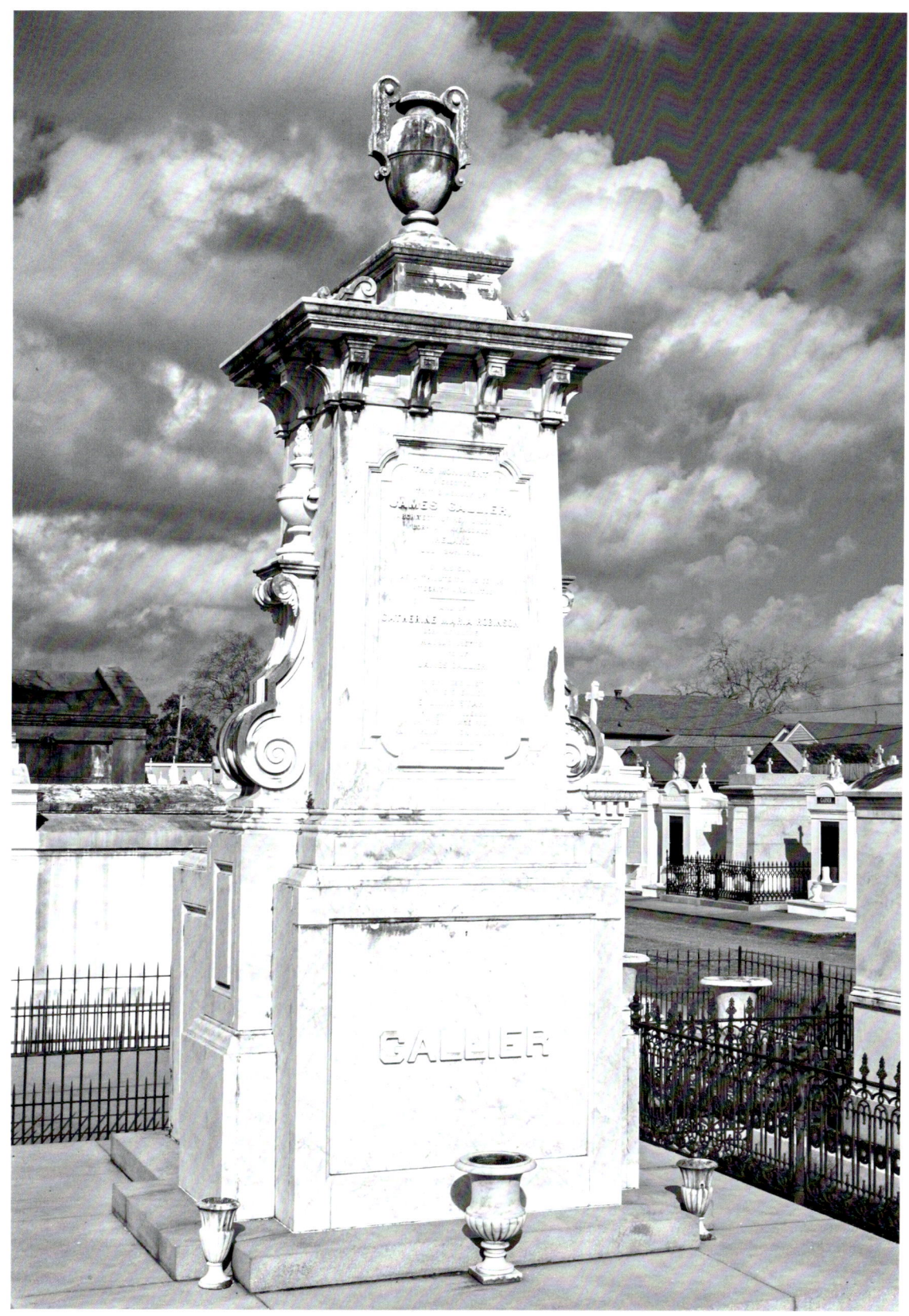

St. Louis Cemetery #3

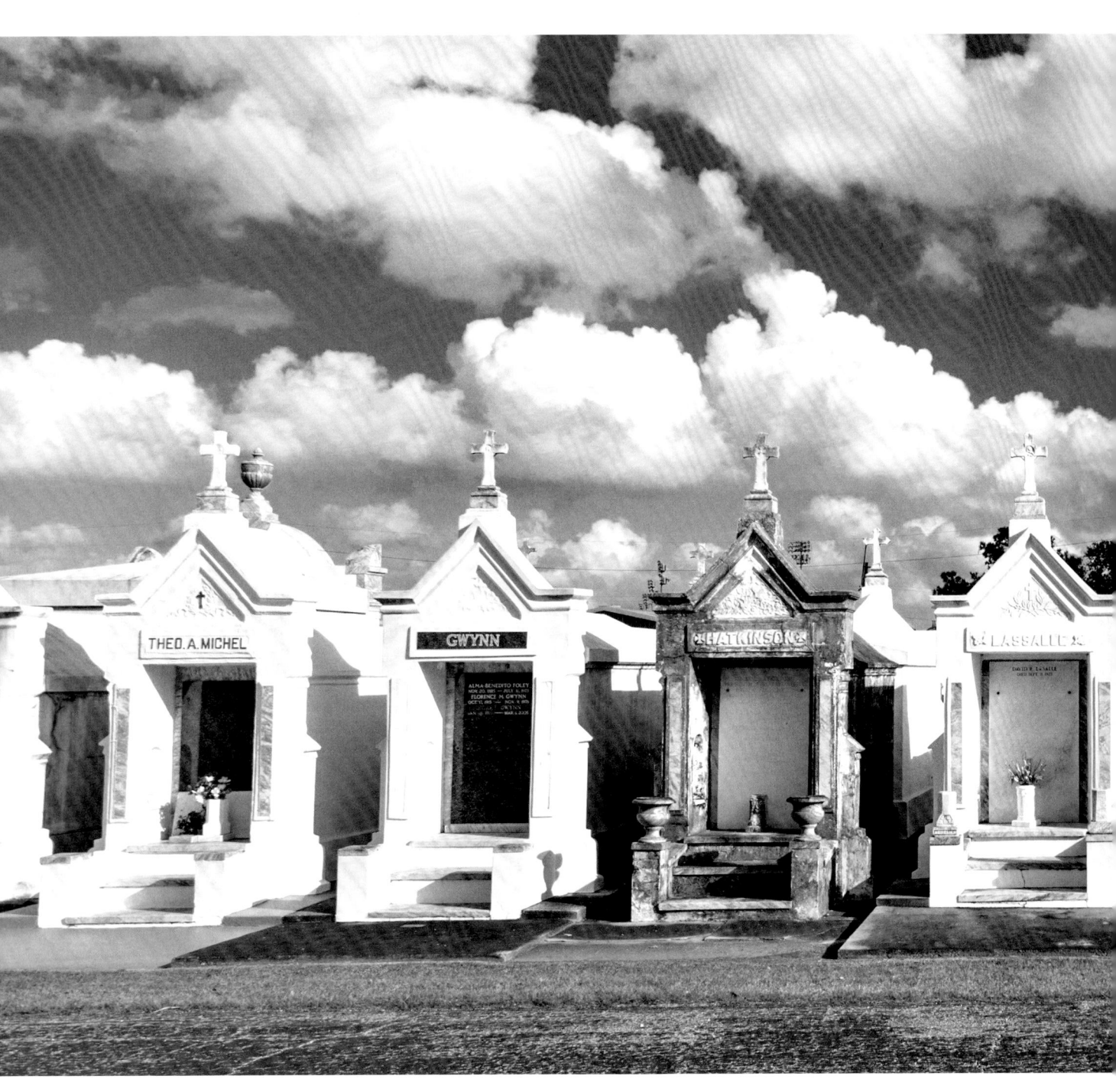

St. Louis Cemetery #3

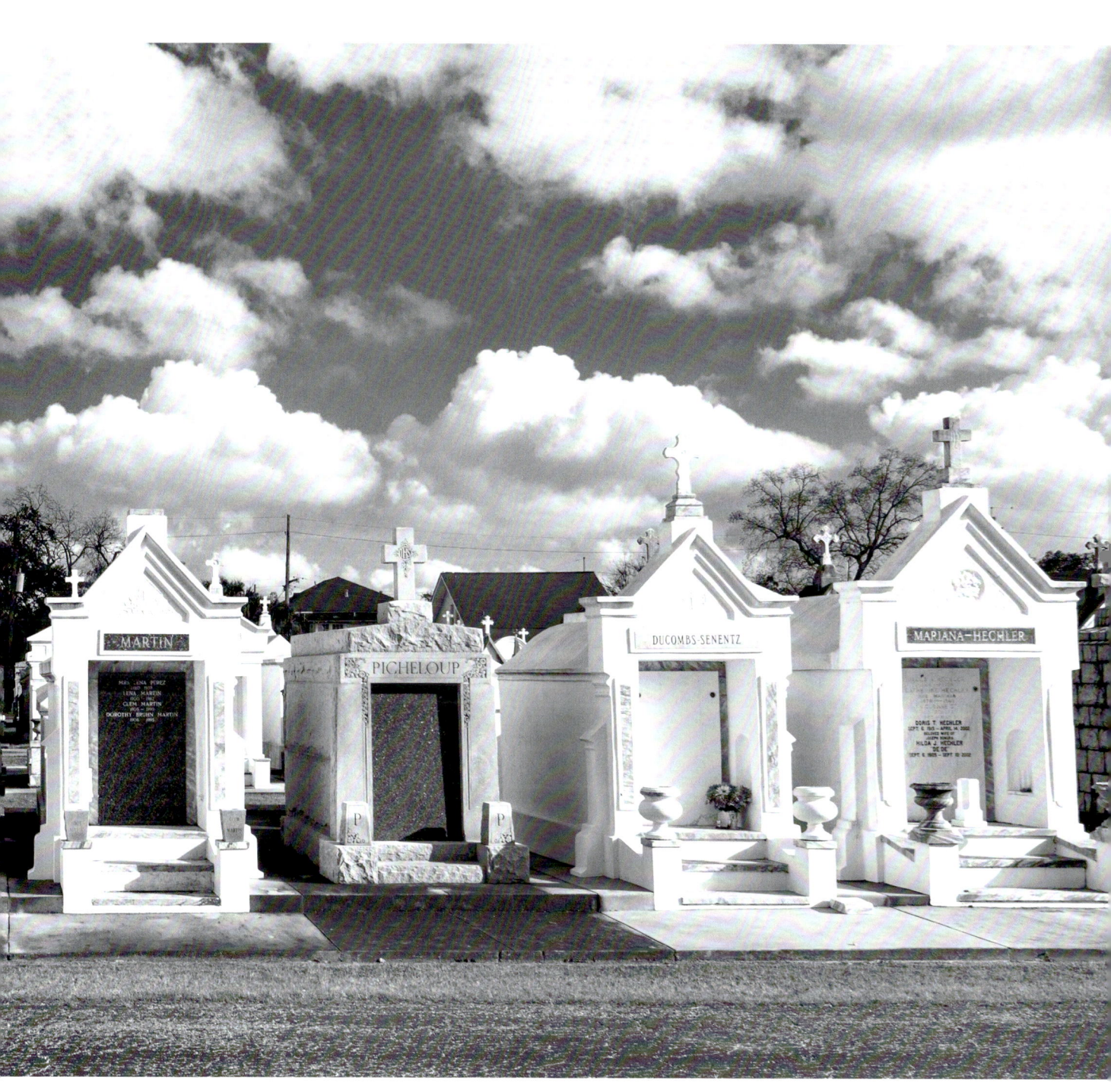

St. Patrick's Cemetery #1 & #2

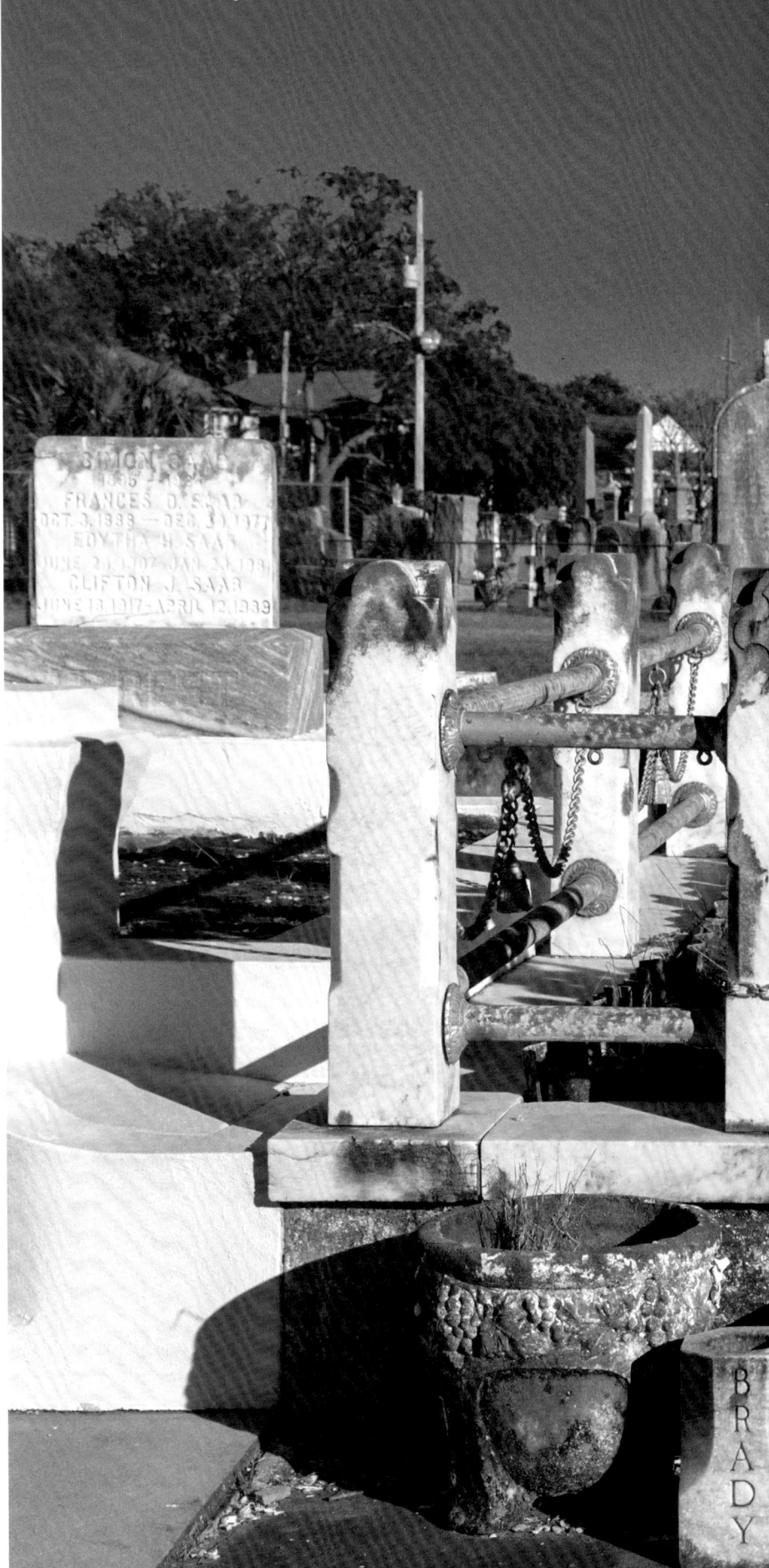

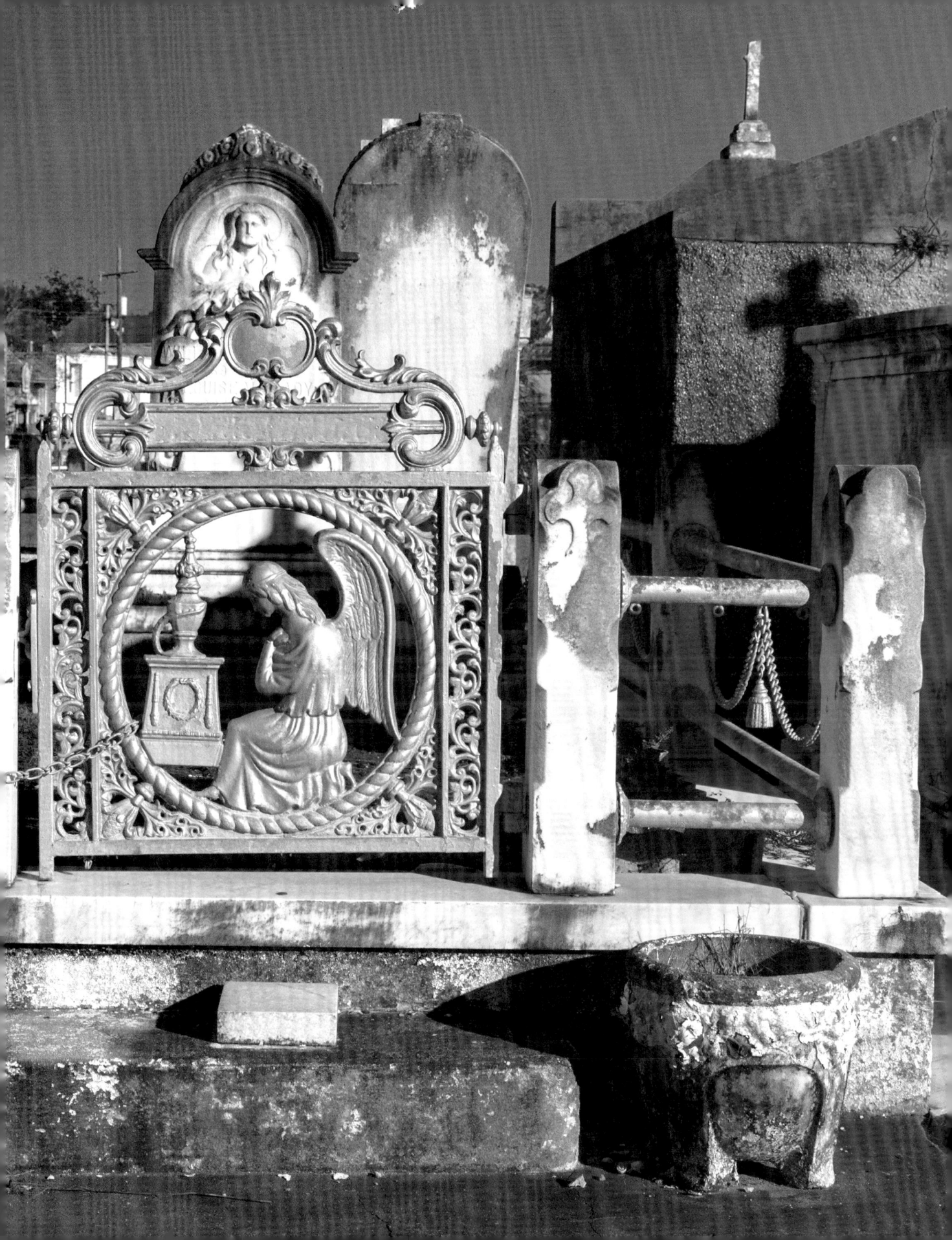

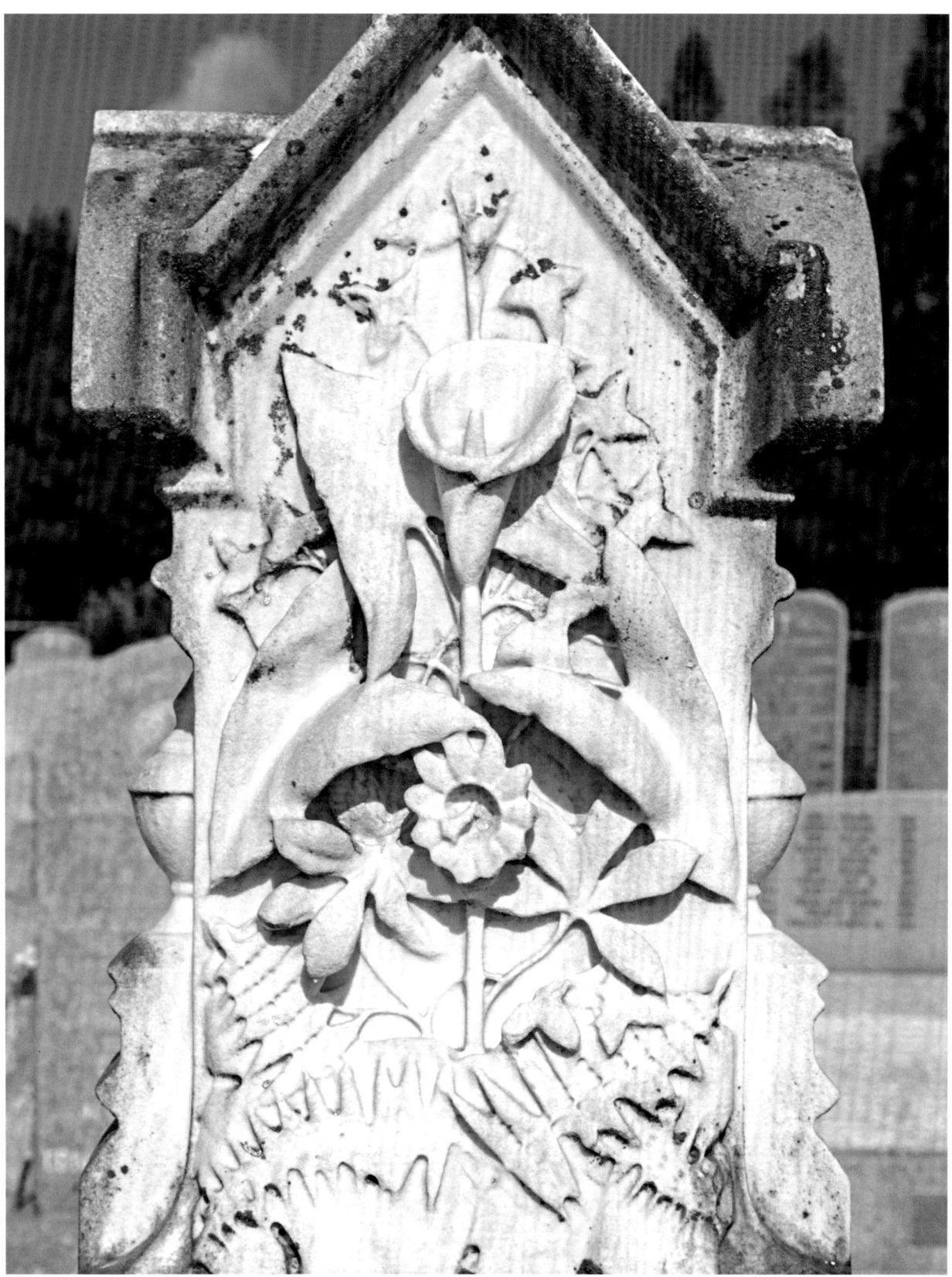

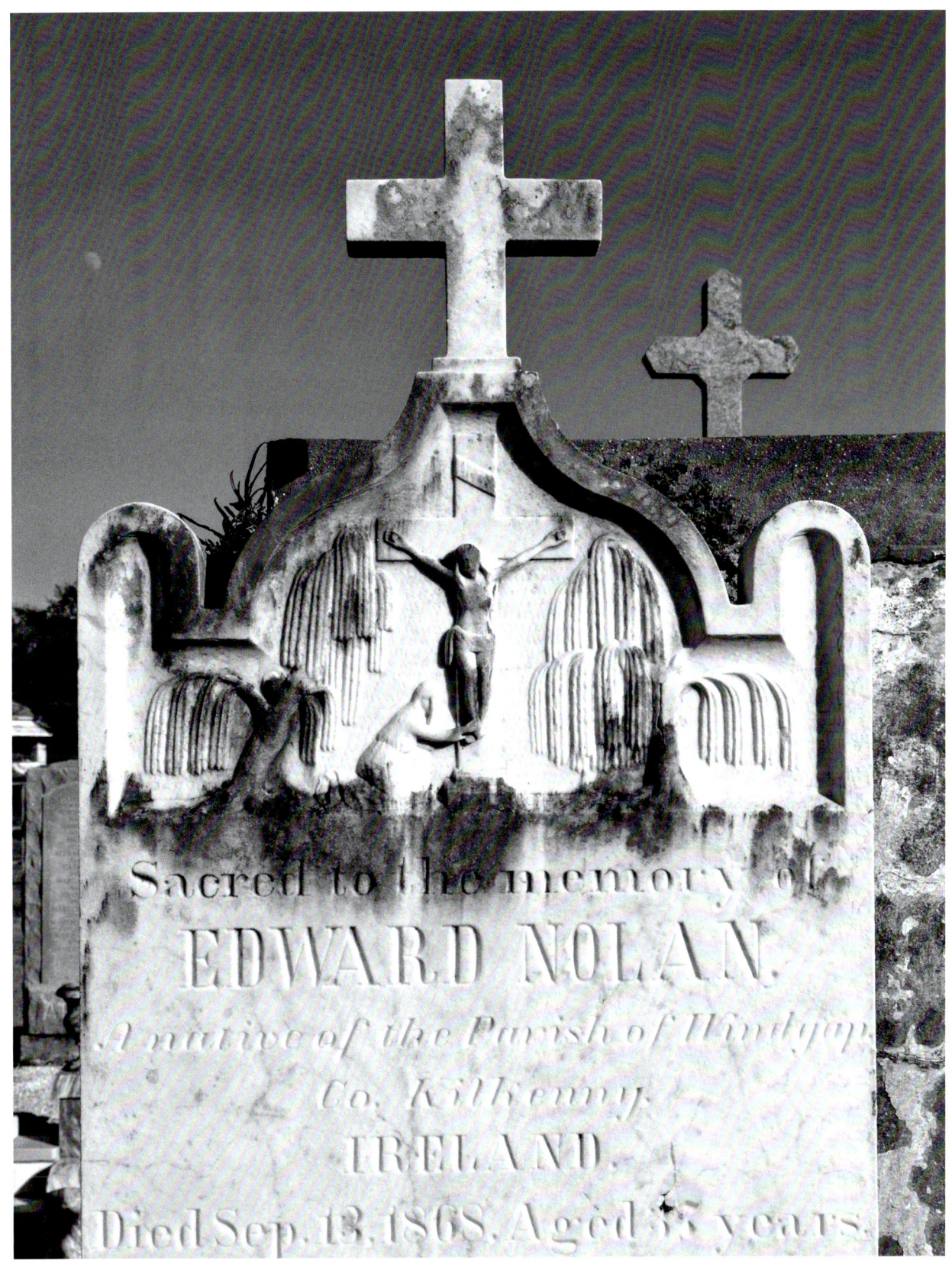

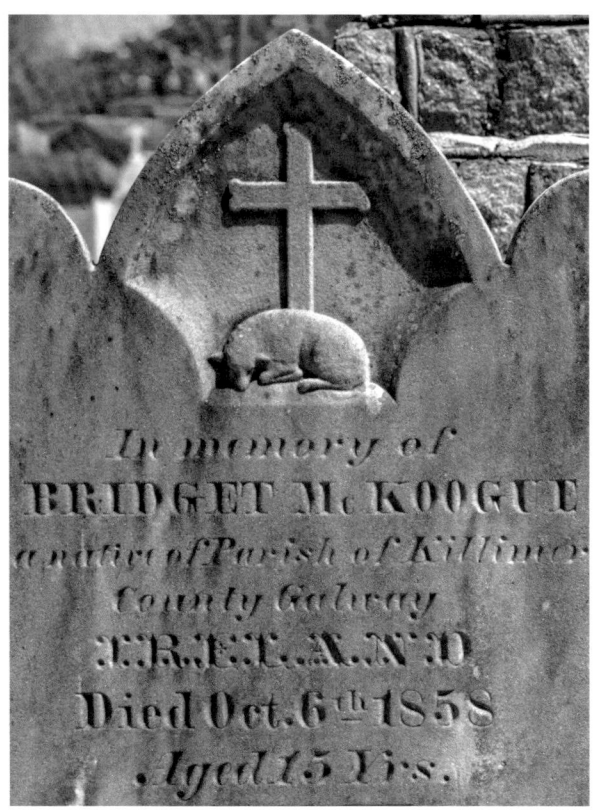
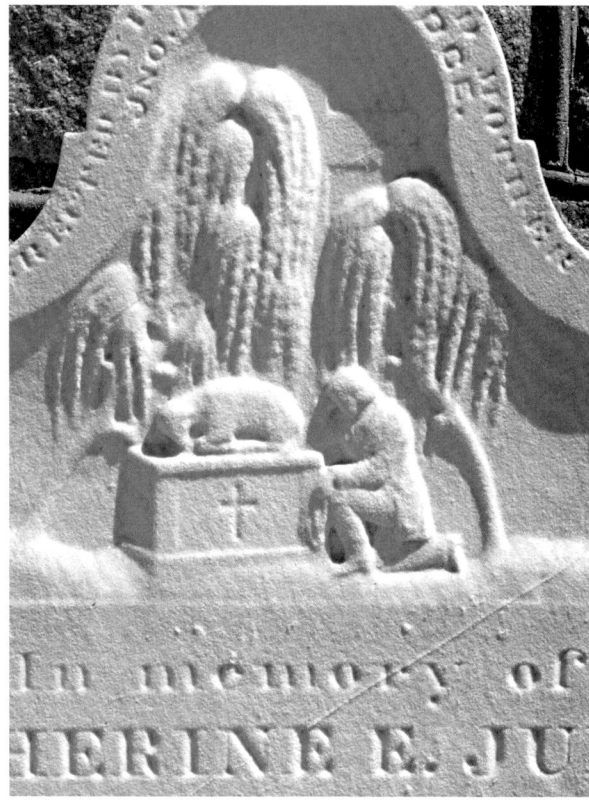
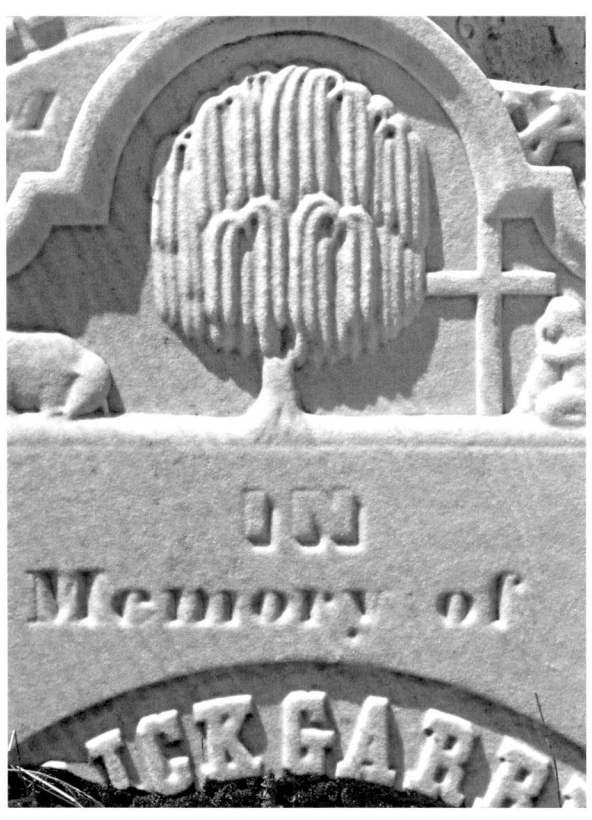
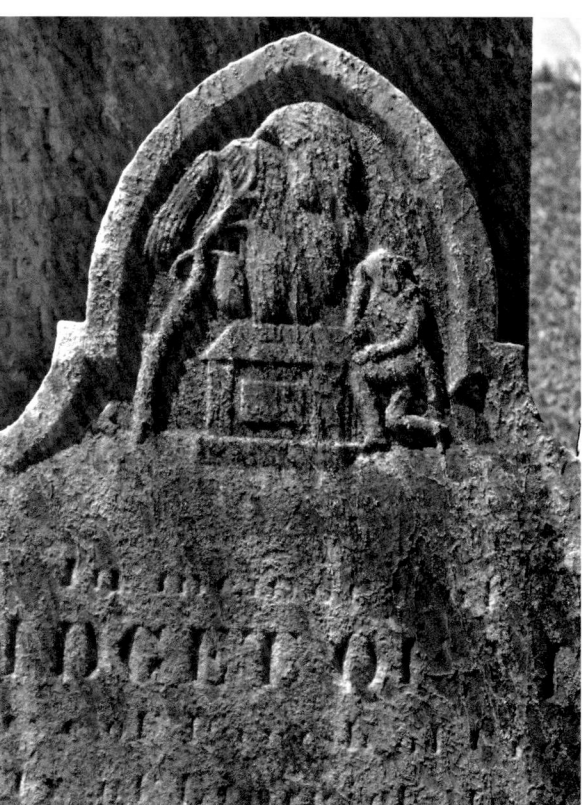

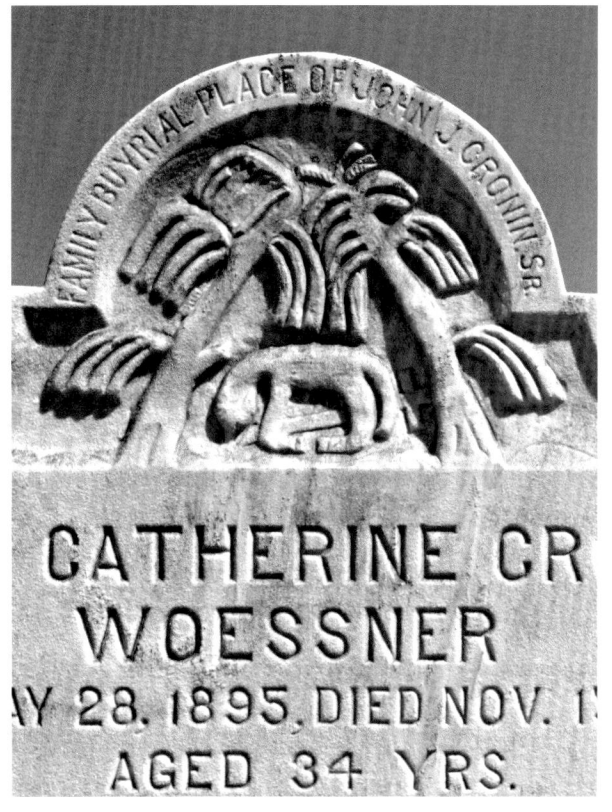
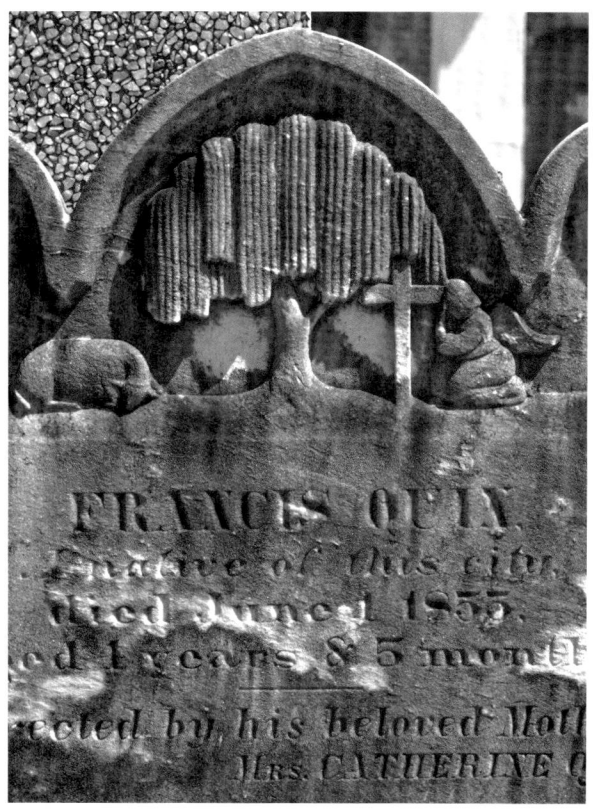
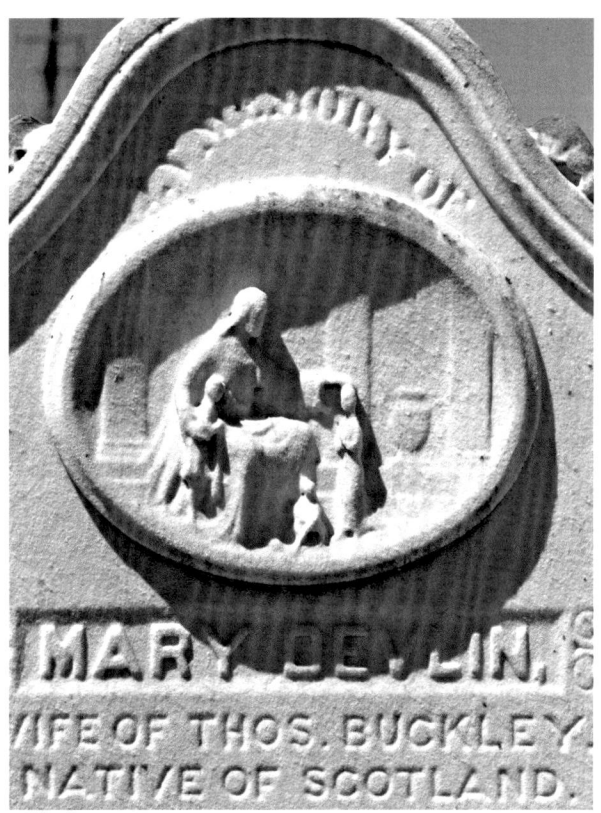
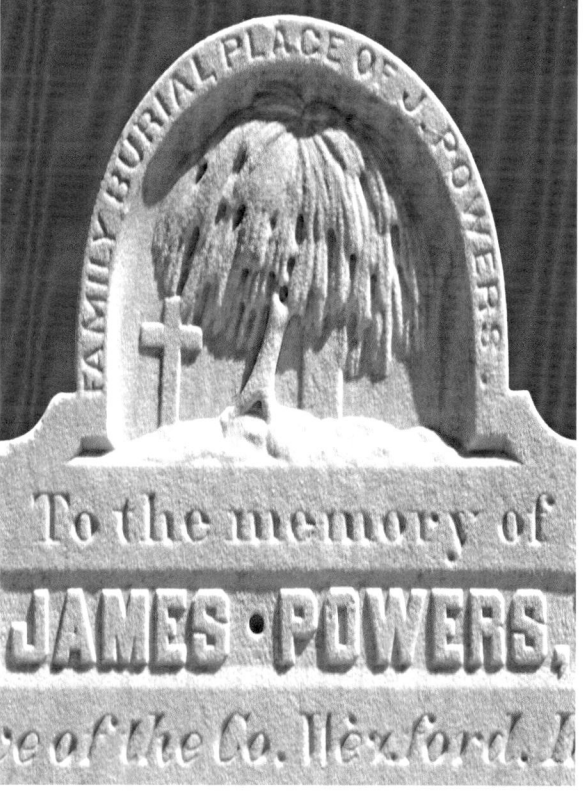

St. Patrick's Cemetery #2

Additional Cemeteries

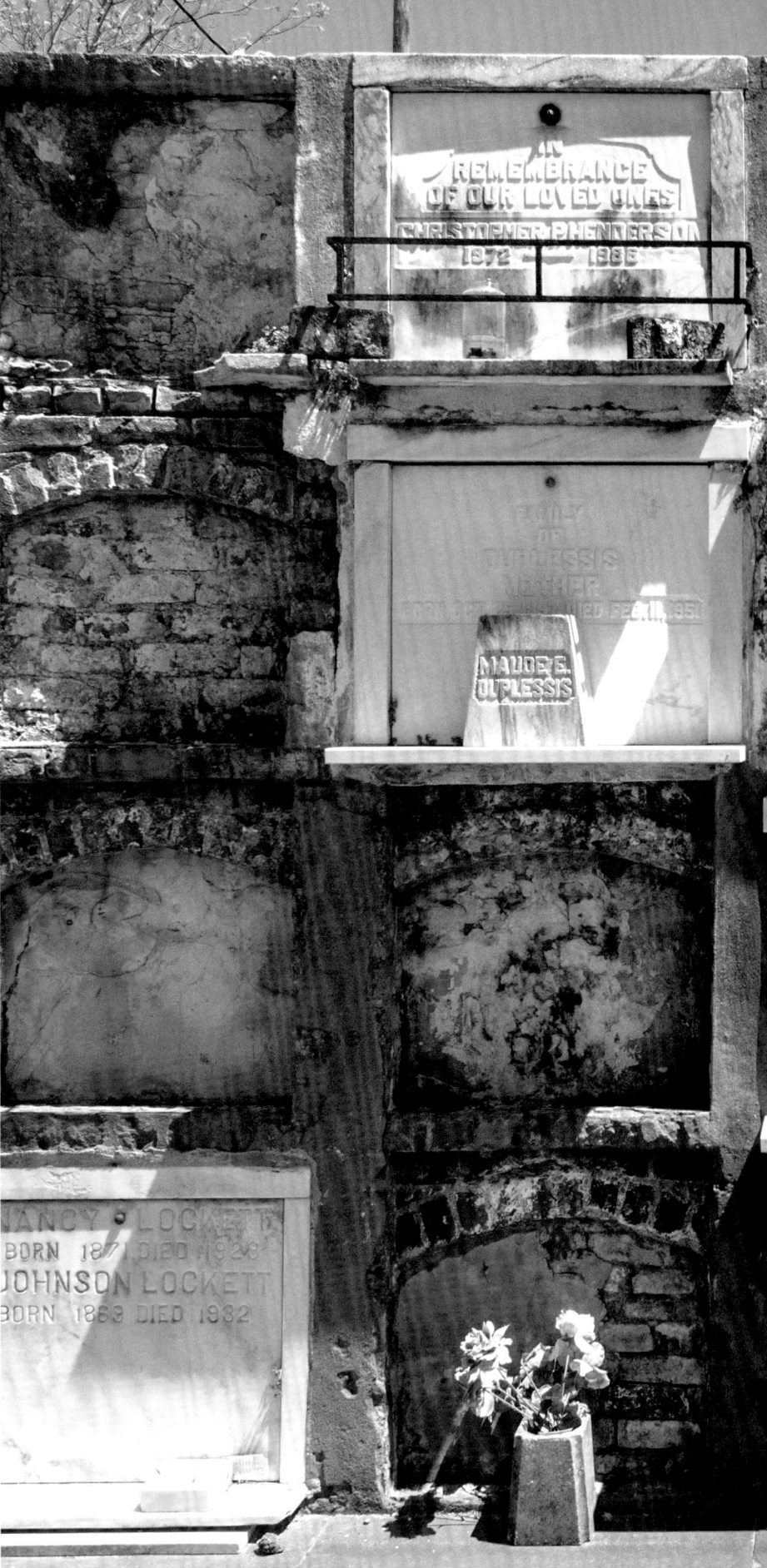

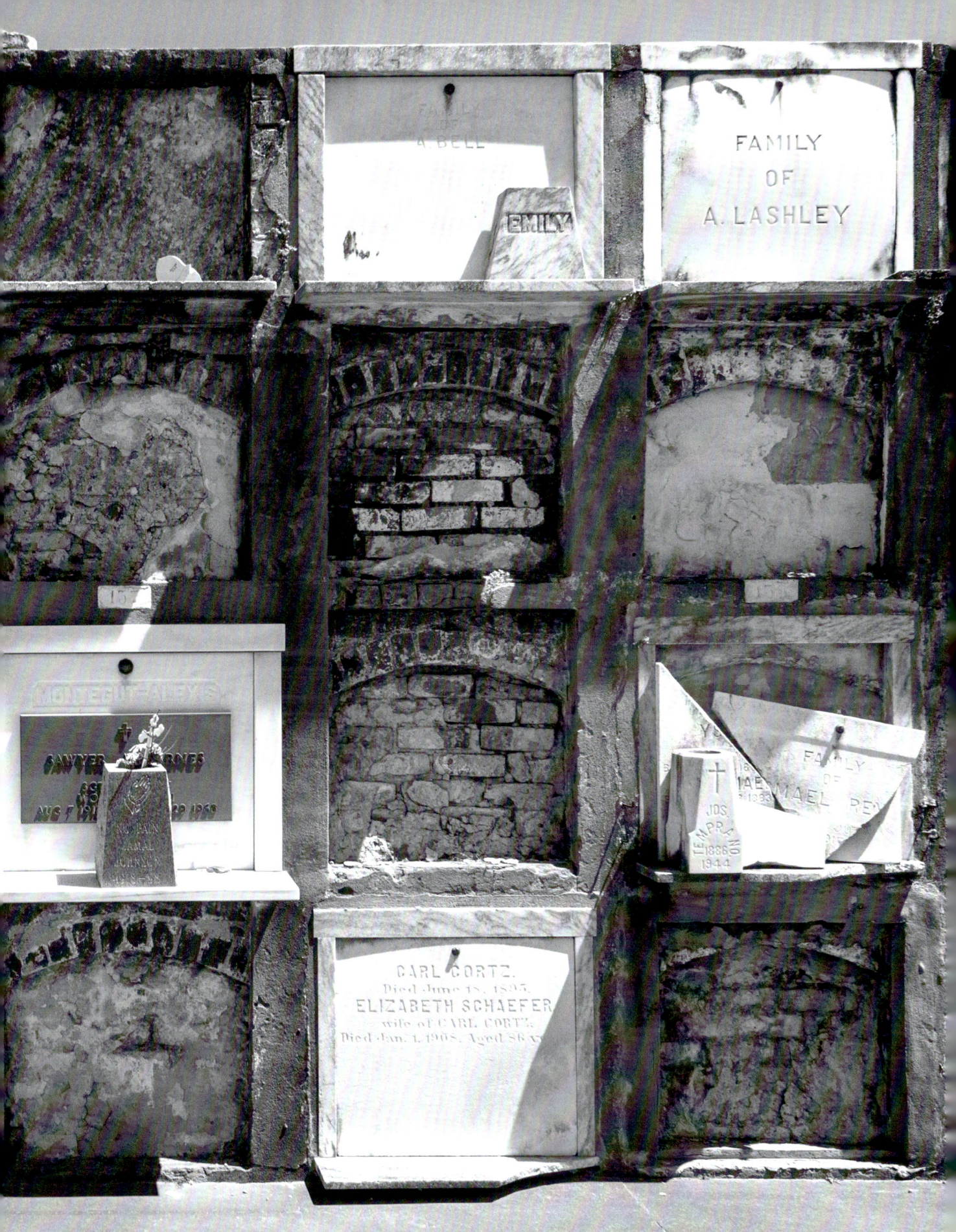

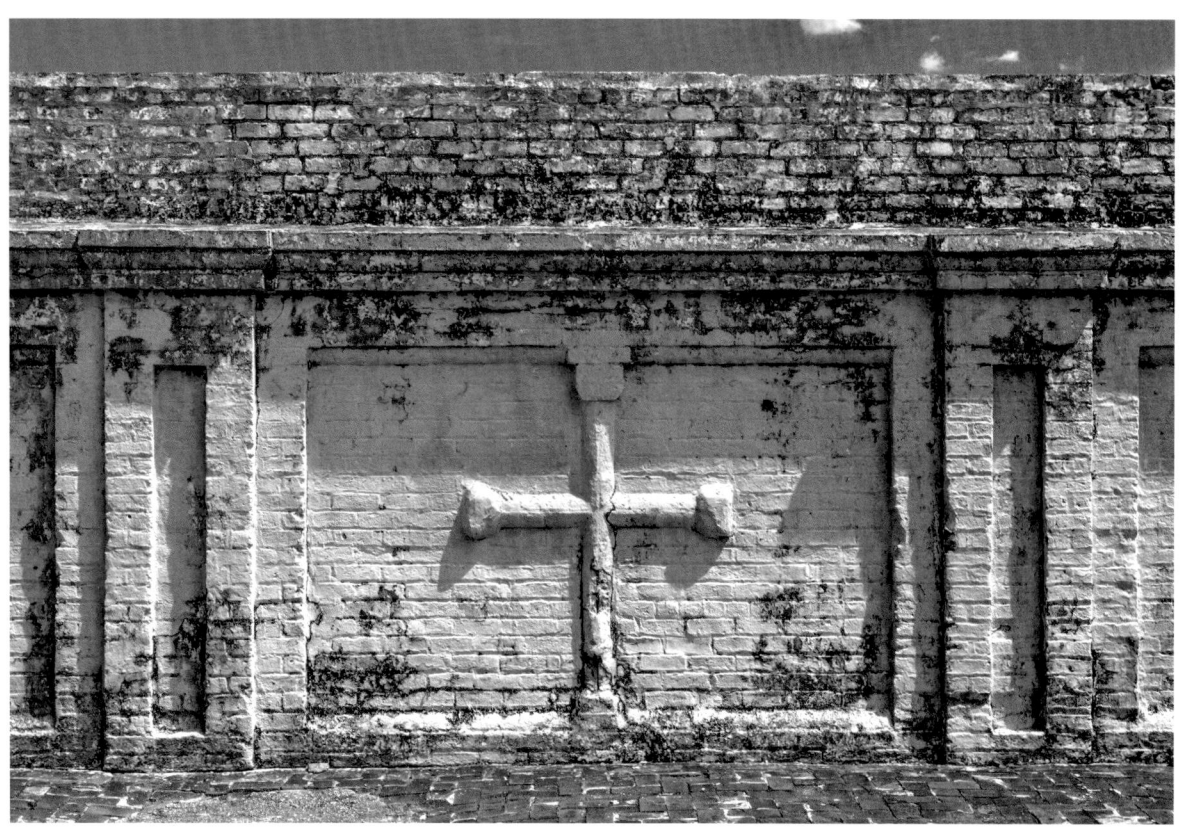

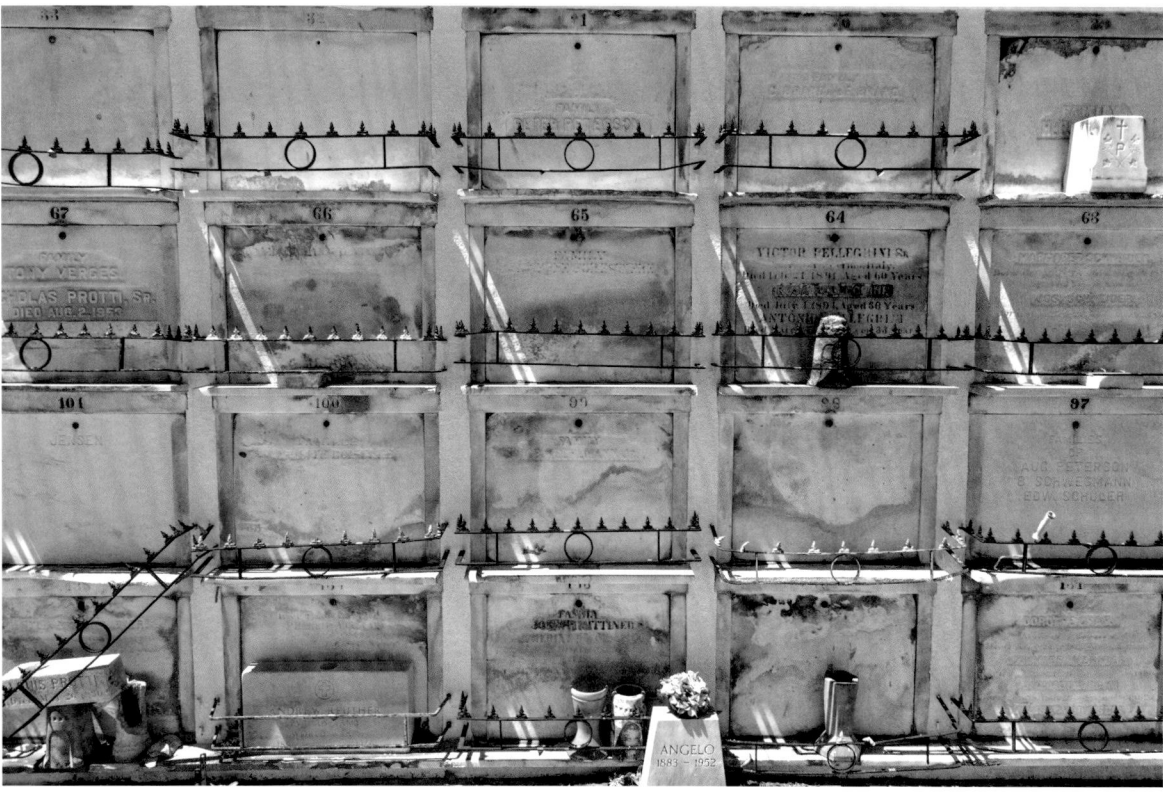

St. Vincent de Paul Cemetery #1

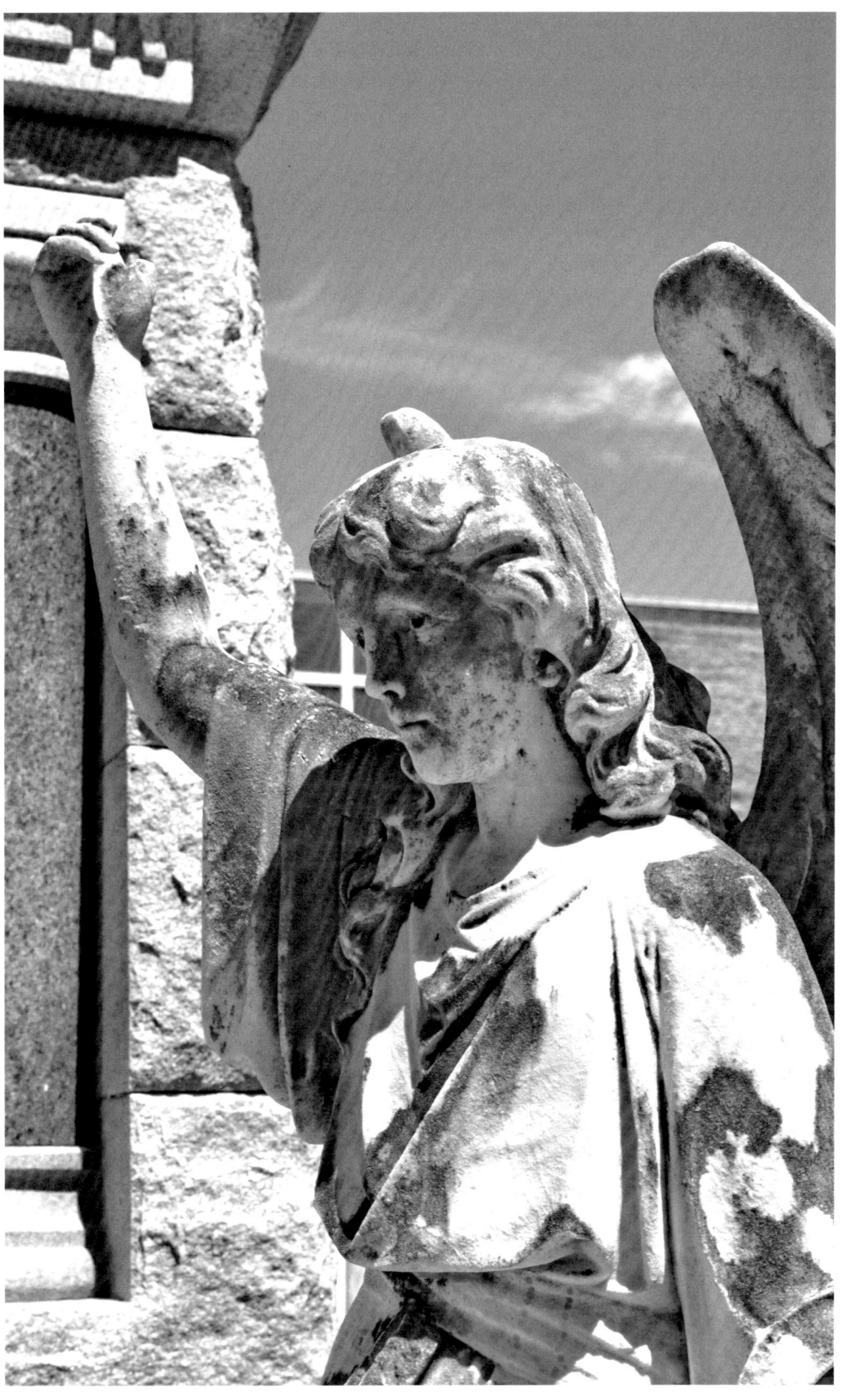

St. Vincent de Paul Cemetery #2   173

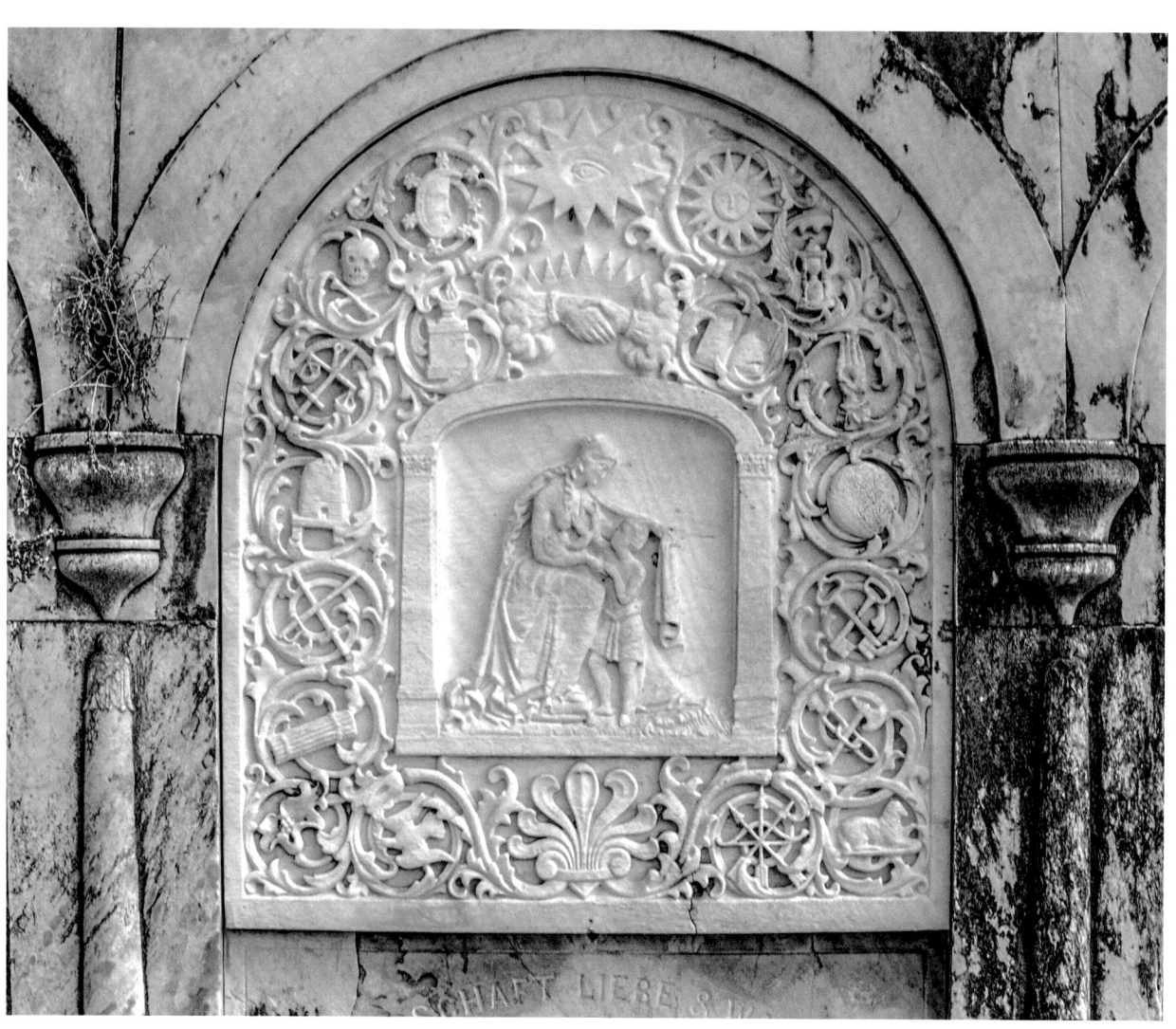

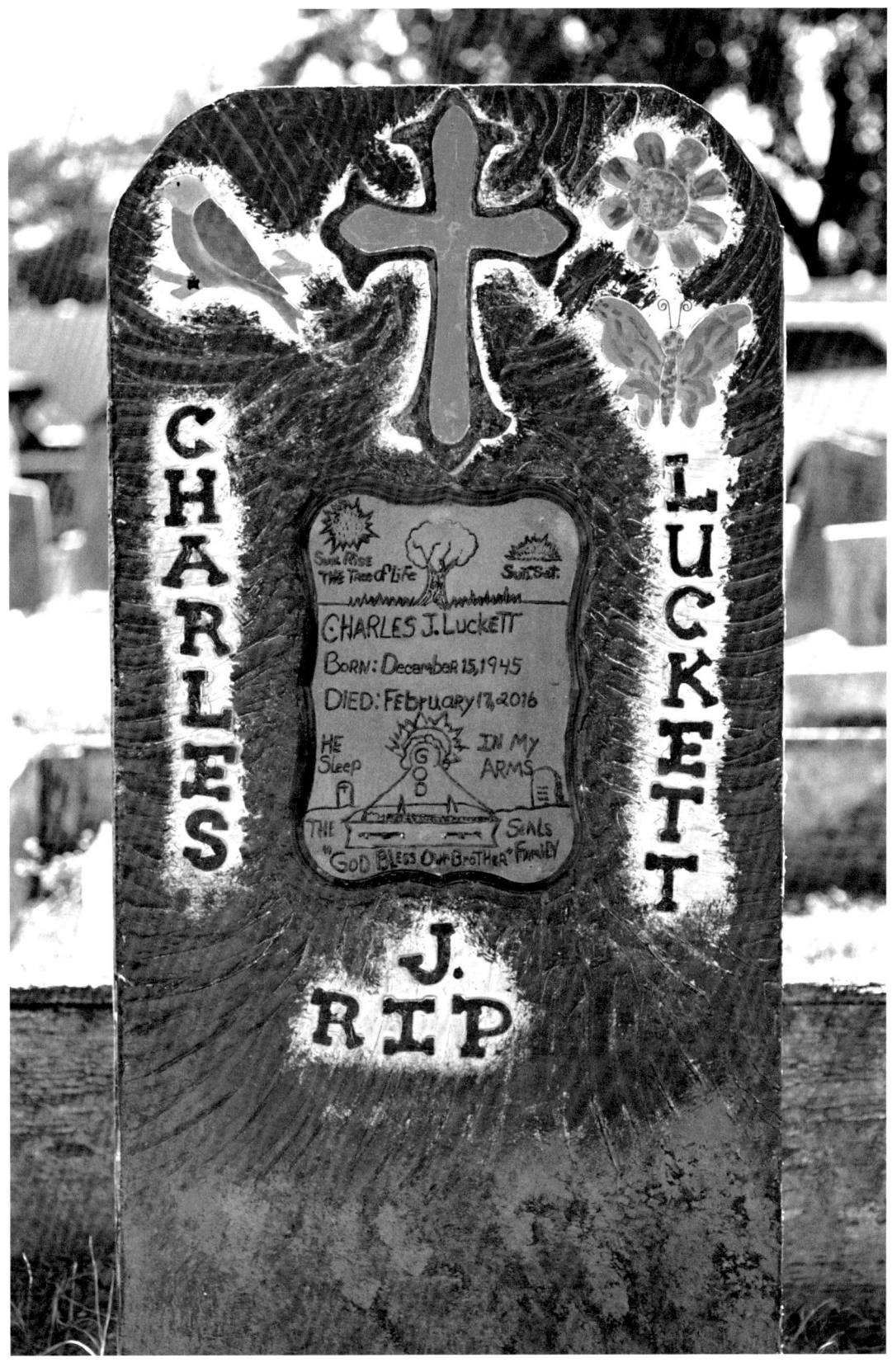

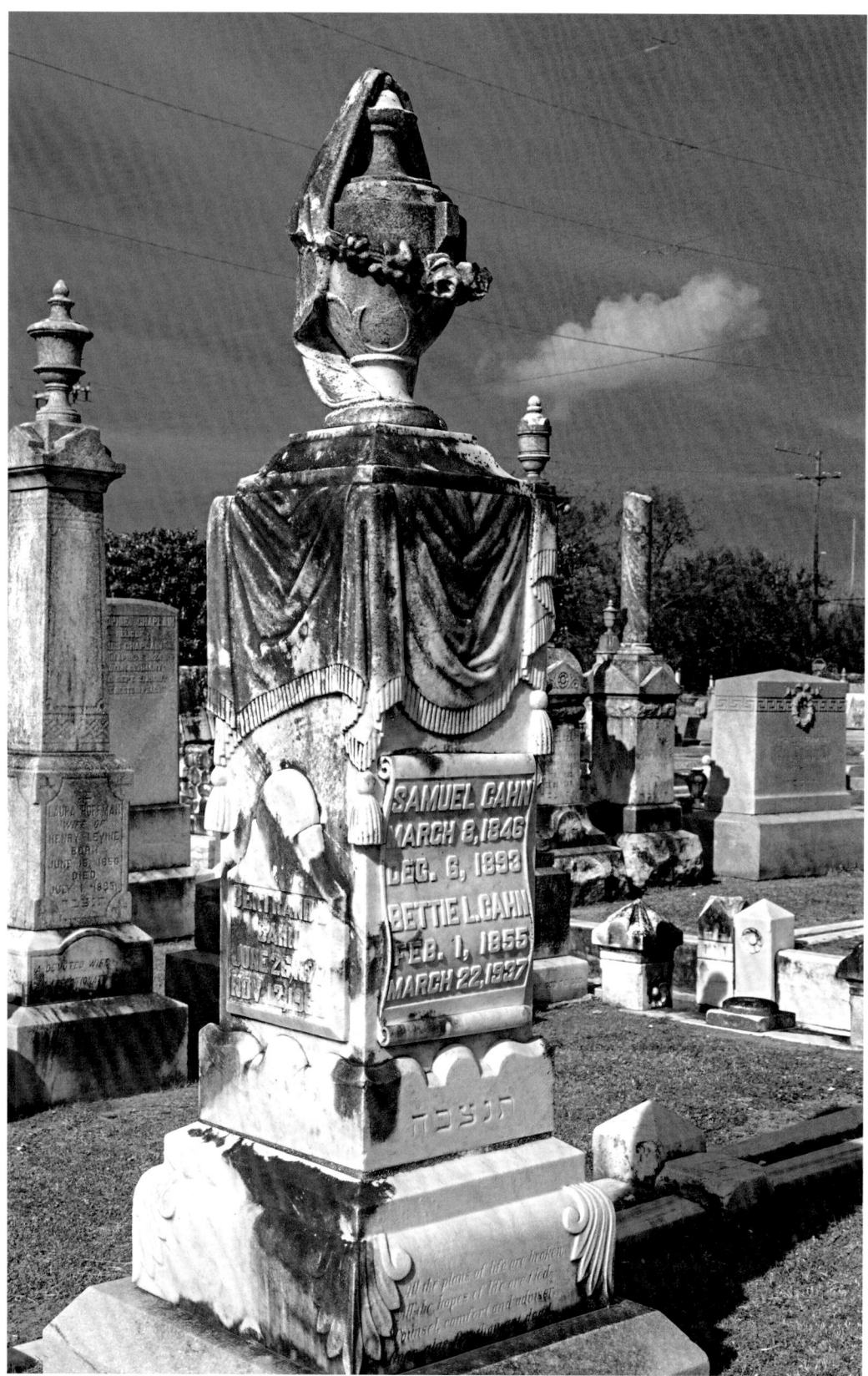

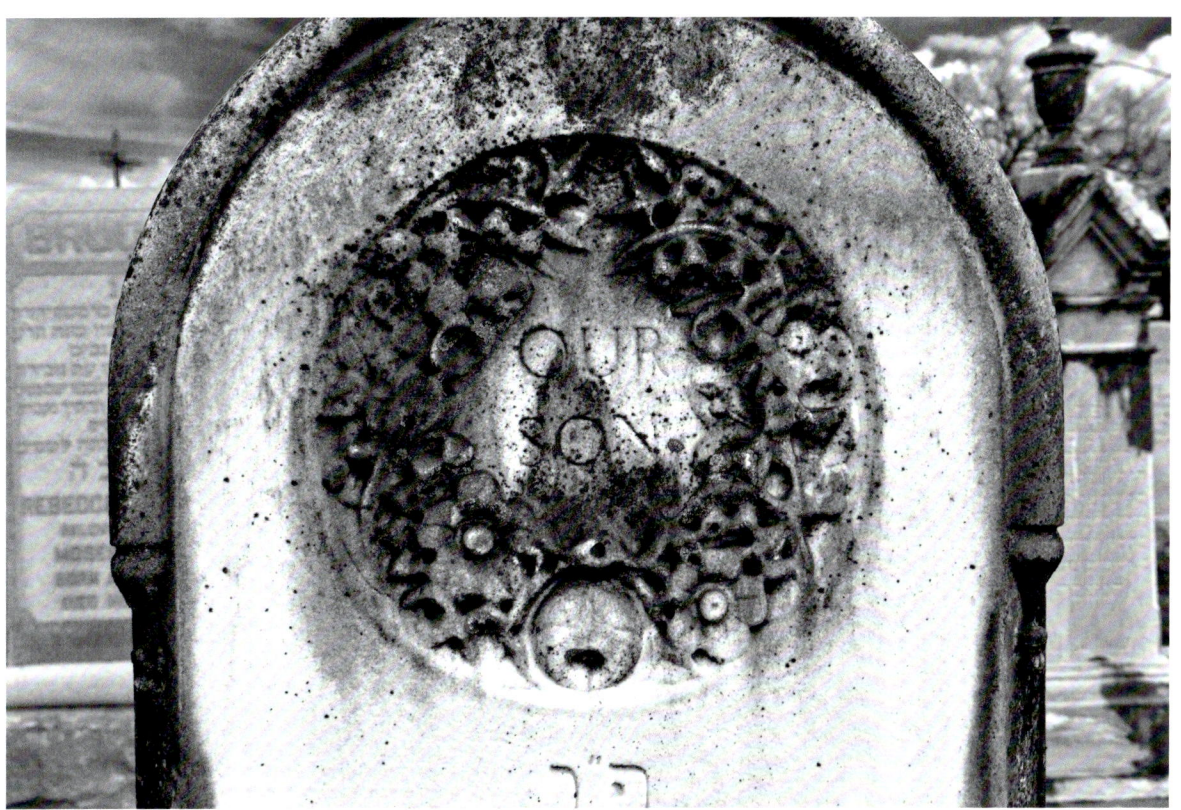

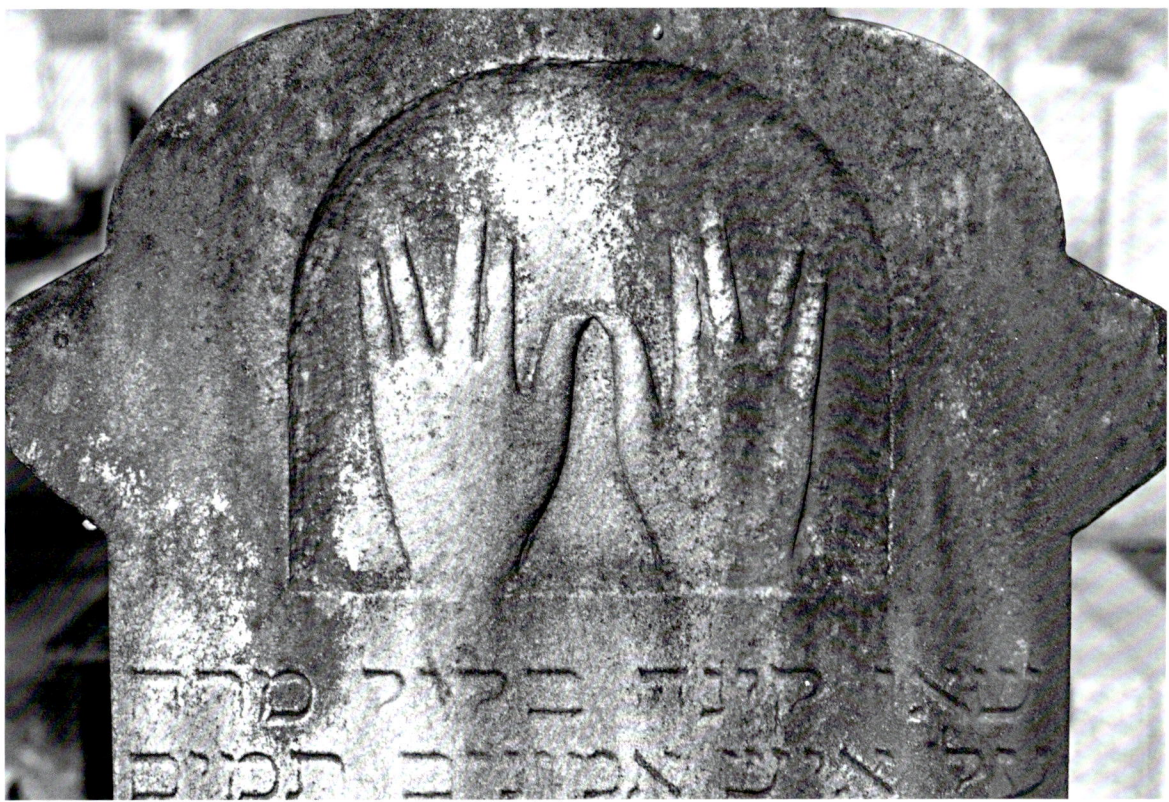

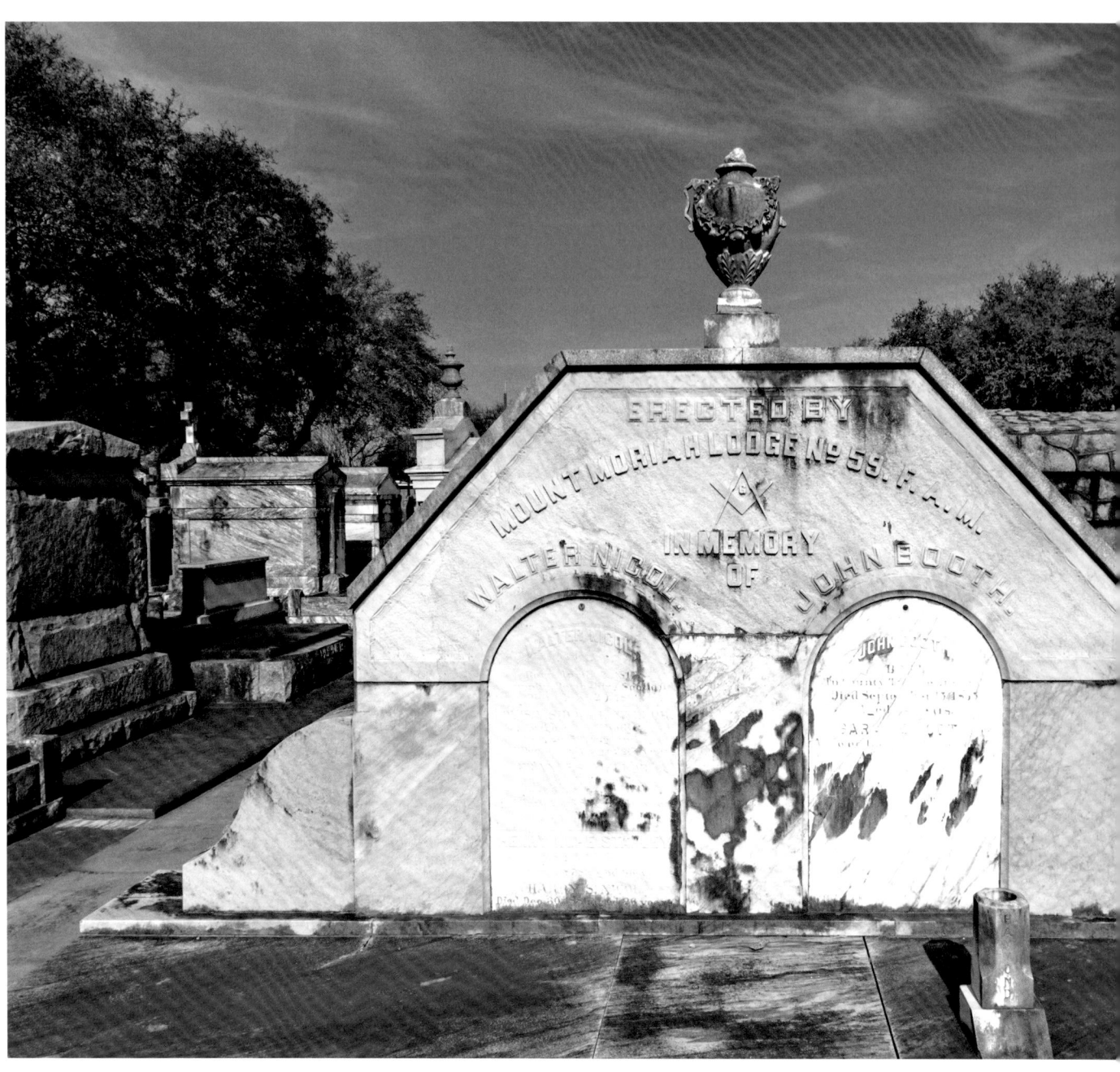

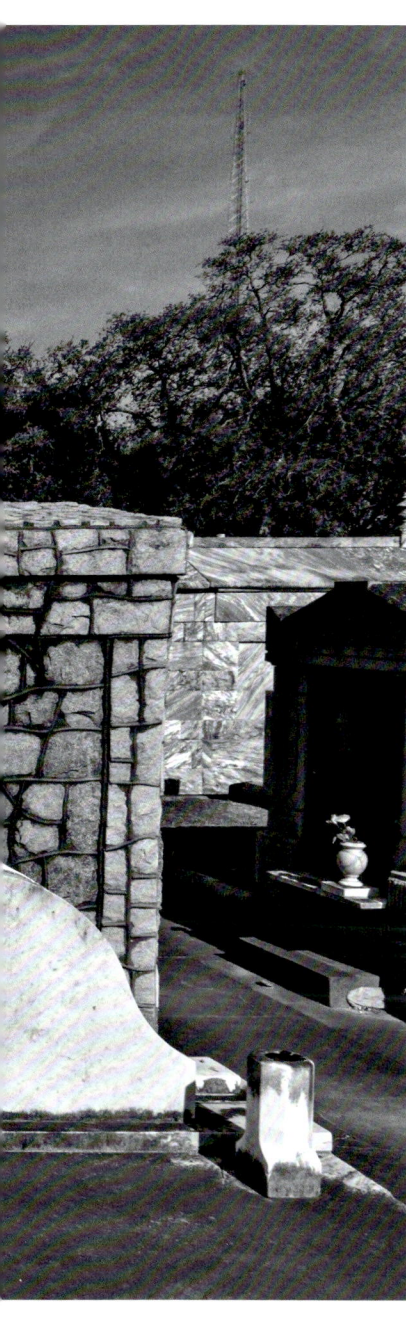

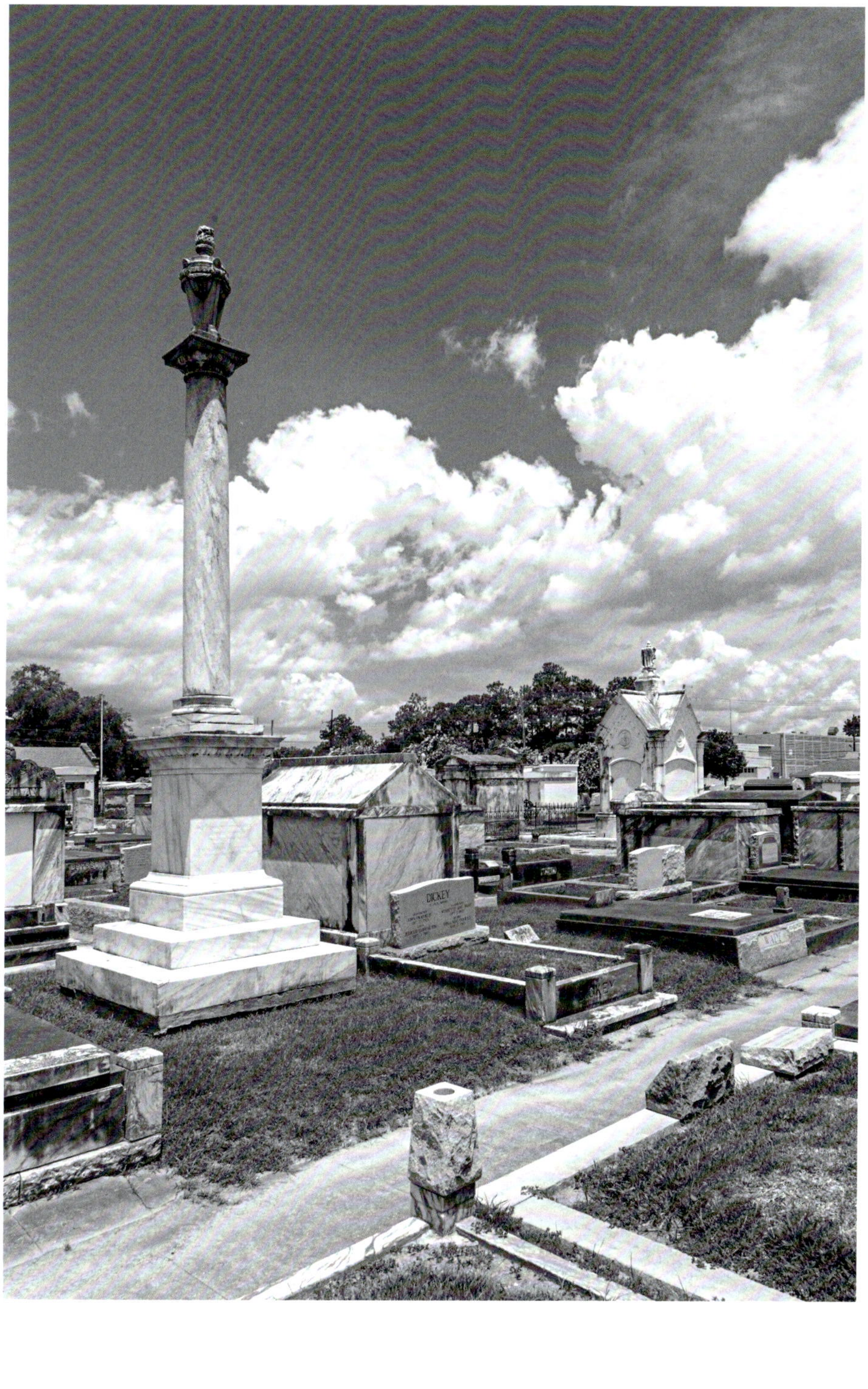

Masonic Cemetery #1 179

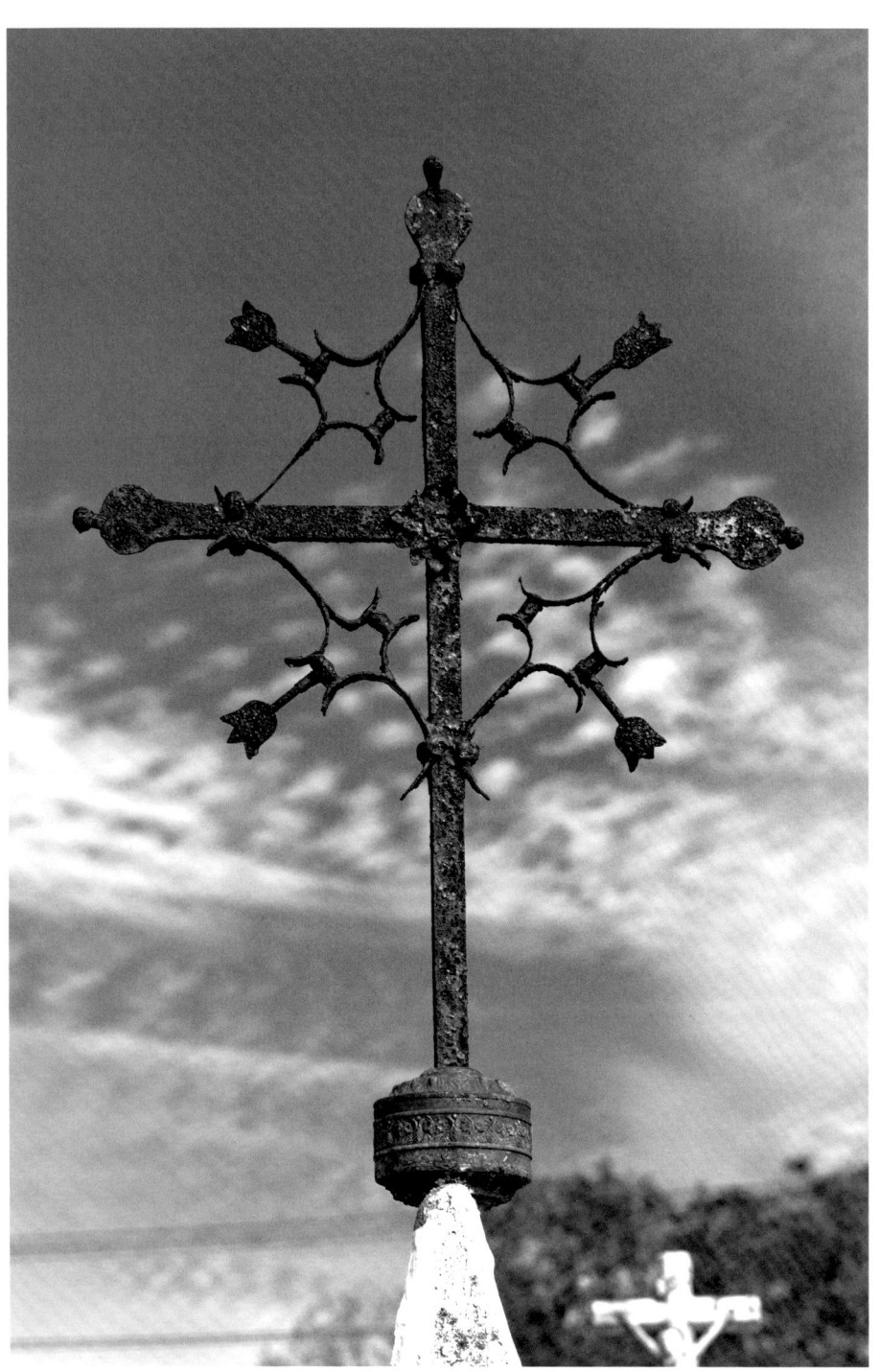

St. Joseph's Cemetery #1

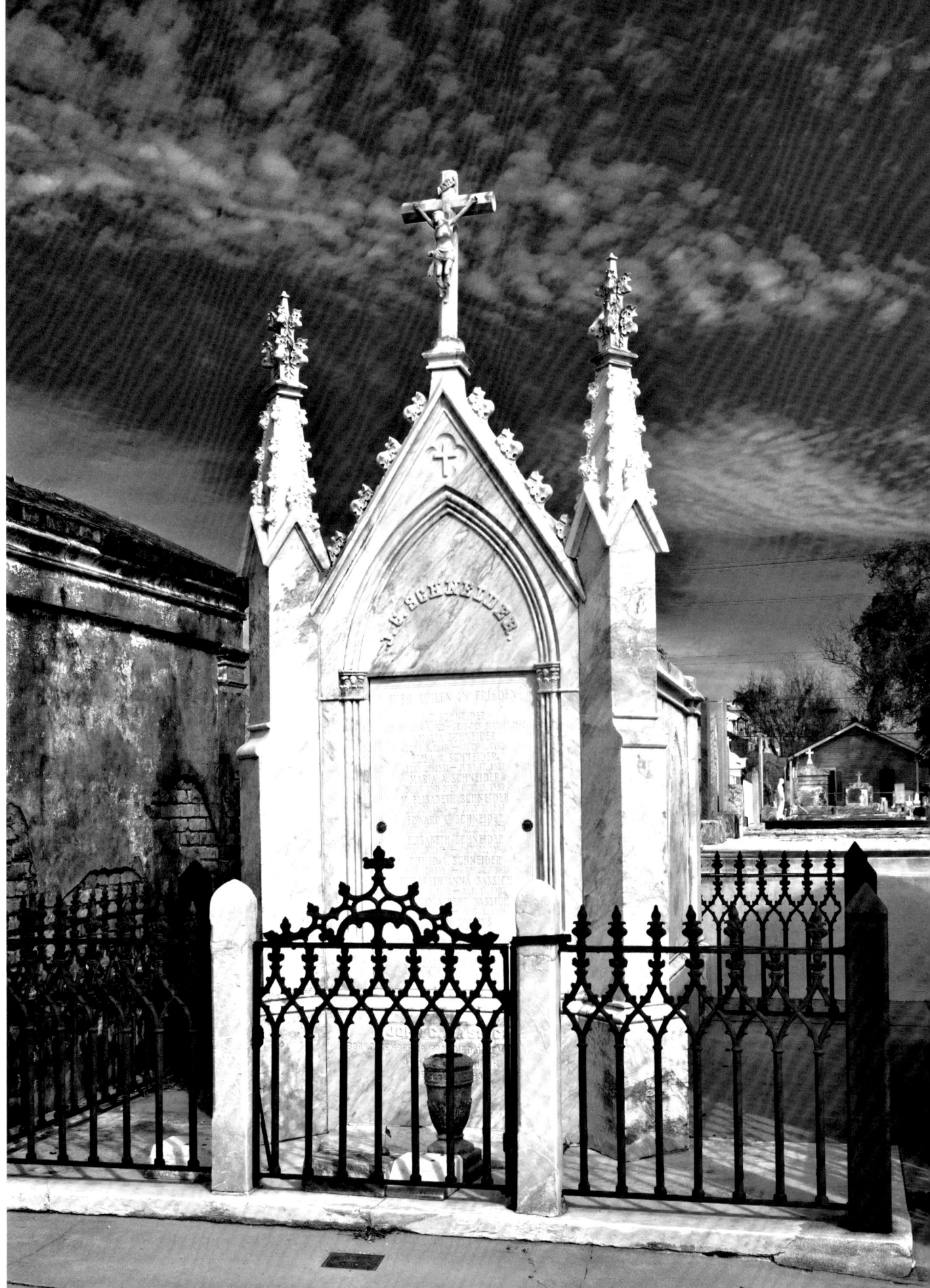

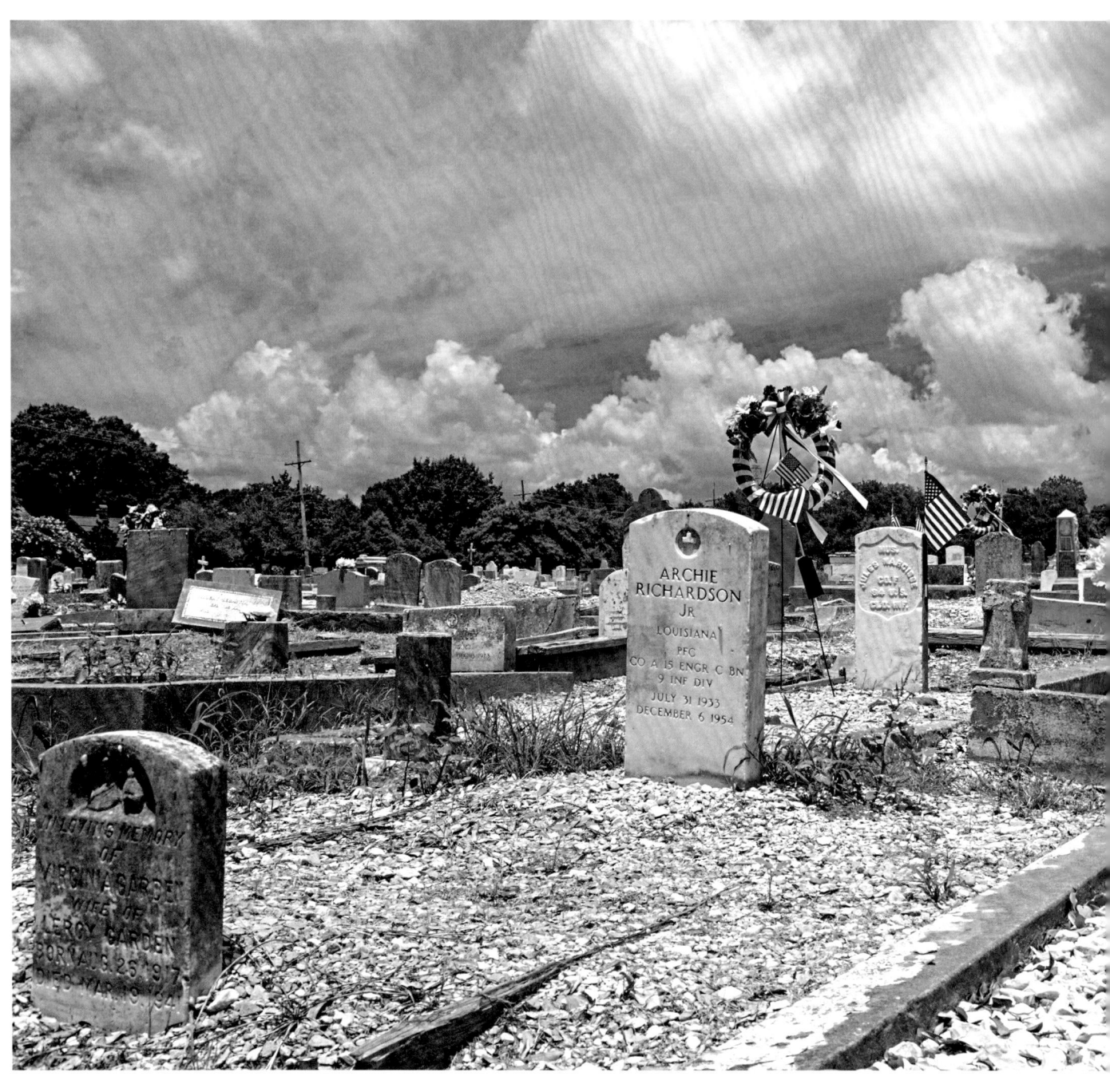

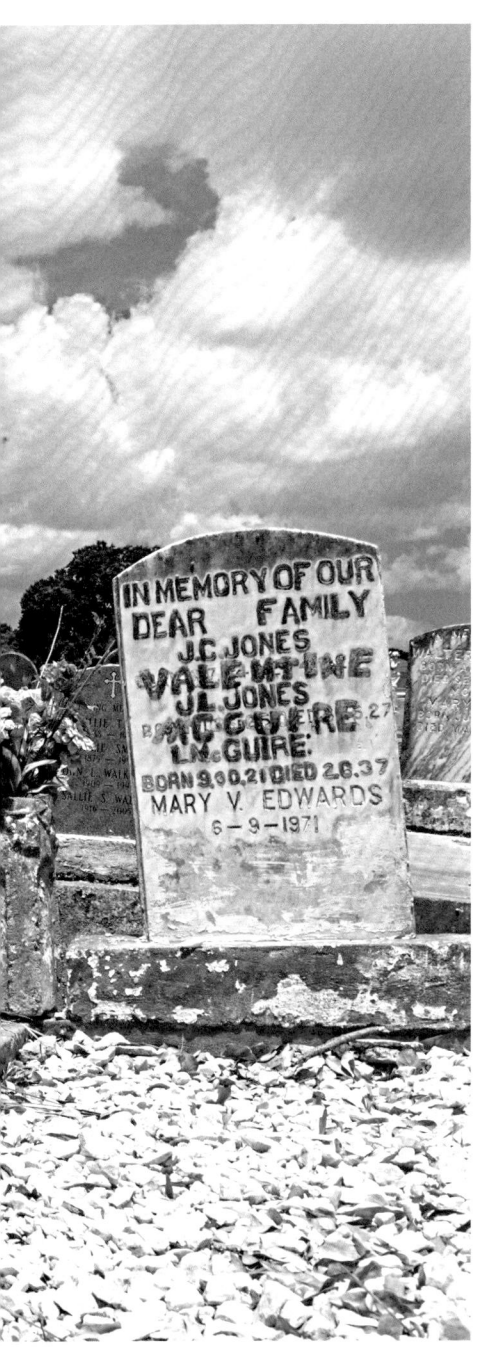

Carrollton Cemetery #1

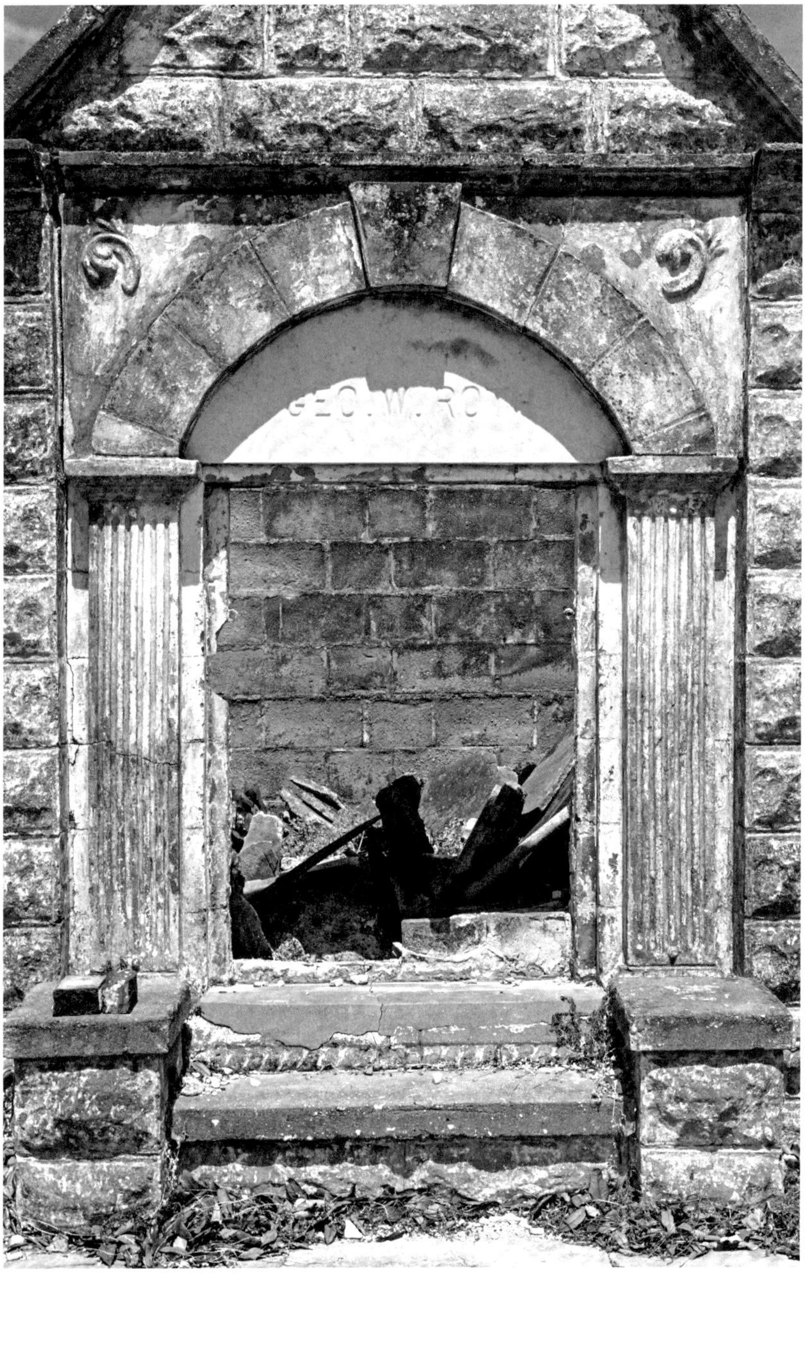

A Photographer's Vision

Une tombe est un monument érigé à la limite de deux mondes.
—Jacques-Henri Bernadin de Saint-Pierre
Études de la Nature (1784)

A photographer sees the tangible and tries to make it into something intangible—the photograph. It is the essence of the person, place, building, or landscape that the photographer is trying to capture, wanting the viewer to see what they see. Personal? It is next to impossible to explain one's vision, to communicate in words how one sees in rectangles and squares and the detail that is found within them. The light as it plays across an object creating shadows and shades of color, how light and darkness seem to compromise to form the shadows that mirror the objects they play about. An artist sees this in minute detail, every nuance, and tries to share this experience by simply pressing a small button that releases a shutter, capturing the moment. Light, shadow, and dark pass through a piece of glass and paint their dance onto film (or a sensor), freezing it in time.

In my body of work, I strive to capture the rigidity of stone or brick against the softness of grass, trees, clouds, and sky—each possessing its own sense of self in relationship with the others, together revealing to the observer their beauty and being and reliance upon one another. They cannot exist without companions, as the dark and the shadows cannot exist without the light. Nothing can exist without its opposite, the yin and yang of all existence made evident to all every day in the presence of the light and the dark. It is magnificence incarnate, the simplicity of being.

The images in this book are intended not to document the cemeteries but to offer my visual interpretation of their artistic value. They portray almost two hundred years of life and craft. I do not see the tombs, mausoleums, wall vaults, and monuments as utilitarian structures but rather as works of art that comprise an outdoor museum. These structures, statues, urns, crosses, ironworks, and delicately carved figures and symbols were created to speak to the fragility of life, each one unique. They speak to us about lives lived and the love that was and is bequeathed to the departed, even by a simple carving of a name and date. They are art in a true form, placed with the deepest love and honor. These works represent the joy and pain hidden within the marble, bronze, iron, and stone.

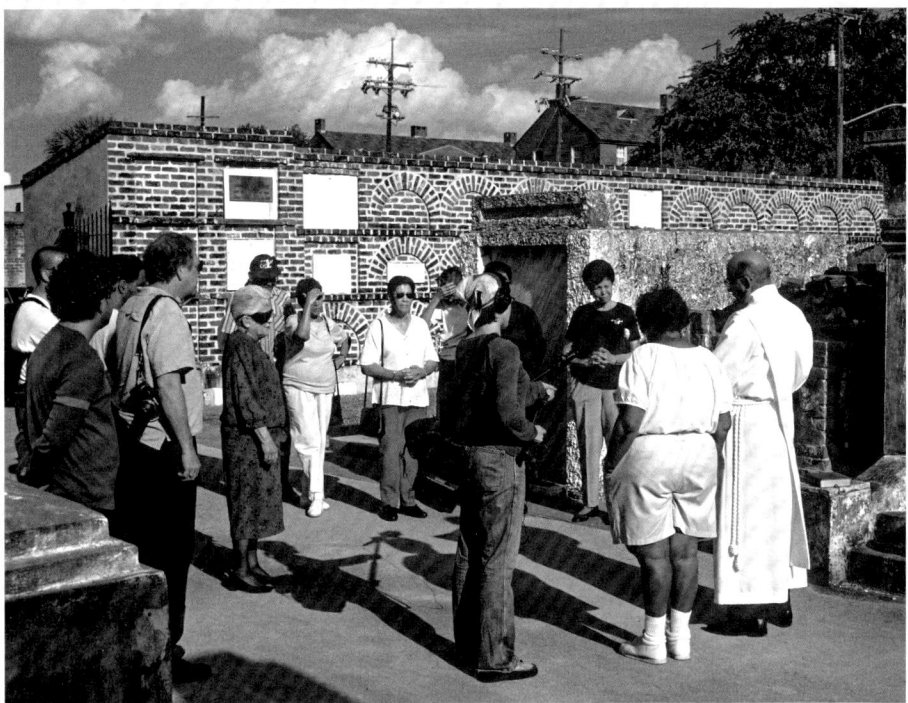

Blessing of the tombs, All Saints' Day, St. Louis Cemetery #2, Square 3
Photograph by Jan White Brantley

An artist is not defined by the identity of painter, sculptor, or photographer but by a dedication to craft and profession. When a skilled surgeon operates, an attorney pleads a case, an electrician wires a building, or a pilot maneuvers through a storm, their dedication and devotion to their work defines them as artists. They are forever seeking to achieve perfection in their work and knowing that it can never be attained—a destination constantly remaining over the horizon, beyond reach.

My own journey has been a long path filled with kindness from many—parents who gently guided and knew to let me be free, close friends, mentors who made it all possible, and my wife, Jan White Brantley, deceased in life though not in heart, a love that is joined at the soul and in spirit, a loss that created a pain more agonizing than I had ever known existed. The images in this work are rooted in all of the experiences of my life and the lessons learned through perseverance and stubbornness. These images are the legacy of their influence and as well as that of the subjects within them. I have tried to bring life into the subject that is called death, as if it were a termination of the journey. It is not. It is simply the door we walk through to look out on another endless horizon and the adventure that lies there.

It is my wish and prayer that all those who see these images are moved by the lives represented in them and realize that this photographer is just a messenger.

Robert S. Brantley
August 30, 2018

Index of Plates

St. Roch Cemetery #1

PAGE 68
Angels looking over the cemetery's entrance gates (they lost their wings in a hurricane)

Cypress Grove Cemetery

PAGE 70
Tomb of Taylor family

PAGE 72
Identical tombs of John Hughes and Mark Thomas families

PAGE 73
Tomb of Brady and Stone families

PAGE 74
Basket of flowers in white marble, symbolizing hope and eternal memory; tomb of John Cottle family

PAGE 75
Heartbreaking depiction in white marble of a mother holding her deceased infant above a baptismal font; tomb of Rodd family

PAGE 76
Tomb of Kohn family

PAGE 77
A cast-iron dolphin with a lion's head signifying salvation, love, courage, and strength; tomb of Leeds family

PAGE 78
Tomb of Robert Slark family

PAGE 79
Tomb of William H. Letchford family

PAGE 80 TOP
Tombs of Johnson and Walker families

PAGE 80 BOTTOM
Remains of tomb of Joshua James family

PAGE 81
Tomb of Alexander Harris family

PAGE 82
Shield emblem of the women's auxiliary, the Woodmen Circle of the Fraternal Society, Woodmen of the World; tomb of Etta Smith

PAGE 83 TOP
Steam pumper fire engine; monument of Irad Ferry

PAGE 83 BOTTOM
Wall vault tablet with pump fire engine; tomb of J. F. Krieg

Dispersed of Judah Cemetery

PAGE 84
Three monuments of White family

PAGE 86
Monument of Michael Levy

PAGE 87
Marble column topped by a draped urn symbolizing the vessel of the soul and its passage to heaven; monument of Louis A. Davidson

PAGE 88
Three monuments of Solomon family

PAGE 89 TOP
Monument of Emma Franck Wolf

PAGE 89 BOTTOM
Ferns signifying humility; the lilies, purity, mercy, and innocence; detail of Alexander Morales monument

Greenwood Cemetery

PAGE 90
Side panels bearing daffodil for divine love, morning glory for resurrection, rose for unfailing love and wisdom, and tulip for love and passion; tomb of Walker and Behan families

PAGE 92
Cast-iron tomb of C. A. Miltenberger family

PAGE 93
Lady Justice, represented in white marble, holding the scales of fairness and the sword of authority; tomb of German General Worker Society

PAGE 94
Panorama, row of tombs, Myrtle Avenue

PAGE 96
Tomb of Josephine Mesa

PAGE 97 TOP
A classically dressed woman leaning against a headstone and holding a laurel, overcome with grief; tomb of James J. Glennan

PAGE 97 BOTTOM
Flowers referring to the brevity of life surrounding clasped hands (wife on left, husband on right) signifying love, affection, and unity after death; tomb of John Janeway family

PAGE 98
Wreath of oak and laurel leaves on a Latin cross. Oak represents strength, honor, and faith; laurel, victory and immortality. Tomb of Washburn and Pruves families

PAGE 99
Seated Buddha in the single lotus position, representing peace in a turbulent world; tomb of Gee Nee Tong

PAGE 100 TOP
Winged cherub head carved by the Barret brothers, gracing a small monument to Hazel Mallory, who died at the age of ten months and nine days

PAGE 100 BOTTOM
Tragic portrayal in marble of the death of an infant, with a heart-wrenching epitaph; monument of Robert Roberts

PAGE 101
Cherub representing divine wisdom, with its index finger pointing up, the passage into heaven. The cherub stands above a blank sheet, representing a life cut so short, there was little to write. Monument of Philip C. Alberstadt, died aged four years

PAGE 102 LEFT
Monument of Captain George Smith

PAGE 102 RIGHT
Tomb of Daniel and Sarah Edwards family

PAGE 103
Folk art tomb of John McCarthy

PAGE 104
Crescent and star police badge with cap in white marble; society tomb of Police Mutual Benevolent Association

PAGE 105
White marble pediment with crescent and star police badge and accoutrements, along with urns topped by the eternal flame; society tomb of Police Mutual Benevolent Association

Lafayette Cemetery #1 & #2

PAGE 106 #1
Tombs, main aisle, Square 1

PAGE 108 #1
Tomb of D. R. Godwin family

PAGE 109 #1
Wrought-iron fence with projectile points

PAGE 110 TOP #1
Roses signifying unfailing love, wisdom, beauty, hope; morning glory, love, resurrection; and ivy, eternal life and love. Buds represent a child or a young life. Tomb of David R. Godwin

PAGE 110 BOTTOM #1
Tablet detail; tomb of Jan White Brantley

PAGE 111 #1
Grieving woman holding her loved one's ashes. This statue was formerly atop the adjacent Zimmerman family tomb.

PAGE 112 TOP #2
Variety of tomb types

PAGE 112 BOTTOM #2
Society tomb of German Craftsman Association

PAGE 113 TOP #2
Society tomb of the Butchers Benevolent Society

PAGE 113 BOTTOM #2
Society tomb of Young Men Olympian Benevolent Association

PAGE 114 #1
Tomb of yellow fever victims, mostly children

PAGE 115 #1
Tombs of Brennen and McNeil families

PAGE 116 TOP #1
Winged hourglass suggesting the rapid passage of time. The oak and laurel wreath signifies strength, honor, victory, and glory. Tomb of Jacob U. Payne

PAGE 116 BOTTOM #2
Heart within a wreath, the symbol of the Pure in Heart Benevolent Association, an African American society organized in New Orleans, 1878

PAGE 117 TOP #2
Tomb of the Coachmen Benevolent Association, an African American labor society organized in Philadelphia in the 1820s

PAGE 117 BOTTOM #2
White marble tympanum of the African American society tomb of the Ladies Pride of Louisiana Benevolent Association

PAGE 118 #2
Angel holding wreaths above two kneeling figures, one presenting a scroll with the names of honored dead and the other the urn of eternal life; society tomb of German Craftsman Association

PAGE 119 TOP #1
Pediment detail, pump fire engine; society tomb of Jefferson Fire Company No. 22

PAGE 119 BOTTOM #1
Pediment of John J. E. Aurich tomb

PAGE 120 LEFT #1
Laurel leaves signifying honor and achievement; tomb of the Poydras Female Orphan Asylum

PAGE 120 RIGHT #1
Urn symbolic of the vessel of the soul, with the flame representing the eternal soul; tomb of Anton Eriksenn

PAGE 121 #1
Tomb of Adam Bensel family

Metairie Cemetery

PAGE 122
White marble sphinx and reflection guarding the entrance to the Egyptian-style pyramid mausoleum of the Lucien N. Brunswig family

PAGE 124
The mausoleum of Lucien N. Brunswig, a romanticized Egyptian pyramid guarded by a marble sphinx, opposite a classically dressed woman in mourning

PAGE 125
A blazing star centered over the entrance, signifying rank as a mason. Two columns are capped by floral baskets, one with an orb displaying signs of the zodiac and the other, a globe. Mausoleum of Charles Francis Buck

PAGE 126
Mausoleum of William Henry Dark Brook family, framed by two cedars. This Greek Revival tomb is capped by palmettes representing immortality.

PAGE 127
Two griffins acting as supports on a sarcophagus, representing the dual nature of Christ and the power of the divine. A scallop shell symbolizes spiritual journey. Monument of Eugene Lacosst

PAGE 128 TOP LEFT
Russian Orthodox cross on a Moorish Revival tomb with stained glass; tomb of Larendon-Beauregard families

PAGE 128 TOP RIGHT
Ornate bronze cross, a combination of the Celtic and Latin crosses. The center of the cross is inscribed with "IHS," abbreviation for the Greek ΙΗΣΟΥΣ, meaning Jesus, while the base is ornamented with the Book of Revelation's title of God, Alpha and Omega. Mausoleum of Bernard C. Carbajal family

PAGE 128 BOTTOM LEFT
Monument of Mary Cardinale-Maggio

PAGE 128 BOTTOM RIGHT
Celtic Cross engraved with "IHS," meaning Jesus; tomb of George H. Terriberryen

PAGE 129
Portrait of Christ in white bisque recessed into the center of a Latin cross. The crown of thorns symbolizes his love for humanity.

PAGE 130 TOP LEFT
Urn with a broken handle above a tympanum of white marble with wreath and Celtic cross; tomb of Johanna Lilienthal family

PAGE 130 TOP RIGHT
Bronze draped urn with flame, one of two outside the mausoleum of John Dibert family

PAGE 130 BOTTOM LEFT
Grapes, symbolic of Holy Communion and the blood shed by Jesus during the crucifixion, with leaves representing the Christian faith; tomb of Caswell P. Ellis family

Index of Plates

PAGE 130 BOTTOM RIGHT
Draped urn representing death and the passage between this life and the next, with an eternal flame reminding us of the eternal nature of the soul; tomb of Boothby family

PAGE 131 TOP LEFT
Ornate, white marble draped handled urn with an eternal flame; tomb of Michael Frank

PAGE 131 TOP RIGHT
Carved bay laurel motif symbolizing wisdom and eternal life; monument of Eugene Lacosst

PAGE 131 BOTTOM LEFT
White marble planter; tomb of Dr. John P. R. Stone family

PAGE 131 BOTTOM RIGHT
White marble draped and handled urn with eternal flame, decorated with garland symbolizing mourning; tomb of August Geiger

PAGE 132
Center figure is a representation of the virtue Hope, seen with an anchor; N. Miller family

PAGE 134
Tomb of Jules Aldigé

PAGE 135
Row of marble angels atop tombs on Avenue A

PAGE 136 TOP
Statue of Christopher Columbus pointing toward the New World, standing atop the Societa Cristoforo Colombo's society tomb, built in the 1890s

PAGE 136 BOTTOM
Bronze statue depicting General Albert Sidney Johnston sitting atop his horse, Fire Eater, moments before his death on April 6, 1862, at the Battle of Shiloh; mausoleum of the Army of Tennessee, Louisiana Division

PAGE 137
The angel Gabriel with his horn (trumpet); tomb of the great bandleader Louis Prima

PAGE 138
Rough-cut Latin cross with the figure of an angel holding a wreath; monument of Mattingly family

PAGE 139 LEFT
Statue of Terpsichore, the muse of dance, at the entrance of the Lucien Denapolis tomb

PAGE 139 RIGHT
Bronze figure of Grief with roses, erected by Albert Weiblen; tomb of Kimmel family

PAGE 140
St. Joseph holding a lily atop the society tomb of Società Italiana di Mutua Beneficenza San Giuseppi

PAGE 141
The martyred St. Bartholomew atop the society tomb of Congregazione Fratellanza Italiana di San Bartolomeo Apostolo

PAGE 142
Monument of Benjamin Saxon Story

PAGE 143
Rear detail; mausoleum of Bestoff family

———

St. Louis Cemetery #1, #2 & #3

PAGE 144 #1
Society tombs and other tomb styles

PAGE 146 #1
According to legend, tomb of alleged voodoo queen Marie Laveau

PAGE 147 TOP #1
Tomb of Italian Mutual Benevolent Society

PAGE 148 #1
Figure of a kneeling woman in prayer for the souls of the departed; society tomb of Portuguese Benevolent Association #2

PAGE 149 #1
Grief-stricken woman in classical dress holding the inverted torch of lives extinguished; Society Tomb of Portuguese Burial Society

PAGE 150 TOP LEFT #1
Draped urn on a pedestal with olive branches for peace, victory, and God's forgiveness. The sun symbolizes light and eternal life. Tomb of St. Cyr family

PAGE 150 TOP RIGHT #1
Urn of the infant John J. Dos Ramos

PAGE 150 BOTTOM LEFT #1
Ironwork and marble tomb of Laurent Millaudon family.

PAGE 150 BOTTOM RIGHT #1
Monument of Armand and Marie Varney

PAGE 151 #1
Often called the Little Weeper, a white marble statue of an anguished child sits atop the tomb of wealthy grocer Alexander Bergamini and his family.

PAGE 152 TOP LEFT #1
Wrought-iron cross; tomb of Enoul Livaudais

PAGE 152 TOP RIGHT #1
Wrought-iron gate and cross; tomb of Appolinaire Perrault

PAGE 152 BOTTOM LEFT #1
Wrought-iron cross; tomb of Hippolite Tricou

PAGE 152 BOTTOM RIGHT #1
Early wrought-iron Greek-style cross with fleurée terminals, fashioned by an unknown blacksmith, circa 1800; Zenon tomb

PAGE 153 #1
Decaying tombs, St. Louis Cemetery #1

PAGE 154 #2, Square 1
Tomb of J. C. De St. Rome family

PAGE 156 TOP #2, Square 3
Wall vaults; tomb of William Bailey

PAGE 156 BOTTOM #2, Square 3
Abandoned tombs

PAGE 157 #2, Square 3
An unusual treatment of Grief in bas-relief above a fireplace mantel; tomb of Sylvanie Brunnette Leon

PAGE 158 #2, Square 2
Tomb of Jean Martial Lapeyre

PAGE 159 #3
White marble sculpture of an anguished mother holding her dead child, one of the most heart-wrenching monuments in the city; tomb of Fourchy family

PAGE 160 #3
Tomb of Cyprien Dufour family

PAGE 161 #3
Cenotaph of James Gallier Sr.

PAGE 162 #3
Panorama of tombs on St. Paul's Avenue

St. Patrick's #1 & #2

PAGE 164 #2
Cast-iron gate with an angel praying before an incense altar, referring to Revelation 8:4, "The smoke of the incense, together with the prayers of God's people, went up before God from the angel's hand"; tomb of William A. Brady family

PAGE 166 #1
Intricate carving in white marble: calla lily for purity, ferns for the victory over death, ivy for life and love eternal, and passion flower for the suffering of Christ; monument of Arthur McCauley

PAGE 167 #2
Mary Magdalene crying before the crucified Christ, surrounded by weeping willow trees; headstone of Edward Nolan

PAGE 168 TOP LEFT #2
Latin cross with sleeping lamb signifying purity, innocence, and the sacrifice by Christ; headstone of Bridget McKoogue

PAGE 168 TOP RIGHT #2
Three Latin crosses depicting Calvary and Christ's love. The sleeping lamb symbolizes faith in Christ; a grieving man leans over the tomb. Monument of Catherine Judge

PAGE 168 BOTTOM LEFT #2
Sleeping lamb representing faith in Jesus and Latin cross with a praying angel indicating intercession for the soul of the departed; monument of Patrick Garric

PAGE 168 BOTTOM RIGHT #2
Broken monument depicting a grieving husband at the grave of his wife; tomb of Bridget Quaid

PAGE 169 TOP LEFT #2
Marble monument of John J. Cronin family depicting the legend of the donkey at Christ's crucifixion

PAGE 169 TOP RIGHT #2
Angel praying beneath a cross for intercession of the departed soul; headstone of Francis Quin

PAGE 169 BOTTOM LEFT #2
Latin cross above the marble monument, one of a few with a dove representing the Holy Spirit. Below is a bas-relief of children gathering about Jesus. Tomb of Mary Devlin Buckley

PAGE 169 BOTTOM RIGHT #2
Weeping willow symbolizing mourning in cemetery scene with Latin cross; monument of James Powers

Additional Cemeteries

St. Vincent de Paul Cemetery #1 & #2

PAGE 170 #2
Desire Street wall vaults

PAGE 172 TOP #1
Exterior wall of St. Vincent de Paul Cemetery #1

PAGE 172 BOTTOM #1
Louisa Street wall vaults

PAGE 173
Angel pointing toward heaven, indicating that the soul has risen; tomb of Dr. William Nothacker

Odd Fellows Rest Cemetery

PAGE 174
Marble bas-relief; society tomb, Teutonia Lodge No. 10

Holt Cemetery

PAGE 175
Folk art monument of Charles J. Luckett

Hebrew Rest Cemetery

PAGE 176
Monument of Samuel Cahn family

Anshe Sfard Cemetery

PAGE 177 TOP
Daffodil representing divine love and youth; lily of the valley, innocence and purity; monument of Lester S. Pailet

Chevra Thilim Cemetery

PAGE 177 BOTTOM
Cohanim hands, a motif that originated with the priestly tribe of Aaron in Judaism, uplifted to allow the blessings of God to flow into the congregation; monument of Aron Weingrun

Masonic Cemetery #1

PAGE 178
Society tomb of Mount Moriah Lodge No. 59, Free and Accepted Masons

PAGE 179
Overview; monument of Samuel M. Todd

St. Joseph's Cemetery #1

PAGE 180
One-of-a-kind Latin wrought-iron cross resting atop the tomb of Mrs. Mary J. Breen. Knob terminals signifying life emerging from death are in the form of tulips, her love and passion.

PAGE 181
Tomb of J. C. Schneider

Carrollton Cemetery #1

PAGE 182
Graves, Indigent Square #218

PAGE 183
Abandoned tomb of George W. Roth

LAST PAGE:
Legends abound with this bronze figure of Grief holding roses, originally the tomb of the Storyville madam Josie Arlington, now that of the Morales family, Metairie Cemetery.

Index of Plates 189

Acknowledgments

No matter the endeavor, no one gets from the beginning to the end without aid and advice, and this work is no exception. I want to tender my appreciation and heartfelt gratitude to Jan Cigliano Hartman for her never-ending faith, advice, and critical eye throughout this project. I would also like to extend warm thanks to my friend S. Frederick Starr for being the first to see the importance in the work and for his guidance along the way. There are times when it seems to an author that he or she is asking far too much of people. I cannot thank my dear friends Mary Lou Eichhorn and Scott Gallinghouse enough for their research assistance, spot-on critiques, and kindness during the entire journey that has been this work, and for their warmth of spirit. I would like to thank Heather Veneziano for her incredible knowledge of funerary art and symbology, which was so essential to this book. A special thanks to Sherri Sison Peppo, director of Catholic Cemeteries of the Archdiocese of New Orleans and Harold Bailey, gatekeeper and gentle soul of St. Louis Cemetery #1. I wish to thank Amanda Blake of Save Our Cemeteries and Emily Ford of Oak and Laurel for their help. I am indebted to Lynette Slaughter Vinet for her research and article on Nicolas Mioton and for allowing me the honor of using the material in his biography. To my close friend and fellow photographer John Menszer for his honest assessment of the images in this volume. Richard Vallon for his friendship and encouragement and for the use of his drone for an aerial photograph. By no means last is my gratitude to my editor, Sara Stemen, for her gentle manner and adroit skills in helping to shape this work. I would also like to thank all the people who work every day in what seems an uphill struggle for the preservation of the cemeteries of New Orleans.

Robert S. Brantley
February 2019

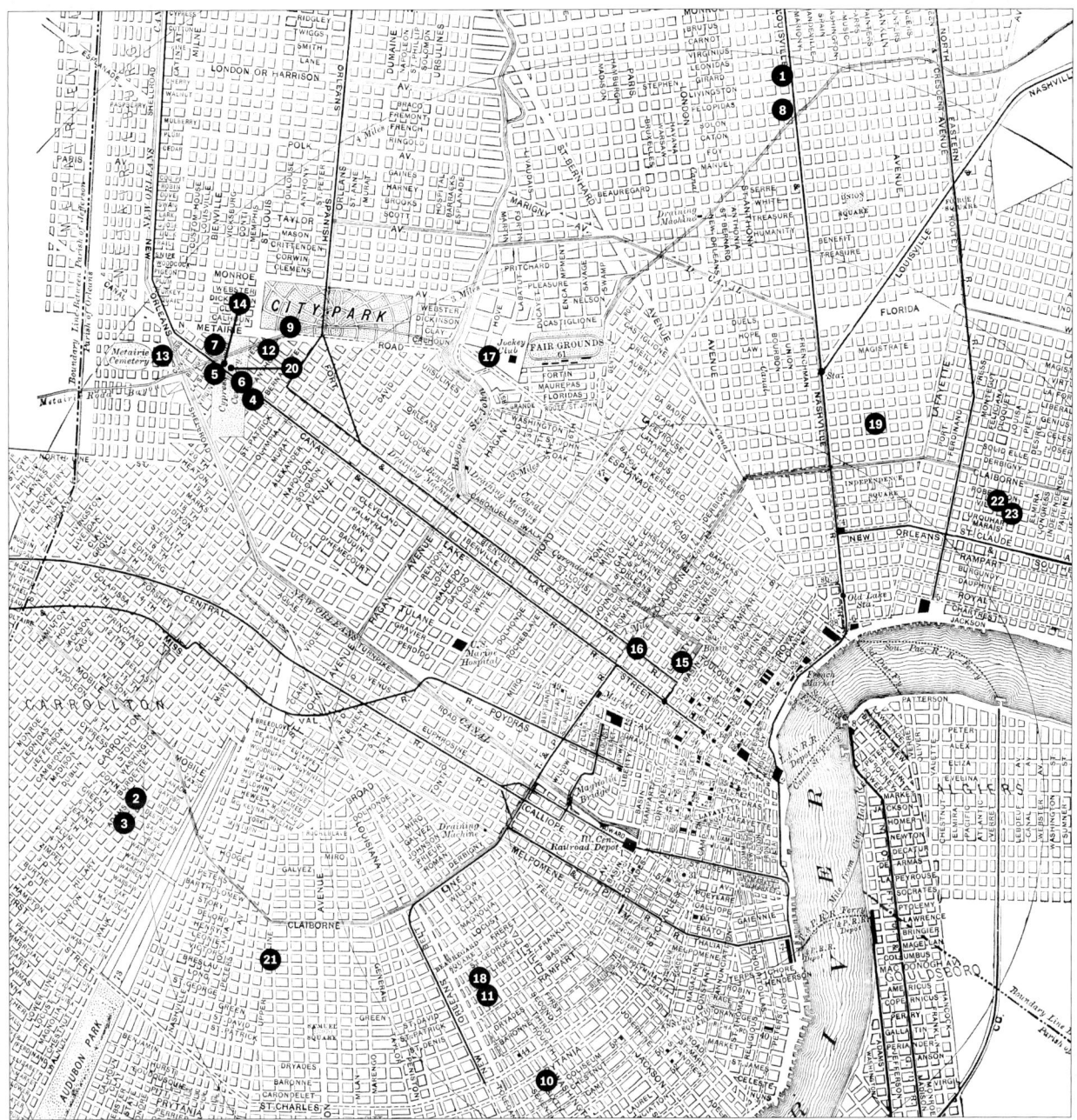

Cemetery Locations

1. **Anshe Sfard**
   4300 block, Frenchmen St.
2. **Carrollton #1**
   1701 Hillary St.
3. **Carrollton #2**
   1900 block, Hillary St.
4. **Chevra Thilim**
   4800 block, Canal St.
5. **Cypress Grove**
   Corner of Canal St. &
   City Park Ave.
6. **Dispersed of Judah**
   4937 Canal St.
7. **Greenwood**
   City Park Ave. & Canal St.
8. **Hebrew Rest**
   4100 block, Frenchmen St.
9. **Holt**
   527 City Park Ave.
10. **Lafayette #1**
    1400 block, Washington Ave.
11. **Lafayette #2**
    2110 Washington Ave.
12. **Masonic #1**
    400 block, City Park Ave.
13. **Metairie**
    5100 Pontchartrain Blvd.
14. **Odd Fellows Rest**
    5055 Canal St.
15. **St. Louis #1**
    425 Basin St.
16. **St. Louis #2**
    200 to 400 blocks,
    North Claiborne Ave.
17. **St. Louis #3**
    3421 Esplanade Ave.
18. **St. Joseph's #1**
    2220 Washington Ave.
19. **St. Roch**
    1725 St. Roch Ave.
20. **St. Patrick's #1 & #2**
    5000 block, Canal St.
21. **Valence Street**
    4600 block, Valence St.
22. **St. Vincent de Paul #1**
    1400–1500 block, Louisa St.
23. **St. Vincent de Paul #2**
    1500 block, Piety St.

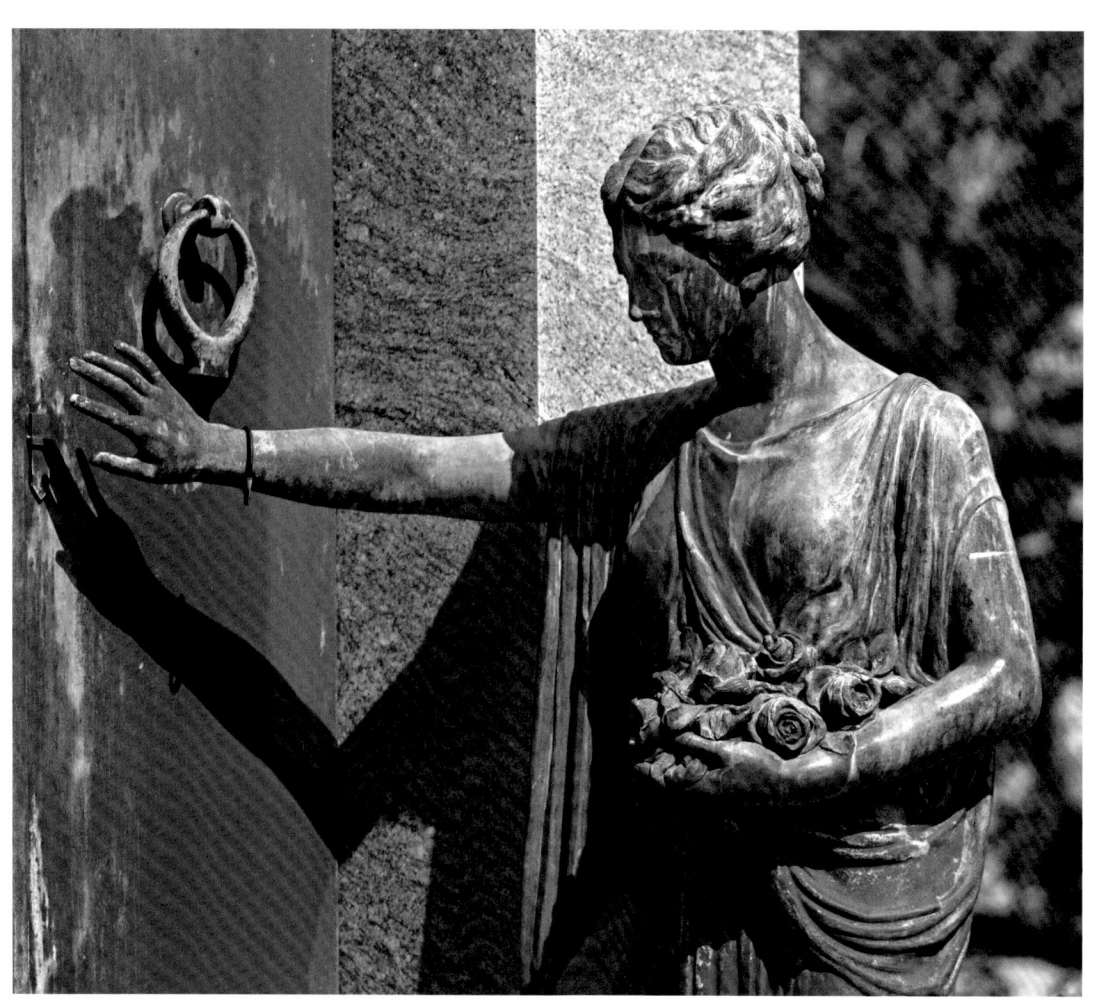